UNDERSTANDING THE RELIGIOUS PRIESTHOOD

UNDERSTANDING THE RELIGIOUS PRIESTHOOD

HISTORY, CONTROVERSY, THEOLOGY

CHRISTIAN RAAB, OSB

Foreword by Brian E. Daley, SJ

The Catholic University of America Press

Washington, D.C.

The paper used in this publication meets the minimum requirements of American National Standards for Information Science—Permanence of Paper for Printed Library Materials, ANSI Z39.48-1984.

∞

Library of Congress Cataloging-in-Publication Data
Names: Raab, Christian, author.
Title: Understanding the religious priesthood : history, controversy, theology / Christian Raab, OSB ; foreword by Brian E. Daley, SJ.
Description: Washington, D.C. : The Catholic University of America Press, [2021] | Includes bibliographical references and index.
Identifiers: LCCN 2020041707 | ISBN 9780813233239 (paperback)
Subjects: LCSH: Priesthood—Catholic Church. | Pastoral theology—Catholic Church. | Balthasar, Hans Urs von, 1905–1988.
Classification: LCC BX1913 .R235 2021 | DDC 262/.1—dc23
LC record available at https://lccn.loc.gov/2020041707

In memory of my father,
Edward Raab, who first introduced
me to monks

CONTENTS

FOREWORD

BRIAN E. DALEY, SJ

Christian faith and practice constantly confront us with paradoxes. The spiritual tradition of the church seems to oscillate between inviting us to find God in splendor and to find him in simplicity, in the aesthetic elaboration of our worship and in a cultivated austerity; between calling Christians to flee the world and to embrace it in loving concern; to serve our poor and isolated brothers and sisters and to seek, in silence and solitude, the universal presence of God. Instinctively, we find ourselves saying over and over that there is room for both approaches, for all ways of seeking God, not least because the person of Christ our Lord is itself a paradox: God the Son, living among us as a vulnerable human being; a Jewish man, giving fully human form and face to the Son's eternal reality.

The history of institutionalized Christian religious consecration and ministry shows traces of this same tendency toward an inner tension between apparently competing instincts and styles. Since the fourth century, at least, when Christians, no longer living in fear of government oppression, were able to shape their lives more openly to reflect their deepest desires, men and women of faith began to seek out places of peaceful refuge, away from home and the distractions of everyday life, where they could focus their time and energies entirely on seeking God. So the origin of what we usually think of as "religious" or monastic life seems to lie in the withdrawal of Christian believers into a pattern of life—sometimes solitary, sometimes in a larger community of like-minded people—that was centered on prayer and focused Biblical meditation, on manual work, and on a cultivated simplicity of human needs, all under the direction of an older ascetic who had already weathered some of the struggles of living this way.

What we call in the West "religious life"—a pattern of life consecrated to following Christ as a full-time occupation—has its origin, then, not in forms of community service and leadership, but in the attempt to escape from the claims of individual and communal responsibility, however serious and legitimate they may have been, in order to seek out the company of God. So early Christian spiritual writers sensed, in the centuries in which religious life was first being shaped, that such a life was, in principle, incompatible with normal human commitments, both to family and to formal, ordained church leadership. John Cassian, the fifth-century Latin monk whose writings on the ideals of the religious life were to play a dominant role in shaping the Western church's understanding of this emerging tradition, famously remarks in his *Institutes of the Common Life*:

> Here is an old saying of the fathers that is still current . . . : a monk must by all means flee from women and bishops. For neither permit him, when once they have bent him to familiarity with themselves, to devote himself any longer to the quiet of his cell, or to cling with most pure eyes, through insight into spiritual matters, to divine contemplation.[1]

In both the attractions of the opposite sex and the attractions of church office, as given by a bishop in ordination, Cassian sees fatal sources of distraction for a serious would-be monk.

And yet, as we know, monks were sought out, more and more, to accept church office as the centuries went on: to be ordained as bishops—heads of local churches—probably because of their years of serious immersion in the life shaped by the ideals of the gospel and eventually also to be ordained presbyters (priests), who could not only assist the

1. John Cassian, *The Institutes of the Common Life* 11.18, trans. Boniface Ramsey, Ancient Christian Writers 58 (New York and Mahwah, N.J.: Newman Press, 2000), 247–49. In the course of discussing the principal vices or imperfections that stand in the way of full commitment to a spiritual life, Cassian is here speaking about the dangers of vainglory (*kenodoxia*). Like sexual attraction, the attraction to the power and "empty honor" implied in office is for him clearly deceptive, an obstacle to single-minded religious dedication.

local bishop, but also remain in their monastic communities and minister to the liturgical needs of their fellow ascetics. The advantages of having trained sacramental ministers within a community were undeniable, especially if the community had been established in a remote place. Yet the dangers, both for the monk-priest himself and for the rest of the community, were also obvious: a priest might expect to be shown special deference that contradicted the democratic spirit of the monastic fraternity or assume that his role of liturgical leadership would be automatically extended beyond the eucharistic assembly. So the *Rule of Benedict*, composed in Italy perhaps a century after Cassian, exhibits the same sensitivity that Cassian shows toward the spiritual danger of holy orders, now from the perspective of the whole community:

> If anyone in priestly orders should ask to be received into the monastery, permission shall not be granted to him too readily. Nevertheless, if he persevere firmly in his petition, let him know that he will have to observe the full discipline of the Rule, and that nothing will be abated for him.... However, let him be allowed to take rank next to the abbot to pronounce blessings, and to celebrate Mass, provided that the abbot give him permission. Otherwise, let him not presume to do anything, knowing that he is subject to the discipline of the Rule; but let him give to all an example of humility.[2]

Two chapters further on, in the same cautious spirit, the *Rule* goes on to consider the possibility of a monk, who is in the community already, being ordained for liturgical service:

> If any abbot wishes to have a priest or deacon ordained for his monastery, let him choose out one of his subjects who is worthy to exercise the priestly office. But let the one who is ordained beware of elation or pride, and let him not presume to do anything but what is commanded him by the abbot.... Let him always keep that place which is his according to the time of his entry into the monastery, except in his duties at the altar.[3]

Clearly, for these early writers on the ascetic life, the central danger of a monk's holding any ecclesiastical office was that it might breed a spirit

2. *Rule of St. Benedict* 60, trans. Justin McCann (London: Sheed and Ward, 1970), 66.
3. *Rule of St. Benedict* 62; McCann trans. 68.

of arrogance and personal ambition in the holder, which would be in dramatic contrast to the simple dedication to discipleship that lay at the origin of monastic observance. Clericalism, even at the origins of religious life, and the claim to precedence that can flow from holding church office, was seen as one of the main internal forces opposed to the ascetic spirit.

As the centuries went on, however, the role of the ordained leader in the Christian community, especially in the Latin church, came to be identified more and more closely with the personal call to holiness and union with God, to which religious consecration was understood to be a response. In the late sixth century and afterward, the role of the ordained bishop and presbyter came to be identified more and more as one of sacramentally representing Christ in his offering of himself to the Father: once and for all in his sacrifice of himself on the cross, but continuingly in the church, his body, through the commemorative sacrifice of the Eucharistic celebration. As the presiding minister of the Eucharist, every priest came to be seen as Christ's representative in the contemporary world, speaking Christ's words and offering Christ's unique and infinitely efficacious sacrifice now, in a sacramental way that makes it concretely and actively present for the world.[4] Along with this change of emphasis, which grew clearer in the theology of the Carolingian period and of the High Middle Ages, the term "priest" (*sacerdos*) now came to be applied first of all to presbyters rather than primarily to bishops, as in the patristic age; and the defining role of a priest was seen in the presbyter's power to offer to God the sacrifice of Christ by presiding at the Eucharist.[5] Priesthood, in the West, was in the process of being transformed from a ministry of community leadership to a unique opportunity for powerful intercessory prayer, rooted in the ongoing mediation of Christ himself.

All of this clearly affected the way Western Christians understood

4. See, for example, Gregory the Great, *Dialogues* 4.55–59, emphasizing through a variety of anecdotes the effectiveness, for the living and the dead, of the sacrifice of the Mass offered for particular people by individual priests.

5. For a classic expression of this understanding, see Thomas Aquinas, *Summa Theologiae* III, q. 37, a. 2: "The sacrament of order is directed to the sacrament of the Eucharist, which is the 'sacrament of sacraments.' . . . Hence, the distinction of orders is derived from their relation to the Eucharist."

the relationship of ordained priesthood to a life devoted to discipleship and contemplative prayer. From the fourth century on, it became increasingly common for bishops, such as Augustine, to encourage their clergy to live with them, in a life of regular, common prayer, practical obedience, and shared possessions. In the British Isles, early medieval bishops often gathered their clergy around them into communities living under a monastic rule, in effect transforming the diocese into an extension of the monastery. For the canons regular of the Middle Ages, the new "apostolic" communities of the thirteenth century such as the Dominicans and Franciscans, and even for Reformation-era active religious communities such as the Society of Jesus, the life of prayer and contemplation in a community of shared goods and simple lifestyle, under the direction of a religious superior as well as of the local bishop, became increasingly the context for a newly energized preaching and sacramental ministry to the world outside the community's walls. Although not all the members of these new, actively ministerial communities were sacramentally ordained, priesthood had become central to their understanding of the role of consecrated religious men in the world. For the Jesuits of the sixteenth century and later, in fact, only tested and qualified priests could be admitted to full profession as members of the religious community.

With the decrees of the Second Vatican Council, and in the twentieth-century theological ferment in which they grew, new questions began to be asked about this long-standing hybridization of religious charisms and ministerial leadership in the Catholic Church. As in many of its attempts at renewing the life of the church, the Council's decrees on the ministry of priests (*Presbyterorum Ordinis*) and on the renewal of religious life (*Perfectae Caritatis*) emphasize the importance of recapturing the "original" idea of these institutions as the best guide to their contemporary revitalization. In outlining the role of the ordained within the church, the Council makes it clear that all the baptized, as members of Christ's ecclesial body, are called to realize, in a variety of ways, Christ's priestly and sanctifying presence in the wider world.[6] The particular role of the ordained within the church is clearly presented as

6. See, for example, *Lumen Gentium* (*LG*) 10; *Presbyterorum Ordinis* (*PO*) 2.

one of enlightened, noncoercive leadership, realized through preaching the Word of God and celebrating the sacraments, in union with their bishops.[7] Although the Council emphasizes the central importance of the disciplined pursuit of holiness in the life of the priest—of celibacy, obedience to his bishop, simplicity of life, and even voluntary poverty,[8] as ways of growing in personal union with Christ, whose work in the world he is ordained to continue—the perspective from which the Council approaches priesthood is clearly that of the priest's distinctive *function*: his active role of ministry, rather than his spirituality. And the one mention of ordained members of religious congregations in the Council's decrees stresses their similarity to diocesan clergy in terms of their basic work in the church:

> Thus they may be said in a certain sense to belong to the diocesan clergy inasmuch as they share in the care of souls and in the practice of apostolic works under the authority of the bishops.[9]

The Council's model for priestly ministry is clearly that of the diocesan clergy.

Vatican II's document on religious life, *Perfectae Caritatis*, is considerably shorter and more general in its teaching, presumably because of the wide variety of forms and institutions in which Christians, through the centuries, have sought inspiration and support for following Jesus. The emphasis is on the importance, for every institute, of rediscovering its founder's charism: the particular vision of holiness and active discipleship from which the institute has grown; it is precisely in their variety that all of these institutionalized charisms together enrich the church.[10] But given the history of the interweaving of religious life in men's institutes with the public prayer and ministry of priests, it is

7. PO 4–5, 13.

8. See especially PO 15–17.

9. Decree on the Ministry of Bishops (*Christus Dominus*) 34, in Second Vatican Council, *The Basic Sixteen Documents: Vatican Council II; Constitutions, Decrees, Declarations*, trans., ed. Austin Flannery (Northport, N.Y.: Costello, 1996), 306.

10. So *Perfectae Caritatis* (*PC*) 2: "It is to the Church's advantage that each institution has its own proper character and function. Therefore the spirit and aims of each founder should be faithfully acknowledged and maintained, as indeed should each institute's sound traditions, for all of these constitute an institute's heritage"; Decree on the Ministry of Bishops, 387. See also *PC* 7–8.

striking how little attempt is made in these documents to reflect in a positive way on the relationship between them. *Perfectae Caritatis*, in fact, simply observes that in religious institutes containing both lay and ordained members, all should be "on an equal footing and with equal rights and obligations, apart from those arising from sacred orders."[11] The ancient fear that the ordination of monks might lead to ambition and class distinctions within the religious community seems to have reappeared.

In short, the paradox of ordained members of religious communities—of institutional office and personal spiritual commitment—continues to challenge us. To be effective in their witness to the gospel and in their role of leading others to Christ, the ordained members of the community need to cultivate many of the qualities and practices that have been part of religious life since the early church: humility, radical control of their human drives for sexual gratification and power, simplicity of life, readiness to listen and accept direction, simple charity, singleness of heart. Yet from the earliest days of the Christian community, ordination itself has been a way of designating its leaders, not of calling its members to deeper discipleship. The religious or monastic life, on the other hand, has had as its purpose the pursuit of personal and communal holiness, which need not involve the direct service or leadership of others. How can we understand the relationship of these two ways of life as distinct yet complementary? Is the insistence today on sacramental ordination for effective liturgical and community leadership within a religious or monastic body simply a relic of a clericalist past, as some recent scholars suggest? Does membership in a religious community add anything of substance to the preaching and ministry that is to be expected of any sincere and well-trained deacon, priest, or bishop? Does the ordination of vowed religious as priests compromise the powerful effect of their charismatic life itself within the church?

In this book, Christian Raab has opened an inviting and challenging new way for us to consider this ancient problem. Fr. Christian is himself a Benedictine monk and priest from St. Meinrad's Archabbey in Indiana and is engaged in forming future diocesan and monastic priests at

11. *PC* 15, 397.

St. Meinrad's School of Theology. He is also a student of the work of the late Swiss theologian Hans Urs von Balthasar, whose highly original synthesis incorporated elements of German romantic philosophy, a wide range of literary and musical sources, and Balthasar's own pastoral and spiritual experience as a Jesuit formed in the *Spiritual Exercises* of St. Ignatius into his view of the long tradition of Christian theology. Balthasar was never willing to accept a hard distinction between spiritual vision and theological learning, prayer, and creative analysis, the existential and the objective realms of reality. So his theology, in all its comprehensive breadth, remains a reflection, by a man of deep aesthetic sensibility, of long spiritual experience and peerless erudition, on the human encounter with the ineffable, unimaginable God.

The various forms of the religious life always engaged Balthasar. From his own long education and reading and from his years as a priest and spiritual director, he developed a typology, based on New Testament figures, that enabled him to distinguish and characterize different forms of discipleship and ministry in concrete terms. Fr. Christian here suggests we can find in Balthasar's imaginative use of these iconic spiritual types a fruitful approach to answering the ancient doubts and anxieties about the place of religious priesthood in the church of today. And looking beyond Balthasar's synthesis to the writings of Pope St. John Paul II, Fr. Christian powerfully suggests one possible answer to this age-old dilemma:

> The religious priest has a double signification of radical discipleship and objective, official, apostolic ministry. John Paul stated rather dramatically that "he reproduces in his life the fullness of the mystery of Christ," i.e., both Jesus' subjective lifestyle and his objective office with the saving grace it brings [*Vita Consecrata* 30]. By signifying both mysteries, the religious priest also shows their union [chapters 7 through 10 of this volume].

As is usually the case with paradoxes, the truth seems to lie in the middle of things: affirming both sides of the apparent contradiction at once, thus showing that it is really not a contradiction at all. As in the Mystery of Christ's own person, we simply have to learn to think of God and his creation in a new way.

This is a rich, learned book, engaging an ancient, central problem in the life of organized Christian discipleship with a breadth and depth that will both challenge our suppositions and lead us to new possibilities of understanding. We can only be indebted to Fr. Christian Raab for leading us on a journey that promises to draw us into a deeper appreciation of God's ever-present gifts in the life of his church.

PREFACE

My interest in the theology of religious priesthood grew out of my own vocation. I am a Benedictine monk and priest of St. Meinrad Archabbey in southern Indiana. This means I belong to a religious family that was not founded by a priest. In accord with St. Benedict's original intention, male Benedictine communities are typically mixed, meaning they have both ordained and nonordained members. Although I entered the monastery already having a strong desire to be a priest and was grateful when I was allowed to pursue that desire to its end in ordination, I still had to think about how the monastic vocation and priestly vocation might be integrated into a single vocational identity.

Complicating matters, my community, like many others, had, in the not too far distant past, responded enthusiastically to Vatican II's call to eliminate differences of status between ordained and nonordained members. On the one hand, this was certainly a positive development. Earlier generations had had entirely separate formational tracks for those intending to be priest monks and those intending to be brothers. Priests and brothers had slightly different clothing. They did not socialize much with each other. Clerics even had posher place settings at meals. After the Council, these class distinctions thankfully disappeared. On the other hand, because the onus of vocational identity was now placed so strongly on simply being a monk, for this emphasized what we all had in common, the answer to the question of how a priestly vocation fit with being a monk remained quite murky.

Furthermore, one of St. Meinrad's founding missions, which continues to this day, was to operate a seminary for the formation of clergy for the Catholic Church. Historically, the vast majority of our seminarians have been diocesan students, and there has been a reasonable, built-in pressure to gear the seminary education there toward diocesan clergy. As a monk in formation, however, this meant that where the formation I received in my religious community did not speak much about priestly identity, the formation I received on the seminary side did not speak much about monastic identity. The integration of these two identities was something left up to the individual monk. For me it remained a persistent question, leading to the research that resulted in this book.

In the decade since my ordination, I have discovered that the questions that motivated my research have been and continue to be shared by many other religious priests and seminarians. This is a book for them. Its humble purpose is to provide some theological insights for integrating a religious and priestly identity. Second, but only second, it is a book on Hans Urs von Balthasar's theology, which I have found very helpful for thinking about religious priesthood. In no way is it an attempt to exhaustively systematize his thought or to speak a final word about his theology of vocations and states of life. It simply strives to illuminate and apply some helpful insights he provides that I believe help us appreciate more fully the meaning of religious priesthood, its importance for the church, and the privilege of being called to it.

ACKNOWLEDGMENTS

With deepest gratitude, I thank all those persons who supported me professionally and personally as I researched and wrote this book. I am especially grateful to Christopher J. Ruddy, for his theological mentorship; to Msgr. Paul McPartlan and Nicholas J. Healy, who served as my first readers, for their time, attentiveness, and invaluable feedback; and to Fr. Brian Daley, SJ, for the thoughtful foreword he authored for this volume. I am also greatly indebted to Fr. Regis Armstrong, OFM Cap, Fr. John Beal, Fr. Patrick Cooney, OSB, Fr. Thomas Gricoski, OSB, Fr. Christopher Hadley, SJ, Fr. Dan Horan, OFM, Fr. Austin Litke, OP, and James Ware for reviewing portions of the manuscript at various stages; and Jonathan Ciraulo, Michael Dunnigan, Andrew Krema, and Casey Lilley for their help with foreign language sources. Any remaining errors in content or translation are mine. Thanks as well to Br. Joel Blaize, OSB, for his help with formatting; and to John Martino and everyone at CUA Press for their work in publications.

Over the course of my research and writing, I was privileged to engage in informal conversations with various religious and priests about my topic. These conversations sometimes led to great research leads. They always contributed greatly to my perspectives on priesthood and religious life. Many of these same people have also been wonderfully supportive friends. I wish to acknowledge Fr. Matthew Luft, OSB, Sr. Jeana Visel, OSB, the Benedictine Sisters of Bristow, VA, Br. Richard Oliver, OSB, Fr. Quinn Connors, O.Carm, Fr. Jude DeAngelo, OFM Conv, Fr. Justin Ross, OFM Conv, Fr. Marek Stybor, OFM Conv, Br. James Moore, OFM Conv, Fr. Andrew Hofer, OP, Sr. Maria Frassati Jakupcak, OP, Sr. Stephen Patrick Joly, OP, Sr. Teresa Christi Balek, OP, Sr. Mariana McGlynn, OP, Sr. Chau Nguyen, OP, Fr. David Thayer, SSP, Br. Peter

Killeen, FSC, Sr. Ruth Harkins, IHM, the Paulist Fathers of Washington, D.C., Fr. David Alcade Morales, Fr. Ildefonso Figueres, Fr. Michael Witczak, Fr. John Galvan, Fr. Edwyn Dwyer, Fr. Steve LaFlamme, and Fr. Peter Marshall. Thanks also to Joseph Cardinal Tobin, CSsR, Bishop Brendan Leahy, and Fr. John O'Malley, SJ, who took time from their very busy schedules to offer perspective and/or pointers on my project.

I am very grateful to Fr. Archabbot Kurt Stasiak, OSB, Fr. Prior John McMullen, OSB, Ret. Abbot Justin DuVall, OSB, and all the monks of St. Meinrad Archabbey, without whose witness this book would not have been inspired and without whose support and sacrifice it would never have been completed. I especially thank Fr. Harry Hagan, OSB, and Fr. Guerric DeBona, OSB, for their role in my monastic formation; Fr. Colman Grabert, OSB, for giving me his Balthasar library and for his encouragement; and Fr. Ephrem Carr, OSB, Fr. Guy Mansini, OSB, Fr. Mark O'Keefe, OSB, Fr. Denis Robinson, OSB, and the late Fr. Cyprian Davis, OSB, for their teaching and/or scholarship, which I have had the privilege to cite in this book.

Finally, thanks to the many other persons who supported me with their love, friendship, and encouragement as I researched and wrote this book: especially, the Raab family, Nick and Melissa Hladek, Megan and Ernie Freund, the good people in CUA's Office of Campus Ministry, Fr. Raymond Studzinski, OSB, and all the priests and residents of Curley Hall, and everyone at Saint Meinrad Seminary and School of Theology.

ABBREVIATIONS

Balthasar's Trilogy

GL (1–7)	*The Glory of the Lord: A Theological Aesthetics*, vols. 1–7
TD (1–5)	*Theo-Drama: Theological Dramatical Theory*, vols. 1–5
TL (1–3)	*Theo-Logic*, vols. 1–3

Other Works by Balthasar

CSL	*The Christian State of Life*
DGO	*Die Grossen Ordensregeln*
ET (1–4)	*Explorations in Theology*, vols. 1–4
EWG	*Engagement with God: The Drama of Christian Discipleship*
FG	*First Glance at Adrienne von Speyr*
JT	*"Johannine Themes in the Rule and Their Meaning Today"*
LAIC	*Love Alone Is Credible*
LLC	*The Laity and the Life of the Counsels*
OPSC	*The Office of Peter and the Structure of the Church*
OT	*Our Task: A Report and a Plan*
PS	*Priestly Spirituality*
PSC	*Paul Struggles with His Congregation*
TH	*A Theology of History*
TSS	*Two Sisters in the Spirit: Thérèse of Lisieux and Elizabeth of the Trinity*

Vatican II Documents

AA *Apostolicam Actuositatem*

AG *Ad Gentes*

CD *Christus Dominus*

GS *Gaudium et Spes*

LG *Lumen Gentium*

PC *Perfectae Caritatis*

PO *Presybterorum Ordinis*

SC *Sacrosanctum Concilium*

John Paul II Documents

CL *Christifideles Laici*

FC *Familiaris Consortio*

PDV *Pastores Dabo Vobis*

PG *Pastores Gregis*

RD *Redemptionis Donum*

VC *Vita Consecrata*

Other Magisterial Documents

CCC *Catechism of the Catholic Church*

CIC *Code of Canon Law* (1983)

FLC *Congregation for Institutes of Consecrated Life and Societies of Apostolic Life, Fraternal Life in Community*

MR *Sacred Congregation for Religious and for Secular Institutes, Mutuae Relationes*

RCC *Rites of the Catholic Church*

VS *Congregation for Institutes of Consecrated Life and Societies of Apostolic Life, Verbi Sponsa*

English quotations from magisterial documents are taken from the Vatican website (http://w2.vatican.va/content/vatican/en.html) unless otherwise indicated.

Ancient and Medieval Works

FA:ED	Francis of Assisi, *Francis of Assisi: Early Documents*
RB	Benedict of Nursia, *The Rule of St. Benedict*
RM	The Master, *The Rule of the Master*
ST	Thomas Aquinas, *Summa Theologica*

English quotations from sacred scripture are taken from the NABRE unless they are included in a quote from another author in which case they are quoted as presented by that author. Quotations from *The Rule of St. Benedict* are taken from Timothy Fry, ed., *RB1980: The Rule of St. Benedict in Latin and English with Notes* (Collegeville, Minn.: Liturgical Press, 1981), unless otherwise noted.

UNDERSTANDING THE RELIGIOUS PRIESTHOOD

Introduction

Those called to combine the religious vocation with ordained ministry have always faced a tension. Early monks commonly perceived the duties that accompanied ordination to be a threat to their spiritual quest. Ordained medieval friars faced major questions as to how they fitted into diocesan structures. In the last fifty years, however, this tension has arguably erupted into an identity crisis for religious priests.[1] There are at least four reasons for this crisis.

First, the Second Vatican Council left the identity and mission of religious priests in an ambiguous state. Although the theology of priesthood, both ordained and lay, is ubiquitous throughout the Vatican II documents, it is conspicuously absent in the Council's discussions of religious life. Similarly, there is little discussion of religious priests where the theology of ordained ministry is presented. Religious priests appear to be, at best, a hybrid of two vocations discussed separately by the Council. Second, as John O'Malley has pointed out, the Council and postconciliar magisterial teaching so strongly encourage the diocesan priest to embrace the evangelical counsels, which typically specify the religious state, that these no longer appear to differentiate the religious priest from his diocesan counterpart in a meaningful way.[2]

Third, as O'Malley also points out, the Council and subsequent magisterial teaching most often present ordained ministry according to the model of diocesan clergy: Priesthood is paradigmatically envi-

1. For more on the background of this crisis, which will be elaborated in part II of this book, see Paul K. Hennessy, ed., *A Concert of Charisms: Ordained Ministry in Religious Life* (New York: Paulist Press, 1997).

2. John W. O'Malley, "Priesthood, Ministry, and Religious Life: Some Historical and Historiographical Considerations," *Theological Studies* 49 (1988): 223–67.

sioned as being exercised within a parochial setting as ministry to a stable community of the faithful in cooperation with the diocesan bishop. This does not account for the history of ministry of religious priests, who have often exercised their ministry outside of typical parochial structures, frequently to the non-evangelized and, to varying degrees, exempt from local episcopal jurisdiction. When priesthood is presented exclusively according to the diocesan type, the religious vocation appears to compromise the priestly one.

Fourth, there is also a question as to whether ordaining religious threatens the integrity of the religious life. Since the Council, some thinkers have contended that ordination introduces hierarchical class structures into religious life antithetical to the desires of religious founders (e.g., Benedict and Francis), that it requires additional formation that inevitably distances one from his religious identity, and that it compromises the prophetic charism of religious by creating a double set of allegiances to one's religious community and superior, on the one hand, and to one's presbyterate and bishop, on the other.[3]

Pope John Paul II once assured religious priests that they could find a "profound and dynamic unity" between their religious and priestly vocations.[4] The question is, "How?" Is there a way to understand the identity and mission of the religious priest that honors both what he shares with the diocesan priest and nonordained religious and what differentiates him? Is there a way to do this that does not appear to compromise either the religious or priestly vocations?

To answer these questions, this book will look especially to Hans Urs von Balthasar (1905–88), a major twentieth-century theologian who reflected upon the meaning of religious priesthood. Balthasar's ecclesiology is unique because it not only does not exclude religious priests,

3. See, for example, the arguments of Sandra M. Schneiders, *Religious Life in a New Millennium*, vol. 1, *Finding the Treasure: Locating Catholic Religious Life in a New Ecclesial and Cultural Context* (New York: Paulist Press, 2000), esp.264–81; Doris Gottemoeller, "The Priesthood: Implications in Consecrated Life for Women," in Hennessey, *Concert of Charisms*, 127–38; and Ghislain Lafont, "The Theology of Priesthood in the Context of Monasticism" (audiocassette), Monastic Institute Tapes: Benedictine Federation of the Americas, n. 8105 (Richardton, N.Dak.: Christian Life Center, 1981).

4. John Paul II, Apostolic Exhortation *Vita Consecrata* (March 25, 1996), 30 (hereafter *VC*).

but arguably requires them. While some aspects of his ecclesiology have been systematized and advanced by subsequent scholars—most notably by Dermot Power regarding the Petrine office and diocesan priesthood[5] and by Brendan Leahy regarding the Marian profile and the laity[6]—there has not yet been much theological reflection on Balthasar's vision of religious priesthood, which he puts forth under the emblematic figures of the Apostles John and Paul.

Besides his fame[7] and influence on popes John Paul II,[8] Benedict XVI, and Francis,[9] there are two reasons Balthasar is an ideal theologian from whom to develop this theology of the religious priesthood. First, his personal history offered him a unique and rare "insider's perspective" on various ecclesial vocations. Second, his theological style shares characteristics of Vatican II and thus can be brought easily into a fruitful dialogue with the Council.

5. Dermot Power, *A Spiritual Theology of the Priesthood: The Mystery of Christ and the Mission of the Priest* (Washington, D.C.: The Catholic University of America Press, 1998).

6. Brendan Leahy, *The Marian Profile in the Ecclesiology of Hans Urs von Balthasar* (Hyde Park, N.Y.: New City, 2000).

7. Fergus Kerr observed in 2007 that Balthasar "is widely regarded as the greatest Catholic theologian of the [twentieth] century" and is "by far the most discussed Catholic theologian at present"; Kerr, *Twentieth-Century Catholic Theologians: From Neoscholasticism to Nuptial Mysticism* (Malden, Mass.: Blackwell, 2007), 121 and 144.

8. In 1984, John Paul II awarded Balthasar the International Pope Paul VI prize for theology and then, four years later, in 1988, named him a cardinal (though Balthasar died three days before the honor was officially bestowed). The same pope adopted one of the hallmark features of Balthasar's ecclesiology, the interplay of the church's Marian and Petrine profiles, citing the Swiss theologian on this point in the apostolic letter *Mulieris Dignitatem* (hereafter *MD*) (August 15, 1988), 27. Balthasar's notion of the church's Marian and Petrine profiles also appears in the *Catechism of the Catholic Church* (*CCC* 773). For more on Balthasar's impact on John Paul II, see John McDade, "John Paul II and His Ecclesiology," in *The Legacy of John Paul II*, ed. Gerald O'Collins and Michael Hayes, 51–70 (London: Burns and Oates, 2008).

9. For discussion of Balthasar's influence on popes Benedict XVI and Francis, see Tracey Rowland, *Benedict XVI: A Guide for the Perplexed* (New York: T. and T. Clark, 2010), and Massimo Borghesi, *The Mind of Pope Francis* (Collegeville, Minn.: Litirgical Press Academic, 2018).

Life

Balthasar's life would have sensitized him in a particular way to the significance of the various states of life and vocations to the church's life and mission.[10] Hans Urs von Balthasar was born in Lucerne, Switzerland, in 1905, to an observant Catholic family of noble stock. Three of his immediate family members were distinguished lay people whose vocational paths included visible ecclesial dimensions: His father was an architect who designed Lucerne's St. Karli-Kirche, a trend-setting work of modern church architecture. His mother was one of the founders of the Swiss League of Catholic Women, for which she also served as the first general secretary. His younger brother became an officer in the Vatican's Swiss Guard. With the possible exception of Yves Congar, Balthasar reflected more extensively and profoundly on the laity's role in the church than any other twentieth-century theologian. His sensitivity to the significance of the layperson's vocation was surely formed at an early stage by his own family's high level of ecclesial involvement.

Balthasar also wrote extensively about religious life. He was fortunate, therefore, to have intimate personal exposure to many of the traditional orders. His family tree included "abbots and abbesses, canons, and a Jesuit provincial in Mexico."[11] In his youth he attended liturgies at

10. The most complete biography of Balthasar available in English is Peter Henrici, "Hans Urs von Balthasar: A Sketch of His Life," in *Hans Urs von Balthasar: His Life and Work*, ed. David L. Schindler, 7–43 (San Francisco: Ignatius Press, 1991). There are book-length biographies in Italian: Elio Guerriero, *Hans Urs von Balthasar* (Milan: Edizione Paoline, 1991); and German: Manfred Lochbrunner, *Hans Urs von Balthasar und seine Theologen-kollegen* (Würzberg: Echter, 2009). Most introductions to Balthasar's theology begin with biographical information and give special attention to his intellectual formation and influences. See Rodney A. Howsare, *Balthasar: A Guide for the Perplexed* (London: T. and T. Clark, 2009); Edward T. Oakes and David Moss, eds. *The Cambridge Companion to Hans Urs von Balthasar* (Cambridge: Cambridge University Press, 2004); Oakes, *Pattern of Redemption: The Theology of Hans Urs von Balthasar* (New York: Continuum, 1994); Aidan Nichols, *Divine Fruitfulness: A Guide through Balthasar's Theology beyond the Trilogy* (Washington, D.C.: The Catholic University of America Press, 2007); and Nichols, *The Word Has Been Abroad: A Guide through Balthasar's Aesthetics* (Washington, D.C.: The Catholic University of America Press, 1998). For Balthasar's own brief sketch of his early life, see his *Our Task: A Report and a Plan*, trans. John Saward (San Francisco: Ignatius, 1994), 35–44 (hereafter *OT*).

11. Henrici, "Hans Urs von Balthasar," 8

a Franciscan church, where he sang in the choir. His sister Renée was a member of the Franciscan Sisters of Sainte-Marie des Anges and served as the community's Superior General from 1971 to 1983. Balthasar had even greater exposure to Benedictine life. He attended the *Gymnasium* (equivalent to the American high school) at the abbey of Engelberg, where he enjoyed studying music and literature. Later, in between Balthasar's departure from the Jesuits and his incardination into a diocese, Balthasar renewed his vows to observe the evangelical counsels before the abbot of Maria Laach abbey in Germany. When Balthasar established his publishing house, Johannes Verlag, he located it in the village at the base of the ancient Swiss abbey of Einsiedeln.

Balthasar's most important involvement with religious life, though, came through his years as a member of the Society of Jesus. In 1921, Balthasar transferred from the Benedictine school at Engelberg to the Jesuit college at Feldkirch, Austria. From there, Balthasar moved on to study *Germanistik*, "an interdisciplinary field of German studies, encompassing both literary and philosophical approaches to the canonical German authors," at the state-run University of Zurich.[12] Balthasar gravitated back to the Jesuits after participating in a thirty-day Ignatian retreat in 1927. The retreat awakened in him a sense of religious vocation for the first time. After completing his doctorate in German studies with a thesis on the "History of the Eschatological Problem in German Literature," he entered the Jesuits in 1929. After a novitiate at Paluch and theological studies at Fourvière, Lyons, in France, Balthasar was ordained a priest in 1936.[13]

Balthasar left the Jesuits in 1950, just before he would have made final vows.[14] Before saying something about why that fracture took place, it is important to note that the Jesuits always remained for Balthasar "a beloved homeland"; he described the necessity of leaving them as strik-

12. Oakes and Moss, *Cambridge Companion to Hans Urs von Balthasar*, 3.

13. He spent the first four years of his priesthood contributing to the Jesuit journal *Stimmen du Zeit* and concentrating on his own writings. In 1940, Balthasar was given the choice "of going either to Rome as a professor at the Gregorian University or to Basel as a student chaplain." He chose the latter, says Henrici, "because pastoral work was closer to his heart than lecturing"; Henrici, "Hans Urs von Balthasar," 14.

14. By canonical exception, the Jesuits are the only religious community in which final religious vows can succeed ordination.

ing him "like a blow."[15] Long after Balthasar's departure from the Jesuits, he remained deeply connected to the Society's spirituality. Balthasar continued to direct Ignatian retreats, and he believed the secular institute he helped found was under Ignatian inspiration and a natural development of Ignatian ideals.[16] As Werner Löser has shown, the influence of St. Ignatius can be detected in many of Balthasar's theological writings, especially his reflections on states of life and vocations.[17]

Secular institutes are a third ecclesiological category with which Balthasar had intimate familiarity. Balthasar's involvement with secular institutes emerged through his association with Adrienne von Speyr, a lay married physician and religious visionary Balthasar met in 1940. After facilitating her conversion to Catholicism, he served as her spiritual director and was convinced of her authenticity as a mystic. Balthasar eventually moved in with von Speyr's family and transcribed sixty volumes of her dictations of her mystical experiences and insights. Five years after their first encounter, Balthasar and von Speyr founded a secular institute, *Johannesgemeinschaft*, or the Community of St. John. The mission of the community was to provide a way for lay persons, living in the world, to combine the embrace of secular work with full commitment to the evangelical counsels. Balthasar hoped that his theology would never be considered apart from his common mission with von Speyr in the establishment of this secular institute.[18]

At that time, secular institutes were still very new in church life and somewhat misunderstood. It was unclear, for example, whether their members should be considered lay or religious. They needed a theorist. Balthasar rose to the task. In 1955, he wrote that the foundation of the

15. Balthasar, *First Glance at Adrienne Von Speyr* (hereafter *FG*), trans. Antje Lawry and Sergia Englund (San Francisco: Ignatius Press, 1981), 43.

16. *FG* 51–55, and *OT* 21–22. The Community of St. John requires its members to undergo St Ignatius's spiritual exercises. Its rule contains many references to their use. See *OT* 119–75, esp. 136, 158, and 175. Balthasar stated, "What Ignatius wanted in his time clearly meant for me and from then on, 'worldly community' (secular institute); the difficult sacrifice demanded by the transition was accompanied by the certainty of serving the same idea with greater exactness"; Balthasar, *Rechenschaft 1965* (Einsiedeln: Johannes, 1965), 35.

17. Werner Löser, "The Ignatian *Exercises* in the Work of Hans Urs von Balthasar," in Schindler, *Hans Urs von Balthasar: His Life and Work*, 103–20.

18. *OT* 13.

secular institute was the "ecclesial action that has been assigned to me, which I myself have not chosen. This is the center; everything else, even if developed earlier, has been placed around it."[19] These words illuminate the central place the theology of secular institutes has in his work. Importantly for our purposes, in order for Balthasar to provide and defend a theory of secular institutes, he had to think through a whole theology of states of life and vocations. This theology in turn sheds light on the meaning of religious life and priesthood.

To Balthasar's great disappointment, the Jesuits were unwilling to support his work with the secular institute and were uncomfortable with his association with von Speyr. Balthasar, however, had come to believe that his mission to develop the secular institute was from God and was inseparable from his relationship with von Speyr. Therefore, in 1950, Balthasar left the Society of Jesus.[20]

Every priest must be attached to either a diocese or to an institute of consecrated life. Balthasar was no longer a Jesuit, and secular institutes were not yet considered institutes of consecrated life, so he needed to find a diocese in which to incardinate. Openly committed as Balthasar was to the work of advancing secular institutes, he initially struggled to find a diocese that would allow him the freedom to continue with von Speyr and the *Johannesgemeinschaft*. He finally incardinated into the diocese of Chur, Switzerland, in 1956, and spent the remaining thirty years of his life as a diocesan priest. Diocesan priesthood is thus a fourth ecclesial category, or vocation, that Balthasar experienced firsthand.[21]

Balthasar's life as a diocesan priest, however, was atypical. He served as a student chaplain, writer, publisher, spiritual director, speaker, and retreat master. He was singularly dedicated to advancing the Community of St. John. He was never assigned to a parish and never actually lived in the diocese to which he belonged. Up to the end of his life, he longed to be reconciled with the Jesuits. Paradoxically, then, the ecclesial category in which Balthasar spent most of his life was, in some sense, the one with which he had the least affinity.

19. Balthasar, *My Work: In Retrospect*, ed. Cornelia Capol (San Francisco: Ignatius, 1993), 43.

20. Balthasar narrates the story in *OT* 79–80.

21. See Lochbrunner, *Hans Urs von Balthasar und seine Theologen-kollegen*, 178, for some details about Balthasar's attempts to be incardinated in various dioceses.

Dermot Power argues that Balthasar's vision of diocesan priesthood is marked by a degree of ambivalence and lack of concrete realism because of his personal circumstances.[22] Nonetheless, as Power's own book shows, Balthasar's view of diocesan priesthood should not be dismissed. Even if he never felt quite personally at home in the vocation, he had a deep love and esteem for diocesan clergy. He was troubled both by anti-authority attitudes in the church and by mediocrity in the priesthood. He therefore devoted much of his thought to defending the dignity of the priesthood, both diocesan and religious, and to exhorting priests to holiness. Reflecting his expertise on the priesthood, he was summoned in 1971 to Rome to the Synod of Bishops to serve as a "*peritus* on the question of the priestly office."[23]

Balthasar died in 1988. In 1985, just three years before his passing, the reconciliation with the Jesuits he had long hoped for almost happened. Unfortunately, it had to be jettisoned once again over the thorny issue of Balthasar's commitment to secular institutes.[24] While he may have died feeling like an outsider to his beloved Jesuits, Balthasar's long life's journey had provided him a unique insider's view of lay life, religious life, secular institutes, and diocesan priesthood. This experience would enrich his theology.

His Style

Unlike some of the other great theologians of the twentieth century, Balthasar neither attended nor advised the Second Vatican Council, his influence only being felt in the decades afterward. Nevertheless, his theological style, what one may call his aesthetic approach, matches well the teaching style of the Council and can help fill out areas neglected by the Council, such as religious priesthood. As John O'Malley and Avery Dulles have pointed out, the theological style adopted by the Council was a departure from the style of previous councils, and this

22. Power, *Spiritual Theology of the Priesthood*, 7–8.

23. Louis Roberts, *The Theological Aesthetics of Hans Urs von Balthasar* (Washington, D.C.: The Catholic University of America Press, 1987), 19. Balthasar drafted the synod's chapter on priestly spirituality.

24. Nichols, *Word Has Been Abroad*, xviii.

change was as significant to the Council's teaching as the content of its documents. Heretofore, most church councils had been called in order to deal with specific doctrinal or disciplinary controversies. Hence, they operated either like "juridical bodies that heard cases and rendered judgment" or like "legislative bodies that issued ordinances, to which were attached, as with any law, penalties for failure to comply."[25] Vatican II, however, was not called to deal with any specific controversy, but to present the church's teaching anew to the modern world. Hence, the Council "issued no canons, no anathemas ... in so speaking, it marked a significant break with past councils."[26]

The theological style adopted by the Council, says O'Malley, can be identified as panegyric, or as *ars laudendi*, the art of praising. "Panegyric is the painting of an idealized portrait in order to excite admiration and appropriation."[27] This style, which is more literary than philosophical and more aesthetic than legal, was employed in antiquity by the church fathers and had been revived by twentieth-century protagonists of *la nouvelle théologie* such as de Lubac and Congar. The purpose of the panegyric style

> is not so much to clarify concepts as to heighten appreciation for a person, an event, or an institution and to excite emulation of an ideal. Its goal is the winning of internal assent, not the imposition of conformity from outside. It teaches, but not so much by way of propositions and pronouncements as by suggestion, insinuation, and example.[28]

The key to accomplishing this purpose is to hold up ideals, describe them in an aesthetically powerful way, and only then "draw conclusions from them and spell out practical consequences. This is a soft style compared with the hard-hitting style of canons and dialectical discourse. It is rightly described as 'pastoral' because it was meant to make Christian ideals appealing."[29]

25. O'Malley, *What Happened at Vatican II* (Cambridge, Mass.: Belknap Press, 2008), 44.

26. O'Malley, *What Happened at Vatican II*, 45.

27. O'Malley, *What Happened at Vatican II*, 47.

28. O'Malley, *What Happened at Vatican II*, 47.

29. O'Malley, *What Happened at Vatican II*, 47. It is appropriate to recall here that

Not by condemning or legislating, but by holding up ideal images, the Council "manifests what it holds to be the church's inner reality" and "thereby indicates how the church will, ideally, behave and 'do business.'"[30] In commenting on the Council's style, Dulles explains how its use of images is just as, if not more, effective than juridical anathemas or scholastic distinctions in leading the audience toward the truth, attitudes, and actions it seeks to elicit:

> Images function as symbols. That is to say, they speak to man existentially and find an echo in the inarticulate depths of his psyche. Such images communicate through their evocative power. They convey a latent meaning that is apprehended in conceptual, even a subliminal way. Symbols transform the horizons of man's life, integrate his perception of reality, alter his scale of values, reorient his loyalties, attachments, and aspirations in a manner far exceeding the powers of abstract conceptual thought. Religious images, as used in the Bible and Christian preaching, focus our experience in a new way. They have an aesthetic appeal, and are apprehended not simply by the mind but by the imagination, the heart, or more, properly, the whole man.[31]

Images, therefore, can be exceedingly powerful. They "suggest attitudes and courses of action; they intensify confidence and devotion. To some extent they are self-fulfilling; they make the Church become what they suggest the Church is."[32]

Vatican II was a council of images. It provided portraits not only of

---

in the speech that opened the Second Vatican Council, Pope John XXIII asked the Council to present the fullness of the church's teaching in a positive manner that would be attractive to the modern world. Rather than condemning errors through canons and anathemas or proving assertions through scholastic discourse, the Council should provide an inviting presentation of Christian truths. During the course of the Council, John's speech was often recalled and the Council fathers strove to produce evangelical, pastoral documents more reminiscent of sacred scripture and the church fathers than of dry theological manuals. See Gérard Philips, "Dogmatic Constitution on the Church: History of the Constitution," in *Commentary on the Documents of Vatican II*, ed. Herbert Vorgrimler, trans. Lalit Adolphus, Kevin Smyth, and Richard Strachan (New York: Herder and Herder, 1967–69), 1:108.

30. O'Malley, *What Happened at Vatican II*, 49.

31. Avery Dulles, *Models of the Church*, rev. ed. (New York: Image, 1987), 20.

32. Dulles, *Models of the Church*, 20–21.

the church, but also of the various vocations and states of life within the church: the lay person, the deacon, the priest, the bishop, and the religious. This panegyric style must be understood for the ramifications of the Council's teaching regarding religious priesthood to be fully appreciated. With respect to religious priesthood, the Council did not provide specific imagery of religious priesthood, and its directive images for priesthood and religious life appeared mutually exclusive. This could only tend toward a sense that religious priesthood represented a compromise of either religious life or priesthood. If images truly have the power O'Malley and Dulles suggest, then it is not surprising that religious priesthood experienced an identity crisis after the Council.

In many ways, Balthasar shared the Council's panegyric approach. He described his seven-volume theological aesthetics as "an attempt to develop theology in light of the third transcendental, that is to say: to complement the vision of the true and the good with that of the beautiful."[33] He believed that, when perceived in faith, the beauty of revelation has transformative power for the beholder. Balthasar's first theological goal is to be transformed himself by the encounter with divine revelation. His second goal is to illuminate revelation's content in such a way that those who engage his theology will be led to their own personal transformation through contact with Christ in relation to whom Balthasar hopes his own theology is transparent.[34]

The first volume of Balthasar's theological aesthetics is entitled *Seeing the Form*, a pithy way of describing how Balthasar perceives the first task of theology. Where Dulles and O'Malley speak of images, Balthasar speaks of form (*Gestalt*). Form is that which mediates beauty, splendor, and glory. Form has a structure somewhat like that of a sacrament. Sacraments contain what they signify. Beauty similarly resides in an object's form.[35] Also, just as sacraments affect those who receive them, the form impresses itself on the one contemplating. The more one beholds

33. Balthasar, *Glory of the Lord: A Theological Aesthetics*, vol. 1, *Seeing the Form*, trans. Erasmo Leivà Merikakis (Edinburgh: T. and T. Clark, 1982), 9 (hereafter, *GL* 1).

34. See Angelo Scola, *Balthasar: A Theological Style* (Grand Rapids, Mich.: Eerdmans, 1996), 2.

35. Balthasar states, "Light does not fall on this form from above and from outside, rather, it breaks forth from the form's interior.... The content (*Gehalt*) does not lie behind the form (*Gestalt*), but within it"; *GL* 1:151.

in wonder a beautiful form, the more one becomes impressed by this form.

For Balthasar, theology has as its "primary object of perception, God's self-disclosure in the form of Christ,"[36] a form that is the "unique, hypostatic union between archetype and image."[37] Christ is archetype because all creaturely beauty derives from and reflects divine glory. He is image because he is the perfect concrete particularization of transcendent beauty. The form of Christ reveals the ultimate meaning of the world, man, and, most importantly, the truth of God's interpersonal trinitarian life. The form of Christ is most radically unveiled in the Cross, which, through its "deformity" (*Ungestalt*), best expresses God's glory by unveiling the radical extent of God's kenotic love.[38]

The theological task is completed by faithfully displaying the content of revelation with the Christ-form at its center.[39] Balthasar's method is accordingly highly scriptural: He seeks to "identify the contours" of Christ's form as it is communicated in Holy Writ and explicate it for the church.[40] This can mean that Balthasar's corpus is marked by a "preponderance of description over argument."[41] However, his work is not simply a repetition of scripture. According to Balthasar, the theologian must himself be transformed by his contemplative encounter with the form. Impressed by revelation's scriptural expression, he can present it in new, illuminating ways to others. He can make connections and highlight aspects of revelation particularly necessary for his age. The theologian's task is to present revelation in a beautiful way and thus to help foster the communication of form. For Balthasar, theology is "on

36. Robert Koerpel, "The Form and Drama of the Church: Hans Urs von Balthasar on Mary, Peter, and the Eucharist," *Logos: A Journal of Catholic Thought and Culture* 11, no. 1 (2008): 76.

37. *GL* 1:432.

38. Chau Nguyen, "The Church and the Eucharist in Light of the Marian Principle according to the Thought of Hans Urs von Balthasar," unpublished paper presented in Eucharist and Church course, The Catholic University of America, Washington, D.C., April 12, 2010, 2–3; See also Dermot Power, *A Spiritual Theology of the Priesthood*, 29–31.

39. *TD* 1, 125f.

40. Bevil Bramwell, "Hans Urs von Balthasar's Theology of Scripture," *New Blackfriars* 86, no. 1003 (2005): 314.

41. Karen Kilby, *Balthasar: A (Very) Critical Introduction* (Grand Rapids, Mich.: Eerdmans, 2012), 147.

the one hand an obedient repetition of the expression of revelation imprinted on the believer, and on the other, a creative, childlike, free sharing in the bringing-to-expression in the Holy Spirit … of the mystery which expresses itself."[42]

Balthasar's panegyric theology can thus be a helpful conversation partner for Vatican II and its interpreters. As a theologian who was not present at the Council, his theology can be a resource for recovering images not highlighted by the Council but that further illuminate the meaning of the church and its various vocations and, ultimately, that of religious priesthood. In John and Paul especially, suggests Balthasar, one may "see the form" of religious priesthood, with John as a symbol of contemplative monastic priesthood, whereas Paul serves as a symbol for itinerant religious priesthood.

To understand how the images of these early apostles help us to answer our contemporary questions about the religious priesthood, we will examine this theology more thoroughly in part III of this book. We must set the groundwork that will make these questions sharper and the answers more meaningful.

Plan of the Book

The questions this book will set out to answer with Balthasar's help are twofold. First, what is the ecclesial identity and mission of religious priesthood? More precisely, how is religious priesthood distinct from, and how does it overlap with, the vocations of nonordained religious and nonreligious priests? Is religious priesthood merely a hybrid of religious life and priesthood, or does it have its own integrity as a differentiated charismatic mission? Second, does the vocation to religious priesthood compromise either the vocation to religious life or the vocation to priesthood? If not, why not? If so, is it worth the tensions it involves?

These questions are nothing new in the history of the church. Part I (chapters 1–3) provides a concise history of the relationship between the priestly and religious vocations. It demonstrates how religious priest-

42. Balthasar, *Glory of the Lord*, vol. 2, *Studies in Theological Styles: Clerical Styles*, trans. Andrew Louth, Francis McDonough, and Brian McNeil (Edinburgh: T. and T. Clark, 1984), 28 (hereafter *GL* 2).

hood, from its earliest monastic forms to its nineteenth-century incarnations, has always involved certain tensions but also positive characteristics that have benefited the church. Additionally, the chapter clarifies how, historically, different theologies and spiritualities of religious life and priesthood have functioned to affirm or deny the compatibility of religious life and priesthood. It concludes with a summary sketch of the historical identity and mission of religious priesthood and a description of its outstanding challenges.

Part II (chapters 4–5) brings this discussion up to date, establishing and analyzing the current state of the question of religious priesthood in dialogue with the documents of the Second Vatican Council, postconciliar magisterial teaching, and contemporary theological reflections on the relationship between ordained priesthood and religious life. It attends particularly to the teaching of the Second Vatican Council on priesthood and religious life and to the reception of that teaching by theologians and by religious communities. It substantiates the claims that Vatican II's portrait of priesthood adopts a diocesan type, while its portrait of religious life is that of a nonordained religious. It shows how Vatican II's teaching has been interpreted by many contemporary theologians in such a way that religious priesthood now seems to violate the integrity of either priesthood or religious life.

Part III (chapters 6–8) turns to Balthasar for a fresh approach to the question. Chapter 6 introduces the Swiss thinker's theology of vocations and states of life by outlining his key concepts of "mission," "constellation," and "state." Chapter 7 explains the analogical nature of Balthasar's theology of vocations. It then shows how this analogical approach gives Balthasar's ecclesiology a flexibility and intrinsic openness to religious priesthood lacking in other ecclesiological approaches that imagine the church's paradigmatic vocations (lay life, religious life, and priesthood) as mutually exclusive categories. Chapter 8 presents and analyzes Balthasar's use of the apostles John and Paul as types of the identity and mission of religious priesthood. It concludes by examining how Balthasar sees in John and Paul types of two different kinds of religious priesthood. John is a symbol of contemplative monastic priesthood, whereas Paul serves as a symbol for itinerant religious priesthood. Through these figures, Balthasar is able to establish certain characteristics of religious priesthood and demonstrate that religious priesthood cannot ultimately be a compromise of either priesthood or religious life.

Moving from a study of Balthasar to a systematic theology of the religious priesthood, part IV (chapters 9–12) completes this book by presenting four enduring marks of religious priestly identity and mission. It provides theological support for each characteristic by bringing Balthasar's insights into dialogue with other thinkers on the critical questions concerning the relationship of religious life and ministerial priesthood. Chapter 9 presents religious priesthood as a double sign of radical subjective discipleship and official apostolic ministry. Chapter 10 shows religious priesthood as a mediating vocation between the hierarchical institution of the church and movements of charismatic-prophetic renewal. Chapter 11 explores and grounds the missiological importance of the religious priest as one who typically exercises an extraparochial and transdiocesan ministry. Chapter 12 defends religious priestly ministerial identity as concentrated in the ministerial functions of sanctifying, preaching, and teaching. Within each chapter of part IV, the outstanding questions raised in part II are reintroduced and answered by appeal to Balthasar's theology. These answers are further developed through the support of insights from theologians such as Yves Congar, Brian Daley, Guy Mansini, Jean-Marie Tillard, and John Paul II to provide a durable model of the identity and mission of religious priesthood.

These investigations will show that religious priesthood is charismatically differentiated from both nonordained religious life and diocesan priesthood. Its unique mission is to signify the unity and complementarity of objective ministry and subjective discipleship, to mediate between charism and hierarchy, and to provide a ministry of word and sacrament to transdiocesan and extraparochial contexts. This ministry of mediation *does* carry within it certain existential tensions. There are tensions, for example, between ministerial obligations and radical discipleship, between the concern for charismatic renewal dear to religious life and the concern for institutional unity that the priest is especially called to foster, and a tension between the religious priest's ministerial affiliation with the local presbyterate and his membership in the "supra-diocesan" community of religious life.[43] The navigation of these

43. *VC* 47.

tensions by the religious priest is fruitful, however, for both the religious priest himself and for the wider church. Balthasar's theology is helpful for grounding this profile scripturally and theologically and for showing how and why, ecclesiologically, there is no unbridgeable gap between the vocations of religious life and priesthood. Balthasar's vision of religious priesthood is reconcilable with magisterial teaching, liturgy, and canon law. When developed and buttressed by other theologians, it can serve as a basis for a vision of religious priesthood in a postconciliar context. In short, Balthasar's theology is constructive for seeing religious priesthood as an integral charism rather than merely as a compromise.

PART 1

HISTORICAL PERSPECTIVES ON RELIGIOUS PRIESTHOOD

To understand what a thing is now, it is important to perceive what it has been through the ages. To understand why a thing provokes controversy now, it is important to explore whether and why it has always done so. Accordingly, we begin this book with a historical survey of religious priesthood. We seek to uncover what attitudes there have been among key figures in the history of religious life toward this vocation. We will see that some saw religious priesthood as a compromise, while others supported it as a calling and charism. We will investigate the theologies and spiritualities that guided these attitudes. We will also explore what religious priesthood has looked like in terms of concrete lifestyle and ministerial practice across the ages. Although this survey is not an exhaustive history, it is sufficient to set the stage for investigating the contemporary state of the question of religious priesthood in part II.

In order to proceed in the most concise way, the scope of this presentation has been narrowed. The focus here is primarily on the tradition of religious priesthood in the West, although some attention will be paid to the East in the first millennium. With due apologies to men in other religious families, I attend heavily to the Benedictine, Franciscan, Dominican, and Jesuit experiences. I hope that other religious priests from other traditions will find enough analogies to their own experience in these stories.

This survey begins with a discussion of the relation between priesthood and monasticism from antiquity to the Middle Ages (chapter 1). Next, it explores priesthood among the mendicant orders, especially the Franciscans and Dominicans, that came to the fore in the thirteenth century (chapter 2). Last, it investigates the relationship of the religious and priestly vocations among the Jesuits, who date from the sixteenth century, and the apostolic congregations that followed in their wake (chapter 3). Chapter 3 ends with some summary observations about the tensions that religious priesthood has always faced and offers a preliminary sketch of the historical identity and mission of religious priesthood.

CHAPTER 1

Monastic Priesthood

Priesthood and Monasticism in Antiquity

The story of religious priesthood begins in the fourth century, a century that witnessed the emergence of both the presbyter as a well-differentiated ecclesial office with a specific role of ministerial leadership and monasticism, the first recognizable movement of religious life. At the beginning of the fourth century, priesthood and monasticism were largely parallel institutions, evolving separately and somewhat in distinction to each other. By the end of the same century, increasing numbers of monks were being ordained to the priesthood.

The Emergence of Priesthood and Monasticism

At first, Christians did not refer to their leaders as priests. Initially, they applied the language of priesthood to the community as a whole—for instance, the "royal priesthood" mentioned in 1 Pt 2:9—and to the unique mediatory role of Jesus Christ "the High Priest of our confession" (Heb 3:1).[1] The first leaders of the Christian community were

1. Brian E. Daley, "The Ministry of Disciples: Historical Reflections on the Role of Religious Priests," *Theological Studies* 48 (1987): 608. My account of the early history of ministerial priesthood relies heavily on Daley and is supplemented by the accounts found in Raymond E. Brown, *Priest and Bishop: Biblical Reflections* (Eugene, Ore.: Wipf and Stock, 1970); Aidan Nichols, *Holy Order: Apostolic Priesthood from the New Testament to the Second Vatican Council* (Eugene, Ore.: Wipf and Stock, 1990), 5–66; Jean-Pierre Torrell, *A Priestly People: Baptismal Priesthood and Priestly Ministry*, trans. Peter Heinegg (Mahwah, N.J.: Paulist Press, 2013), 60–127; and Kenan B. Osborne, *Priesthood:*

called "apostles," a term that applied originally and typologically to the Twelve, but that was expanded, as in the case of Paul and Barnabas, to include other authoritative preachers who had witnessed the risen Lord and were commissioned by him to engage in missionary travels and found churches.[2] In addition to apostles, there were other itinerant evangelists who spread the gospel but whose authority appears to have been subordinate to the apostles. These were called "prophets" and "teachers" (1 Cor 12:28).

There is also evidence from the New Testament that from very early on, stable local structures of governance existed alongside and functioned in tandem with the itinerant apostles, prophets, and teachers who traveled in and out of the local communities.[3] The Pauline and deutero- Pauline letters refer to the local offices of *episkopoi* (overseers), *presbyteroi* (elders), and *diakonoi* (servants or ministers). The *Didachē*, which probably dates to early second-century Syria and so is one of the earliest nonscriptural Christian sources, testifies to the coexistence of itinerant preachers and local leadership. In that document, "wandering 'apostles,' 'prophets,' and 'teachers' are to be welcomed and revered in the community, if their doctrine and life are credible (11:3–12; 11:13)."[4] At the same time, the community elected bishops to lead at the local level. Members of both groups seem to have been accepted as presiders at the Eucharist.[5]

Ignatius of Antioch, most likely writing around 115, more clearly defines the offices of *episkopos*, *presbyteros*, and *diakonos*. Just twenty years earlier, in the First Letter of Clement, a Roman document that dates from about the year 96, the exact functions and relationship of

A History of Ordained Ministry in the Roman Catholic Church (Eugene, Ore.: Wipf and Stock, 1989), 40–160.

2. For discussions of the criteria for the designation of the term "apostle," see Francis Sullivan, *The Church We Believe In: One, Holy, Catholic and Apostolic* (Mahwah, N.J.: Paulist Press), 155–57.

3. Rom 12:6–8, 16:1–2; Phil 1:1–2; 1 Thes 5:12–13; 1 Tm 3:1–13, 4:14, 5:17–25; Ti 1:5–9; Acts 14:23, 20:17. See Nichols, *Holy Order*, 10–30, for a discussion of these two groups.

4. Daley, "Ministry of Disciples," 609n12.

5. Hervé-Marie Legrand, "The Presidency of the Eucharist according to the Ancient Tradition," in *Living Bread, Saving Cup*, ed. R. Kevin Seasoltz, 196–221 (Collegeville, Minn.: Liturgical Press, 1987).

the *episkopoi, presbyteroi,* and *diakonoi* were rather ambiguous. The terms "*episkopoi*" and "*presbyteroi*," especially, were used somewhat interchangeably. While it is possible that, already in that earlier stage, the council of elders (*presbyteroi*) exercised a collective oversite of the local church with one of them acting as a sort of president of the council or chief overseer (*epispkopos*), it is clear from Ignatius's writings that by his time each church had one definite *episkopos,* set clearly above the other *presbyteroi.* Ignatius exhorted his audience to remain always in union with the *episkopos,* or bishop, who represented "the center of the community's liturgical and social activity" and served as the face of its unity.[6] As the community's clear leader, the bishop was the normal Eucharistic presider, though he sometimes appointed *presbyteroi* to preside in his place.[7] Otherwise, the presbyters' main role was to serve as members of an advisory council to the bishop.[8] The deacons were the "active workers" within the community.[9] Their role probably included social outreach, preaching, teaching, and some liturgical functions, though not, apparently, presiding at the Eucharist.[10] In Ignatius, itinerant evangelists are no longer mentioned.

The third-century writings of Hippolytus, Tertullian, Cyprian of Carthage, and the Syriac *Didascalia apostolorum* strongly emphasize that the community's Eucharistic ritual was a continuation of the sacrificial self-offering of Jesus, and they explicitly describe the role of Eucharistic presider as priestly. To the vocabulary of ministry (*episkopos* and *presbyteros* and *diakonos*), the Latin title of *sacerdos* and the Greek title of *hiereus,* both meaning "priest," were now added. These titles were most frequently applied to the bishop. However, in third-century ordination rites, presbyters, like bishops, are described as being ordained

6. Daley, "Ministry of Disciples," 610.

7. Daley, "Ministry of Disciples," 611n20. In "Epistle to the Smyrnaeans," Ignatius writes, "Only consider that Eucharist valid which is held by the bishop or one whom he delegates" (*Smyrn* 8.1). The translation is Daley's.

8. Aidan Nichols thinks presbyters may have also had an important role in teaching during this period; *Holy Order,* 40.

9. Daley, "Ministry of Disciples," 610.

10. For more on the role of deacons in the ante-Nicene era, see W. Shawn McKnight, *Understanding the Diaconate: Historical, Theological and Sociological Foundations* (Washington, D.C.: The Catholic University of America Press, 2018), 111–44.

for "priestly service,"[11] and eventually it is the presbyter rather than the bishop who will be given the shorthand title of "priest." Presbyterial capacity to offer the Eucharistic sacrifice like the bishops will make possible the developments of the fourth century.

The last of the great imperial persecutions of Christians occurred in 304 under Diocletian. Christianity transitioned from being a persecuted minority group to being first, in 313, a legal religion in the empire and then, in 389, its official religion. This new status yielded ecclesiastical changes. Once, all the Christians of a given city could easily gather in a central place for worship with the bishop presiding at their worship. Now, exponential growth in the number of Christians required the construction of myriad churches throughout each urban environ, and bishops delegated presbyters to preside regularly in their place at these "satellite" Eucharistic assemblies.[12] Bishops remained the supreme ecclesial authorities over all the churches of their provinces, and deacons continued to carry out an important social ministry in the distribution of charity, but more and more presbyters assumed responsibilities of presiding, preaching, and teaching within particular assigned congregations. According to Brian Daley, the fourth century "was really the century of the presbyter, the century when the presbyter's quasi-episcopal role, as delegated head of the neighborhood community or parish, became established."[13]

In the fourth and early fifth centuries, theologians such as Ambrose, Augustine, and Chrysostom further exalted the status of priesthood by closely identifying the priest with Christ in their reflections on the church's sacramental life. They expressed "that it is Christ himself who touches us [through the priest] in the holy rites of the Church: Christ who baptizes, Christ who offers us his flesh and blood as Eucharistic food."[14] As the instrument of these mysteries, the priest enjoyed an esteemed role as the one who made Christ's salvific activity present to the people. Chrysostom went so far as to express that because the "priest could literally confer salvation through baptism and Eucharist," he was

11. Hippolytus, *Trad. Apost.* 3 and 4. The translation is Daley's.
12. Daley, "Ministry of Disciples," 612.
13. Daley, "Ministry of Disciples," 612.
14. Daley, "Ministry of Disciples," 612.

"in a position superior to the angels."[15] The priest was also elevated sociologically at this time. With the change in relation between church and state that began with Constantine, the Christian *clerici* inherited the privileges previously enjoyed by the pagan priests, such as "exemption from civil and military service, from subjection to civil courts, and from taxation."[16] The clergy, the leaders of a heretofore persecuted minority, were now a distinct and privileged group.

Meanwhile, the fourth century also witnessed the birth of monasticism. There had certainly been Christian ascetics before this period: men and women who practiced celibacy or virginity, intense prayer, austerity of diet, and material simplicity. These persons, however, often lived with their families and, in large part, remained active members of both society and the local church.[17] In the fourth century something new occurred: great numbers of those with the ascetical impulse withdrew to the desert and other rural places to practice a life set apart from both society and even nonmonastic Christians. This ideal of withdrawal, though it varied in intensity depending on time period and location and rarely if ever meant complete separation, is the best way of distinguishing the monastic movement from other ascetics and celibates who preceded them.[18]

The most important reason for the growth of monasticism during the fourth century was the change in relation between the church and the state. Whereas Christian faith had once been inherently risky, it was now increasingly safe and even necessary for social or political advancement. The end of persecution and the rise of privilege meant an un-

15. George E. Demacopoulos, *Five Models of Spiritual Direction in the Early Church* (Notre Dame, Ind.: University of Notre Dame Press, 2007), 13. See Chrystostom, *On the Priesthood*, 3.15.

16. Bernard Cooke, *Ministry to Word and Sacraments: History and Theology* (Philadephia: Fortress, 1976), 559.

17. Joseph T. Lienhard, "Signs of the Times: Signs, Symbols and Meanings in Religious Life," in *Apostolic Religious Life in America Today: A Response to the Crisis*, ed. Richard Gribble, 91–107 (Washington, D.C.: The Catholic University of America Press, 2011).

18. According to Mark Sheridan, the emphasis on withdrawal can even be found in authors such as Basil and Augustine, even though they simultaneously presented a vision of monasticism that was more engaged in apostolic work; Sheridan, "The Origins of Monasticism in the Eastern Church," in *RB 1980: The Rule of Saint Benedict in Latin and English with Notes*, ed. Timothy Fry, 3–41 (Collegeville, Minn.: Liturgical Press, 1980).

avoidable change in the profile of Christians themselves: Many persons were entering the church for reasons of personal gain rather than out of sincere conversion. Commentators of the time lamented the rise of secular "worldly" values among Christians. Monasticism arose, in this context, "to provide an outlet for those who were not satisfied with a mediocre Christianity."[19] In the words of Joseph Ratzinger, "The journey into the desert was a departure from the solid interconnected structure of the local Church, a departure from a Christianity more and more adapted to the needs of worldly life."[20]

Monastic Priesthood in Egypt

The first great pioneers of monasticism were in Egypt. Here, the movement took two characteristic forms. First, in Lower Egypt, St. Anthony of the Desert (c. 251–356) and his many imitators established themselves in informal colonies of hermits, pursuing a life of intense asceticism and solitary contemplation under the tutelage of charismatic spiritual masters, the desert *abbas* and *ammas*. Second, in Upper Egypt, St. Pachomius (c. 292–348) created highly structured cenobitical communities with a formal rule of life, dedicated to the practices of common prayer and communal virtue. In both locales, the question of whether or not it was appropriate for a monk to be ordained to the ministry appeared almost immediately.

There were both internal and external pressures to make monks official ministers of the church. The internal pressure was a practical matter. Monks had to travel each week from their secluded retreats to the urban churches to celebrate the Eucharist. Since the large, urban, episcopally led churches were already beginning to be supplemented by satellite churches led by presbyters, it seemed possible, and perhaps desirable, to also have satellite Eucharistic assemblies in the desert, led by monastic priests. This would relieve the burden of a long weekly sojourn out of the desert.[21]

19. Sheridan, "Origins of Monasticism in the Eastern Church," 16.

20. Joseph Ratzinger, *Pilgrim Fellowship of Faith: The Church as Communion*, trans. Henry Taylor (San Francisco: Ignatius Press, 2005), 192.

21. Adalbert de Vogüé, "Priest and Monastic Community in Antiquity," *Cistercian Studies* 22 (1987): 17–24.

External pressures were twofold. On the one hand, monks were becoming renowned for their virtues and charismatic gifts, which led the people to push monks to enter official ecclesial leadership, particularly as bishops. On the other hand, there was a growing need to maintain unity between the Christians of the city and the Christians of the desert. The desert ascetics sometimes chided the lifestyles of the urban Christians, and the desert *abbas* occasionally set themselves up as alternative authorities to bishops who they portrayed, fairly or unfairly, as overly worldly. Complicating the situation, some monastic communities were suffused with heresies such as Melitianism, Arianism, and later, Pelagianism and Donatism.[22] Because bishops had difficulty monitoring the monastic communities, which were often at a distance from the urban diocesan centers, a solution was to ordain reliable, orthodox monks to exercise ecclesiastical discipline in the desert, thus bringing ascetic Christians more firmly in line with the bishops while simultaneously drawing them away from competing heretical groups.[23]

Early Egyptian monks raised several objections to the prospect of ordaining monks.[24] The hermits' objections were mainly two. First, by accepting the duties of official ministry, the monk would no longer be able to pursue with the same intensity the contemplative goal to "pray without ceasing" (1 Thes 5:17); rather, he would be burdened with looking after other people's salvation.[25] Although the hermits were often

22. See Demacopoulos, *Five Models of Spiritual Direction in the Early Church*, 35, 98–105.

23. See David Brakke, *Athanasius and the Politics of Asceticism* (Oxford: Clarendon Press, 1995), 81–82.

24. Monks who successfully avoided ordination include Theodore of Phermae, Isaac of the Cells, Macarius the Great, and Pachomius. John Cassian lamented having been ordained, and Dracontius of Nitiria retreated back to the desert after ordination only to be admonished for doing so by Athanasius. See Daley, "Ministry of Disciples," 605–6 and 605n2, for references.

25. John Cassian most famously quipped, "A monk ought by all means to fly from women and bishops. For neither of them will allow a person who has once become bound by them ... to care, any longer, for the quiet of his cell, or to continue with pure eyes in divine contemplation, rapt in his vision of holy things"; *De institutis*, 11.18, trans. Daley. For a discussion of the spirituality of the desert hermits and the single-minded devotion to prayer and penance it entailed, see Cyprian Davis, "Prayer as a Battle: The Monastic Contribution," in *The Tradition of Catholic Prayer*, ed. Christian Raab and Harry Hagan, 51–62

engaged in informal teaching and placed great value on providing hospitality to others, they framed their vocation as a primarily solitary endeavor of prayer and penance that could be derailed by too much pastoral responsibility. Second, they associated the desire for ordination with a temptation to vainglory. The monk was supposed to be a humble man who had renounced everything. Given the exalted status of priesthood at this time, ideas of obtaining ecclesial rank and exercising its influence were assumed to be suggestions of the Devil.[26]

In the Pachomian cenobitical tradition of Upper Egypt, the objection to ordination was slightly different. Pachomius had been inspired by the vision of ecclesial life described in Acts 2:42 and 4:32.[27] He thus promoted *koinonia*, a common life marked by the sharing of goods and the practices of common prayer and community virtues, as an ideal of monastic life. He organized large, highly structured monasteries of numerous monks dedicated to the cultivation of *koinonia*. Additionally, his monks engaged in a certain degree of service to outsiders such as sheltering the elderly and orphans, care for the sick, and distribution of food to the hungry.[28] They even built churches for the neighboring Christians in which, by some accounts, they sometimes taught or preached.[29] Despite the more active orientation of Pachomian monasticism, Pachomius viewed monastic priesthood to be harmful to religious common life. He refused ordination for himself and for any of his monks because

(Collegeville, Minn.: Liturgical Press, 2007), and Joseph A. Jungmann, *Christian Prayer through the Centuries*, trans. Joseph Coyne (Mahwah, N.J.: Paulist Press, 2007), 9–13.

26. As Abba Moses put it, "Sometimes on a plea of building the faith of many and winning souls for religion, he [Satan] incites us to want to be ordained, and so snatches us from the humility and the discipline of our way of life"; quoted in Owen Chadwick, ed., *Western Asceticism* (Philadelphia: Westminster, 1958), 210.

27. "They devoted themselves to the teaching of the apostles and to the communal life, to the breaking of the bread and to the prayers"; "The community of believers was of one heart and mind, and no one claimed that any of his possessions was his own, but they had everything in common."

28. See Sheridan, "Origins of Monasticism in the Eastern Church," 27–28.

29. Eoin de Bhaldraithe, "Daily Eucharist: The Need for an Early Church Paradigm," *American Benedictine Review* 41 (1990): 401; Davis, "Monasticism and Priesthood in the Egyptian Desert" (audiocassette), Monastic Institute Tapes: Benedictine Federation of the Americas, n. 8102 (Richardton, N.Dak.: Christian Life Center, 1981).

he believed it would introduce ambition and envy into the community, thereby upsetting its spirit of unity and equality.[30]

Entwined with these spiritual and moral concerns, and perhaps running deeper than them, was an objection, shared by both hermits and cenobites, concerning church order. Clerics and monks, it was thought by many, occupied fundamentally different places in the church. The former were ordained for service within particular churches to which they were attached. Although "at large" ordinations took place, these were generally frowned upon and even forbidden by the Council of Chalcedon in 451. Priests were expected to administer the sacraments, uphold orthodoxy through doctrinal instruction, distribute charity, and exercise formal ecclesial discipline within urban or suburban churches. The basis of their authority was ordination. Monks had withdrawn from the daily networks and associations of the urban churches; they constituted an alternative milieu in the desert. Although monks continued to depend on the clergy for sacraments and, to varying degrees, ecclesial discipline, they also had their own leaders, the desert *abbas* whose authority was based not on ordination, but upon their own ascetical development and the possession of charismatic gifts such as the discernment of spirits.

Initially, and until monasteries started to host their own satellite Eucharistic assemblies, ordination meant assuming duties in urban or suburban churches removed from the desert milieu entirely. Though a man could continue to identify himself as a monk and was expected to carry himself with the comportment of a monk, ordination pulled him from his monastic retreat. It is obvious why monks, especially those of the most contemplative type, would have resisted ordination. Similarly, a priest who wished to take up the monastic life was expected to renounce his clerical office, since it was attached to duties in a church to which he would no longer minister. Such a move was a morally ques-

30. "No one among them had clerical rank in the holy church. Indeed, our father Pachomius did not want any clerics in his monasteries for fear of jealousy and vainglory"; Armand Veilleux, ed., *Pachomian Koinonia*, vol. 1, *The Life of Saint Pachomius* (Kalamazoo, Mich.: Cistercian, 1980), 47n51. See also Bruce Lescher, "Laybrothers: Questions Then, Questions Now," *Cistercian Studies* 23 (1988): 83.

tionable act.[31] For these reasons, many persons in the fourth century concluded that the two vocations were incompatible.

Nonetheless, by the late fourth century, monasteries increasingly formed their own Eucharistic assemblies with their own priests. Communities then had to navigate the question of whether or not a strictly charismatic leadership could or should be maintained. Two solutions appeared. The first solution, which was adopted at Nitria, Skete, and a vast number of other eremitical colonies, was to make it a matter of course to have the charismatic leadership ordained, so that the spiritual fathers of the community were also in charge of both its sacramental administration and formal ecclesiastical discipline.[32] A second solution, followed by Pachomius, was to continue to disallow the ordination of monks, maintain the practice of dependence on the secular clergy (who would now travel out to the desert to provide sacraments to the monks), and continue the tradition of lay charismatic leadership.[33]

Basil of Caesarea

In Asia Minor, as in Egypt, the ecclesiastical situation was similarly marked by a tension between monastic Christians, on the one hand, and lay Christians and clergy, on the other.[34] St. Basil (327–79) was motivated to bridge the gap between the two groups. By the time he was ordained bishop in 370, he had already written two community "rules," the *Moralia,* which was not much more than a compilation of New Testament passages, and the *Small Asketikon,* in which he worked out more thoroughly his own theories. After his elevation to the See of Caesarea, Basil established several communities of monks and nuns and issued a third rule, the *Great Asketikon,* which was a further expansion of the second.[35] Notably, Basil does not speak in his rules about monks, but rather about Christians in general. Basil probably initially chose this language because he was trying to write an ascetical rule that he

31. See Demacoupolos, *Five Models of Spiritual Direction,* 27–28.

32. Sheridan, "Origins of Monasticism in the Eastern Church," 21–22.

33. Terrence Kardong, "Lack of Ministry: A Problem as Old as the Rule of Benedict," *American Benedictine Review* 35 (1984): 98.

34. Daley, "Ministry of Disciples," 607.

35. See Kardong, *Pillars of Community: Four Rules of Pre-Benedictine Monastic Life* (Collegeville, Minn.: Liturgical Press, 2010), 7–14.

thought could be kept by the whole church and serve as a basis for its reform. However, Basil soon realized that not all the faithful could be expected to practice discipleship in the same way,[36] and he wrote the *Small* and *Great Asketikons* more specifically targeted at monastic audiences.[37] Interestingly, he maintained the language of "Christians" even in his later rules. Perhaps this was because he wanted to assert the common bond between monastics and the faithful. When Basil referred to monks as Christians, he reminded monks of their fundamental unity with the church, and he also pointed to them as an ideal for the imitation of the rest of the church.[38]

Basil's monasticism had several remarkable characteristics that set it apart from the Egyptian tradition, particularly the eremitical form. First, Basil's community intentionally blended the ascetic life with the apostolic life.[39] Basil framed his rule around the great dominical commandments, love of God and love of neighbor. Claiming that work could be carried out with a "remembrance of the presence of God," Basil explicitly disagreed with those in the eremitical tradition who disparaged active service as a distraction from prayer.[40] Second, for Basil, charitable outreach, rather than being somewhat "ad-hoc" as it had been in Egypt, constituted a formal element of the religious life.[41] Basil's monks and nuns operated schools that taught not only their own monks, but also lay students in both religious subjects and secular trades. Additionally, they ran hospitals, a diocesan guest house, and shelters for the needy. They also seem to have had churches that provided liturgy and sacraments to both monks and outsiders.[42]

Third, the needs of the church determined the apostolates of the

36. Ratzinger, *Pilgrim Fellowship of Faith*, 192–93.

37. Kardong, *Pillars of Community*, 17.

38. Ratzinger, *Pilgrim Fellowship of Faith*, 192–93; Ephrem Carr, "Basil and Chrysostom: Apostolic Activities for Monks" (audiocassette), Monastic Institute Tapes: Benedictine Federation of the Americas, n. 7907 (Richardton, N.Dak.: Christian Life Center, 1979).

39. Characteristics 1–4 and 6 have been taken from Carr's Conference "Basil and Chrysostom."

40. Kardong, *Pillars of Community*, 33.

41. Carr, "Basil and Chrysostom."

42. De Bhaldraithe, "Daily Eucharist," 403.

monastery. For Basil, the monastery was not separate from the church but a presence within the church oriented toward its service. It was "a small group to give life to the whole."[43] Importantly, the service of religious was not to be contained within the parameters of their own community. For Basil, says Ephrem Carr, "love of neighbor ... cannot be held within the monastery walls; it reaches out to the church."[44] Fourth, these apostolic works were carried out from within the context of monastic stability. Like Pachomius, Basil was inspired by the vision of *koinonia* in Acts 2 and 4. Praying and working in common made *koinonia* possible. The schools, hospitals, retreat houses, and shelters that the monks and nuns staffed were adjoined to the monastery so that monks could continue to live the common life in some degree of separation from the world while engaging in active apostolates.

Fifth, although the monastic superior assigned specific tasks to monks, the community was in close association with the bishop, who served as an external overseer. It was Basil, after all, as bishop, who established the communities to assist with pastoral goals. This arrangement, where monasteries had their own superiors but were overseen and employed for pastoral tasks by the local bishop, remains the norm in the Eastern Church today.[45]

Sixth, Basil believed that only those who trained in prayer in asceticism could effectively minister. Following a classical scheme, he contended that purgation was the first step in the spiritual life and naturally preceded active charity. He was particularly concerned that his religious be purified from the temptation to vainglory before they could become part of the community's outreach. Though his Egyptian contemporaries agreed with this order, a primary difference between them and Basil was that the latter was confident monastic life would transform a monk or nun sufficiently and quickly enough that he or she could perform ministerial services without a near lifetime of ascesis being required beforehand.

43. Jean Gribomont, "Obéissance et Évangle selon S. Basil Le Grand," *Vie Spirituelle*, suppl. no. 21 (1952): 192.

44. Carr, "Basil and Chrysostom."

45. Ronald G. Roberson, "The Profile of Eastern Monasticism Today," *Melita Theologica*, suppl. no. 21 (1994): 102.

There were priests in Basil's community. In contrast to the Egyptian scene, their presence seemed to provoke little controversy. There are several reasons that monasticism and priesthood did not appear to be in inherent conflict here. For one thing, Basil's determination to emphasize the common identity of all Christians probably lessened any tensions that might have emerged from the clerical status of some members. More importantly, he envisioned religious life in such a way that it was ordered internally to ministry or apostolate. By conceiving of religious life as a mixed life oriented to the service of the church and closely associated with the public ministry of the bishop, priesthood no longer appeared to compromise the religious life. At the same time, by locating ministerial services within or adjacent to the communal complex, priests had a situation in which they could carry out apostolic activities without compromising their monastic commitment. Last, by recognizing ascetical foundations as necessary for effective ministry, the religious vocation appeared as a fitting preparation for priesthood and priesthood could be conceived as a fulfillment, or at least an expression of the religious vocation.

Augustine of Hippo

In the Western part of the church, Augustine of Hippo (354–430) pioneered yet another form of "ministerial monasticism."[46] After his conversion, he joined with some friends in an intentional ascetic and contemplative community. After he was ordained a priest, he continued to live a monastic lifestyle, founding a "garden monastery" at Hippo.[47] Like Pachomius, "the main emphasis in Augustine's idea of monasticism seems to have been on prayer, poverty, and the sharing of goods in common life—a model consciously drawn from the picture of the early Christian community in Acts 4:32."[48] When Augustine was ordained bishop he moved out of this monastery, yet he soon longed again for the monastic lifestyle and turned the bishop's house into a "monastery of clerics,"[49] priests liv-

46. Daley, "Ministry of Disciples," 619.

47. Kardong, *Pillars of Community*, 156.

48. Daley, "Ministry of Disciples," 619.

49. Augustine, Sermon 356.3. The translation is Kardong's, in *Pillars of Community*, 156.

ing the common life. Augustine's clerical monks not only provided him with fraternity, but were also "an indispensable aid to Augustine's episcopal ministry.... They provided the hospitality expected of a bishop and carried out many of the duties of his assistant clergy, as well as being a model of evangelical community life for the wider world."[50] Ten of these clerics eventually became bishops in their own right, many of whom followed Augustine's example and created similar monastic-style communities of clerics.[51] In the eleventh century, these communities became the inspiration for the canons' regular movement.[52]

It is important to note that despite his innovation of "ministerial monasticism," Augustine seemed to uphold the traditional African ideal of monasteries as having an exclusively contemplative purpose that was not to be compromised too much by pastoral responsibilities. He conceived of his monastic-style clerical community as being something new and different from monasteries in their proper sense. His monastic-style clerical communities were populated by men whose first responsibility was to pastoral ministry and who adopted a monastic style of life as support for that ministry and for prayer.[53]

Augustine provided in this context an early theology of religious priesthood. In his commentary on John 21, he contrasted the contemplative life of the monk with the active life of the priest and bishop. The monk is symbolized by the gospel figure of John who "remains" with the Lord. The cleric is symbolized by Peter, who must feed the Lord's flock. According to Augustine, his clerical monks combined the vocations of John and Peter. By virtue of their monastic style of life, they were called to a common life of contemplation. By virtue of their ordination, they

50. Daley, "Ministry of Disciples," 619.

51. See Kardong, *Pillars of Community*, 158.

52. C. H. Lawrence, *Medieval Monasticism: Forms of Religious Life in Western Europe in the Middle Ages*, 3rd ed. (Harlow, UK: Longman, 2001), 160–64.

53. Augustine chastised more than one monk for accepting ordination because it removed them from the cloister, and he congratulated an abbot on avoiding ordination and the many pastoral responsibilities it entailed; Demacopoulos, 87–88. More significantly, Augustine departed from the more traditional "garden monastery" upon his ordination as bishop because he felt his own pastoral responsibilities would disrupt the rhythms of his fellow monks' lives; Kardong, *Pillars of Community*, 156.

were called to ministry.[54] This way of framing things, where the call to ministry comes from orders, while religious commitment pertains mainly to prayer and common life, contrasts somewhat with Basil's vision of religious life as ordered from within to apostolic service. Augustine's framework would have a long legacy in the Western Church.

Benedict of Nursia

Although St. Benedict (c. 480–547) was influenced by the Egyptian masters, as well as by Basil and Augustine, the primary source for his rule was the writings of an obscure early sixth-century Italian figure known to history only as the Master. Like Pachomius, the Master prohibited the ordination of monks and even forbade priests to join the community. He justified this course by arguing that God had, in fact, established two different kinds of "houses," churches and monasteries.[55] The two institutions possessed parallel and equal systems of authority. Churches were governed by bishops, priests, and deacons; monasteries by abbots and deans. The two hierarchies and their spheres of governance were sharply demarcated.[56]

When Benedict authored his rule, he incorporated much of the Master's teaching, but he notably altered the Master's policy on monastic priests. Benedict allowed priests to join the monastery and allowed monasteries to have some of their members ordained, but placed monastic priests firmly under the authority of the abbot, who was typically a lay monk. At the same time, the monastery as a whole was accountable to its diocesan bishop, who could remove a wicked abbot from office and set up someone else in his place.[57] This situation of lay abbots having au-

54. Enrico Castellucci, "I Religiosi Presbiteri Nella Chiesa: *Excursus* Storico," *Sequela Christi* 2 (2009): 86–119, esp. 92–93.

55. Luke Eberle, trans., *The Rule of the Master* (Kalamazoo, Mich.: Cistercian Publications, 1977), chapter 11 (hereafter *RM*).

56. Priests were not to "lay claim to any part in God's organization or government or administration" of the abbey whatsoever. They were to be "considered outsiders (*peregrini*) in the monastery," for they "retain and exercise their presidency and preferment in churches"; *RM* 83.1–2. According to Kardong, the Master envisions monasteries as "enclaves closed to the jurisdiction of the clergy, and which possess their own separate authority"; Kardong, "Lack of Ministry," 102.

57. Benedict extends the same force of accountability to the local faithful and other abbots; *RB*, chapter 64.

thority over monastic priests ended when monasteries, for reasons to be discussed later, became heavily clericalized during the medieval period.

Although, unlike the Master, Benedict allowed for monastic priests, he voiced the same cautions that had been first expressed in the fourth-century desert. He exhorted monastic priests that they must serve as "an example of humility" and "guard against conceit or pride."[58] They must not become distracted from their pursuit of holiness but "make more and more progress toward God."[59] Both priest and community were to take special care to avoid double standards for priests so that the unity and equality of the community could be preserved.[60]

Exactly what kind of ministry Benedict's priests engaged in is debated. The only ministerial roles for the priest mentioned in the Rule are administering blessings and celebrating Mass, "provided that the abbot bids him."[61] The pastors of the community were the abbot, prior, and deans, whose authority was not based on ordination. Although Benedict's rule mentions monks sometimes working away from the monastery, it does not tell us what they were doing.[62] These factors have led scholars such as Adalbert de Vogüé to conclude that Benedict's priests were primarily, if not exclusively, for the purpose of internal sacramental ministry.[63]

Other scholars say it is possible to take a wider view of the purpose of monastic priesthood for Benedict. Gregory the Great's description of Benedict in the *Dialogues* is the only source we have for the life of the saint. Even if it is not entirely historically accurate, it is at least typologically significant for the Benedictine charism. The portrait locates Benedict within the largely pagan environment of rural Italy in the mid-sixth century.

58. *RB* 60; *RB* 62.

59. *RB* 62.

60. A priest entering the monastery "will have to observe the full discipline of the rule without any mitigation"; *RB* 60.2. He must not "make any exceptions for himself"; *RB* 60.5. The priest's rank in the community, meanwhile, "corresponds to the date of his entry into the community and not that given him out of respect for his priesthood'"; *RB* 60.7. "Any higher rank is given to a priest because of 'the goodness of his life' (*RB* 62.6) not because he is ordained"; Kevin W. Irwin, "On Monastic Priesthood," *American Benedictine Review* 41 (1990): 226.

61. *RB* 60.4.

62. *RB* 50.

63. See Adalbert de Vogüé, "Eucharist and Monastic Life," *Worship* 59 (1985): 498–510; de Vogüé, "Priest and Monastic Community in Antiquity," 17–24.

Benedict and his monks lived there a life of prayer, ascetical withdrawal, *and* apostolic action. Gregory mentions Benedict preaching twice, in both cases to pagans.[64] Benedict also heals a local man's servant, raises a dead boy to life, and exorcises a demon from a visiting cleric. Benedict and his monks built two churches for the people of the rural area, one of these churches being a converted pagan shrine. He sent two monks to preach in them.[65] According to Jean LeClercq, Gregory's portrait of Benedict fits what is known about "the Christianization of the countryside" in sixth-century Italy after the barbarian invasions. It was carried out by ascetical "volunteers" for life in a rural pagan world.[66] In its earliest stage, Benedictine monastic life already had a missionary dimension.

By describing Benedictine life as a mixed life of prayer and apostolic action, rather than as an exclusively contemplative life, Gregory's *Dialogues* widen the potential scope of Benedictine priesthood. Although Benedict and the majority of his monks were lay, descriptions of their apostolic activities suggest that these are not inappropriate works for Benedictine monks.[67] Since Benedict both admits priests into the monastery and allows monks to be ordained, it is only a short leap to accepting that monks could be ordained for such work. Eoin de Bhaldraithe thinks there is reason to believe this was in the mind of Benedict himself. Monks in rural places were sometimes entrusted with the care and staffing of preexisting but decaying churches. Other times they built new churches, as Gregory describes. These churches served the needs of the people of the area as these became Christian through the monk's evangelizing work. According to de Bhaldraithe, *RB* 62 can be read from this vantage point. When the Rule says the abbot can have a monk ordained, it is not simply to provide for the monastery's own needs. It is to provide for the monastic community and for all those to whom the monastery collectively ministers.[68]

64. Jean LeClercq, "Monachisme, sacerdoce et missions au Moyen Age: Travaux et résultats récents," *Studia Monastica* 23 (1981): 307–23, esp. 313–14 and 323.

65. Kardong, *The Life of St. Benedict by Gregory the Great: Translation and Commentary* (Collegeville, Minn.: Liturgical Press, 2009).

66. LeClercq, "Monachisme, sacerdoce et missions au Moyen Age," 314.

67. See Irwin, "On Monastic Priesthood," 237.

68. See De Bhaldraithe, "Lay Abbots: Should We Return to the Earlier Church Practice?" *American Benedictine Review* 59 (2008): 316–31, esp. 325.

Monastic Priesthood in the Medieval West

From the end of the Roman Empire through the early Middle Ages, monks were heavily involved, often at the behest of the papacy, in missionary efforts to the Germanic, Celtic, and Slavic tribes. St. Patrick, St. Augustine of Canterbury, St. Boniface, St. Cyril, and St. Methodius, for example, led missions that brought Christianity to the new peoples of Europe. These monastic missionaries usually brought with them teams of monks, both ordained and lay.[69] While establishing the church in the mission lands, the groups continued the common life. Their leaders assumed a dual role as both the monks' superior and the head of the local church that grew up around the monastic foundation. Sometimes, the ecclesiastical structures they left in their wake were unusual. Although the figures mentioned earlier were appointed bishops, not every head of a missionary monastery was a bishop; however, he was still the effective head of the local church. The monastery and its environs, which fell outside the bounds of any diocese, were nonetheless like a diocese, headed by a monk-priest who was not a bishop, with a team of monastic clergy serving the people of the area. This situation appeared in both Ireland and Gaul and still exists today in the form of the "abbey *nullius*, or territorial abbey."[70]

The great period of missionary monasticism had peaked by the eighth century and ended by the eleventh. In the now-Christian Europe, more familiar diocesan and parochial structures were planted, and the number of diocesan clergy exploded such that there was much less demand for monks to engage in active ministry. Monks withdrew, by and large, from active apostolic engagement, and monasticism assumed a more and more exclusively contemplative form.[71] Inasmuch as monks continued to engage in an active ministry, there was a decided effort to prevent them from doing so. The First Lateran Council, in 1123, forbade monks the exercise of the care of souls. Even the confessions of pilgrims to monasteries needed to be heard again by the parish pastor or bishop. The Third Lateran Council, in 1179, explained that monks were not to

69. LeClercq, "Monachisme, sacerdoce et missions au Moyen Age," 316–19.

70. De Bhaldraithe, "Lay Abbots," 329.

71. See Ernest Skublics, "A Contemplative Ministry?," *Worship* 45 (1971): 480–87.

live alone in a villa parish or town. With such decisions, monks were increasingly confined to the cloister.

Ironically, the decline in monastic ministerial outreach occurred at the same time as an increase of the number of clerics in monasteries. Although monastic missionary efforts required a number of monks to be ordained, at the end of the eighth century, priests and deacons still only constituted about 20 percent of the Western European monastic population. During the Carolingian period in the West (c. 800–1000), monasticism underwent a process of clericalization so that by the tenth century approximately 75 percent of monks were ordained.[72] The primary reason for this increase was not increased external pastoral activity but, rather, increased liturgical activity within monasteries.

In antiquity, Christians might receive communion on a daily basis, but the celebration of the Eucharist was limited to Saturdays and Sundays. This situation began to change with Gregory the Great. In his *Dialogues*, Gregory described a vision he had had of freeing a man from purgatory by offering Mass for him, and he used this vision to suggest that masses be said daily, even in private by the priest if need be, for the benefit of the souls of the living and dead. When, in about 700, the circulation of Gregory's *Dialogues* rose, particularly in Rome, it inspired popular demand for more masses; the Eucharistic sacrifice, applied to specific intentions, was seen as an incomparable source of grace for souls. As Ghislain Lafont puts it, "The principle of 'the infinite value of a single Mass' led paradoxically to the multiplication of Masses."[73]

When Charlemagne (742–814) rose to power over much of Western Europe in 800, he wanted the entire church there to imitate the Roman Church's liturgical practices, which now included multiple daily and private masses. He and his successor, Louis the Pious (778–840), employed the monks Alcuin (d. 804) and Benedict of Aniane (747–821) to pioneer a reform of the monasteries. These promoted a vision of the monastery as a little Rome, with a high level of liturgical activity. The monastery's role in the culture was to do penance and to pray for the church. Because the Mass was considered the perfect and most efficacious prayer, it made sense for the monks to be committed to the liturgy

72. Congar, *Études d'ecclésiologie médiévale* (London: Varorium, 1983), 154.

73. Lafont, "The Eucharist in Monastic Life," *Cistercian Studies* 19 (1984): 306.

and ordained to say the Mass. The people of the time literally *bought* into the system, donating monies and lands to the monks in exchange for being remembered at Mass. This spiritual economy catalyzed the clericalization of the monasteries.[74]

Furthermore, changes were taking place in liturgical theology that allowed the great number of priest-monks ordained to say private masses to appear more plausible. The patristic period had closely linked the Eucharistic body of Christ and the body of Christ in the assembly. A primary purpose of the Eucharist was to join the community to one another and to God in a common celebration of thanks and praise. A private Mass, isolated from an assembly, was scarcely imagined. Furthermore, the one who presided over the Eucharist ought to have had a community over which he also exercised, alone or as part of a team, since the two Christic bodies were so closely linked. Along these lines, Chalcedon forbade "at large" ordinations and expected priests to be attached to churches. Monasteries of antiquity typically had only a few priests, enough to serve the community's public liturgies.[75]

The Carolingian debate between Radbertus and Ratramnus led theologians to make a strong distinction, even a separation, between the "true" body of Christ, the Eucharist, and the mystical body of Christ, the church. Faced with a heresy denying the real presence, theologians of the Carolingian era intensified their defense of the Eucharistic elements as the true body and celebrated the priest's real power to transform them. It became far less important to the Carolingians that the priest have a church to which he was attached and a community over which he would preside than that he could truly confect the elements and manifest the perfect prayer of the church, even if he did so alone.[76] In the Carolingian imagination, the priest's action of sanctifying the Eucharistic elements began to dwarf his roles of preaching, teaching, and leading in a community context.[77] A monk offering a private Mass for the souls in purgatory seemed to be as much of a priest as the busy par-

74. See Lafont, "Eucharist in Monastic Life," 300–307.

75. See De Bhaldraithe, "Daily Eucharist," 407–14.

76. See Irwin, "On Monastic Priesthood," 225–26; Lafont, "Eucharist in Monastic Life," 302–6.

77. Daley, "Ministry of Disciples," 614.

ish pastor, and there ceased to be an intelligible reason not to ordain as many monks as possible.

The medievals worked out a spirituality in which the monastic and priestly vocations formed a tight symbiosis. The two vocations meshed because the primary monastic work was to pray, and priesthood was now being conceived in such a way that it too was a vocation to pray the perfect prayer of the Mass. Brian Daley explains, "As a man of God whose life was dedicated to God's praise in a kind of continual sacrifice," the monk was a fitting priest; "he seemed more suited than the ordinary parish pastor to offer Christ's Eucharistic sacrifice to the Father."[78] This was a contemplative vision of priesthood, "an understanding of sacramental ministry that saw the offering of the Eucharistic sacrifice as the culmination of a life of contemplative prayer, and that regarded ordination as a kind of sacramental seal placed on a holy life, for the benefit of the monastic community and for the deeper sanctification of the monk himself."[79] With this spirituality in hand, even the most contemplative monastic communities, such as the Cistercians and Carthusians, had a justification for ordaining many of their members, and were, in fact, heavily clerical orders.[80]

It is important to note, however, that monks of this period did not withdraw entirely from active apostolic work. Charlemagne, believing monasteries could offer the education and moral example that would serve as a spiritual foundation of society, encouraged monasteries to establish external schools. Abbeys such as St. Gall, Bobbio, and Cluny were at the forefront of this effort.[81] By this time, most monks were priests or deacons, and, according to Bernard Cooke, "teaching was apparently considered an appropriate expression of the ordained minister's special call to service in the church."[82] Additionally, some monastic priests were occupied as *capilani*, or chaplains to royal courts.[83] When the Cistercians arrived on the scene in the twelfth century, they

78. Daley, "Ministry of Disciples," 617.

79. Daley, "Ministry of Disciples," 617–18.

80. For more on the clericalization of the contemplative orders, see Augustine McGregor, "Monastic Life and the Priesthood: A Historical Study," *Hallel* 7 (1979): 101–16.

81. See Lawrence, *Medieval Monasticism*, 137–42.

82. Cooke, *Ministry to Word and Sacraments*, 368.

83. Cooke, *Ministry to Word and Sacraments*, 367.

were often employed by the papacy as its official preachers, inquisitors, and legates.[84] Furthermore, monasteries continued to provide pastoral care for the people who lived and worked on or near their estates. Perhaps the most prominent area of monastic outreach, however, was tending to the needs of pilgrims. The years 1000–1400 were the great years of this movement. Thousands of pilgrims traveled across Europe to Rome, Jerusalem, and Compostela, as well as to countless other saints' shrines in order to visit relics, pray at holy places, and receive indulgences. Monasteries were often constructed at or near martyrs' or Marian shrines and along pilgrimage routes. Bishops entrusted monasteries with the care of pilgrims. In large part this was corporal care, such as feeding and housing, but the monks also provided spiritual care, such as public liturgy and spiritual direction.[85]

By the end of the twelfth century, monasticism had assumed most of the forms that would characterize it through the second millennium. Under the title of monk, we find hermits and cenobites, Basilian and Augustinian ministerial monks, Benedictine missionaries and teachers, liturgically focused Cluniacs, contemplative Cistercians, and high medieval stewards of reliquaries/hosts to pilgrims. While the ordination of monks could sometimes be controversial, priesthood eventually managed to find a home in all of these expressions of monasticism. The synthesis or priesthood and religious life achieved by monasticism will be both challenged and deepened with the advent of the mendicant orders in the thirteenth century.

84. See Yves Congar, "De la communion des églises a une ecclésiologie de l'église universelle," in *L'Épiscopat et L'Église Universelle*, ed. Yves Congar and B. D. Dupuy, Unam Sanctam 39 (Paris: Cerf, 1962), 227–60.

85. See Jonathan Sumption, *The Age of Pilgrimage: The Medieval Journey to God* (Mahwah, N.J.: HiddenSpring, 2003). The ministry of monks to pilgrims is somewhat understudied, but Sumption provides ample examples of this important monastic work in his book.

CHAPTER 2

Priesthood among the Mendicants

The Emergence of the Mendicants

In the thirteenth century a new form of religious life arose in the church: the mendicant orders, which included the Franciscans, Dominicans, Carmelites, Augustinian Friars, and Servites.[1] In terms of numbers and immediate influence, the Franciscans and Dominicans were the greatest of these. Like monks, the mendicants, or friars, as their male members were called, embraced a life of prayer and chaste celibacy. There were important differences, however. Monastic community life had been inspired above all by the description of the Jerusalem Church in Acts 2 and 4. It was a stable common life of prayer, liturgy, learning, work, and the sharing of goods. The majority of its ministries were carried out on monastic property. The friars, in contrast, sought to imitate the life and ministry of Jesus and his disciples on the road to Jerusalem. The friars identified themselves as itinerant preachers: they were mobile, poor, and driven to take the gospel to the ends of the earth.

The mendicants reflected a larger reform movement of the High Middle Ages. Pope Gregory VII (1073–85) sought to correct clerical corruption, particularly the common practices of nicolaitanism (concubinage), simony (buying and selling ecclesiastical offices), and nepotism

1. For more on the mendicant orders besides the Franciscans and Dominicans, see Frances Andrews, *The Other Friars: The Carmelite, Augustinian, Sack and Pied Friars in the Middle Ages* (Woodbridge, UK: Boydell, 2006).

(the passing on of offices within families and estates). Ecclesiastical offices were coveted because they were attached to benefices, or fixed salaries. Secular authorities often insisted on choosing the men who would receive ecclesiastical office in their realms and on investing them with the symbols of their offices. Frequently, they appointed uneducated and unsuitable cronies. Among his reforms, Gregory advanced the church's legal autonomy from the encroachment of secular regents and secured the church's right to choose its own ministers. This reform was supported by the emerging systematization of canon law, which theorized that the pope and bishops had a power of jurisdiction over the church's inner workings similar to the divine right kings held to rule temporally. This theory, we shall see later on, had immense influence on the subsequent development of the theology of holy orders. Finally, Gregory appealed to lay people to demand more from their clergy, even permitting them to refuse the sacramental administrations of corrupt priests.[2]

Empowered by the Gregorian Reform and inspired by their own reading of the gospel, numerous urban lay Christians of the twelfth century showed their hunger for a purer church by organizing into small communities dedicated to what they called the *vita apostolica*, the apostolic life, characterized by gospel poverty and preaching. The movement almost immediately caused conflict. Some individuals and groups were overly critical, subjective, and even heretical in their bent. A large number of the faithful, who had long suffered the failures of incompetent clergy and were thus themselves poorly catechized, latched onto extreme and heretical messages.[3] Secular authorities and bishops responded by arguing against the legality of the groups, saying that public preaching required formal permission from bishops, that such a mandate was usually restricted to clergy, and that learning was a prerequisite to preach publicly.[4]

2. See Dominic Monti, "Gospel Preaching and Gospel Life: Similarities and Differences," in *Franciscan Evangelization: Striving to Preach the Gospel*, Washington Theological Union Symposium Papers 2007, ed. Elise Saggau (St. Bonaventure, N.Y.: Franciscan Institute, 2008), 17–18.

3. See C. Colt Anderson, "Clerics, Laity and Preaching the Gospel among the Early Franciscans," in Saggau, *Franciscan Evangelization*, 33–54, esp. 39; Simon Tugwell, ed., *Early Dominicans: Selected Writings* (Mahwah, N.J.: Paulist Press, 1982), 8–9.

4. Monti, "Gospel Preaching and Gospel Life," 22.

It was not enough, however, for the church's leadership simply to clamp down on the extremes of the reform movement. The church had to meet its concerns. In 1215, the Fourth Lateran Council, recognizing the sorry state of the clergy, asked for "suitable men" to help the bishops preach and catechize the people.[5] Beginning with Innocent III (1198–1216), a series of far-sighted popes recognized that if the good zeal of one or two of the groups committed to the *vita apostolica* could be combined with proper education, formation, and organization, perhaps they could become the "suitable men" for whom the church was looking.[6]

Religious Life and Priesthood among the Early Franciscans

Around 1204, Francis of Assisi (1181–1226), like other enthusiasts for the *vita apostolica*, committed himself to a life of evangelical poverty. The charismatic figure soon attracted a group of like-minded disciples. They shared a common life of itinerancy, informal preaching, simple labor, occasional begging, and engagement in corporal works of mercy for the benefit of the poor.

Francis was on friendly terms with the bishop of Assisi, so he and his brothers were allowed to move about rather freely within the diocese. Francis, however, felt compelled to imitate Christ and the apostles just

5. Canon 10 of the Fourth Lateran Council states, "Among the various things that are conducive to the salvation of the Christian people, the nourishment of God's word is recognized to be especially necessary, since just as the body is fed with material food, so the soul is fed with spiritual food.... Now it often happens that bishops by themselves are not sufficient to minister the Word of God to the people.... We therefore decree by this general constitution that bishops are to appoint suitable men (*viros*) to carry out with profit this duty of sacred preaching, men who are powerful in word and deed and who will visit with care the peoples entrusted to them in place of the bishops, since these by themselves are unable to do it, and will build them up by word and example"; Norman P. Tanner, ed., *Decrees of the Ecumenical Councils* (Washington, D.C.: Georgetown University Press, 1990), 1:239–40.

6. Regarding the contribution of various popes to the mendicant cause, see Laureito Landini, *The Causes of Clericalization of the Order of Friars Minor: 1209–1260 in the Light of Early Franciscan Sources* (Chicago: privately published, 1968), 56–76; and Regis Armstrong, J. A. Wayne Hellmann, and William Short, eds., *Francis of Assisi: Early Documents* (New York: New City, 1999), 1:558–77; hereafter, *FA:ED*.

as their lives were described in the gospels. As such, he wished to "go into the whole world" (Mk 16:15) and "make disciples of all nations" (Mt 28:19). His bishop (Guido II of Assisi) cautioned him that, if he extended beyond Assisi, Francis might run into trouble with other bishops. Francis decided to go to Rome to seek out papal blessing for his group. It is likely he did so because he believed the pope, as successor to Peter, the chief of apostles, could authorize a mission of universal range.[7]

Innocent saw in Francis a man who combined the best zeal for the *vita apostolica* with a strong instinct for communion with the hierarchy of the church.[8] In short, Francis was precisely what the church needed. He could serve as a bridge by which the institution would benefit from the energy of reform and by which the reform movement could be harnessed and steered. Innocent gave Francis and his brothers the papal blessing and official permission to move about and preach publicly beyond the boundaries of Assisi. The visible sign of this blessing was the Friars' reception of the tonsure.[9]

Consistent with its origins in the lay penitential movement, Francis did not initially envision his community as a clerical order. However, within fifty years, nearly every friar was ordained or in formation for ordination. The reasons for this shift are complex and disputed.[10] Francis was not a priest, though he may have been ordained to one of the minor

7. Cyprian Rosen, "Fostering the Patrimony of the Order of Friars Minor Capuchin: A Study in the Mutual Responsibility of the Order and the Apostolic See (Canons 576 and 631)" (JCD diss., The Catholic University of America, 2009), 39; Monti, "'Deservedly Approved by the Roman Church': The Context for Papal Recognition of Francis's *Forma Vitae*," in *The Rule of the Friars Minor, 1209–2009: Historical Perspectives, Lived Realities*, ed. Daria Mitchell, 3–31 (St. Bonaventure, N.Y.: Franciscan Institute , 2010).

8. The opening chapters of both Franciscan rules, *Regula Non Bullata* 1221 and *Regula Bullata* 1223, include promises of obedience by Francis to the pope and his successors. See *FA:ED* 1:63 and *FA:ED* 1:99.

9. According to Laureito Landini, "These 'small tonsures' were a device of the moment, inspired by Innocent or one of the cardinals, whereby Francis and the others might more easily be recognized as being associated somehow with the hierarchy of the Church and as belonging to some approved order, that they might more easily carry out their apostolate of preaching penance"; Landini, *Causes of Clericalization of the Order of Friars Minor*, 32.

10. For the current state of the question, see Daniel P. Horan, *Franciscan Priesthood: The Possibility of Franciscan Presbyters according to the Rule and Tradition* (Brighton, Mass.: Koinonia, 2012).

orders.[11] He opened membership in his fraternity to anyone, ordained or not, who would assume his humble way of life. Francis originally intended that each member would contribute to the community by exercising the gifts, talents, and skills with which he had come to the brotherhood. For a priest-friar, this meant ministerial work. For lay-friars, it would take other forms such as trades or domestic service. Eventually, a number of clerics entered Francis's band of followers, and some scholars have argued that these clerics soon enough co-opted the fraternity and marginalized the nonordained members to the extent that there was little meaningful future for them in the order.

Another likely reason for clericalization was the desire of the friars to preach more freely and widely and the concurrent desire of ecclesiastical authorities such as the pope to utilize the friars to advance evangelical goals.[12] When Francis first visited Innocent, he sought and received explicit permission to preach informal, spiritual, and moral sermons in squares and on street corners, but not permission to preach formal dogmatic homilies in churches. The freedom of any Christian to bear witness to his or her faith is something that today we would see as stemming from baptism and confirmation, and so it is not so astounding that Innocent recognized Francis and his brothers' right to carry out this activity. In fact, the pope had already previously recognized a right to preach informally for lay groups such as the Poor Catholics and the *Humiliati*.[13] Francis's tonsuring, however, was a new development. At that time, men preparing for holy orders received tonsures as the first step of their initiation into the clerical state. By giving Francis the tonsure,

11. Francis referred to himself as a cleric, and popular hagiography has long described Francis as a deacon. Horan and others do not find this claim to be justifiable based on the best historical sources and think that at most Francis was ordained into one of the minor orders such as subdeacon or acolyte. Since tonsuring was the point of initiation into the clerical state (juridically conceived), it is possible that, sacramentally speaking, Francis never received more than a haircut. See Horan, *Franciscan Priesthood*, 15–16; Michael F. Cusato, "Francis of Assisi, Deacon? An Examination of the Claims of the Earliest Franciscan Sources 1229–1235," in *Defenders and Critics of Franciscan Life: Essays in Honor of John V. Fleming*, ed. Michael F. Cusato and G. Geltner (Leiden: Brill, 2009), 9–39.

12. See *FA:ED* 1:558–77, for papal bulls extending privileges to the friars that reflect the ecclesiastical desire to make use of the Franciscan movement.

13. Monti, "Gospel Preaching and Gospel Life," 24–25.

it marked Francis and his followers as doing more than bearing private witness by their preaching. It could be read as Innocent's intention to associate them in some way with the hierarchy's own mission. When, just a few years after Francis's meeting with Pope Innocent, the Fourth Lateran Council called for "suitable men" to assist the bishops in their evangelical mission, it likely seemed to both the bishops and the friars that the friars were a natural fit for that role, for they had already begun to fill it.

Still, there was no reason that either the tonsuring or the request for "suitable men" to assist the bishops in proclaiming the word of God necessitated clericalization of the order. The friars could have remained a group of mostly lay preachers associated with the pope and bishops in some other way. In another era, religious profession might have been seen as enough to establish the friars in a public ecclesial mission. However, the bishops had a bad taste in their mouths from those members of the lay penitential movements who had been hypercritical. Also, lay penitential preaching often enough broached dogmatic questions and sometimes slid into heresy. Thus, the bishops increased pressure that anyone who bore any kind of public witness should not only have express permission to do so, but the kind of education that was reserved for clerics.[14] So there was an external pressure on the friars to clericalize. Meanwhile, assuming the best intentions, it is likely that many of the friars perceived that they could do a lot of good if more of them were formally trained, educated, and ordained so that they could preach not only informally, but dogmatically, and in churches.

Ordination was also necessary to offer the sacrament of penance. In antiquity, penance had been a public, communal rite reserved for grave sinners and almost always administered by the bishop. During the early medieval period, Irish monks, mostly lay, introduced the practice of private confession to the masses. The episcopacy initially resisted this development, but a compromise worked out during the Carolingian era permitted ordinary priests to administer penance for most sins.[15] By

14. See Monti, "Gospel Preaching and Gospel Life," 22–30; Monti, "Deservedly Approved by the Roman Church," 18; Darleen Pryds, "Preaching Women: The Tradition of Mendicant Women," in Saggau, *Franciscan Evangelization*, 57–65.

15. See James Dallen, *The Reconciling Community: The Rite of Penance* (New York: Pueblo, 1986), 110–13.

the High Middle Ages, private confession was becoming a more universal practice of Christians. The Fourth Lateran Council introduced, for the first time, the requirement of all Christians to confess their sins yearly, at least. This greatly increased the need for well-trained confessors. While only an indirect cause of their clericalization, the Franciscans assumed this task of administering penance and were a valuable instrument in meeting this growing need of the church.[16]

As is probably apparent, clericalization tested some early Franciscan ideals, the first being humility. As earlier noted, Francis wanted every friar to remain in the hierarchical state he had at the time of entry; the only priests of the order were to be those who were already clerics when they joined the fraternity. Francis had named his group the "friars minor," or "lesser brothers," because he believed every friar should consider himself lesser than others, never seeking positions of authority or power. Francis associated the ambition for formal education, increasingly a prerequisite for ordination, with vanity, and so prohibited it for the lay friars. They should remain with the amount of education they had at the time of entry.[17] After a time, however, Francis changed his policies. He allowed lay-friars to study and pursue ordination, though he cautioned against their becoming inflated.[18] However, and paradoxically perhaps, Francis consistently exhorted the friars to revere and submit to priests and bishops. As more priests entered the fraternity and more and more friars were ordained, it was potentially difficult for the nonordained brothers not to put the fathers on a pedestal and for the fathers not to assume it. Francis's own teaching and example of profound reverent submission toward priests meant it would be a challenge for priests of the order to maintain the humble position they were expected as Friars Minor to occupy.[19]

A second, related test was to the inclusion of the nonordained friars in the community and to their equality within it. Francis desired a

16. Landini, *Causes of Clericalization of the Order of Friars Minor,* 142–44.

17. *FA:ED* 1:105.

18. *FA:ED* 1:107; see also Augustine Thompson, *Francis of Assisi: A New Biography* (Ithaca, N.Y.: Cornell University Press, 2012), 112–13; and Neslihan Senocak, *The Poor and the Perfect: The Rise of Learning in the Franciscan Order, 1209–1310* (Ithaca, N.Y.: Cornell University Press, 2012).

19. Landini, *Causes of Clericalization of the Order of Friars Minor,* 50–55.

mixed brotherhood of ordained and nonordained friars with a spirit of true fraternity among them. Francis promoted equality within the order by making very few distinctions in his First Rule between ordained and nonordained by chastising priests who clamored for authority and by promoting two nonordained friars as his first and second successors as head of the order.[20] However, the clerics were the most educated members of the brotherhood and expected to be able to lead. As the number of clerics increased, the nonordained were quickly relegated to second-tier status, rarely occupying positions of authority after 1239.[21] Then, as the church increasingly called upon the order to undertake clerical tasks such as doctrinal preaching and the hearing of confessions and as the order embraced these tasks, the lay friars significantly decreased. The shift was a source of consternation for some of Francis's original followers, such as Thomas of Celano.[22] Within a century, disputes regarding the place for the nonordained brother in the order factored into the splintering of the Franciscans between the "Conventuals," "Spirituals," and "Observants." Three hundred years later, it factored again into the emergence of the Capuchins who, like the earlier "Spirituals" and "Observants," were dedicated to recovering the inclusion and equality of the lay friars, a value they felt the Conventuals had lost.[23]

The final test was of poverty. The friars were to be itinerant mobile preachers; neither the community as a whole nor individuals within it were to own any property.[24] Training for priesthood, however, required stable dwellings, books, and a healthy financial situation so that the friars did not have to spend each day begging or engaging in the menial tasks by which they acquired their bread. In order to bring these

20. Cusato, "Francis of Assisi, Deacon?," 37.

21. See Landini, *Causes of Clericalization of the Order of Friars Minor*, 123–26.

22. Landini, *Causes of Clericalization of the Order of Friars Minor*, 98–100.

23. See Rosen, "Fostering the Patrimony of the Order of Friars Minor Capuchin," 90–125, esp. 95 and 116–20. As Rosen notes, inclusion and equality of the lay-friars was by no means the only concern of either the thirteenth- or sixteenth-century Franciscan reform movements.

24. For fresh perspectives on the meaning of Franciscan poverty, see Jacques Dalarun, *Francis of Assisi and Power* (St. Bonaventure, N.Y.: Franciscan Institute, 2007); and Cusato, "The Renunciation of Power as a Foundational Theme in Early Franciscan History," in *The Early Franciscan Movement, 1205–1239: History, Sources, and Hermeneutics* (Spoleto: Fondazione Centro Italiano di Studi Sull'alto Medioevo, 2009), 29–48.

necessities into alignment with the Franciscan ideal, Francis arranged for others outside the order to claim formal ownership of the buildings and books the friars used and to donate monies, considered alms rather than wages, in exchange for pastoral services. There was no question, however, that having access to these things represented and influenced a change in Franciscan lifestyle.[25]

The priesthood, therefore, within the Franciscan order, held a paradoxical place. On the one hand, it was helpful, arguably necessary for involvement in the tasks of official preaching and hearing of confessions that Franciscans had begun to engage. On the other hand, it presented challenges to Franciscan ideals such as humility, inclusion and equality, and poverty.

Religious Life and Priesthood among the Early Dominicans

Before he created the Order of Preachers, St. Dominic Guzman (1170–1221) was a canon regular of the diocese of Osma, Spain. The canons regular were an outgrowth of the Gregorian Reform. As part of his campaign to abolish simony and nicolaitanism, Pope Gregory VII encouraged the secular clergy to embrace a common life of committed celibacy, prayer, and shared property. In many places, but particularly in Northern Italy and Southern France, urban secular clergy organized themselves, or were organized by their bishop, into clerical houses observing the regular life. The arrangement was very similar to the one St. Augustine had established centuries before, and the canons regular now adopted Augustine's rule.[26]

Between 1203 and 1206, Dominic twice accompanied Diego of Osma, who was both the see's new bishop and the original prior of its canons, on ambassadorial journeys to Denmark. Passing through Southern France during their second journey, the pair encountered a team of Cistercian papal legates combating the Albigensian heresy. The

25. For details, see Cajetan Esser, *Origins of the Franciscan Order* (Chicago: Franciscan Herald, 1980), 165–68; and Lawrence M. Clopper, "Langland and the Franciscans on *Dominium*," in Cusato and Geltner, *Defenders and Critics*, 85–104.

26. See Lawrence, *Medieval Monasticism*, 160–64.

heretics, who embraced radical poverty, were winning many converts. Diego grasped that the heretics' austere lifestyle gave credibility to their message, and so he encouraged the legates to adopt it, as well. Combining orthodox preaching and radical poverty, Diego, Dominic, and the three papal legates worked for a short while together and were able to return many persons back to orthodoxy. Diego died in 1207, and the group continued with success before eventually dissipating. Soon after, Fulk, the bishop of Toulouse, invited Dominic to organize, within his diocese, a group of clergy dedicated explicitly to the life of radical poverty, evangelization of heretics, and catechizing of the faithful.[27]

In 1215, Dominic accompanied Fulk to the Fourth Lateran Council, where, as we have already seen, the bishops requested "suitable men" to assist them as auxiliary preachers and teachers. Dominic understood that his own work in Toulouse corresponded to this request and that his task therefore might not be limited to a single diocese. Confirmed by a vision in which Sts. Peter and Paul called him and "his sons" to evangelize the whole world,[28] Dominic requested and received in 1216 and 1217 from Pope Honorius (1216–27) Bulls that instituted the Order of Preachers and commissioned them to an apostolate of universal evangelization.[29]

It is easiest to see the uniqueness of the Dominican vocation by comparing it with the other forms of religious life that were present at that time in history. Dominican roots were in the canons regular, but they differed from them in some important respects. First, the Dominicans embraced the more austere poverty that was characteristic of the *vita apostolica* movement. Because the canons were attached to the cathedral and parishes, they still received benefices that they then held in common. The Dominicans renounced parochial offices that came with benefices. They survived only by way of alms, which they usually received in conjunction with pastoral work. Second, the Dominicans were

27. See Tugwell, *Early Dominicans*, 11–16.

28. William A. Hinnebusch, *The History of the Dominican Order*, vol. 1, *Origins and Growth to 1500* (New York: Alba House, 1965), 49.

29. Tugwell, *Early Dominicans*, 14–16. For more on the genesis of the Dominican order, see Benedict M. Ashley, *The Dominicans* (Eugene, Ore.: Wipf and Stock, 1990), 2–24.

not territorially bound. The canons, like monks, were stable (though not strictly cloistered) within a locale and vowed obedience to a local superior. The Dominicans were itinerant. They moved back and forth between different locations in different dioceses. They vowed obedience not to a local superior but to a superior general in Rome who himself was accountable to the holy father.[30]

Though the Dominicans shared many things in common with the Franciscans, they also stood distinct from them. According to Simon Tugwell, there is a subtle difference in the Franciscan and Dominican approaches to the *vita apostolica*. For Francis, the stronger emphasis was on the *vita*—that is, on embracing a life that was a strict imitation of Christ. Francis embraced preaching because he considered it integral to the life of discipleship. For Dominic, the stronger emphasis was on the *apostolica*, on being sent to evangelize.[31] Though his love for poverty was sincere, he embraced the *vita* in part because he understood it aided his preaching.[32] The Dominicans also had a much stronger clerical identity from the beginning. Franciscans had emerged from the lay penitential movement, but Dominic was a cleric who had been formed in the tradition of canons. Dominic accepted lay members, but these were very few; hence, the Dominicans did not struggle through the same tensions between ordained and nonordained members as early Franciscans did.[33] Furthermore, everything in Dominic's order was to support preaching for the salvation of souls. Since books and stable

30. For Comparisons of the Dominicans with the Canons Regular, see Tugwell, *Early Dominicans*, 20–21, and Hinnebusch, *History of the Dominican Order*, 1:46–47, 120–27.

31. While the *apostolica* certainly takes pride of place, the imitation of Christ was nonetheless of great importance to Dominican life: see Ulrich Horst, "Christ, *Exemplar Ordinis Fratrum Praedicantium*, according to Saint Thomas Aquinas," in *Christ among the Medieval Dominicans: Representations of Christ in the Texts and Images of the Order of Preachers*, ed. Kent Emery and Joseph P. Wawrykow, 256–70 (Notre Dame, Ind.: University of Notre Dame Press, 1998).

32. Tugwell, *Early Dominicans*, 18–19. For more on Dominic's interpretation of poverty, see Guy Bedouelle, *Saint Dominic: The Grace of the Word*, rev. ed., trans. Mary Thomas Noble (San Francisco: Ignatius Press, 1987), 138–54.

33. Hinnebusch, *History of the Dominican Order*, 1:125. For a comprehensive history of Dominican brothers, see Thompson, *Dominican Brothers: Conversi, Lay, and Cooperator Friars* (Chicago: New Priory Press, 2017).

dwellings were needed in order to form good, well-educated preachers, they were permitted from the beginning, and were never considered a compromise of poverty.[34]

Dominicans contrasted even more with monks, particularly monks of the High Middle Ages who were moving away from active ministry toward a more exclusive focus on liturgy (for instance, Cluny), cloister, solitude, and silence (e.g., Camaldolese, Cistercians, and Carthusians). Dominic departed from monastic customs in several ways: time spent on either manual labor or *Lectio divina* (spiritual reading) could be replaced by time in academic study; the divine office should be recited briefly and succinctly so as not to overly interfere with study and preaching; attendance at chapter, common meals, and even choir could and should be dispensed with for a friar who was preaching. Most importantly, friars could move in and out of the cloister more easily so as to be more available for ministry.[35] From some monastic points of view, these changes appeared to compromise the integrity of regular life,[36] but Dominic, following the line of thought established by Basil and others, saw a mixed life of contemplation and action as superior to either contemplation or action in isolation.[37]

Dominic's genius was to recognize that whether something is considered a compromise depends on the ideal one is trying to uphold. By ordering the elements of religious life to explicitly pastoral ends, the priesthood did not appear to compromise religious life. Instead, it ful-

34. Hinnebusch, *History of the Dominican Order*, 1:146–51.

35. Hinnebusch, *History of the Dominican Order*, 1:46–47, 84, 121. See also Bedouelle, *Saint Dominic*, 104–18.

36. Tugwell, *Early Dominicans*, 21. Tugwell notes that the Cistercians accused the Dominicans of being "Pharisees," a word that means "divided." In the eyes of the Cistercians, Dominicans were men divided between the cloister and the world, the contemplative and active lives.

37. Hinnebusch, *History of the Dominican Order*, 1:84. The classic defense of this comes in St. Thomas Aquinas, *Summa Theologiae*, II-II, q. 188, a. 6 (hereafter *ST*): "Accordingly we must say that the work of the active life is twofold. One proceeds from the fullness of contemplation, such as teaching and preaching. Wherefore Gregory says (Hom. v in Ezech.) that the words of Psalm 144:7, 'They shall publish the memory of . . . Thy sweetness,' refer 'to perfect men returning from their contemplation.' And this work is more excellent than simple contemplation. For even as it is better to enlighten than merely to shine, so is it better to give to others the fruits of one's contemplation than merely to contemplate."

filled it. Nor did religious life appear to compromise the priesthood. Rather, it supported it.

Conflict between Friars and Seculars

It is unlikely the friars could have existed before the High Middle Ages. After the fall of Rome, Europe reverted to being a mostly rural, agrarian society. People lived in small villages on landed estates. Feudal structures bound people closely to both the soil, as serfs and lords, and one another, as vassals held by oaths of fealty. It was a society in which each one had a determined place. The church mirrored the feudal structure.[38] The *bannus parochialis* system assigned everyone in Christendom to parishes to which the faithful were required to contribute from their resources in exchange for ministerial services. Pastors were supported economically by this system.[39]

The twelfth century saw great changes. The crusades, popular pilgrimages, and the rise of international trade created a much more mobile society. Mercantilism with its monetary economy created a middle class. The middle class had resources and yet were not bound to the soil as either lords or serfs. They were enfranchised and independent and joined voluntary ecclesial and social societies such as guilds and confraternities rather than simply finding their place within the estate to which they had been born. These were denizens of the new, rising cities.[40]

The life of the friar depended on and reflected this new society. The friars were mobile, international in membership, democratic in their structures, and dependent on the voluntary support of the Christian faithful.[41] They could not have survived as itinerant beggars among the earlier agricultural estates. With the emergence of cities, their style of life became possible.

Above all, it was the friars' mobility, the practical requirement of

38. See Lester K. Little, "Saint Louis' Involvement with the Friars," *Church History* 33 (1964): 125–48, esp. 125–26.

39. See Landini, *Causes of Clericalization of the Order of Friars Minor*, 108.

40. Congar, "De la communion des églises," 242–43.

41. Congar, "De la communion des églises," 243.

their vocation to spread the gospel to the ends of the earth, that inevitably led them into conflicts with secular clergy. There had been tensions between monks and the secular clergy, but, in a rural world, these were far fewer. Monks were bound to landed estates in a world of people bound to landed estates. They less frequently crossed into the seculars' territory. Friars wished to set up churches and mission sites that fell within already established parochial boundaries and to move between them as preachers, teachers, and confessors. Although many bishops appreciated and sought out the friars,[42] more than a few saw them as competitive interlopers whose lifestyle was all too reminiscent of heretics such as the Albigensians.[43] The friars' success drew people away from parish churches, and with them, of course, went monies and bequests.[44] Additionally, within a few decades of their foundation, the friars secured faculty positions at places like the University of Paris, positions held a century before by canons and secular clergy. Moreover, the friars were drawing recruits from the university, capable men who may have otherwise joined the diocesan ranks.[45]

The friars depended on the popes to defend their rights to preach and minister beyond the fixed boundaries of a particular diocese. In turning to the papacy in this way, the mendicants were continuing a trend begun among monasteries, most importantly Cluny and the Cistercians, which had been granted jurisdictional autonomy by the Holy See and placed under its protection in order to preserve them from the excessive interventions of local bishops and lay magistrates, who often demanded the right to appoint abbots and otherwise interfered in the monasteries' inner workings. The friars' association with the papacy reaffirmed the connection between religious life and the Holy See, but in this case, the reason for the alliance was less for the sake of internal governance than for the purpose of external ministry.[46]

The popes, in turn, saw in the friars an opportunity to advance re-

42. See Lawrence, *Medieval Monasticism*, 264. For example, Robert Grosseteste invited the friars into his diocese to preach and hear confessions.

43. Hinnebusch, *History of the Dominican Order*, 1:58.

44. Lawrence, *Medieval Monasticism*, 265.

45. See Little, "Saint Louis' Involvement with the Friars," 137.

46. See O'Malley, "Priesthood, Ministry, and Religious Life," 236.

form and bolster their own influence.[47] Nearly every pope of the thirteenth century issued bulls that exhorted the bishops to welcome the friars into their dioceses and granted the friars extensive privileges that effectively allowed them to preach and hear confessions universally and to support themselves through alms collected in conjunction with this ministry. The same popes, meanwhile, began to use the friars as a sort of "papal clergy," appointing them as legates, mediators, preachers of crusades, and inquisitors.[48]

An exception to thirteenth-century papal support of the friars was Innocent IV (1243–54). Apparently, he was troubled by an attempt among the Franciscans to popularize a thesis, stemming from Joachim of Fiore, that the church was entering a new phase of history in which "the secular clergy would no longer serve any useful purpose in society" and "would be superseded by barefooted mendicants who lived in imitation of the Apostles."[49] In response to this effort and to the constant complaints of the secular clergy about the encroachment of the friars on their territory, Innocent issued the Bull *Etsi Animarum* (1254), which prohibited the friars from any longer admitting laypeople to their churches; from administering the sacrament of penance without the local ordinary's permission; from preaching at the same time a bishop was preaching; and from preaching within parochial boundaries without an invitation from the local pastor.[50]

Only sixteen days after he had issued *Etsi*, however, Innocent died. His successor, Alexander IV (+1254–61), returned to the friars their full range of privileges. Alexander's action incited William of St. Amour (c. 1200–72), a secular canon teaching at the University of Paris, to publish works in which he called the very existence of the friars into question. William argued that there are only two ministerial orders in the church: bishops succeed the twelve apostles, while parish priests succeed the seventy-two disciples of Luke 10. According to William, these are the only two orders commissioned and sent by the Lord. The friars are the "pseudo-preachers," described in Matthew 24:24, who preach without a

47. See Congar, "De la communion des églises," 239–43.

48. Landini, *Causes of Clericalization of the Order of Friars Minor*, 67.

49. Little, "Saint Louis' Involvement with the Friars," 138.

50. Landini, *Causes of Clericalization of the Order of Friars Minor*, 72.

divine commission.[51] It made little difference to William that the popes had permitted the friars to preach. He said that the popes did not have the authority to send the friars into dioceses against the wishes of the local bishops. Furthermore, he said that pastors had as much authority within their parishes as bishops did within their dioceses. Hence, pastors could not be compelled to accept friars preaching within their parish boundaries.[52] William completed his argument by saying that the friars belonged to the ranks of religious, not of the clergy. William adopted a distinction made by Pseudo-Dionysius that located monks and clergy within two different hierarchies. The former belong to the hierarchy of those being perfected (laity and religious), the latter to the hierarchy of those who perfect others (the clergy). As religious, the friars were clearly followers rather than leaders in the church. As such, they should follow the pattern of monks, fasting and praying in seclusion and supporting themselves by manual labor, not by begging (since St. Paul prohibited it for able-bodied persons), nor by alms collected in conjunction with ministerial work (since the friars had no real right to engage in such work).[53]

The Responses of Thomas Aquinas and Bonaventure

The task of responding theologically to William was taken up by the Dominican St. Thomas Aquinas (1225–74) and by the Franciscan St. Bonaventure (1221–74). In responding to William, the two great scholastic masters developed sophisticated theologies of religious priesthood.[54]

51. Robert J. Karris, Introduction to *Works of St. Bonaventure: Disputed Questions on Evangelical Perfection*, trans. Thomas Reist and Robert J. Karris (St. Bonaventure, N.Y.: Franciscan Institute, 2008), 11.

52. Landini, *Causes of Clericalization of the Order of Friars Minor*, 74.

53. Congar, "De la communion des églises," 244; Karris, Introduction to *Works of St. Bonaventure*, 12.

54. Thomas's and Bonaventure's theologies of religious priesthood have been laid out by David N. Power, upon whose summary this section relies. See Power, "Theologies of Religious Life and Priesthood," in Hennessy, *A Concert of Charisms*, 61–103, esp.71–76.

Thomas Aquinas

Aquinas accepted William's basic Dionysian distinction between religious and clergy as a distinction between those who are perfected and those who perfect. Unlike William, however, Thomas recognized a bridge between the two Dionysian hierarchies in the person of the bishop. The bishop stands atop the hierarchy of those who perfect, but because he must be perfect to perfect others, he himself also must stand atop the ranks of the perfected. Therefore, it is appropriate for bishops to have taken a vow, analogous to that made by religious, "to oblige themselves to those things which pertain to perfection."[55] According to Thomas, such a vow established the bishop in a permanent state of life by which he committed his whole self, for the whole of his life, to "the service of the flock entrusted to him."[56] Thomas did not extend the same definitive requirement for subjective commitment to holiness to priests and deacons, nor did he appear to see them occupying a state of life distinct from the ordinary faithful. His stance likely stemmed from a historical situation in which priests and deacons sometimes were married, often had duties in addition to ministry, and could abandon their ministerial responsibilities to join monasteries or simply to retire.[57] Nonetheless, by associating bishops and religious in the same or similar state of life, Thomas established a link, unrecognized by William, that made the religious state a fitting foundation and preparation for ministry.

Thomas conceived of priesthood primarily according to its relation with the Eucharist. Through the sacrament of orders, the priest was stamped with the character of Christ by which the priest could efficaciously transform bread and wine into Christ's body and blood and offer these in sacrifice. Other ministerial functions, such as preaching, teaching, and ruling, had a more indirect relationship to orders. For Thomas, ordination communicated grace for the exercise of these functions, but their legitimate use required not only ordination but a canonical mandate bestowed by the bishop to whom these functions most properly

55. *ST* II-II, q. 184, a. 5.

56. Balthasar, *The Christian State of Life*, trans. Mary Frances McCarthy (San Francisco: Ignatius Press, 1977), 302; hereafter *CSL*.

57. David Power, "Theologies of Religious Life and Priesthood," 71–72; Balthasar, *CSL*, 302; *ST* II-II, q. 184, a. 6, ad.3.

belonged.[58] In this way, Thomas made a distinction between what was given ipso facto through the power of ordination—that is, the ability to sanctify (especially to confect the Eucharistic elements)—and what was given through the power of jurisdiction held by the bishops, which was a mandate to preach, teach, or rule.[59]

Thomas appealed to the pope's unique power of jurisdiction to respond to William's concerns about the friars' encroachment on the territory of the seculars. As the "first among bishops," the pope had universal right of jurisdiction and could "intervene with authority in every church without restriction," which he did, for example, by sending the friars on a transdiocesan mission.[60] The pope, however, had not acted arbitrarily. The needs of the time demanded "preachers and confessors who lived holy lives and who were well versed in doctrine and the knowledge of the scriptures in a way that many parochial clergy were not."[61] Nor had the pope acted alone, for, again, the Fourth Lateran Council called precisely for such "suitable men." Thomas further justified the existence of the friars by appealing to New Testament descriptions of itinerant apostles, preachers, and teachers unassigned to particular churches. Thomas said there could and should still be those in the church delegated by the pope and bishops to come "to the aid of local priests" without themselves being "attached to a local church."[62]

William had also attacked the identity of the friars as religious. His

58. David Power (and many others) claim that St. Thomas did not recognize preaching or ruling as related in any way to sacramental ordination; see Power, "Theologies of Religious Life and Priesthood," 72. Guy Mansini has demonstrated that this is an overstatement and that the hard division of the power of orders and the power of jurisdiction was not made by St. Thomas but by his later interpreters; see Mansini, *The Word Has Dwelt among Us: Explorations in Theology* (Ave Maria, Fla.: Sapientia, 2008), 164–69.

59. David Power, "Theologies of Religious Life and Priesthood," 72. See also Lafont, *Imagining the Catholic Church: Structured Communion in the Spirit*, trans. John J. Burkhard (Collegeville, Minn.: Liturgical Press, 2000), 50–52.

60. Congar, "De la communion des églises," 246; Thomas Aquinas, *Contra Gentiles* IV.76, *Sent.* IV, d. 7, q. 3, a. 1. ad. 3; *Sent.* IV d. 24, q. 3, a. 2, sol. 3.

61. David Power, "Theologies of Religious Life and Priesthood," 72. Congar explains that Thomas was insistent that the canonical mission came not just from the pope but from the bishops; see Congar, "De la communion des églises," 246.

62. David Power, "Theologies of Religious Life and Priesthood," 72; *ST* II-II, q. 188, a. 4, ad 4.

vision of religious life was an exceedingly narrow one of monks "clearly separated from the local Church, living strictly within and unto themselves and serving only for contemplation."[63] Thomas defended religious life taking a more active form on the basis that "the religious state is directed toward the perfection of charity," which includes love of both God and neighbor.[64] The contemplative life was good, he said, but became better when its fruits were shared with others.[65] Furthermore, of all forms of active charity, the greatest were those that contributed most directly to another's spiritual, and not just corporeal, good. Therefore, the highest form of religious life could be found among the friars who combined the contemplative and active dimensions of life and whose active service was the preaching of the gospel that pertained so directly to salvation. Among the friars, the ministry of the word was supported by contemplation and study, and contemplation and study reached an evangelical goal through preaching and teaching.

Thomas saw mendicant religious life and pastoral ministry as a fitting combination, but he was careful not to conflate the two. The observances of religious life such as prayer, study, and commitment to the evangelical counsels made the friars suitable for ministry. However, it was not religious life itself that inducted a man into a mission to teach and preach, but a mandate from those holding proper jurisdiction. The responsibility for the care of souls ultimately remained the duty of bishops.[66] The bishops, however, could delegate the care of souls, or parts of it, to secular and religious clergy who assisted them. The friars did not assume the full care of souls as a parochial pastor would, but "only that portion of diocesan ministry that could be called *salus animarum* (the saving of souls) through preaching, teaching, and the hearing of confessions."[67] The friars were not attached to local parishes, did not typically govern stable communities of the faithful, and did not receive benefices (which is why they

63. Ratzinger, *Pilgrim Fellowship of Faith*, 197.

64. *ST* II-II, q. 188, a. 3.

65. *ST* II-II, q. 188, a. 6.

66. David Power, "Theologies of Religious Life and Priesthood," 73; *ST* II-II, q. 188, a. 4, ad 2.

67. Basil Cole and Paul Conner, *Christian Totality: Theology of the Consecrated Life*, rev. ed. (New York: Alba House, 1997), 340.

needed to rely on alms).[68] Their aim was not to compete with the secular clergy but to assist them for the good of the faithful.

Bonaventure

Also responding to William of St. Amour, Bonaventure advanced theses similar to those of Thomas Aquinas, though with important nuances. According to Bonaventure, the friars were justified in their priestly ministry by the needs of the day: widespread sin, ignorance, confusion incited by heretics, and a shortage of competent prelates to deal with these problems.[69] As Bonaventure saw it, the pope had formally recognized the role of religious orders taking on "the office of preaching and hearing confessions in order to rush aid to perishing souls.... This was necessary because of the need of the people and the insufficiency of priests."[70] Rather than being in competition with the secular clergy, the friars were answering the request of the Fourth Lateran Council for such "suitable men" to help in some tasks of pastoral ministry. William had charged that religious could not perform ministerial tasks proper to diocesan clergy. Bonaventure responded that they could because they were doing the bidding of higher authority.[71] Like Thomas, he appealed to the power of jurisdiction to justify the friars' ministry. He claimed that:

> Members of religious orders could take on the ministerial functions of the diocesan clergy if they were given the mission to do so by legitimate authority. Since the Fourth Lateran Council had identified the pope and the local ordinary as the two authorities that could delegate such a mission, Bonaventure firmly grounded the preaching ministry of the friars in canon law without prejudicing episcopal privileges.[72]

68. See O'Malley, "Priesthood, Ministry, and Religious Life," 231–37.

69. Anderson, "Clerics, Laity, and Preaching the Gospel among the Early Franciscans," 51. See also Bonaventure, *Quare fratres minors praedicent et confessions audient*, n. 9, in *Opera Omnia* 8:377

70. Anderson, "Clerics, Laity and Preaching the Gospel among the Early Franciscans," 51.

71. Anderson, "Clerics, Laity and Preaching the Gospel among the Early Franciscans," 49

72. Anderson, "Clerics, Laity and Preaching the Gospel among the Early Franciscans," 49; see Bonaventure, *Quare fratres minors praedicent et confessions audient*, in *Opera Omnia* 8:275–81.

Some bishops, however, were not open to the friars' ministry. In this case, Bonaventure depended on a strong doctrine of papal primacy to defend the friars' mission. The apostles were succeeded by bishops who were princes of local churches. Among the apostles, one, Peter, was the highest and was obeyed by the apostles. Among the bishops, the pope stood in the place of Peter and should be similarly obeyed. Bonaventure reasoned that because the church was a single body, it needed a single head. If authority could not be ultimately reduced to one principal authority, the church would collapse into division, chaos, instability, and weakness. Bonaventure supported this teaching with the Dionysian understanding that the ecclesial hierarchy mirrored the celestial hierarchy. In the spiritual order, all things derived from God and emanated from God and were ordered in obedience to God. Pseudo-Dionysius identified the bishop as holding the place of God in the ecclesial hierarchy. Bonaventure presented the fullness of ecclesial power as residing in the papacy: all power and jurisdiction derived from him and emanated from him. All in the church must obey him. When there was a conflict between friars and bishops, the friars could proceed based upon privileges granted by the papacy.[73]

In explaining and defending the friars as a new form of religious life in the church, Bonaventure said the friars combined three commitments previously envisioned as exclusive: the contemplation of the hermits, the virtue of the cenobites, and the apostolate of priests.[74] "According to Bonaventure, the ministry of preaching and of hearing confessions becomes a task of the order through religious profession, this then being a community goal and purpose, which of its nature required both ordination and learning."[75] In formulating things this way, Bonaventure arguably departed from Francis and made priesthood integral to, and a culmination of, the Franciscan charism. Meanwhile, he defined the Franciscans against the hermits and cenobites, whom he depicted as lacking any intrinsic apostolic dimension.

For Bonaventure, religious life and priesthood formed a highly

73. Bonaventure, *Disputed Questions on Evangelical Perfection*, q. 4

74. Bonaventure, *Opusculum* XIII.1.1; *Cur sanctus Franciscus novam Regulum institut*, in *Opera Omnia* 8:338.

75. David Power, "Theologies of Religious Life and Priesthood," 74.

symbiotic relationship. At the time, there were several minor orders to which a man was ordained (today we say instituted) as steps along the way to the priesthood. Bonaventure framed this ascension according to the classical patristic scheme of the spiritual life as a progression through the purgative, illuminative, and unitive stages. For example, the first step in ascending the ladder of orders was reception of the clerical tonsure, which, according to Bonaventure, "represented a total dedication to the service of God, cutting off temporal appetites and elevating the mind to God."[76] It was followed by elevation to the office of the psalmist in which the mind was illuminated by engagement with the scriptures.[77] The culminating ordination to the priesthood in which a man was stamped with priestly character corresponded to union with Christ in the ordinand's heart. Ascending through the hierarchy of sacramental orders therefore was a spiritual journey. As such, it was completely compatible with the goals of religious life. The fact that friars, like secular clergy, were initiated by reception of the tonsure bolstered the sense that the Franciscan life was fulfilled in priesthood. On the other hand, by describing the tonsure explicitly as an ascetical symbol, Bonaventure suggested that the best candidates for ordination were those who begin their journeys with renunciation.[78]

Along the same lines, Bonaventure emphasized poverty as both the heart of the spiritual life and the best foundation for ministry. To be poor was to live in closer union with Christ, who was humble and who loved universally without possessing. Francis's great material and spiritual poverty united him with Christ to the point of total identification expressed in the stigmata. Bonaventure extrapolated from the example of Francis that the avarice of attachments is the primary obstacle to recognizing Christ and being uniting to him. He thereby encouraged all clergy to practice material and spiritual poverty. With avarice removed,

76. David Power, "Theologies of Religious Life and Priesthood," 74; Bonaventure, *Breviloquium*, Pars VI, cap. XII.

77. At the time, tonsuring and the office of the psalmist were seen as "sub-orders" one received before receiving the minor orders of exorcist, acolyte, lector, and porter, and the major orders of presbyter, deacon, and subdeacon. See Bonaventure, *Breviloquium*, Pars VI, cap. XII; see also Nichols, *Holy Order*, 79–81.

78. David Power, "Theologies of Religious Life and Priesthood," 74–75.

the cleric would better understand the truth he was to teach and preach and would love with the very heart of Christ.[79]

Thus, Thomas and Bonaventure responded to William of St. Amour and so provided theologies of religious priesthood that have considerable merit even today. They explained how religious priesthood had scriptural antecedents and juridical justification, how religious life could support ministry and find a certain fulfillment in priesthood, and how religious priests performed an essential ecclesial service. Their theologies were heavily influenced by the mendicant life they lived as a Dominican or Franciscan. The itinerant ministry their orders initiated would also come to characterize most of the forms of religious life that followed in their wake.

79. David Power, "Theologies of Religious Life and Priesthood," 75–76; Bonaventure, *De Excellentia Magisterii Christi* III.

CHAPTER 3

Priesthood in Apostolic Congregations

Late Medieval Developments

By the sixteenth century, the church was once again in need of reform. The fourteenth-century plague (Black Death), which killed between 30 and 60 percent of Europe's population, decimated the tight, stable, and reliable ecclesial and social communities that had developed over the course of the medieval centuries. Persons, quite understandably, turned their attention more and more away from community-centered concerns toward their own private well-being.[1] The clergy, meanwhile, were once again enmeshed in problems that did not put them in good position to inspire the faithful back to ecclesial engagement. Clerical absenteeism, concubinage, buying and selling of church offices, and lack of education among the clergy resurfaced as problems that undermined trust in ecclesial structures and ecclesiastical authorities.[2] Indeed, the Avignon papacy (1309–76) and the Great Western Schism (1378–1417) brought the stability of the papacy itself into question. Last, abuses in popular piety diminished the credibility of practices that had once served as lifeblood for Christian spirituality and culture. In what began as an attempt to invigorate the church, the hierarchy offered indulgenc-

1. See John Kelly, *The Great Mortality: An Intimate History of the Black Death, the Most Devastating Plague of All Time* (New York: Harper, 2005).

2. See Lu Ann Hozma, "The Religious Milieu of the Young Ignatius," in *The Cambridge Companion to the Jesuits*, ed. Thomas Worcester, 13–31 (Cambridge: Cambridge University Press, 2008).

es to those who completed pilgrimages or other pious acts. Noting the throngs of pilgrims who seemed to approach their journey as little more than tourism, many critics questioned whether the various external acts to which indulgences were attached were of real spiritual worth. Complicating matters, indulgences, which were technically remission from temporal punishment due to sin, were often misunderstood as guarantees of salvation that could be earned through external acts. When indulgences began to be given in exchange for monetary donations to the church, the situation created the appearance that salvation itself was being bought and sold. The church had never before seemed so corrupt and so uninspiring of allegiance.

Figures associated with the late Medieval *Devotio Moderna*, of which Thomas à Kempis (1380–1471) is the most well-known example, responded by encouraging a spirituality of private prayer and individual virtue over and against corporate expressions of popular piety and other ritual performances. In the sixteenth century, the great leaders of the Protestant and Catholic Reformations continued and developed these themes. They popularized a spirituality that emphasized interior dispositions over merely external acts, the possibility of an immediate relationship with God that did not depend so much on a then visibly weak clergy, and personal reading of scripture, which was now possible for the first time on a broad level owing to the invention of the printing press. The Protestant Reformers, of course, went further than their Catholic counterparts in shifting the center of Christian spirituality from the community to the individual, from the clergy to the laity, from external rites to interior dispositions, and from public liturgy to private reading of scripture. Nonetheless, late medieval and early modern reform, whether Catholic or Protestant, is similarly characterized by heightened attention to the individual's personal relationship with God, the interior emotional and imaginative dynamics of that relationship, and the use of the scriptures as a doorway into that relationship.[3]

3. See Denis Robinson, "The Counter-Reformation: Age of Imagination," in Raab and Hagan, *Tradition of Catholic Prayer*, 89–105.

Priesthood and Religious Life among the Early Jesuits

Among the many great Catholic figures of the sixteenth century, Ignatius Loyola (1491–1556) stands out as the one most important to the history of religious priesthood. Ignatius, a member of the Basque nobility by birth, had his career as a soldier prematurely ended when he was critically wounded at the Siege of Pamplona in 1521. During his long period of recovery, he read Ludolph the Carthusian's *Life of Christ*, as well as various lives of saints. He noticed a sense of joy and energy when he imagined living a life similar to the ones of Francis and Dominic. He equally noticed a lack of inner peace when he imagined returning to the life of soldiering. Resolved to change his life in a positive direction, when Ignatius healed enough to move again, he made a pilgrimage to Jerusalem as penance for his sins.

On the road, Ignatius began work on his classic text, *The Spiritual Exercises*, which was the fruit of his reflections on God's work in his own conversion. It was a guide to discerning one's particular path of discipleship. It invited the one praying to place himself or herself imaginatively in the presence of Jesus within particular gospel stories. By conversing with the Lord in the context of these narratives and by attending (with the help of a spiritual director) to the affective experience of the Spirit's activity in one's heart, one could discover the action one should take. This text became the foundation of Ignatian spirituality, a new spirituality in the church. The *Exercises* were a Catholic expression of the sixteenth-century direction of reform toward individual piety and scriptural engagement. In time, they would be promoted, just as the Jesuits themselves would be promoted, as a Catholic answer to Protestantism.[4]

In 1523, Ignatius reached Jerusalem. He stayed for two weeks and then journeyed to Spain. Ignatius was now determined to commit his life to the corporal and spiritual works of mercy and to sharing the *Spir-*

4. For discussions of the Jesuits' relation to the Reformation, see John Patrick Donnelly, *Ignatius of Loyola: Founder of the Jesuits* (New York: Pearson-Longman, 2004), 152–59; O'Malley, *The First Jesuits* (Cambridge, Mass.: Harvard University Press, 1993), 272–83.

itual Exercises. However, he discovered that he would be taken more seriously, particularly as a preacher and teacher, if he were a priest with formal training.[5] He began studies in philosophy and theology in Spain before shifting to Paris. There in 1534, Ignatius, together with six of his fellow students, formed a company that committed itself to traveling to Jerusalem to perform charitable acts. These seven, plus three more, were ordained in Venice in 1537 and reached Rome in 1539. The political situation of the time made the mission to Jerusalem impossible, so they offered themselves to the service of the pope. In 1540, Pope Paul III instituted the group, with Ignatius as its leader, as the Society of Jesus.[6]

In preparing to meet the holy father, the group created a document, the *Formula of the Institute,* as the original expression of their way of life, which was the basis for the later *Constitutions.* The text explained the group's purpose as the "propagation of faith and progress of souls," which they intended to accomplish through "public preaching, lectures, and any other ministrations whatsoever of the Word of God, and further by means of the *Spiritual Exercises,* the education of children and unlettered persons in Christianity, and the Spiritual consolation of Christ's faithful through hearing confessions and administering the other sacraments." The text went on to say that the Society was committed to "reconciling the estranged ... holily assisting and serving those who are found in prisons and hospitals, and indeed performing any other works of charity according to what will seem expedient for the glory of God and the common good."[7] This text highlights a strong ministerial and priestly identity at the very foundation of the Society. More than monks, and even more than mendicants, who would have surely included common prayer and common life in such a mission statement, the Jesuits appeared to be assembling, above all, for the express purpose of ministry, whether that was preaching, teaching, leading the *Spiritual Exercises,* administering sacraments, or engaging in corporal works of mercy.

5. See William Harmless, "Jesuits as Priests: Crisis and Charism," *Studies in the Spirituality of Jesuits* 19, no. 3 (1985): 1–47, esp. 36–37.

6. Robinson, "Counter-Reformation," 92.

7. Quoted in O'Malley, *First Jesuits,* 5.

The high priority of ministry in the Jesuits' purpose and self-conception is reflected in their approach to religious life. The Jesuits made numerous decisions about their lives as religious based on what they perceived as being most efficacious for ministry. The most striking of their innovations was their abolishing common recitation of the Liturgy of the Hours in Choir. They abandoned this practice precisely because they felt it took too much time and made them less available for ministry. Using the same criteria, they dropped enclosure in convents and monasteries and moved into houses. These were closer to the people. Outsiders could enter the houses rather freely to receive ministry, and Jesuits could exit them without hassle whenever an invitation to serve arose.[8]

Ministry also affected the Jesuits' practical interpretation of the traditional vows. As a result of their ministerial emphasis, the Jesuits were a more diffuse, independent group than the monks, and even the mendicants, had been. They therefore were to be held accountable by a more intense obedience. They were required to make a daily examination of conscience and report, in a spirit of total transparency, all their struggles to their superiors.[9] The shape of Jesuit poverty, on the other

8. See O'Malley, *First Jesuits*, 53, 67, 135–36 (choir), 67–68 (convents). Abandonment of choir and cloister were the two marks that most distinctively set the Jesuits apart from monks and mendicants, but other aspects of their life also came as a result from their desire to maximize availability for ministry. For example, they dropped both the distinctive religious habit and obligatory fasts particular to religious because they believed these placed unnecessary obstacles to associating with the people. Also, Ignatius did not continue the practice of religious "chapters," councils made up of those in solemn vows to provide guidance to the religious superior. He replaced chapters with a monarchical system so that fewer Jesuits would be burdened with internal governance and more would be available for external ministry. The Jesuit's strong ministerial identity not only caused them to drop practices that had heretofore characterized religious life, but also transformed some of the elements of traditional religious life the Jesuits did maintain. For example, ministry impacted formation. Like monks and mendicants, Jesuits went through an intense initial period of formation, the novitiate. In those orders, however, the novitiate was primarily a time of prayer and asceticism. Because the Jesuits considered ministry so central to their identity, they introduced ministerial experiences into the novitiate. This allowed both the community and the candidate to take the latter's ministerial experiences into account in the discernment of his vocation. Similarly, the Jesuits postponed solemn vows until after several years of testing in ministry.

9. See O'Malley, *First Jesuits*, 352–55.

hand, had to be rethought when it became an obstacle to ministerial service. Schools, for example, quickly became a central ministry of the Jesuits. These required money, books, buildings, and a stable staff. Although Ignatius, like Francis, initially desired the Jesuits to embrace a more radical itinerant poverty, Ignatius determined that the ministerial advantages of operating the schools were worth the changes the schools inevitably forced upon the Jesuit lifestyle.[10]

Another important element in the Jesuits' identity as religious was their innovation of a fourth vow, a special vow of obedience to the holy father. Because they themselves were an international body ("of different provinces and realms," as the *Constitutions* of the order expressed it), and because they sought to exercise an international ministry that would reach out not only to those who needed them within the church but also to those who were outside Christendom (this being the Age of Discovery that opened pathways to missions far beyond Europe), they sought to align themselves with the holy father, whom they believed could, as universal shepherd, authorize their mission and help them determine where, in and beyond the church, they would best serve.[11] In closely associating themselves with the papacy, the Jesuits were, of course, following the example of religious before them, but they were the first to express it in terms of a vow.

The Jesuits were not only religious, but also, for the most part, priests.[12] However, they expressed their priesthood in a particular

10. See O'Malley, *First Jesuits*, 374–76.

11. Quoted in O'Malley, *First Jesuits*, 299. For more on the Fourth Vow, see O'Malley, "The Fourth Vow in Its Ignatian Context: A Historical Study," *Studies in the Spirituality of Jesuits* 15, no. 1 (1983): 1–59; Brian E. Daley, "In Ten Thousand Places': Christian Universality and the Jesuit Mission," *Studies in the Spirituality of Jesuits* 17, no. 2 (1985): 1–32.

12. The place of priesthood in Jesuit identity is a complicated issue. One could say that the Jesuit vocation was strongly oriented toward the priesthood but not exhausted by the priesthood. The Society was oriented toward the priesthood because the first ten Jesuits were all priests, and they founded their Society to engage in ministries, some of which, such as the administration of penance, required ordination to carry out. Though the Jesuits have always had large numbers of nonordained members, this stems primarily from the fact that their formation is exceptionally long. The vast majority of nonordained members, at any time in history, were preparing for priesthood, a process that could take longer than a decade. Those destined to remain nonordained were called "temporal coadjutors." Nonetheless, the Jesuit self-concept was not exhausted by the priesthood because the Jesuits always placed greater emphasis on their identity and mission as Jesuits

way.[13] The Jesuits consistently rejected attempts to make pastors with a stable *cura animarum* (care of souls of a particular and usually geographically determined section of the church), and they did so for three primary reasons. First, the office of pastor came with a benefice that the Jesuits believed violated their observance of evangelical poverty. Second, the Jesuit vocation, like that of the mendicants, entailed a commitment to itinerancy that could not be maintained if one were bound to a particular assembly of the faithful as pastors were. Third, such an office entailed a ministry to those whose pastoral needs were already being met by diocesan structures; the Jesuits did not want to compete with the diocesan clergy but, rather, desired to reach those who were not being, and perhaps could not be, reached by the parish priests.[14]

The Jesuits conceived of themselves, as is evident in the *Formula* of 1540, primarily as evangelists, as ministers of the word. In their early days, they preached in "public squares and markets, in hospitals, in prisons, aboard ships in dock, in fortresses, on playing fields," and "in hospices or hostels."[15] As the Jesuits became more organized and structured, they published books and catechetical materials, gave formal lessons to children and adults, and operated parish missions. Eventually, they focused their energies into the two primary ministries of retreat centers, where they offered the *Spiritual Exercises*, and schools,

---

than on their specific identity and mission as priests. Jerónimo Nadal, Ignatius's special assistant, emphasized that Christ called the Twelve by name and sent them out on missions before they were "ordained" at the Last Supper. The Jesuits, similarly, derived their identity and mission upon entrance to the Society, with ordained ministry being a later event that sealed rather than bestowed this identity and mission; O'Malley, *First Jesuits*, 79–80, 157–59. On the place of priesthood in Jesuit identity, see also Harmless, "Jesuits as Priests"; Michael J. Buckley, "Jesuit Priesthood: Its Meaning and Commitments," *Studies in the Spirituality of Jesuits* 8, no. 5 (1985): 135–66; and Donald L. Gelpi, "Theological Reflections on the Priestly Character of our Jesuit Vocation," *Studies in the Spirituality of Jesuits* 19, no. 3 (1987): 49–63.

13. In his discussion of the Jesuit approach to priesthood, contrasted the relative attention Jesuits give to each of the classical *tria munera* of ministry Michael Buckley: the prophetic (*munus docendi*), priestly (*munus sanctificandi*), and royal (*munus regendi*). Buckley concludes that the Jesuits primarily exercise a "prophetic priesthood"; see Buckley, "Jesuit Priesthood," 148–51.

14. See O'Malley, *First Jesuits*, 74.

15. O'Malley, *First Jesuits*, 93.

which they regarded as an excellent medium of evangelization.[16] Additionally, they were at the forefront of the church's sixteenth- and seventeenth-century foreign missions. In all these endeavors, the Jesuits tended particularly to those groups whose needs were unmet by parochial structures, either because these persons would not or could not attend the parish assembly (e.g., the indigent, soldiers and sailors, prostitutes, non-Christians, those in hospitals and prisons), or because these persons were looking for spiritual enrichment above and beyond what the parish typically offered (e.g., those who came to the Jesuit retreat houses to make the *Spiritual Exercises*).[17]

Like all priests, the Jesuits were, of course, also administrators of the sacraments, but they were so in a limited fashion. They did not, for example, except in rare circumstances, administer marriage, baptism, or extreme unction. These, they reasoned, belonged to the office of pastors, which they generally did not hold.[18] They modeled themselves after Paul, the itinerant preacher, who came "to preach," rather than "to baptize" (1 Cor 1:17).[19] They celebrated the Eucharist among themselves and for others who wished to attend their churches, but the primary sacrament they offered the people was reconciliation. The Jesuits were particularly attracted to this sacrament because it fit with their desire to lead people through deep interior conversion and because it afforded the opportunity to give people a "private sermon," and so, once again, emphasized their identity as ministers of the word.[20]

Like the early mendicants, however, the Jesuits had to defend themselves against numerous objections to their ministry. Some ecclesial figures suspected the Jesuits of being guilty of the excesses of Protestantism; in their eyes, the *Spiritual Exercises* promoted a spirituality in which an individual could depend solely on an inner light from God and disregard the institutional church.[21] Also, in a scene that was highly

16. For a full discussion of Jesuits' ministry of the Word, see O'Malley, *First Jesuits*, 91–133.

17. See O'Malley, *First Jesuits*, 74.

18. See O'Malley, *First Jesuits*, 134–35.

19. On the example of Paul for the life of the Jesuit, see O'Malley, *First Jesuits*, 73, 271, 349, and 362.

20. Jerónimo Nadal, Ignatius's special assistant, quoted in O'Malley, *First Jesuits*, 133.

21. See Donnelly, *Ignatius of Loyola*, 148–49.

reminiscent of William of St. Amour's attack on the friars, the faculty of the University of Paris, in 1554, charged the Society with faultily dismissing traditional forms of religious life and infringing on the "pastoral rights of bishops, pastors of parishes, universities and other religious orders."[22] As the friars had done, the Jesuits appealed to their papal privileges to defend their style of life and rights to minister.

The Jesuits therefore recapitulated many of the features of religious priests before them. They served as a conduit between a reform movement of the age and the office of the church that legitimized it; they attempted to integrate the ideals of religious life with the goals of active ministry; they sought a close relationship with the papacy; they ministered in a way that transcended parochial and diocesan boundaries; and they gravitated toward the ministerial functions of preaching/teaching and sanctifying, without becoming pastors who exercised the full *cura animarum*.

The Council of Trent on Religious Life and Priesthood

At the same time the Jesuits were emerging, the sixteenth and seventeenth centuries witnessed a much-needed renewal in the diocesan priesthood that, perhaps unavoidably, posed questions to the ongoing relevance of religious priesthood. The two great movements for the renewal of diocesan clergy were the Council of Trent (1545–63) and the French School of Spirituality.

In its formal decree on religious life "Concerning Regulars and Nuns," the Council described religious as those who make the three vows: poverty, chastity, and obedience. The Council exhorted religious to prayer, penance, fasting, and stability in a cloister. In this decree, the Council gave no acknowledgment or encouragement to religious ministries. Despite the recent introduction of the Jesuits and several centuries of mendicant activity, the Council presented a vision of religious life as primarily stable, cloistered, and contemplative, without active apostolates.[23]

22. O'Malley, *First Jesuits*, 289.

23. Twenty-Fifth Session, "Concerning Regulars and Nuns," Chapter I, in H. J, Schroeder, *The Canons and Decrees of the Council of Trent* (Charlotte, N.C.: TAN, 1978),

In its decree on Holy Orders, the Council presented the sacrament as a rite imparting a character that empowered the one who received this character to confect the Eucharistic elements and to offer the Eucharistic sacrifice. It neglected to speak of the pastoral or preaching dimensions of the priesthood.[24] This lacuna reflects theological developments of the late scholastic period. We have seen how Thomas Aquinas and Bonaventure emphasized that the power of jurisdiction, possessed by the bishops and pope, allowed these men to delegate preaching, teaching, and shepherding functions to priests. While Thomas, at least, still recognized that the sacrament of orders communicated grace (though not a mandate) for the preaching/teaching and ruling functions, later scholastics lost sight of this entirely. They taught a sharp division between the power of orders and the power of jurisdiction. Orders gave only the capacity to sanctify. The power to preach, teach, and rule came exclusively from the power of jurisdiction that was held by the pope and bishops. The bishops, and above all the pope, held this power not through episcopal ordination but as a result of authority granted directly by God akin to the divine right of kings to rule.[25] The divorce of the power of order and the power of jurisdiction in late scholastic theology, coupled with the necessity of defending the authenticity of the Eu-

221. All citations from the Council can be found in Schroeder. The Council's few references to religious ministries in other places fall in juridical canons that reasserted bishops' rights and duties to oversee ministry within their dioceses. There, the Council attempted to bring some balance to several centuries of papal privileging of religious vis-à-vis the bishops. The Council acknowledged bishops' authority over all preaching in their dioceses and exhorted bishops to monitor preaching to see that it was informed, orthodox, and beneficial. They were to carry out this supervision even if the preachers were religious. The Council determined that religious preachers needed the "blessing" of the local bishop to preach in their own churches, and they needed explicit permission to preach in a church that did not belong to their order; see Fifth Session, Chapter II, in Schroeder, *Canons and Decrees*, 27–28. Similarly, religious priests needed express permission to hear confessions within a particular diocese from the local bishop (Twenty-Third Session, Chapter XV, in Schroeder, *Canons and Decrees*, 175). None of these canons represented a definitive obstacle to the ministry of religious priests, but they did send a strong message to religious clergy that they did not have free range to operate independently from local episcopal authority.

24. See Twenty-Third Session, "Sacrament of Order," in Schroeder, *Canons and Decrees*, 162–64.

25. See Mansini, *Word Has Dwelt among Us*, 164–70.

charistic sacrifice against Protestant challenges, explains the way Trent presented its doctrine of orders as pertaining only to the sanctifying function. The Council did, however, have much to say and encourage about ordained ministers as pastors and preachers in its juridical canons describing the requirements and expectations of priests. Therefore, at least in terms of describing what priests do, it is erroneous to conclude that the Council presented a one-dimensional portrait.[26]

Trent's one-sidedness lay rather in its high degree of attention to diocesan and parochial ministries and in its corresponding neglect of religious priests and the kinds of ministry they offered. With the Protestant Reformation making gains, Trent sought to overhaul the diocesan system and to renew the church. Trent called for a series of initiatives in this direction. First of all, despite having defined priesthood exclusively in regard to the sacraments of Eucharist and reconciliation, the Council was forceful that priests needed to preach as well as catechize.[27] To preach and teach well, one needed to live a holy life and be educated. To this end seminaries would be established that would educate young men, form them in holiness, and train them to preach and teach. Bishops were given authority to draw funds from parishes to build these seminaries as well as the right to compel appropriate men of the clergy to teach in them.[28]

Ignorant, weak, corrupt priests were to be disciplined or removed. Above all, clerical absenteeism was to be eradicated. The Council saw this problem, rampant in the sixteenth century, as the most pernicious of all the church's difficulties. People without a resident pastor were deprived of adequate pastoral care. Trent exhorted priests to live among the people and bishops to live in their dioceses in order to know and love and care for them. The priest needed to be a good shepherd living among his sheep.[29] The Council even revived the sixth canon of Chal-

26. For an example of this common, but somewhat incomplete, interpretation, see Alexandre Ganoczy, "Splendours and Miseries of the Tridentine Doctrine of Ministries," in *Office and Ministry in the Church*, ed. Bas van Iersel and Roland Murphy (New York: Herder and Herder, 1972), 75–86.

27. See Twenty-Fourth Session, Chapter VII, in Schroeder, *Canons and Decrees*, 200.

28. See Twenty-Third Session, Chapter XVIII, in Schroeder, *Canons and Decrees*, 180.

29. See Thirteenth Session, Chapter I, and Twenty-Third Session, Chapter I, in Schroeder, *Canons and Decrees*, 80 and 166.

cedon, which forbade at-large ordinations. Trent stated, "No one shall in the future be ordained who is not assigned to that church or pious place for the need or utility of which he is promoted, where he may discharge his duties and not wander about without any fixed abode."[30]

The Council took steps to make sure that not only priests, but also the people were attached to and present in the parishes. The faithful were exhorted to attend their parish churches in order to hear the preaching there. They were also mandated to receive their sacraments there and discouraged from receiving the sacraments elsewhere.[31] Since there were questions in some cases about where one's home parish was, parish boundaries were to be erected where they did not yet exist. If a particular parish had too many faithful to attend to, the bishop was to assign more priests to that parish. If the people did not have a parish close enough to them, the bishop or closest rector was to ensure that new churches were built.[32]

It is somewhat remarkable that Trent turned almost exclusively to the diocesan/parochial system when it sought to renew the church. It did not appeal to religious priests or ministries for help as the medieval world had done. Rather, its entire program was based on invigorating the parochial clergy and the parish system. A reform and strengthening of the diocesan priest and parish was needed and probably long overdue. It was also very effective, for after Trent the problems of absenteeism, concubinage, and lack of education among the clergy greatly diminished.

From the perspective of religious priesthood, however, Trent left much to be desired. According to O'Malley, "The Council sent the church on a long journey that by the twentieth century meant that when people thought of 'church' they thought of 'parish' and when they

30. Twenty-Third Session, Chapter XVI, in Schroeder, *Canons and Decrees*, 176.

31. "The holy council commands the bishops that, for the greater security of the salvation of the souls committed to them, they divide the people into definite and distinct parishes and assign to each its own and permanent parish priest, who can know his people and from whom alone they may licitly receive the sacraments; or that they make other more beneficial provisions as the conditions of the locality may require"; Twenty-Fourth Session, Chapter XIII, in Schroeder, *Canons and Decrees*, 206–7.

32. See Twenty-First Session, Chapter IV, in Schroeder, *Canons and Decrees*, 140.

thought of 'priest' they thought of 'pastor.'"[33] It largely ignored the ministry of priests who were not pastors, and it also ignored the ways in which people received ministries that were not parish-based—through, for example, their voluntary associations with "monasteries, priories, shrines, manor chapels, oratories, guilds, confraternities, third orders, sodalities, schools, and collegiate churches (to which list 'retreat houses' would at a certain point be added)."[34]

The French School

Trent had called for a holier, better educated, more confident diocesan clergy. In France, Pierre Bérulle (1575–1629), Jean-Jacques Olier (1608–57), and Jean Eudes (1601–80) founded the French Oratory, the Society of St. Sulpice, and the Congregation of Jesus and Mary, respectively, to take the lead in articulating a specifically priestly spirituality and advancing the new seminary system.

The French School promoted an exalted vision of the priest that was closely identified with the incarnate person and mission of Jesus Christ. On this matter, Aidan Nichols helpfully summarizes the teaching of Bérulle, who was truly the pioneer among these figures:

> The eternal Word had assumed humanity so that there might be a mediator between God and man. Through the humanity of Jesus Christ, the world gives glory to the Father, and the Father acts to transform the world, reconciling it to himself. Similarly, the ministerial priest is, in a double sense, a continuing mediator between God and man. For, on the one hand, he offers the worship of the faithful to the Father by uniting it with Christ's sacrifice through the Mass. And on the other hand, he acts as God's instrument in the transformation of the world, through evangelizing and passing on the divine teaching, especially in the context of the direction of souls, and by dispensing the mysteries of Christ's Body and Blood, and administering the other sacraments of the Church.[35]

33. O'Malley, "Priesthood, Ministry, and Religious Life," 247.
34. O'Malley, "Priesthood, Ministry, and Religious Life," 247.
35. Nichols, *Holy Order*, 112.

With their own particular emphases, each of the members of the French School upheld this exalted vision of the priest as mediator and "angel" who goes back and forth between the realms of God and man, offering love from one side to the other.[36]

For the French School, the priest's sublime function demanded a high degree of personal perfection. His internal, subjective disposition needed to approach the two-directional love of Christ himself. For the priest's sanctification, he was given the graces of priestly consecration and sacramental orders that united him closely to the person of Jesus. This union was strengthened through the priest's prayer, active ministry, and, most especially, through his offering of the Eucharist, where "the divine Son draws the priest each day into the unity of his own person, joins him to his deified humanity, and makes him, through the Eucharistic gifts, the dispenser of the Holy Spirit."[37]

A special feature of the communities established by the French School, communities that eventually were fitted into a new canonical category of societies of apostolic life, was that they did not take formal religious vows. The initial reason for this decision was their particular pastoral goal: they aspired to assist, educate, and model holiness to the diocesan clergy. Since the diocesan clergy did not make religious vows, these new communities would not, either. However, they ultimately attempted to provide theological and spiritual justification for this decision. Bérulle claimed that the first order in the church, the apostles, were priests rather than religious. Therefore, the priest, by virtue of his participation in this "first state" of the church, through the consecration and sacrament of orders, has a bond to Jesus that is "greater and stronger than that of a solemn vow."[38] The French School did not disparage the vows. De Condren, who was Bérulle's successor as leader of the Oratory, explained that they embraced the vows implicitly by "entering the sublime state of the priesthood."[39] Nonetheless, it was primarily be-

36. William M. Thompson, introduction to *Bérulle and the French School*, ed. William M. Thompson, trans. Lowell M. Glendon (New York: Paulist Press, 1989), 57.

37. Nichols, *Holy Order*, 114.

38. Quoted in William M. Thompson, introduction to *Bérulle and the French School*, 57.

39. *Lettres de Condren* (Paris: Guyot et Roidot, 1857), 168–69, quoted in Eugene Aloysius Walsh, *The Priesthood in the Writings of the French School: Bérulle, De Condren,*

cause priests bore the character of the only Son of God imprinted upon their souls, through baptism and holy orders, that they should be motivated for discipleship.[40] Given the pastoral aim of the French School to promote the dignity of the diocesan priest, who did not make vows, this way of framing things makes some sense. However, it does beg the question of whether and how explicit religious vows add to the pursuit of sanctity for a religious priest.

A final important characteristic of the French School was that it encouraged priests to commit to exercising all three of the classical ministerial *munera*: preaching/teaching, sanctifying, and governing. Here, they reflected the influence of Trent, which defined priests in terms of the sanctifying *munera* but heavily exhorted the clergy to become better pastors and preachers. Christ had been priest, prophet, and king. Today's priests were his associates and must likewise hold together all three functions.[41] For the clergy to effectively minister as priests, preachers and pastors, they needed to recover the holiness of monks and the learning of the schoolmen, both of which had been too long neglected in priestly formation.[42]

The French School, though its immediate concern was reform of the diocesan clergy, was important to the history of religious priesthood in two key ways. By developing a priestly spirituality, it portrayed ministerial praxis as a source of grace, a means of sanctification, and a pathway to intimacy with the Lord not only for those the priest served, but for the priest himself. From the perspective of religious priesthood, the upshot of this approach was that priesthood now in no way appeared to compromise the pursuit of holiness. It offered its own spirituality. The downside was that it could make the vows seem superfluous for a priest. Second, the French School promoted a vision of priesthood that argued for the integrated practice of all three *munera*. Again, this was import-

Olier (Washington, D.C.: The Catholic University of America Press, 1949), xiii. The translation is that of Walsh.

40. See William M. Thompson, introduction to *Bérulle and the French School*, 57.

41. This was a particular emphasis of John Eudes. See Gerald O'Collins, *Jesus Our Priest: A Christian Approach to the Priesthood of Christ* (Oxford: Oxford University Press, 2010), 201.

42. See Bérulle's "Pièce 891: A Letter on the Priesthood," in William M. Thompson, *Bérulle and the French School*, 183–85.

ant for diocesan clergy, but it was a vision of priesthood rather different from the more specialized approaches taken by religious priests. Contemplative monastic priesthood had been made plausible by the ability to separate the sanctifying function from the need to also preach, teach, and govern. More active monastic, mendicant, and Jesuit priesthood had exercised the preaching/teaching and sanctifying *munera*, but less frequently the governing insofar as they were not generally pastors.

Missionary Congregations

The final group that can be put under the heading of apostolic congregations are the numerous missionary orders founded within the last four centuries to bring the gospel to the poor and/or those in mission territories. In the seventeenth century St. Vincent De Paul (1581–1660) began the Congregation of the Mission to serve the corporal and spiritual needs of France's rural poor. The Vincentians, as they came to be known, soon assumed missions to Africa and the Middle East. In the eighteenth century, Alphonsus Liguori (1696–1787) founded the Congregation of the Holy Redeeemer in Italy with the similar goal of caring for the rural poor. Within a century, the Redemptorists, too, were heavily involved in foreign missions.

In the nineteenth century, the number of such missionary congregations grew considerably. The Missionary Oblates of Mary Immaculate (founded in 1815), Congregation of the Holy Cross (1840), Congregation of the Holy Spirit (1842), Salesians of Don Bosco (1845), Congregation of the Immaculate Heart of Mary (1862), St. Joseph's Society for Foreign Missions (1866), Comboni Missionaries (1867), Missionaries of Africa (1868), and Society of the Divine Word (1875) were men's religious communities dedicated to missionary work. There were also numerous women's missionary congregations such as the Marist Missionary Sisters (1857), Congregation of Our Lady of the Missions (1861), Salesian Sisters of Don Bosco (1872), Franciscan Missionaries of Mary (1877), Holy Spirit Missionary Sisters (1889), and the Missionaries of the Sacred Heart (1900).[43]

43. See William R. Burrows, "Catholics, Carey's 'Means,' and Twenty-first-Century Mission," *International Bulletin of Missionary Research* 34 (2010): 131–38, 138n10. For a

The bulk of these congregations showed the influence of the Jesuits in various ways. They had been founded with a strong sense of ministerial purpose. Their lifestyle was communal but somewhat less cloistered (particularly the men) than the mendicant or monastic orders. They could move about rather independently, but they had been prepared for this by a long formation that cultivated a strong sense of obedience and fidelity to the church and to one another. Like the Jesuits, they were "close partners of the pope." Though they did not make the "fourth vow," "their constitutions were all approved by Rome and contained clauses that inculcated loyalty to the Holy See and obliged the orders to undertake missions at the direction of the Holy See's central missionary coordination agency, the Congregation for the Doctrine of the Faith."[44]

What was different about these missionary congregations was that where the Jesuits had been founded to provide a broad range of ministerial services to potentially any person in the entire world, the nineteenth-century missionary congregations, perhaps reflecting a new capitalistic age, were much more specialized.[45] They were founded around concrete ministerial tasks such as preaching missions and retreats, teaching in schools and catechetical programs, or, as was often the case with women's orders, hospital work. Each of the orders tended to focus on one or two of these activities. They also tended to target specific audiences. For example, the Paulist Fathers were founded in 1858 to evangelize North America; the White Fathers (1868) were established to preach the gospel in Africa; and the Salesians of Don Bosco were to minister to youth. Finally, a high degree of specificity similarly characterized the spiritualities promoted in their missions. The Passionists (1769), for example, were devoted to "making manifest the love of God shown in Jesus' undergoing his passion and death."[46] The Oblates of

brief history of several founders of modern missionary congregations, see Fabio Ciardi, "Il Ministero Presbitale a Servizio del Carisma: Approfondimenti e Commento All'Esperienza Carismatica Nella Chiesa," *Sequela Christi* 2 (2009): 235–55.

44. Burrows, "Catholics, Carey's 'Means,' and Twenty-first-Century Mission," 133. This section of the Congregation for the Doctrine of the Faith (CDF) has been renamed the Congregations for the Evangelization of Peoples.

45. See Burrows, "Catholics, Carey's 'Means,' and Twenty-first-Century Mission," 133.

46. Burrows, "Catholics, Carey's 'Means,' and Twenty-first-Century Mission," 133.

Mary Immaculate sought to make known the Sacred Heart and the Immaculate Heart of Mary as "supernatural means of regeneration."[47] Each group had a definitive niche and brand.

With respect to the questions of religious priesthood, the missionary congregations had three important features. First, in continuity with the tradition of religious priesthood before them, they had no intention to replace the diocesan clergy. In missionary lands, they built up the church until it could provide its own ministers.[48] In places where the church was already established, they "complemented the work of stable, local clergy" by preaching parish missions, working with youth, teaching in schools, or reaching out to the poor through corporal works of mercy.[49] Second, in discontinuity with prior tradition, some of these communities opted to become societies of apostolic life rather than religious institutes, which is to say, they decided not to make solemn vows of poverty, chastity, and obedience.[50] It is remarkable that, where the original societies of apostolic life had been forged specifically with a mind of being closer to the diocesan priesthood and holding up an example to them, missionary congregations (of both men and women) that were far removed from this work now opted for this canonical possibility.

Third, women religious were highly active in this movement as teachers, catechists, and nurses, operating schools, hospitals, and shelters.[51] This was a bit of a rebirth. In the first millennium, women had

47. 1917 *Catholic Encyclopedia*, "Oblates of Mary Immaculate," New Advent, http://www.newadvent.org/cathen/11184b.htm, accessed April 19, 2019.

48. In most nineteenth-century missionary initiatives, eventual handing over of parochial and diocesan structures to indigenous clergy was the stated ideal. On the other hand, there were many cases in which, long after the local church had been established, religious remained in parochial ministry, either because they wanted to or because bishops pressured them to do so. For experiences of parochialization among the Redemptorists and Paulists, see David J. O'Brien, *Isaac Hecker: An American Catholic* (New York: Paulist Press, 1992), 112–15, 174–75; for several case studies of similar experencies among the Franciscans, see Benedikt Mertens, "Franciscans in Parochial Ministry: Past and Present Aspects of a Debated Question," *Antonianum* 75 (2000): 523–54.

49. David Power, "Theologies of Religious Life and Priesthood," 79.

50. For example, the Missionaries of the Precious Blood (founded in 1815), the Paulist Fathers (1858), Glenmary Home Missionaries, and the Maryknoll Fathers and Brothers (1911).

51. This aspect of the nineteenth-century missionary congregations has been highlighted by Ratzinger; see his *Pilgrim Fellowship of Faith*, 200.

been engaged in informal "ministry" as charismatic ammas. In cenobitical communities, nuns operated schools and hospitals and provided service to pilgrims, much like their monastic brethren.[52] Beginning in the Carolingian era, however, monasticism became an increasingly internal affair focused on liturgy. Because women could not offer the Mass, popular support for women's religious life waned somewhat, and the number of women's monasteries decreased.[53] Women were involved in the early stages of the mendicant movement as informal preachers. This quickly came to an end, however, due to concerns about women moving about freely and the increasing alignment of preaching with ordination and juridical mandates.[54] The female branch of the mendicant tradition soon became a cloistered affair. The lifestyle of Franciscan and Dominican nuns was very similar to that of Benedictine women of the time: prayer, seclusion, and ascetical practice. Women seeking an ecclesial vocation had two possibilities: They could make vows as religious nuns in a cloistered convent, or they could dedicate themselves to charitable work in affiliation with a confraternity or third order. Many women who chose the latter option were privately committed celibates (either virgins or widows), but they were not in formal vows. Technically speaking, there were no female active religious. A woman in vows had to be enclosed.[55]

Societies of Apostolic Life had advanced the notion that there could be associations of committed celibates who were not under formal religious vows. Though this innovation was introduced with priests in mind, Vincent de Paul soon applied it to a community of women he was founding, the Daughters of Charity. Because these women made promises rather than vows, they did not have to be fully cloistered nuns and could engage in external apostolates. In later years, more and more women's communities were founded that adopted the same or similar approaches. They made promises or simple vows, rather than the sol-

52. See Susan E. Smith, *Women in Mission: From the New Testament to Today* (Maryknoll, N.Y.: Orbis, 2007).

53. See Joseph H. Lynch, *The Medieval Church: A Brief History* (London: Longman, 1992), 212–15.

54. Pryds, "Preaching Women," 55–77.

55. See Lawrence, *Medieval Monasticism*, 217–35.

emn vows that would have canonically restricted them to the cloister. This legal loophole allowed them the latitude they needed to minister more freely in the church.[56]

For our purposes, this trajectory reveals as much about attitudes toward religious life and priesthood as it does about attitudes toward women. For centuries, the bias had been that religious life commits one to the personal pursuit of evangelical perfection, but not necessarily to the church's mission or its ministry. If one was a religious priest, it had seemed to be the case that it was the priestly part of one's identity that commissioned one to the apostolate. The emergence of nineteenth-century missionary women deeply challenged that assumption. They were not priests, they could not be priests, and yet they were at the forefront of the church's apostolic work.[57]

Conclusion to Part I

It is now possible to note several characteristics of religious priesthood that have remained relatively consistent throughout the church's history. First, religious priesthood has often had to navigate a tension between the call to radical discipleship and the duties of the priestly office. This tension emerged first as a tension between the active and contemplative lives. With monasticism conceived as a life of radical withdrawal for the purpose of prayer and penance and with priesthood conceived as a function of preaching/teaching, sanctifying, and governing in congregations, the duties of priesthood appeared to compromise the fullness of the religious vocation. When more active forms of religious life

56. Communities of active women living a vowed life were finally formally recognized as religious by Leo XIII's apostolic constitution *Conditae a Christo* (December 8, 1900). For more on the complicated history of vows and promises in women's communities, see Council of Major Superiors of Religious Women, *The Foundations of Religious Life: Revisiting the Vision* (Notre Dame, Ind.: Ave Maria, 2009); M. Prudence Allen and M. Judith O'Brien, "The Decree on the Appropriate Renewal of Religious Life: *Perfectae Caritatis*," in *Vatican II: Renewal within Tradition*, ed. Matthew L. Lamb and Matthew L. Levering, 251–70 (Oxford: Oxford University Press, 2008).

57. "The women were never in fact bishops or priests, but they were among those who carried forward the apostolic life and its universal task"; Ratzinger, *Pilgrim Fellowship of Faith*, 200.

emerged, the spiritual ideal was conceived more as a combination of the contemplative and active lives. Therefore, priesthood, with its ministerial duties, appeared to be less of a compromise of the spiritual ideal.

However, even in communities with a more active dimension, priesthood still stood in tension with other spiritual values. Pachomius, Benedict, and Francis shared concerns that priesthood would compromise the dynamics of religious communities committed to equality and humility. Additionally, early Franciscans wrestled with the implications of clericalization for evangelical poverty.

The Dominicans and Jesuits do not seem to have had to contend as much with the tensions between priesthood and the values of radical discipleship. As heavily clerical orders from the beginning, every member was more or less on equal footing. Moreover, these orders were conceived explicitly for ministerial ends that their founders believed justified changes in traditional religious practices. The later missionary congregations were also likely helped by the French School's vision of priestly spirituality, which portrayed ministerial practices as spiritually advantageous, advancing the sanctification not only of those ministered to, but also of the minister himself.

Second, religious priests have lived and ministered in a way that transcended parochial and diocesan boundaries. The mendicants and the Jesuits were international bodies that could not easily be fitted under the governance of any particular local bishop. Moreover, they had a goal of ministering back and forth between dioceses and local churches and ultimately beyond them to mission lands where the church had not yet been planted. For both these reasons they forged alliances with the Roman pontiff, whom they saw as a universal shepherd who could legitimize their itinerant existence and authorize their mission. The missionary congregations followed this same trajectory.

When religious priests ministered within local churches, it was usually in ways that were not parochial. They often had churches that were highly attended by the faithful, but these were not often parishes (at least before the twentieth century), and religious did not usually have the official *cura animarum* of those who came to them. They also ministered in other ways: "through schools or soup kitchens, through retreats or running houses for reformed prostitutes, through books and journals, or through street preaching and 'revivals.'"[58]

Looking backward, monasteries appear, at first, to differ from this phenomenon. Basil's community was commissioned by a local bishop and served the local church. Benedict similarly conceived the monastic community as lying within a local church and as accountable to a local bishop. On the other hand, monasteries were employed in the first millennium by the Holy See to carry out foreign missions. In doing so, they moved beyond the boundaries of local churches. Meanwhile, a number of monasteries sought and received autonomy from local bishops whose interference in their internal affairs had become overreaching. They were thus the pioneers of the alliance of religious with the papacy that protected them. Furthermore, even during the phases of monastic life that seemed to involve the least active pastoral outreach, they were often the place within the diocese where those from outside the diocese were likely to be found. Abbeys had the task of hospitality to those pilgrims who came into the local church but were not of the local church.

Third, religious priesthood has often stood at a nexus between the official, stable institution of the church and the movements of reform. Fourth-century monks, thirteenth-century mendicants, and sixteenth-century Jesuits all belonged to currents of reform. In each case, that reform needed to be harnessed and directed so that it did not become sectarian and so that the larger church could harvest its fruits. Religious priests, by virtue of their relationship with the church's official hierarchy, brought the reform movements into closer relationship with the ecclesial institution. This was seen, for example, in the movement to ordain monks in fourth- century North Africa and in the clericalization of the Franciscans insofar as they were emblematic of the *vita apostolica* movement. At the same time, the ordination of religious reformers gave legitimacy to certain of their activities. This was certainly the case for Ignatius and for the early Franciscans who accepted ordination, at least in part, because it gave them credibility and license to minister as they desired.

58. O'Malley, "Priesthood, Ministry, and Religious Life," 255.

Fourth, religious priesthood has depended upon the distinction and even the separation of the classical *tria munera* that belong to sacramental orders: preaching/teaching, sanctifying, and governing. Contemplative orders that did not exercise active apostolates were able to embrace priesthood because the sanctifying *munus* was separated from the preaching/teaching and governing *munera*. It was possible to be a priest who confected the Eucharist as part of a contemplative vocation to pray. Such a priest did not also have to be an active preacher, teacher, or pastor. More active monastic communities, the mendicants, Jesuits, and missionary congregations relied on a similar ability to separate the preaching/teaching *munus* from the governing *munus*. They could be preachers and teachers (as well as priests offering the Eucharist), but they did not also have to be pastors.

Religious priesthood, then, has exhibited four important historical characteristics. It combines the pursuit of radical discipleship with official ecclesial ministry and accepts the navigation of tensions this combination entails. It ministers in such a way that it transcends diocesan and parochial boundaries. It bridges charismatic reform and institution. It has often depended on the distinction and separation of the *tria munera*. Our next step is to examine how religious priesthood was impacted by the Second Vatican Council and its reception.

PART 2

RELIGIOUS PRIESTHOOD AT AND AFTER VATICAN II

Part I demonstrated that religious priesthood has been marked by some important historical characteristics. First, religious priests have had to navigate tensions between their commitment to the ideals of religious life and to the duties of ecclesial ministry. Second, they have typically ministered in ways that transcended traditional parochial and diocesan boundaries. Third, they have served as a bridge between the church's institutional hierarchy and charismatic movements of reform and renewal. Finally, religious priests have depended on a distinction of the *tria munera* that allowed them to focus on sanctifying, preaching, and teaching and less on ruling.

The history described in part I extended through the nineteenth century. In this second part of the book, we will examine the impact of the Second Vatican Council (1962–65) on religious priesthood (primarily as a theological question and secondarily as a lived experience).[1] Chapter 4 provides a survey of Vat-

1. For historical background, textual analysis, and theological

ican II's ecclesiology and then describes Vatican II's teaching on priesthood and its implications (potential and realized) for religious priests. Chapter 5 provides a similar analysis of the Council's teaching on religious life and its implications and concludes with a summary of the contemporary state of the question of religious priesthood.

Inspired by the method of St. Thomas Aquinas, I have used these two chapters to bring the theological objections to religious priesthood clearly into focus so that I can respond to them later. Thus, I have chosen to highlight figures and lines of thought in these two chapters that tend to maximize the problem of religious priesthood. Voices that contribute to a constructive solution will be dealt with at greater length in part IV.

---

interpretation of the Council, there are four major commentary series: Herbert Vorgrimler, ed. *Commentary on the Documents of Vatican II*, 4 vols (New York: Herder and Herder, 1967–69) [hereafter *Commentary*]; René Latourelle, ed., *Vatican II: Assessment and Perspectives; Twenty-Five Years After (1962–1987)*, trans. Leslie Wearne, 3 vols (New York: Paulist Press, 1988–89); Guiseppe Alberigo, ed., *History of Vatican II*, English version, ed. Joseph Komonchak, 5 vols (Maryknoll, N.Y.: Orbis, 1995–2006); and Peter Hünermann and Bernd Jochen Hilberath, eds., *Herders Theologischer Kommentar zum Zweiten Vatikanischen Konzil*, 5 vols. (Freiburg: Herder, 2004–6).

CHAPTER 4

Vatican II on the Priesthood

Priesthood and religious life find their place within the context of the church as a whole. Therefore, before discussing Vatican II's presentation of priesthood and religious life, it is necessary to say something about the Council's ecclesiology in general. Accordingly, we will spend some time describing the shift the Second Vatican Council made from portraying the church as "perfect society" to portraying the church as "communion." Then, we will acknowledge the principles of Eucharistic ecclesiology that the Council introduced into magisterial teaching and that has implications for how the structure of the church is envisaged today. Although some readers may find this survey of Vatican II's ecclesiology to be a digression, it is necessary. Critics of religious priesthood appeal to Vatican II's theology of the church when they argue that religious priesthood no longer makes much sense. If one wants, as I do, to defend the importance of religious priesthood, one must do it within a postconciliar rather than preconciliar framework.

The Ecclesiology of Vatican II

From Pyramid to Communion

From Trent through the nineteenth century, the image of the church as a "perfect society," *societas perfecta*, dominated ecclesial discourse and consciousness.[1] This notion of the church as "perfect society" was first developed during the medieval Gregorian reforms to promote the

1. See Dulles, *Models of the Church*, 16, 34–46.

church's independence from temporal powers. "Perfect" was not understood here in "the moral sense," but rather meant "complete."[2] By referring to itself as "perfect," the church was claiming that it was "subordinate to no other [power] and lacked nothing for its institutional completeness";[3] it was therefore "fully equipped juridically to run its own affairs."[4] During the Catholic Counter-Reformation, Robert Bellarmine (1562–1621) and other Catholic theologians and canonists further developed the image of the church as "perfect society." Reacting to the perceived individualism of the Protestant Reformers, Catholic thinkers emphasized the nature of the church as a visible, dominically instituted, hierarchically arranged *societas*, the mediation of which was necessary for salvation. After the French Revolution, the image of church as "perfect society" once again became important as a way of supporting the church's autonomy against a now-oppressive state. Up through the middle of the twentieth century, the image of church as "perfect society" was invoked by Catholic pastors and theologians against both secularism and Protestantism.[5]

An important feature of the church as "perfect society" is its pyramidal hierarchical structure.[6] Although Pope Pius XII would contribute significantly to a new vision of the church through his encyclicals *Mediator Dei and Mystici Corporis*,[7] in 1954 he described the church's structure in a way that reflects more the language of pyramidal perfect

2. Paul McPartlan, "Liturgy, Church and Society," *Studia Liturgica* 34 (2004): 150.

3. Dulles, *Models of the Church*, 34.

4. McPartlan, "Liturgy, Church and Society," 150.

5. The first schema of Vatican Council I's Dogmatic Constitution on the Church captured several important features of the church as "perfect society," such as its autonomy, dominical institution, and "set form," which were important in defending the church against secularism and Protestantism. A portion of the text reads, "We teach and declare: The Church has all the marks of a true Society. Christ did not leave this society undefined and without a set form. Rather, he himself gave its existence, and his will determined the form of its existence and gave it its constitution. The Church is not part nor member of any other society and is not mingled in any way with any other society. It is so perfect in itself that it is distinct from all human societies and stands far above them"; quoted in Dulles, *Models of the Church*, 36–37.

6. See Dulles, *Models of the Church*, 39.

7. Pius XII, Encylical Letter *Mystici Corporis Christi* (June 29, 1943); Encyclical Letter *Mediator Dei* (November 20, 1947).

society ecclesiology than the language more commonly used after Vatican II. He stated:

> By virtue of God's Will, the faithful are divided into two classes: the clergy and the laity. By virtue of the same Will is established the twofold sacred hierarchy, namely of orders and jurisdiction. Besides—as has also been divinely established—the power of orders (through which the ecclesiastical hierarchy is composed of Bishops, priests, and ministers) comes from receiving the Sacrament of Holy Orders. But the power of jurisdiction, which is conferred upon the Supreme Pontiff directly by divine right flows to the Bishops by the same right, but only through the Successor to whom not only the simple faithful, but even all the Bishops must be constantly subject, and to whom they must be bound by obedience and with the bond of unity.[8]

Some remarks on this text are necessary. First, the passage begins by strongly dividing the church into two "classes," laity and clergy. This reflects a common post-Tridentine tendency to bypass discussion of the church as a single, unitary subject of mission and, instead, move immediately to the lay-cleric distinction.[9]

Second, characteristic of the clergy is that they participate in some way in sacred power. As discussed in part I, scholastic theologians considered sacred power to be of two kinds: the power of orders and the power of jurisdiction. In other words, to the cleric, something is given by the liturgy of ordination, and something is given by the law itself. Today we would say that the liturgy of ordination gives the necessary capacities to sanctify, preach/teach, and rule, but that a juridical mandate is necessary to do so licitly and, sometimes (depending on the action and circumstances), validly. This mandate is expressed through canonical categories such as ministerial faculties, incardination, and canonical

8. Pius XII, Encyclical Letter *Ad Sinarum Gentem* (October 7, 1954), 12.

9. Needless to say, the relationship between these two parts of the church was often conceived in a rather lopsided fashion. As Pope Gregory XVI (1831–46) put it, "No one can overlook the fact that the Church is an unequal society in which God has destined some to command and others to obey. The latter are the laity, while the former are the clergy"; quoted in Congar, "Moving Towards a Pilgrim Church," in *Vatican II Revisited: By Those Who Were There*, ed. Alberic Stacpoole (London: Geoffrey Chapman, 1986), 133.

mission. The capacity to minister is thus distinguished from the right to use one's capacity to minister. In the scholastic period, however, the sacramental and liturgical basis of the powers of preaching, teaching, and ruling diminished from view so much so that by the sixteenth century, interpreters of St. Thomas like John of Torquemeda, Diego Laynez, and Vio Cardinal Cajetan presented only the sanctifying power, reaching its culmination in the priestly power to confect the Eucharist, as bestowed through ordination. The power to teach and rule over the ecclesial body was considered exclusively a matter of juridical delegation.[10] The power of jurisdiction, held by the bishops and especially by the pope, came, ultimately, not from ordination but by "divine right," and bishops in turn delegated priests to preach, teach, or rule as their representatives.[11] As Henri de Lubac has shown, the sharp division of the two powers reflects a historical situation in which a dynamic sense of Eucharist as "source of the church" had been forgotten and replaced by a restricted notion of the Eucharist as object, simply one of the seven sacraments.[12] This meant that care for the Eucharist (the *corpus verum*) could be easily divided from the care of the church (the *corpus mysticum*). Separation of care of the church from care of the Eucharist actually played into the political goals of "perfect society" ecclesiology. Rather than being conceived sacramentally, the power of jurisdiction was viewed as a "divine right" analogous to the authority of temporal powers in their kingdoms. Because the pope and bishops had this "divine right" to rule in the church, they were entitled to autonomy from secular rule.[13]

The hard division of the two powers had some negative implications.

10. See Mansini, *Word Has Dwelt among Us*, 164–70.

11. The difference of the two powers is made clear in another text of Pius XII: "Christ granted His Apostles a two-fold power: first, the priestly power to consecrate, which was given in full to all the Apostles; second, the power to teach and govern, that is, to communicate to men in God's name the infallible truth which binds them, and to establish the rules which regulate Christian life. These powers of Apostles were passed on to the Pope and Bishops. The Bishops, through the ordination of priests, transmit to others to a precise extent the power to consecrate; the power to teach and govern belongs to the Pope and Bishops"; Pius XII, *Address to the Second World Congress for the Lay Apostolate*, October 5, 1957.

12. McPartlan, "Eucharist as the Basis for Ecclesiology," *Antiphon* 6, no. 2 (2001): 15.

13. See Lafont, *Imagining the Catholic Church*, 48–55; C. C. Pecknold, *Christianity and Politics: A Brief Guide to the History* (Eugene, Ore.: Cascade, 2010), 61–68.

The unity of the *corpus mysticum* appeared to come through the exercise of the power of jurisdiction, and, since the power of jurisdiction was thought to come by divine right rather than by sacramental orders, the unity of the ecclesial body therefore appeared removed from any sacramental source. Additionally, the division of the two powers implied the existence of two different pyramidal hierarchies in the church. At the pinnacle of the power of orders stood the priest, who had the ability to confect the Eucharist. At the pinnacle of the power of jurisdiction stood the pope, who was a universal teacher and had the right of universal governance.[14] The priest and the pope were therefore the two most important figures in this ecclesiology. The bishops and the laity, however, were somewhat "orphaned" by this ecclesiology.[15]

The problem for bishops in this ecclesiology was that they lacked substantial definition. Although many theologians had begun to question it, right up until the Second Vatican Council some still taught that episcopal consecration was not a sacrament.[16] Rather than pertaining to the power of orders, which bestowed the power to confect, episcopal consecration was thought to bestow a share in juridical power over the ecclesial body. This created the impression that bishops were elevated priests to whom "something extra," nonsacramental jurisdictional power, had been "added on."[17] Meanwhile, as the text of Pius (cited previously) indicates, the juridical power of bishops was highly dependent on the papacy. Not only were bishops "subject" to and "bound by obedience" to the "Supreme Pontiff," their power was imagined as being "transmitted" through him. This implied that bishops, rather than being teachers and governors in their own right, were mere vicars of the Holy See.

14. This is particularly evident in the "double proclamation of a universal primacy of jurisdiction of the Roman Pontiff and the infallibility of his doctrinal definitions" in Vatican Council I's (1869–1870) dogmatic constitution, *Pastor aeternus*; Lafont, *Imagining the Catholic Church*, 55.

15. Lafont, *Imagining the Catholic Church*, 62.

16. Kenan Osborne points out that Bellarmine himself had believed in the sacramentality of episcopal ordination. From Trent to the twentieth century, there was a growing consensus that episcopal consecration must be a sacrament. The rationale for seeing it as such, however, was heavily debated. There was no magisterial endorsement of the sacramentality of episcopal orders before Vatican II, which left some scholars free to hold that it was not a sacrament; see Osborne, *Priesthood*, 284 and 325.

17. Mansini, *Word Has Dwelt among Us*, 169.

The problem for the laity in this ecclesiology is that they were mostly ignored. Post-Tridentine ecclesiology has often been criticized for being overly clerical; all ecclesial "power and initiative" seemed to rest with the clergy.[18] The laity appeared as mainly passive figures. It was important to their salvation to profess correct doctrines, receive the sacramental administration of the hierarchy, and be subject to their appointed pastors in obedience. However, before the Catholic Action and liturgical movements of the first half of the twentieth century, little emphasis was placed in post-Tridentine theology on their active and creative participation in the church's life and mission. This neglect of the laity likely stemmed from an overreaction to Protestantism's devaluation of the hierarchy. Catholic ecclesiologists responded by accentuating the elements of the church their opponents were denying. This resulted in what Yves Congar called a "hierarchology": excessive emphasis on the importance of the pope and clergy. Meanwhile, the "two terms" between which the hierarchy mediates, "the Holy Spirit on the one side, the faithful people or the religious subject on the other, were as it were kept out of ecclesiological consideration."[19]

The "perfect society" model of the church therefore had some negative aspects. Some have already been noted. Reflection on the church as a unitary subject of mission was bypassed, the unity the church did have was conceived too juridically and not sacramentally enough, bishops were inadequately differentiated from priests, and laypeople were underappreciated. In addition to these lacunae, Congar's comments indicate another neglected figure—the Holy Spirit. "Perfect society" ecclesiology failed to convey a strong sense of the church's continuing dependence on the living God. As Johann Adam Möhler caricatured this ecclesiology, it appears as if "Christ in the beginning established the hierarchy and by doing so did enough to look after the Church until the end of time."[20] Perhaps as a result of its dearth of pneumatology, the church in this ecclesiology appears lopsidedly institutional. An

18. Dulles, *Models of the Church*, 39.

19. Congar, *Lay People in the Church: A Study for a Theology of the Laity*, rev. ed. trans. Donald Attwater (London: Geoffrey Chapman, 1985), 45.

20. Quoted in Joseph Ratzinger, *Church, Ecumenism, and Politics: New Endeavors in Ecclesiology*, trans. Michael J. Miller (San Francisco: Ignatius Press, 1987), 14.

individual's membership in the church depended on fulfilling certain obligatory duties: confession of right doctrine, reception of (more than participation in) the sacraments, and obedience to the church's pastors. Not enough attention was paid to the interior movements of grace, the participatory dimensions of the liturgy, or the subjective commitment of the faithful to God and to one another.[21]

Vatican II's teaching contributed to a shift away from the pyramidal image of the "perfect society" to an image of the church that was more theocentric, organic, and interpersonal.[22] It would be inaccurate to say that this shift began at Vatican II. In the nineteenth century German theologians like Möhler had presented the church not as a pyramidal perfect society, but as the mystical body of Christ, and this image continued to receive great traction in the first part of the twentieth century through the liturgical movement and in the theology of figures like Romano Guardini. In Pius XII's encyclicals *Mystici Corporis* and *Mediator Dei* it was formally presented in magisterial teaching.[23] Thus, we must see Vatican II not simply as the beginning of something but as

21. See Dulles, *Models of the Church*, 43–44.

22. See Ratzinger, *Church, Ecumenism, and Politics*, 13–16. Without succumbing to an "hermeneutic of discontinuity," one can recognize that this shift was intentional. According to Gérard Philips, the primary drafter of *Lumen Gentium*, the preliminary schema for Vatican II's constitution on the church reflected the *societas perfecta* model. The bishops rejected it because they desired to stress "the nature of the Church as a community rather than as a society." Council Father Bishop Emiel-Jozef de Smedt of Bruges, Belgium, in particular denounced the juridicism, clericalism, and triumphalism of the first schema. According to Philips, Bishop Léon Elchinger of Strasbourg, France, summed up the desire of the Council fathers for a different articulation of the church when he expressed, "Yesterday the Church was considered above all as an institution, today it is experienced as a community. Yesterday it was the Pope who was mainly in view, today the Pope is thought of as united to the bishops. Yesterday, the bishop alone was considered, today all the bishops together. Yesterday theology stressed the importance of the hierarchy, today it is discovering the people of God. Yesterday it was chiefly concerned with what divided, today it voices all that unites"; Philips, "Dogmatic Constitution on the Church: The History of the Constitution," *Commentary* 1:108.

23. For a discussion of Vatican II's ecclesiology's continuity with *Mystici Corporis* and *Mediator Dei*, see Dulles, "Nature, Mission, and Structure of the Church," in *Vatican II: Renewal within the Tradition*, ed. Matthew L. Lamb and Mathew Levering (Oxford: Oxford University Press, 2008), 25–36, and Pamela E. J. Jackson, "Theology of the Liturgy," in *Vatican II: Renewal within the Tradition*, 101–28.

the synthesizer and developer of already present theological currents.[24]

Still, Vatican II further advanced this shift in many ways. For example, the images of the church as "mystery," "body of Christ," and "temple of the Holy Spirit" in *Lumen Gentium*, Chapter I, highlighted the church's theandric qualities, its participation in and dependence on the living, triune God.[25] The image of the church as People of God in *Lumen Gentium*, Chapter II, emphasized the fundamental unity of the church's members before going on to note distinctions among hierarchy, laity, and religious.[26] The Council's image of the church as "sacrament of salvation" in *Lumen Gentium*, Chapter VII, and in *Ad Gentes*[27] similarly promoted an understanding of church as a Eucharistically centered "unified subject of mission."[28] The Council's affirmation of "the full, conscious, and active" liturgical participation of the laity in *Sacrosanctum Concilium* and its recognition of laypeople's missiological contributions in *Lumen Gentium*, Chapters II and IV, and in *Apostolicam Actuositatem* helped recover their ecclesial position.[29] Last, the Council's teaching on the bishops in *Lumen Gentium*, Chapter III, and *Christus Dominus* brought these neglected figures into the foreground, described the episcopal structure of the church in terms of collegiality, and presented papal power in that collegial context.[30] Congar summarized the effect of these changes on the understanding of the church. There was a "vertical re-centering on Christ, and a horizontal shift away ... from Rome to the episcopal college and from the hierarchical priesthood to the whole people of God."[31] The two primary beneficiaries of this shift

24. See Ratzinger, *Church, Ecumenism, and Politics*, 13–14.

25. Vatican Council II, *Lumen Gentium* (November 21, 1964; hereafter, *LG*). For a discussion of these points, see Aloys Grillmeier, "Dogmatic Constitution on the Church," Chapter 1, "The Mystery of the Church," in *Commentary* 1:141–44.

26. See Congar, *Called to Life*, trans. William Burridge (New York: Crossroad, 1987), 88–89.

27. Vatican Council II, *Ad Gentes Divinitus* (December 7, 1965), 1; hereafter *AG*.

28. Benigno Luigi Papa, "Identità Carismatica Ed Esercizio Pastorale Dei Religiosi Nella Chiesa Particolare: Questioni Aperte," *Sequela Christi* 2 (2009): 162.

29. Vatican Council II, *Sacrosanctum Concilium* (December 4, 1963), 14; hereafter *SC*; Vatican Council II, *Apostolicam Actuositatem* (November 18, 1965); hereafter *AA*.

30. Vatican Council II, *Christus Dominus* (October 28, 1965), hereafter, *CD*; See Ratzinger, "The Pastoral Implications of Episcopal Collegiality," *Concilium* 1 (1965): 29.

31. Congar, "My Path-Findings in the Theology of Laity and Ministries." *Jurist* 32

were bishops who, for reasons we shall see, were "powerfully affirmed and strengthened by the Council," and the laity, whose "active participation in the life of the Church and its mission was, if not created there [by the Council], then fostered—through the Constitution on the Liturgy and the reforms that followed it."[32]

At the 1985 extraordinary assembly of the Synod of Bishops marking twenty years since the close of the Council, the bishops identified "communion" as "the central and fundamental idea in the documents of the Council."[33] A number of theologians have since used the notion of communion as an interpretive key that serves to tie together the many different aspects of the Council's ecclesiology.[34] According to Avery Dulles, the most important aspect of communion ecclesiology is the understanding that the church "is a sacrament that brings people into [interpersonal] communion with God and with one another."[35] Benigno Luigi Papa explained that the ecclesiology of communion

> gives proper primacy to the Christian life as a life in the Spirit, emphasizing the filial relationship of all the baptized with the fatherhood of God, the exercise of fraternal charity among all members of the Christian community (clergy, laity, and religious), the life of prayer, and the centrality of the Eucharist as a sacrament of communion with Christ and with all the faithful.[36]

The Eucharistic Structure of the Church

Joseph Ratzinger, writing just three years after the extraordinary synod, argued that Vatican II's ecclesiology of communion is, above all,

(1972): 181. Congar credits Edward Schillebeeckx with first articulating these two decentralizations.

32. Congar, "My Path-Findings," 181. With respect to the laity, Congar is affirming the fact that the recovery of the place of the laity had already begun in the Catholic Action and liturgical movements and the teachings of recent popes.

33. 1985 Extraordinary Synod of Bishops, "Final Report," II.C.1., *Origins* 15 (December 19, 1985): 448.

34. See Dennis Doyle, *Communion Ecclesiology: Vision and Versions* (Maryknoll, N.Y.: Orbis, 2000).

35. Dulles, "Trends in Ecclesiology," in *Called to Holiness and Communion: Vatican II on the Church*, ed. Steven Boguslawski and Robert Fastiggi (Scranton, Pa.: University of Scranton Press, 2009), 2.

36. Papa, "Identità Carismatica," 162.

a Eucharistic ecclesiology.[37] While some thinkers question whether Vatican II accomplished a fully Eucharistic ecclesiology,[38] the Council can at least be credited with introducing Eucharistic trajectories that would be further developed by both the theological community and the magisterial teaching of popes John Paul II and Benedict XVI.[39] The remainder of this section explores how Eucharistic ecclesiology, as interpreted primarily by Ratzinger, imagines the structure of the church.

According to Ratzinger, Eucharistic ecclesiology establishes the foundation of the church in the covenant-creating last supper, which "renews the covenant of Sinai" and at the same time "anticipates" and "presupposes" the "cross and resurrection."[40] Eucharistic ecclesiology thus grounds the origin of the church in the paschal mystery. The Council articulates this especially in *Lumen Gentium* 3, which envisions the church springing forth "from the Lord's wounded side, from which blood and water flowed."[41] As a supernatural meal, the Eucharist unites the church's members across time to the church's inaugural event and creates a "communion of blood and life between God and man."[42] This means, as Ratzinger states, that "the Eucharist joins human beings together, not only with one another, but also with Christ ... in this way it makes people into the Church";[43] or, as de Lubac put it succinctly, "The Eucharist makes the Church."[44] As a sacrifice, the Eucharist con-

37. Ratzinger stated, "Now a Eucharistic ecclesiology developed that many like to refer to also as *communio* ecclesiology. This *communio* ecclesiology actually became the centerpiece of Vatican II teaching on the Church, the new and yet thoroughly primordial thing that this recent Council wanted to give us"; *Church, Ecumenism, and Politics*, 17.

38. See, for instance, Massimo Faggioli, *True Reform: Liturgy and Ecclesiology in "Sacrosanctum Concilium"* (Collegeville, Minn.: Liturgical Press, 2012); also, Christopher Ruddy, *The Local Church: Tillard and the Future of Catholic Ecclesiology* (New York: Crossroad, 2006), 46–53.

39. See especially John Paul II's Encyclical Letter *Ecclesia de Eucharista* (July 7, 2003), and Benedict XVI's Post-Synodal Apostolic Exhortation *Sacramentum Caritatis* (February 22, 2007).

40. Ratzinger, *Church, Ecumenism, and Politics*, 17.

41. Ratzinger, *Church, Ecumenism, and Politics*, 17.

42. Ratzinger, *Church, Ecumenism, and Politics*, 17. As the Council puts it, "In the sacrament of the eucharistic bread, the unity of believers, who form one body in Christ (cf. 1 Cor 10:17) is both expressed and brought about" (*LG* 3).

43. Ratzinger, *Church, Ecumenism, and Politics*, 17.

44. Henri de Lubac, *Corpus Mysticum: The Eucharist and the Church in the Middle*

tinues Christ's work of redemption and structures the ecclesial community around the central act of common worship, "the service of God"; It includes as well "the service of men, the service that transforms the world."[45] Eucharistic ecclesiology thus moves from juridical ways of conceiving the church's unity, form, and mission to a sacramental vision in which the church draws its being and purpose from a mystical ritual of divine/human communion in which all the church's members participate.

Eucharistic ecclesiology highlights the importance of the local church, since this is the context in which the Eucharist is celebrated. Ratzinger points to *Lumen Gentium* 26 as indicative of the Council's Eucharistic understanding of the local church. This article states that the

> Church of Christ is truly present in all legitimate local congregations of the faithful [where] the faithful are gathered together by the preaching of the Gospel of Christ, and the mystery of the Lord's Supper is celebrated.... In any community of the altar, under the sacred ministry of the bishop, there is exhibited a symbol of that charity and "unity of the mystical Body, without which there can be no salvation." In these communities ... Christ is present, and in virtue of His presence there is brought together one, holy, catholic and apostolic Church. For "the partaking of the body and blood of Christ does nothing other than make us be transformed into that which we consume."

Because "in every celebration of the Eucharist the Lord is entirely present," and it is communion with the Lord that "makes people into the Church," the Council teaches that local Eucharistic assemblies can be legitimately called churches.[46]

Although Ratzinger credited Eastern Orthodox theologians for

Ages, trans. Gemma Simmonds (Notre Dame, Ind.: University of Notre Dame, 2006), 62. The church-generating power of the Eucharist is acknowledged by the Council in *SC* 2, 10; *LG* 3, 11; and *PO* 5.

45. Ratzinger, *Church, Ecumenism, and Politics*, 18. For links the Council makes between Eucharist and mission, see *LG* 11, *SC* 2, *PO* 5, and *AA* 3, 4. As Pope Benedict XVI, Ratzinger strongly affirmed these links in his exhortation *Sacramentum Caritatis*, 55, 70, 83, and 86.

46. See Ratzinger, *Church, Ecumenism, and Politics*, 17–18.

helping recover the theology of the local church, he disputed those among them who reasoned that "every Eucharistic community" is "already wholly the Church because it has Christ wholly."[47] For them, unity with other Christian communities is a positive goal, but "not constitutive for the Church," "because one cannot add anything to the wholeness of Christ."[48] The Catholic position, according to Ratzinger, is more nuanced. It affirms the ecclesial reality of local churches, but asserts that participation in the Lord, who is and always is one, demands communion with all "who are also his body and are supposed to become it ever anew in the Eucharist. Therefore the unity among themselves of the communities that celebrate the Eucharist is not an external addition to Eucharistic ecclesiology; rather, it is its inner prerequisite."[49] The Eucharist therefore calls the church to "surpass the local horizon and enter into the shared element of catholic unity," which extends not only geographically but temporally from the church's apostolic origins to the final Kingdom.[50]

A key to communion between local Eucharistic assemblies is collegiality, which appears especially in *Lumen Gentium* 22 and 23. Although the Council did not make the Eucharistic orientation of collegiality explicit,[51] the Benedictine historian of liturgy Bernard Botte, whom Ratzinger credits with reviving this ancient concept for contemporary ecclesiology, did precisely that.[52] In his scholarship, Botte presented numerous patristic texts revealing "two levels" of "collegiality"

47. Ratzinger, *Church, Ecumenism, and Politics*, 18.

48. Ratzinger, *Church, Ecumenism, and Politics*, 18. For an example of the kind of position Ratzinger is critiquing, see Nicholas Afanasieff, "The Church Which Presides in Love," in *The Primacy of Peter*, ed. John Myendorff (Crestwood, N.Y.: St. Vladamir's Seminary Press, 1992), 91–143; a nice summary of various Orthodox authors on the topic can be found in Ruddy, *Local Church*, 9–30.

49. Ratzinger, *Church, Ecumenism, and Politics*, 20.

50. Ratzinger, *Church, Ecumenism, and Politics*, 23.

51. The Eucharistic orientation of collegiality can be implied from the Council only in the sense that its teaching on episcopal collegiality follows immediately upon its discussion of the bishop as High Priest over a Eucharistic assembly in *LG* 21; see McPartlan, "Eucharist as the Basis for Ecclesiology," 16.

52. Ratzinger, *Church, Ecumenism, and Politics*, 21; Bernard Botte, "Collegiate Character of the Presbyterate and Episcopate," in *The Sacrament of Holy Orders: Some Papers and Discussions Concerning Holy Orders at a Session of the Centre de Pastorale Liturgique, 1955* (London: Aquin, 1962), 75–97.

in the early church: "The first level consists of the fact that the bishop is surrounded by the *collegium* of priests," who "make up the bishop's 'council.'"[53] This idea was present especially in the writings of Ignatius of Antioch in the second century, when most local churches were still small enough to celebrate the Eucharist around one altar. In the fourth century, presbyters were regularly delegated to serve smaller satellite communities, which would today be called parishes. These communities maintained unity with one another through the presbyters' relation to each other and to the bishop. This union was grounded Eucharistically. For example, presbyters were required, by the Councils of Auvergne (535) and Mâcon (581), to come regularly to the "episcopal city to take part in the bishop's Mass."[54] In this way, the idea of the church's being most fully assembled in the Cathedral liturgy with the presbyters around the bishop was preserved. Additionally, the practice of "the sending of the *fermentum*, bread consecrated at the bishop's Mass, marked the link with the episcopal Eucharist."[55]

There also needed to be union among the various local churches, which would today be called dioceses. This is helped by the fact that at the next level the bishops form an *ordo*, or *collegium*, among themselves. Generally speaking, each bishop stands at the head of a local church.[56] Their communion with one another thereby reveals that the "universal Church" is also a "communion of Churches."[57] In the early church, the

53. Ratzinger, *Church, Ecumenism, and Politics*, 21.

54. Botte, "Collegiate Character," 81.

55. Botte, "Collegiate Character," 81.

56. The Council clarifies that not every bishop needs to have charge of a particular church. They may serve as members of the college without receiving canonical jurisdiction over a diocese (*LG* 24). Nonetheless, the bishop as head of a diocese seems to remain the primary analogate for what it means to be a bishop, a sense that is preserved by assigning bishops without dioceses to titular churches.

57. Congar, "De la communion des églises," 230–31. See also Jean Marie Tillard, *Church of Churches: The Ecclesiology of Communion* (Collegeville, Minn.: Liturgical Press, 1992), 29–33. Avery Dulles notes that when this way of envisioning things is inadequately qualified it can lead to neglecting the antecedent unity of the universal church as a single dominically instituted communion; Dulles, "Trends in Ecclesiology," 5–6. This is something Ratzinger himself has been very keen to preserve; see, for example, Ratzinger, *Called to Communion: Understanding the Church Today*, trans. Adrian Walker (San Francisco: Ignatius Press, 1996), 75–103. In 1992, the Congregation for the Doctrine of the Faith, with Ratzinger as its prefect, asserted that the universal church "is not a result

bishops maintained union with one another through the exchange of letters. Their unity was also manifest at synods and ecumenical councils.[58] However, Botte shows that their communion was first grounded in a Eucharistic liturgy. In the Mass of Episcopal Consecration, at least three neighboring bishops were (and are) expected to take part. Their presence reflected recognition by the larger church that the one being ordained shared the common faith, that he was now being brought into apostolic succession and would therefore become part of the order of bishops charged with teaching and governing the church.[59]

The bishop, therefore, emerges as a key figure in Eucharistic ecclesiology. He presides over and unites the local church through the Eucharistic sacrifice, and he stands at the nexus point through which the local church is in communion with the worldwide church. What, then, of the pope? Ratzinger did not treat the pope in this particular essay. Other ecclesiologists, however, have emphasized that the pope is, first of all, the bishop of Rome. Hence, he himself presides over the fullness of the church as it is gathered in his diocese.[60] The pope is also the head of the college of bishops and, accordingly, maintains a universal authority (*LG* 22). This authority, however, can be seen as reflecting "his liturgical role in the midst of the college of bishops."[61] When the college, or parts of it, assembles, the pope presides.[62] Moreover, in every local Eucharist, the pope's name is mentioned along with the local bishop's. Thus, as John Paul II noted in his final encyclical, in the very act of Eucharist that "makes the Church," the local assembly's unity with the heads of both the particular church and the college of bishops is affirmed.[63] Ac-

---

of the communion of the churches [though it is reflected by that communion], but in its essential mystery it is a reality ontologically and temporarily prior to every individual church"; CDF, "Some Aspects of the Church Understood as Communion," 8–9; *Origins* 22 (June 25, 1992): 109. For differing perspectives on the relation of the local churches and universal church, see Ruddy, *Local Church*, 100–109; and Mansini, "On the Relation of the Particular to Universal Church," in *Word Has Dwelt among Us*, 117–28.

58. Congar, "De la communion des églises," 232–33.

59. Botte, "Collegiate Character, 87–88.

60. See McPartlan, "Eucharist as the Basis for Ecclesiology," 17–18; Ruddy, *Local Church*, 117–19; Lafont, *Imagining the Catholic Church*, 166–69.

61. McPartlan, "Eucharist as the Basis for Ecclesiology," 17.

62. John Paul II, Apostolic Exhortation *Pastores Gregis* (October 16, 2003), 57.

63. John Paul II, *Ecclesia de Eucharista*, 39; See also *CCC* 1369.

cordingly, the *Catechism of the Catholic Church* depicts the pope as the "servant of Eucharistic unity" of the churches.[64]

Vatican II and Eucharistic ecclesiology therefore have moved away from portraying the church as a pyramidically constructed perfect society to portraying the church as a divine/human Eucharistically centered communion. It is now possible to explore the implications of this shift for religious priesthood.

The Priest in Vatican II's Ecclesiology

At least twice during the Council sessions there were calls for substantial teaching on the religious priesthood.[65] Unfortunately, however, the Council did not produce a document or even a section of a document devoted to the topic. Apart from a few scattered references in *Lumen Gentium* (art. 43), *Presbyterorum Ordinis* (arts. 1 and 8),[66] *Optatum Totius* (introduction),[67] and *Christus Dominus* (art. 28), scarcely a mention is made of their existence. In only one place (*CD* 34) do religious priests earn more than a single contiguous sentence of reflection, and here the Council emphasizes what religious priests have in common with the diocesan clergy. In order to draw any conclusions about the Council's implications for religious priesthood, it is thereby necessary to consider separately what it says about priesthood, which we will do in the remainder of this chapter, and what it says about religious life, the topic of chapter 5.

The priest in Vatican II's ecclesiology has at least three important characteristics. First, he is always seen in subordinate relation to the order of bishops and often in relation to a local bishop. Second, like the

64. McPartlan, "Eucharist as the Basis for Ecclesiology," 17.

65. During the second session's discussions of the schema of the Constitution of the Church, a number of "superiors of orders and bishops from the ranks of the regular clergy (who formed a good third of the college of bishops)" asked that a "special chapter" of the constitution be "devoted to the regular clergy"; Philips, "Dogmatic Constitution on the Church: The History of the Constitution," *Commentary* 1:125. Again, during the third session's discussions of *Presbyterorum Ordinis*, some fathers voiced concern that religious priests were being neglected; Castellucci, "I Religiosi Presbiteri Nella Chiesa," 101.

66. Vatican Council II, *Presbyterorum Ordinis* (December 7, 1965); hereafter *PO*.

67. Vatican Council II, *Optatum Totius* (October 28, 1965).

bishops, he exercises all three ministerial *munera*. Third, he is a pastoral figure in service to the Christian faithful. Each of these characteristics is important to the Council's teaching on the priesthood, and each one, as will be shown, poses challenges to the traditional understanding of religious priesthood.

A Priesthood Subordinate to the Order of Bishops and to the Local Bishop

The Council's teaching on priesthood must be understood in light of its teaching on bishops. The Council took many important steps in developing a more complete theology of the episcopacy. It bears repeating what the official understanding of the bishop had been during the post-Tridentine period (with the roots of this understanding extending to the Middle Ages). According to Paul McPartlan:

> Priestly ordination was wholly directed towards the Eucharist in the restricted sense of the Eucharistic elements. It conferred the full power to transubstantiate the elements and, since every simple priest had this power and exercised it in the Mass, the priesthood was considered to be what the sacrament of Orders was all about. The three grades of the sacrament of Orders were subdiaconate, diaconate, and priesthood. Episcopal consecration conferred no new faculty with regard to transubstantiation, to the *corpus verum*; therefore, it did not pertain to the sacrament of Orders. What it conferred was juridical power to govern the people, the *corpus mysticum*. In this vision, the bishop floats above the celebration of the Eucharist, which has become rather submerged in a system of seven sacraments. He ordains the priest who celebrates the Eucharist, and when *he* celebrates it, he is functioning as a priest at their level, quite contrary to the early patristic understanding that a priest, or rather, a presbyter, presides at a Eucharist only on behalf of the bishop.[68]

The Council presents a different vision of the bishop, one that is based more on the Eucharistic ecclesiology of the patristic period. According to the Council's first document, *Sacrosanctum Concilium*, the "pre-

68. McPartlan, "Eucharist as the Basis for Ecclesiology," 15.

eminent manifestation of the Church" is the Eucharist presided over by the bishop, "surrounded by his college of priests and by his ministers," with "the full active participation of all God's holy people"; as presider over this Cathedral liturgy, which is the fullest expression of the church, the bishop is "considered as the High Priest of his flock."[69] He is truly ordained, and his ordination, says the Council, is "the fullness of the Sacrament of Orders."[70] Thus, the sacramentality of episcopal consecration was affirmed. Ordained as high priest, the bishop also has "the office of teaching and ruling" the body of believers.[71] In this way, the Council united "care of the Eucharist" and "care of the Church" and thus linked functions that had been long separated.[72] Furthermore, it is ordination, the Council specified, that configures the bishop to Christ, "Teacher, Shepherd, and High priest."[73] This teaching subverted the notion that sacramental power was limited to sanctifying while teaching and governing stemmed only from the power of jurisdiction, affirming instead that all three *munera* had grounding in the sacrament of orders.

The image of "the bishop at the altar surrounded by his presbyters and ministers and the full company of the people,"[74] which *Sacrosanctum Concilium* 41 asserts is the "pre-eminent manifestation" of the church, orients the identity of presbyters in their relationship to the bishop and to one another. In this image of the church, the priest is clearly subordinate to the bishop, something the Council affirms in many places. As "High Priest," the bishop has received the fullness of orders, and the presbyter is his cooperator. Presbyters are "dependent" on bishops "in the exercise of their authority."[75] Their own authority to "build up, sanctify, and rule" the church exists only in subordinate relation to the bishops.[76] Even though presbyters should not be seen

69. *SC* 41.
70. *LG* 21.
71. *LG* 21.
72. McPartlan, "Eucharist as the Basis for Ecclesiology," 16.
73. *LG* 21.
74. McPartlan, "Eucharist as the Basis for Ecclesiology," 16.
75. *CD* 15.
76. *PO* 2.

as mere deputies of the bishops,[77] they are still subordinate agents, the "aid and instrument" of the bishops.[78]

At the local level, presbyters form a college, "an intimate brotherhood," around the bishop who, in turn, views them as "sons and friends."[79] Presbyters, for their part, "stand by their bishops in sincere charity and obedience," willingly serving as his "helpers and counselors" in the care of his flock.[80] This image of presbyteral collegiality is present also in *Lumen Gentium*, Chapter V, "The Universal Call to Holiness," where it says priests grow in charity by maintaining the "bond of priestly communion" with their fellow presbyters and are aided in their own sanctification by "generous co-operation with their bishop." Hence, says Friedrich Wulf, "the priest's spirituality and perfection ... include ... co-operation with the bishop and with his fellow-priests in loving service."[81]

In addition to the strong orientation of the bishop to a local Eucharistic assembly in *Sacrosanctum Concilium*, both *Lumen Gentium* and *Christus Dominus* also consider the bishop in relation to the universal church, as a member of the college of bishops that succeeds the apostles, who must therefore be "solicitous for the whole Church."[82] Along similar lines, the Council acknowledges a distinction between membership in the order of presbyters and membership in a local presbyterate. By ordination one becomes a member of the order of presbyters, cooperators with the order of bishops that cares for the church universal. One becomes a member of a local presbyterate by canonical mission and incardination and attached to a local bishop by these means,[83] as

77. *Lumen Gentium* 28 also refers to priests as "cooperators of the episcopal college." Grillmeier comments on this article, saying, "The consecrated priesthood is truly realized in them [priests] and their title of priest is used in no merely metaphorical sense. And this is in virtue of their ordination, a fully sacramental act, which impresses on them the image of Christ, the prototype of the New Testament priesthood"; Grillmeier, "Dogmatic Constitution on the Church," Chapter III, "Article 28," *Commentary* 1:221.

78. *LG* 28. See also *LG* 21.

79. *LG* 28.

80. *PO* 7.

81. *LG* 41; Wulf, Chapter V, "The Call of the Whole Church to Holiness," *Commentary* 1:269.

82. *LG* 23; *CD* 3, 6.

83. Joseph Lécuyer, "Decree on the Ministry and Life of Priests: History of the Decree," *Commentary* 4:199.

well as through the priestly promise of obedience. The distinction between membership in the order of presbyters and membership in the local presbyterate, along with the Council's acknowledgment that every priest has some pastoral orientation to the worldwide church,[84] seems to open a door, at least in theory, to a priesthood that was not particularly attached to a single local bishop but to the college as a whole, headed by the pope, which could then minister in a transdiocesan way.

If the Council had such an "absolute" priesthood in mind, like the one carried out by medieval mendicants and sixteenth-century Jesuits, it did not make it explicit. To the contrary, the assumption seems to be that a priest will normally minister within a diocesan framework, attached to a local church, its bishop, and presbyterate. *Christus Dominus* 34 asserts that even religious priests "can be said in a real sense to belong to the clergy of the diocese inasmuch as they share in the care of souls and in carrying out works of the apostolate under the authority of the prelates." The same decree, in the very next article, limits the exemption of religious, which had heretofore been the basis by which religious priests ministered across diocesan boundaries, to the "internal order of the communities." Paul VI's postconciliar *moto proprio, Ecclesiae Sanctae* I, specifically "numbers" all priests, including religious, "commissioned for service by the bishop among the presbytery."[85] Canons 678 and Canons 691 of the 1983 Code of Canon Law stipulate that religious priests "are subject to the local bishop in all aspects of their public ministry and worship."[86]

Perhaps most significantly, the 1990 revised Rite of Ordination, approved by Pope John Paul II, requires the religious priest to make a promise of obedience not only to his own superior but also to the di-

84. *Presbyterorum Ordinis* 10 states, "The spiritual gift which priests receive at their ordination prepared them not for a sort of limited and narrow mission but for the widest possible and universal mission of salvation 'even to the ends of the earth' (Acts 1:8).... Priests of such dioceses as are rich in vocations should show themselves willing and ready, with the permission of their own ordinaries (bishops), to volunteer for work in other regions, missions or endeavors which are poor in numbers of clergy."

85. Paul J. Cordes, "Decree on the Ministry and Life of Priests: Commentary on the Decree: Priests as Related to Others," *Commentary* 4:248.

86. Leon F. Streider, *The Promise of Obedience: A Ritual History* (Collegeville, Minn.: Liturgical Press, 2001), 114.

ocesan bishop at the time of ordination.[87] The immediate cause of this innovation seems to have been a number of religious priests after Vatican II seeking and receiving dispensation from religious vows, but not being laicized, and therefore being able to operate independent of ecclesial authority.[88] Leon Streider, however, argues that this is a natural development of the Council's teaching on "the diocese as the local Church, and thus the need for the unity of all pastoral ministry in that diocese under the authority of the local bishop."[89] The "implications" of this development, he says, which not only directly places the religious within a strongly local/diocesan framework but also introduces the potential problem of dual obediences (to bishop and religious superior), "will take generations to comprehend."[90] A question that immediately arises is whether bishops could ever actually bypass religious superiors and order priests to tasks and ministries. Although current law seems to prohibit such an action, one may wonder what further developments will bring.[91]

Vatican II and subsequent magisterial teaching therefore seem to imagine priests as normally ministering as part of a local presbyterate, under the authority of a local bishop. Some commentators have quite reasonably interpreted the Council's teaching in this regard to mean that religious priests must be fully integrated into a local diocesan presbyterate. For Kenan Osborne, Vatican II marks the end of "absolute ordinations" and recovers the ancient value of ministers always being ordained for a specific church; priests now "belong to a regional presbyterium, under the leadership of a very definite, regional bishop."[92] He contends

87. See Streider, *Promise of Obedience*, 110.

88. One can legitimately question why it is so much easier for religious to be dispensed from their vows than it is for marriages to be annulled or priests to be laicized. On this point, see Lafont, *Imagining the Catholic Church*, 121.

89. In particular, Streider sees this as a development of *Christus Dominus* 35, which restricts exemption to "internal organization" because of the "need for harmony in the pastoral ministry of a diocese"; Streider, *Promise of Obedience*, 114.

90. Streider, *Promise of Obedience*, 112.

91. For an analysis of the canonical issues surrounding the dual obedience of religious priests, see Seasoltz, "Institutes of Consecrated Life and Ordained Ministry," 139–68, esp.158–60.

92. Osborne, *Priesthood*, 332–33.

that the only way to conceive of ministry otherwise is to locate ministry within an "undifferentiated," "spiritual," "a-temporal," "a-spatial" context. He argues that "religious order priests" should be considered part of whatever diocesan presbyterate in which they minister, but he provocatively suggests that Vatican II's recovery of the theologies of the local church and presbyterate reintroduces the question of whether religious should be associated with priesthood at all.[93] Enrico Castellucci similarly argues that because "it is difficult, after Vatican II, to conceive of the ministry of a priest divorced from the actual path of a particular Church" under a specific bishop, all priests should be considered part of the local ministerial team.[94] Paul Cordes, himself a *peritus* at the Council, says religious priests and secular priests working outside their own dioceses should form fraternal bonds with the diocesan presbyterate and its bishop and willingly cooperate with the mission to the local church. However, says Cordes, because the bishop is "not in full control" of these priests, it is "always desirable ... that priests engaged in pastoral work be incardinated into the diocese in which they are working."[95] Hence, we can see that for a number of thinkers, religious priesthood's tradition of transdiocesan ministry and functional independence from the local bishop and local presbyterate appears to compromise the Council's vision of priesthood.

A Priesthood Exercising All Three Ministerial Munera

Vatican II presented the priest as participating in the ministerial office of Christ as prophet, priest, and king. The threefold office corresponds to the three ministerial functions (*munera*) of teaching/preaching (*munus docendi*), sanctifying (*munus sanctificandi*), and ruling/shepherding (*munus regendi*). Without denying the requirement of canonical mandates for licit ministry, the Council nonetheless spoke very little of the power of jurisdiction in its theology of priesthood. It emphasized, rather, that the power (if not the permission) to preach/teach, sanctify,

93. Osborne, *Priesthood*, 333; see also Streider, *Promise of Obedience*, 110–21.

94. Castellucci, "I Religiosi Presbiteri Nella Chiesa," 106.

95. Cordes, "Decree on the Ministry and Life of Priests: Commentary on the Decree; Priests as Related to Others," *Commentary* 4:249.

and rule was sourced in the sacrament of holy orders.[96] In this way, the Council recovered the understanding—evident in numerous patristic texts—that the ordained is receiving graces through the liturgy not only to make him able to confect the Eucharist but also to teach, preach, and govern.[97] This understanding is consonant not only with the church fathers, but with the vision of the New Testament wherein Christ selected and commanded his apostles not only to repeat his Eucharistic gestures, but also to proclaim the gospel and govern the church. It assumes that when these same apostles laid hands on their successors they did so with the intention that their successors would preach, teach, and lead the church and not merely confect the Eucharistic elements.[98]

Both bishops and priests are described as sharing in the ministerial office of Christ as prophet, priest, and king. *Christus Dominus*, *Presbyterorum Ordinis*, and *Lumen Gentium*, Chapter III, structure their descriptions of ordained ministry around the exercise of the threefold office, and the image of the minister that emerges is one where the priest or bishop exercises all three *munera*. *Lumen Gentium* 21, for instance, teaches that for bishops the "office of sanctifying" comes together with the duty of "teaching and ruling," and *Lumen Gentium* 28 states that priests are similarly "consecrated to preach the Gospel and shepherd the faithful and to celebrate divine worship."

Reflecting the principles of Eucharistic ecclesiology in which care of the Eucharist is united with care of the church, the Council emphasizes the practical unity of the three functions. Preaching leads to the celebration of the sacraments, particularly the Eucharist.[99] The celebration of the sacraments is itself a proclamation of the gospel.[100] The Eucharist in turn builds a community that the priest or bishop governs as shep-

96. *LG* 21 and 28. Aloys Grillmeier explains, "The sacrament … sets them apart, commissions and equips them the preaching of the word, the guidance of the faithful and the celebration of divine worship—all of course, 'according to the degree of their ministry'"; Grillmeier, "Dogmatic Constitution on the Church," Chapter III, "Article 28," *Commentary* 1:222.

97. For references from the fathers, see Mansini, *Word Has Dwelt among Us*, 161–64.

98. *LG* 20.

99. *LG* 24, 26; *PO* 4–5; *CD* 15.

100. *PO* 4.

herd.[101] The shepherd of the faithful governs by teaching and preaching, by which he assembles men and women for the Eucharist.[102] In these texts the "boundaries between the titles [prophet, priest, and king] are fluid: in many ways they overlap."[103] There is a "theoretical and actual inseparability of the three offices: fundamentally these simply unfold the one, single office of Christ."[104]

Furthermore, the *munera* appear to be united in some way in the very person of the minister. According to the *Nota explicativa praevia* accompanying *Lumen gentium*, the share of the minister in the three functions bestowed by consecration is "ontological."[105] Wulf interprets this to mean that the "existential-ontological sharing in the mission of Christ ... essentially and irrevocably determines the person of the ordained priest."[106] The ontological participation of the minister in the "ministry and mission of Christ" is "so deep" and "so real" that the threefold ministry of Christ himself assumes "sacramental visibility and palpability" in the person of the minister.[107]

A number of theologians have assumed that all three *munera* are now to be identified with the sacramental character of the minister.[108]

101. *CD* 15; *PO* 6.

102. *LG* 27; *PO* 5; *CD* 15.

103. Wulf, "Decree on the Ministry and Life of Priests: Commentary on the Decree," Preface, *Commentary* 4:217.

104. Wulf, "Decree on the Ministry and Life of Priests: Commentary on the Decree," Chapter II, "Priestly Functions," *Commentary* 4:232. The 1978 document *Mutuae Relationes* issued by the Sacred Congregation for Religious and for Secular Institutes makes the striking claim, "since, in the new law, Christ has essentially fused the three functions of Teacher, Priest and Pastor into one, there is only one ministry unique in its origin. Consequently the bishop's ministry is exercised is its different functions in an indivisible way"; Sacred Congregation for Religious and for Secular Institutes, *Mutuae relationes*, "The Relationship of Bishops/Religious Orders," *Origins* 8, no. 11 (August 31, 1978): 161–76, art. 7; hereafter *MR*.

105. Vatican II, *Nota explicativa praevia* 2.

106. Wulf, "Decree on the Ministry and Life of Priests: Commentary on the Decree," Chapter II, "Priestly Functions," *Commentary* 4:234.

107. Wulf, "Decree on the Ministry and Life of Priests: Commentary on the Decree," "Preface," *Commentary* 4:217.

108. See Jean Galot, *Theology of Priesthood*, trans. Roger Balducelli (San Francisco: Ignatius Press, 1984), 208–9; Lafont, *Imagining the Catholic Church*, 159; Sara Butler, "Priestly Identity: 'Sacrament' of Christ the Head," *Worship* 70 (1996): 290–306. This position is possibly supported by *Lumen Gentium* 21, which states, "By means of the im-

Lécuyer and Guy Mansini believe the Council left the question unresolved.[109] Mansini contends that, among other reasons, identifying all three *munera* with the sacramental character would be problematic because the efficacy of the sanctifying function cannot be doubted, questioned, or lost in the same way as the efficacy of the governing and teaching functions can be. To identify the presbyter or bishop with the character of Christ the teacher could imply that every statement he made was infallible. When one considers the fact that nearly every important heresy has involved priests, one sees that Mansini raises an important concern. Mansini would prefer to say that the sacrament of orders bestows the "grace" and "call" for the exercise of the prophetic and royal *munera*, but not the character of Christ as prophet and king (whose teaching and ruling cannot be doubted).[110] Nonetheless, Mansini agrees that the Council teaches that the sacrament of orders must be understood as imparting to each priest and bishop a truly ontological share in the threefold office—not only the power to sanctify, but the "radical capacity to teach and rule as well."[111] These functions cannot be divided in the same way as before, and "it is fitting that all three *munera* are discharged by the same man."[112]

The uniting of the three *munera* in both the ministry and the minister raises an obvious question for religious priesthood. The exercise of priesthood by religious often depended historically on the practical separation of the three classical *munera*. The ministry of contemplative monastic priests was centered on offering the Mass. Although more active monks carried out important preaching and teaching ministries, monasteries did not, generally, expect their priests to be pastors. Men-

position of hands and the words of consecration, the grace of the Holy Spirit is so conferred, and the sacred character so impressed, that bishops in an eminent and visible way sustain the roles of Christ Himself as Teacher, Shepherd and High Priest, and that they act in His person."

109. Lécuyer, "L'Episcopato come Sacramento," in *La Chiesa Del Vaticano II: Studi e commenti intorno alla Constituzione dommatica "Lumen Gentium,"* ed. Guilherme Baraúna (Florence: Vallecchi Editore, 1965), 729–30; Mansini, *Word Has Dwelt among Us*, 183.

110. See Mansini, *Word Has Dwelt among Us*, 177.

111. Mansini, *Word Has Dwelt among Us*, 170.

112. Mansini, *Word Has Dwelt among Us*, 176.

dicant and Jesuit priests administered the sacraments, especially Eucharist and reconciliation, and placed a strong emphasis on apostolic preaching, but they often foreswore pastorates. The practical separation of the *munera* was supported theoretically by the hard division of the two powers: Holy Orders bestowed only the sanctifying *munus*. On the basis of the power of jurisdiction, bishops (or the pope) delegated priests to preach, teach, and lead the church. The preaching/teaching *munus* could be separated from the ruling *munus*, just as both were separated from the sanctifying one. This separation allowed religious such as the mendicants and Jesuits to become preaching and teaching specialists without also being pastors.

If the three *munera* can no longer be divided, can they be at least adequately distinguished in such a way that a single minister could effectively specialize in one or the other without being equally responsible for all three tasks? Castellucci cautions against making such a move. Since the *munera* are "co-essential," not rooted in two powers but one ordination, ordained ministry means participation in the whole ministry entrusted by Jesus to the apostles: prophetic, priestly, pastoral.[113] No hard divisions can be drawn across the threefold ministry—between pastors and preachers, for example.[114] All priests are placed in pastoral relation to some specific church, and all priests equally have a missionary mandate.[115] Though Castellucci admits of certain historical emphases, he rejects identifying religious with preaching and diocesan priests with pastoring in any strong way. "The great effort of Vatican II," he says, "was to bring unity to these tasks."[116]

A Pastoral Priesthood

According to the Council, the exercise of the *tria munera* by sacred ministers is oriented to the service (*diakonia*) of the church as a whole.[117] The Council describes bishops and priests as "shepherds"

113. Castellucci, "I Religiosi Presbiteri Nella Chiesa," 103.
114. Castellucci, "I Religiosi Presbiteri Nella Chiesa," 109–10.
115. Castellucci, "I Religiosi Presbiteri Nella Chiesa," 110, 102.
116. Castellucci, "I Religiosi Presbiteri Nella Chiesa," 110.
117. *LG* 24.

whose ministry has been given to the church by the Lord Jesus for the building up of the church and the salvation of mankind.[118] By framing hierarchical ministry in the context of service to others, the Council subverted the clericalism that characterized much of post-Tridentine ecclesiology. Complementary to this development, the Council recognized the charismatic gifts and missiological contributions of the laity and taught that the laity had their own particular participation in the priestly, prophetic, and royal office of Christ.[119] The hierarchy appears in Vatican II's ecclesiology no longer as aloof princes of the "perfect society" or as purely cultic priests celebrating private masses, but as existing to promote, unite, nurture, and foster the life and mission of the whole Christian faithful.[120]

Along these lines, the Council takes care in several places to present priesthood in relation to the body of the faithful. *Lumen Gentium*'s first substantial treatment of priests places them in a Eucharistic context. The people "present themselves as a living sacrifice, holy and pleasing to God," and the "ministerial priest ... teaches and rules the priestly people."[121] The constitution's second substantial treatment of the priest offers a similar image: "They exercise their sacred function especially in the Eucharistic worship or the celebration of the Mass by which acting in the person of Christ and proclaiming His Mystery they unite the prayers of the faithful with the sacrifice of their Head."[122] The positioning of the priest in relation to the Eucharistic people appears repeatedly throughout the Council documents: Priests "gather together God's family," and "in the midst of the flock they adore him in spirit and truth"; "The Eucharistic action, over which the priest presides, is the heart of the congregation"; "Priests have been placed in the midst of the laity"; They "lead and serve their local community."[123]

Not surprisingly, the parochial pastor emerges as the baseline for the Council's vision of priesthood. *Presbyterorum Ordinis* takes priest-

118. *LG* 20, 21, 24, 28.

119. The priesthood of the faithful is said to differ "in essence and not only in degree" from that of the hierarchical priesthood; *LG* 10.

120. Castellucci, "I Religiosi Presbiteri Nella Chiesa," 105–6.

121. *LG* 10.

122. *LG* 28.

123. *LG* 28; *PO* 5, *PO* 9; *LG* 28.

hood engaged in the *cura animarum*, or care of souls, which historically "has meant and still seems to mean primarily the ministry of pastors of parishes under the bishop" as its norm for priesthood.[124] For example, in its opening paragraph, the decree states, "What is said here applies to all priests. It refers in a special way to those who are engaged in the care of souls." For *Christus Dominus* "pastors of parishes hold first place among the collaborators with the bishops" precisely because they are engaged in the care of souls.[125] In fact, there is a strong parallel between the bishop as shepherd of a diocese and the pastor as shepherd of a parish. *Christus Dominus* 11 states, "A diocese is a portion of the people of God which is entrusted to a bishop to be shepherded by him." Meanwhile, "associated with their bishop in a spirit of trust and generosity, [priests] make him present in a certain sense in the individual local congregations"; "under bishop's authority," they "sanctify and govern ... that part of the Lord's flock entrusted to them."[126]

Care of souls has historically been a diocesan task: "In the care of souls ... the first place is held by diocesan priests who are incardinated or attached to a particular church, for they have fully dedicated themselves in the service of caring for a single portion of the Lord's flock."[127] As for religious, who have typically not had the office of *cura animarum*, the teaching on priesthood is to be applied "with suitable adaptations."[128] For religious priests, the upshot of this statement is that it can be considered an admission that the Council is not forcing them into a parochial framework. The disadvantage is that there is little substantial treatment of priests who are not involved in parochial ministry. "The typical priestly figure" that emerges from these texts is "the pastor engaged in care of souls."[129] Nonparochial priests seem to be, if not a deviation, an exception to what it means to be a priest.

Since the Council, a number of theologians have attempted to make one or the other of the *tria munera* "architectonic"—that is to say, they

124. O'Malley, "Priesthood, Ministry, and Religious Life," 253.

125. O'Malley, "Priesthood, Ministry, and Religious Life," 252; see *CD* 30.

126. *LG* 28.

127. *CD* 28.

128. *PO* 1.

129. Castellucci, "I Religiosi Presbiteri Nella Chiesa," 101.

have attempted to see one of the *munera* as primary with the others in some way ordered to or flowing from it.[130] The Council certainly provides material here and there that could favor an interpretation of any one of the three *munera* as primary. *Presbyterorum ordinis* discusses the prophetic *munus* first and states that "it is the primary duty" of priests to preach the gospel.[131] Thus, Rahner and Ratzinger formulated theologies of priesthood that give the prophetic *munus* priority.[132] In next discussing the sanctifying *munus*, *Presbyterorum Ordinis* 5 notes that "every ministry of the Church and every work of the apostolate, are tied together with the Eucharist and are directed toward it." Congar, Lécuyer, and Mansini accordingly maintain the centrality of the priestly function.[133] Even though the ruling *munus* is discussed last, some have read the decree in such a way that everything the other two *munera* involves reaches its final expression in the royal *munus*, which is the pastoral service of building up of the body. Osborne, Lafont, Jean Galot, Francis George, and Walter Kasper thereby favor seeing this *munus* as primary.[134]

It is important to point out why making the pastoral function primary is attractive and yet, at the same time, to show that it creates the

130. Mansini, *Word Has Dwelt among Us*, 218. For a comparative analysis of these various attempts and further references, see Dulles, *The Priestly Office: A Theological Reflection* (New York: Paulist Press, 1997).

131. *PO* 4.

132. See Karl Rahner, "Priest and Poet," in *Theological Investigations*, vol. 3, *The Theology of the Spiritual Life*, trans. Karl H. Kruger and Boniface Kruger (Baltimore: Helicon, 1967), 307–13; "The Point of Departure in Theology for Determining the Nature of the Priestly Office," *Theological Investigations* 12, trans. David Bourke (New York: Seabury and Crossroad, 1974), 35–36; "The Word and the Eucharist," *Theological Investigations* 4, trans. Kevin Smyth (Baltimore: Helicon, 1966), 260–81; Joseph Ratzinger, *The Open Circle: The Meaning of Christian Brotherhood* (New York: Sheed and Ward, 1966); Ratzinger, *Theological Highlights of Vatican II* (New York: Paulist Press, 1966), 175–78; Ratzinger, "Biblical Foundations of Priesthood," *Origins* 20 (October 18, 1990): 310–14.

133. Congar, *Lay People in the Church*, 152–57; Mansini, *Word Has Dwelt among Us*, 221–24.

134. Osborne, *Priesthood*, 333; Lafont, *Imagining the Catholic Church*, 155–205; Galot, *Theology of Priesthood*, 129–53; Francis George, "The Significance of Vatican II," *Communio* 39, no. 1–2 (Spring–Summer 2012): 14–32, esp. 22–24; Walter Kasper, "A New Dogmatic Outlook on the Priestly Ministry," in *The Identity of the Priest*, Concilium 43 (New York: Paulist Press, 1969), 20–33.

greatest dilemma for religious priesthood to do so. Making the pastoral function primary is attractive because it maintains a clear role and identity for the priest in a contemporary ecclesiology that has, since the twentieth century, recovered the gifts, charisms, and active participation of the laity in the church's life, liturgy, and mission. Attempts to make the pastoral function primary highlight the idea that even in an ecclesiology more affirming of the laity, a figure is still required who can unite, order, and guide the charisms and contributions of the people. Much like a conductor before an orchestra, the priest, writes Kasper, "coordinates" the gifts of the Christian faithful; by doing so, priesthood "serves the unity of the Church. In this respect, it is a particularly essential and distinct ministry designed to abet and correlate the other ministries or services."[135]

Francis George is another theologian highlighting how making the pastoral function primary affirms the laity's contributions while still maintaining a central role for the priest. He writes, "In the Catholic perspective, lay ministers can proclaim the Gospel and do other ecclesial service. We have lay ecclesial ministers. Their call to ecclesial service is based on baptism."[136] For George, what distinguishes priestly ministry, and therefore, what lies at its heart, is governance. According to his reading,

> The fathers of the council placed the priestly power to confect the Eucharist in the context of pastoral authority over the body of Christ. Bishops and priests can make present and give to people the sacramental body of Christ *because* they have pastoral authority over the people as the Mystical Body of Christ. That the priesthood and episcopacy constitute a sacrament for the good governance of the Church is important in discerning vocations. A prospective seminarian must be asked: 'Can you govern?'. . . . If that is not the case, no matter how devotional a man is, no matter how smart he is, no matter how holy he is, he is not called to ordained priesthood.[137]

I am not sure that George's claim that the Council recognized the power to confect as dependent upon the authority to govern is correct. The

135. Kasper, "New Dogmatic Outlook on the Priestly Ministry," 25.
136. George, "Significance of Vatican II," 24.
137. George, "Significance of Vatican II," 24; emphasis mine.

Council teaches that priests are "conformed to Christ the Priest in such a way that they are able to act in the person of Christ the head."[138] It is possible to interpret this statement to mean the opposite of what George says. It could be read as placing Eucharistic presidency (the priestly, sanctifying *munus*) before leadership over the body (the pastoral *munus*), such that priests and bishops have pastoral authority over the people *because* they "make present and give to people the sacramental body," and not the other way around. Nonetheless, George accurately indicates that the Council envisioned a unity of care of the Eucharist and care of the church, and his conclusion that the call to priesthood is equivalent to a call to pastoral leadership is striking, but not unreasonable.

If the pastoral function could be interpreted broadly and analogously, there would be room for religious priests, and any nonparochial priests, for that matter, to express it in ways beyond that of the parochial pastors as spiritual directors, school administrators, or chaplains, for example, as these involve leadership of persons and communities. Even so, to interpret the pastoral function in this broader way would require a better understanding of how ordination enhances such ministries. If the shepherding function is read narrowly, however, as specifically the *cura animarum* carried out by and restricted to canonical pastors, then the openness of the church to many traditional expressions of religious priesthood seems far more limited.

Ghislain Lafont has taken a narrower approach and drawn conclusions that would greatly restrict religious priesthood. For Lafont, the church is a "structured communion in the spirit." Each of the church's members has been given charismatic gifts for the good of the church and its mission in the world. Some of the gifts he recognizes are talents for organizing liturgy, sharing the gospel, preaching, teaching, catechesis, ministry to the sick, spiritual direction, and institutional administration.[139] At the top of this structured communion is the bishop, whose charism it is to moderate and preside over the church in the name of Christ. Priests are "lieutenants" of the bishop, "exercising the pastoral responsibility of Jesus Christ in a portion of the particular

138. *PO* 2.

139. See Lafont, *Imagining the Catholic Church*, 135–53.

church."[140] For Lafont, "the fundamental difference between the apostolic ministry and lay ministry seems to be that the latter is given particular form by the charisms imparted to perform this or that task.... The priest's mission is to stir up, verify, and coordinate these ministries and to gather them together in the unique sacrifice of Christ."[141]

Lafont thinks that if the charismatic gifts and talents of the laity were better affirmed and embraced, there would be need for fewer priests. Lafont's approach has weighty implications for religious. He states:

> The number of priests today would not seem so inadequate if, according to the mentality still found, we did not think that a man could not do anything important in the Church unless he was a priest. As far as male religious are concerned, it is necessary that we give more weight to the fact that the essential charism that defines their foundation is most often not the priesthood. The parallel communities of women religious that sometimes have the same founder and that pursue the same goal by benefitting from the same charism and an analogous formation make this amply clear. This fact would seem to prove that the ministerial priesthood is not of the essence for the corresponding institute for men. Why must one be a priest to accomplish the task of Catholic education, if, in a neighboring school conducted by women religious (who are not priests by definition), they are employed in the same work without benefit of ordination? Such a question seems to have nourished the claim to be ordained by some women. Now, in many cases, the solution to this disparity between men and women beneficiaries of the same charism is not the ordination of women to the priesthood, but rather changing the character of the male religious community in such a way as to restrict access to the priesthood. If it is a matter of religious life, the issue is the declericalization of a number of congregations in which the vast majority of its members exercise the charism proper to them all the better because it is not obscured by the "dignity of the priesthood," which in most cases is not really relevant.[142]

140. Lafont, *Imagining the Catholic Church*, 161.
141. Lafont, *Imagining the Catholic Church*, 162.
142. Lafont, *Imagining the Catholic Church*, 162.

Lafont's comments bring to light crucial questions for this study. How deep is the correlation between the charism of ministerial priesthood and the charisms of religious life? And, if the distinguishing feature of priesthood is parochial pastoral leadership, should men who will likely never be pastors be ordained? If they are ordained, what is the meaning of their priesthood? How does their ordination enhance their apostolic work?

So far we have seen how Vatican II's images of priesthood have provoked many questions and challenges for the traditional understanding of religious priesthood. But this is only half the story. To complete our picture, we must now examine how the Council treated religious life and what the implications of that were and are for religious priesthood.

CHAPTER 5

Religious Life and Religious Priests

In order to complete our discussion of Vatican II's implications for religious priesthood, it is necessary to examine the place of religious life in Vatican II's ecclesiology just as we did with priesthood. Before doing so, however, we must first say something about the understanding of religious life just before the Council.

Developments in the Understanding of Religious Life in the Early Twentieth Century

Religious had held an esteemed place in late "perfect society" ecclesiology. Like clerics, religious were considered "sacred persons," set apart from temporal society.[1] They were also increasingly associated with the church's public mission. At the turn of the twentieth century, in his apostolic constitution *Conditae a Christo* (1900), Pope Leo XIII gave canonical recognition to active women's religious congregations. This was highly significant because, heretofore, magisterial teaching had considered religious life *qua* religious life to be mainly a contemplative endeavor oriented to the sanctification of the religious himself or herself. For male religious, the magisterium often associated their apostolic work with their being priests rather than with their religious profession. For women, only contemplative religious life was formally considered religious life. Active congregations were put either into the category of societies of apostolic life (canonically these are not religious institutes),

1. Lafont, *Imagining the Catholic Church*, 60.

or they existed as "private societies," which were like lay confraternities but with some form of permanent commitment to the evangelical counsels.[2] Through Leo's constitution, "the Church took to herself the apostolic mission of institutes."[3] Leo described religious as "devoted cooperators" and "necessary auxiliaries of the bishop and clergy in the exercise of the sacred ministry and the function of Catholic teaching and preaching."[4]

Although Leo was moving toward an understanding of religious life as inherently missiological, his vision of religious still reflected the division of the two powers that was so characteristic of perfect society ecclesiology. Leo understood the participation of religious in the church's public mission as resulting mainly from juridical delegation. In this sense, Leo's vision of religious life bears a close resemblance to the Catholic Action movement he also inaugurated. Due to the increased secularization of society in the late nineteenth century, Leo and subsequent popes commissioned lay people to become involved in the church's public catechetical and evangelical initiatives. Catholic Action was understood as a juridically delegated "participation of the laity in the hierarchical apostolate of the Church."[5] Although Catholic Action was an important step in recovering a sense of the lay apostolate, its great disadvantage was in portraying this apostolate as dependent on deputization from the hierarchy (rather than stemming from the sacraments of initiation).[6] Leo's vision of religious life shares the same lacuna: the missiological activity of religious remained a result more of

2. Mary Judith O'Brien and Mary Nika Schaumber, conclusion to Council of Major Superiors of Religious Women, *The Foundations of Religious Life* (Notre Dame, Ind.: Ave Maria, 2009), 177.

3. Council of Major Superiors of Women Religious, *Foundations of Religious Life*, 6.

4. Leo XIII, *Au milieu des consolations* (December 23, 1900).

5. Pius XI, handwritten letter to Cardinal Gasparri, January 21, 1927, quoted in Balthasar, *The Laity and the Life of the Counsels: The Church's Mission in the World*, trans. Brian McNeil, with D. C. Schindler (San Francisco: Ignatius Press, 1993), 49. *Laity in the Life of the Counsels* is cited hereafter as *LLC*.

6. For more on the limitations of Catholic Action, see Balthasar, *LLC*, 49–50; Aurelie Hagstrom, *The Concepts of the Vocation and the Mission of the Laity* (San Francisco: Catholic Scholars, 1994), 16–17; Jacques Servais, "The Lay Vocation in the World According to Hans Urs von Balthasar," *Communio: International Catholic Review* 23, no.4 (Winter 1996): 656–76.

juridical delegation than of religious vows or consecration per se. In this system, the difference between the missiological roles of religious life and laity involved with Catholic Action seems to lie in the relative stability and permanence of the juridical delegation of the former.[7]

Pius XI clarified that the apostolate of the laity was rooted in baptism and confirmation.[8] Pius XII subsequently redefined Catholic Action as a "collaboration" or "cooperation" of the laity with the hierarchical apostolate. All Christians had a mission stemming from the sacraments of initiation; Catholic Action was simply a way of legally recognizing and organizing these activities as part of the church's public mission.[9] Pius XII envisioned religious consecration as intensifying the missiological orientation of baptismal life and spoke of evangelical commitment as involving "consecration to God and souls."[10] Therefore, like baptism, religious life *qua* religious life was not merely a matter of personal sanctification, but in some way internally ordered to the church's mission. Noting that "religious life is closely interwoven with the holiness and catholic apostolate of the Church itself," Pius even claimed, in his apostolic constitution, *Provida Mater Ecclesia*, that religious constituted a "state between" the clergy and the laity.[11] In this way, Pius inserted religious into the church's hierarchical structure. By virtue of their holiness and mission, religious came immediately after clergy and before the laity.

The Second Vatican Council continued some of Leo's and Pius's

7. For more on magisterial teaching on religious life in the early twentieth century, see Council of Major Superiors of Religious Women, *Foundations of Religious Life*, 1–9; Allen and O'Brien, "Decree on the Appropriate Renewal of Religious Life," 251–58.

8. "It is the sacraments of baptism and confirmation themselves that impose, among other obligations, that of the apostolate, of spiritual assistance to our neighbor. In fact, by confirmation a man becomes a soldier of Christ"; Pius XI, *Ex officiosis litteris*, quoted in Theodore Hesburgh, *The Relation of the Sacramental Characters of Baptism and Confirmation to the Lay Apostolate* (Washington, D.C.: The Catholic University of America Press, 1946), 32.

9. See Pius XII, Encyclical Letter *Evangelii Praecones* (June 2, 1951), 30–31.

10. Pius XII, Motu Proprio *Primo Feliciter* (March 12, 1948), 7. See also Jean Beyer, "Life Consecrated by the Evangelical Counsels," in *Vatican II: Assessment and Perspectives*, vol. 3, *Twenty-Five Years After (1962–1987)*, ed. René Latourelle, trans. Leslie Werne (New York: Paulist Press, 1988), 3:69.

11. Pius XII, Apostolic Constitution *Provida Mater Ecclesia* (February 2, 1947), 7 and 9.

trajectories and retreated from others. The Council spoke of religious life primarily in two places, *Lumen Gentium*, Chapter VI, and *Perfectae Caritatis*, the Decree on the Adaptation and Renewal of Religious Life. These texts depict religious life as having four important characteristics. First, religious life belongs to the charismatic rather than to the hierarchical dimension of the church. Second, religious life is defined in relation to the evangelical counsels. Third, religious life is inherently apostolic. Fourth, authentic religious life is faithful to the charisms of its founders. Each of these claims has important implications for religious priesthood.

Vatican II on Religious Life

Religious Life as Charismatic

The history of *Lumen Gentium*, Chapter VI, Vatican II's first extensive treatment of religious life, is complex. The initial schema of the constitution dealt with religious in a chapter entitled, "The States of Life Devoted to Acquiring Evangelical Perfection." Reflecting Pius XII's vision, this chapter was positioned between those on the clergy and the laity. This draft was rejected for many reasons.[12] Among the many suggested alterations, a number of fathers requested that more attention be paid to the call of every member of the church, not just religious, to holiness and personal sanctification.[13] A second draft abolished the separate section on religious. Discussion of them was moved "into the chapters entitled, respectively, 'The People of God with Special Reference to the Laity' and 'The Call to Holiness in the Church.'"[14] These two chapters followed initial chapters on the mystery of the church and the hierarchy. Now, however, religious present at the Council began to feel ignored and raised many objections. The final decision was to create again a chapter

12. See Philips, "Dogmatic Constitution on the Church: The History of the Constitution," *Commentary* 1:106–10; Jan Grootars, "The Drama Continues between the Acts: The 'Second Preparation' and Its Opponents," in Alberigo and Komonchak, *History of Vatican II*, 2:408–10.

13. Grootars, "Drama Continues between the Acts," 2:409.

14. Gabriel O'Donnell, "The Renewal of Religious Life," in Boguslawski and Fastiggi, *Called to Holiness and Communion*, 204.

specifically devoted to religious that would be located immediately after a chapter discussing the call to holiness in general.[15]

The final structure of the text of *Lumen Gentium* reflects the Council's vision of the relationship between religious life and the structure of the church. According to Gérard Philips, the *peritus* who served as *Lumen Gentium*'s primary drafter, the constitution has been organized in such a way that "there are always two chapters in unquestionably logical connection."[16] The first two chapters "give the doctrine on the mystery of the Church," the first "its transcendent dimension," the second "its historical realization" in the people of God. "Chapters III and IV then describe the organic structure of the church as Christ instituted it—that is, the functions of the pastors and ministers, and on the other part of the diptych, as it were, the tasks of the laity." In Chapters V and VI, the "schema passes on directly to the finality of the Church, the sanctification of all men."[17] Chapter V deals with the universal call to holiness. Chapter VI describes the religious life as a particular response to the call to holiness and a sign of the church's finality. Chapter VII deals with the church as a pilgrim people on its way to the kingdom, while Chapter VIII describes the eschatological church in glory, Mary, and the saints.

If Chapters III and IV describe the church's dominically instituted hierarchical structure, the placement of the chapter on religious life after the chapter on the universal call to holiness, and thus at a once-removed distance from Chapters III and IV, could be read to imply that religious life lies somewhere outside the structuring categories of the church. This would be a departure from Pius XII's vision of "religious as an intermediate state between clergy and laity."[18] The Council verifies that it is indeed moving away from Pius's framework. It states that the religious life should not be considered "an intermediate state between

15. Philips, "Dogmatic Constitution on the Church: The History of the Constitution," *Commentary* 1:122, 131.

16. Philips, "Dogmatic Constitution on the Church: The History of the Constitution," *Commentary* 1:131–32.

17. Philips, "Dogmatic Constitution on the Church: The History of the Constitution," *Commentary* 1:131.

18. Beyer, "Life Consecrated by the Evangelical Counsels," 3:71.

the clerical and lay states. But, rather, the faithful of Christ are called by God from both these states of life so that they might enjoy this particular gift in the life of the Church and thus each in one's own way, may be of some advantage to the salvific mission of the Church."[19]

According to Philips, the location of Chapter VI at a once-removed distance from Chapters III and IV indicates that religious life is a charismatic rather than hierarchical element in the church.[20] Although the Council did not actually use the word "charismatic" to describe religious life, it refers to religious life as a "particular gift" of God for some persons. This terminology may be read in light *Lumen Gentium* 12, which explains that the Holy Spirit enriches the church through both "sacraments" and "ministries" on the one hand and "special graces" or "charisms" on the other hand. Because *Lumen Gentium* 12 concerns the participation of the people of God in the prophetic office of Christ, there seems to be a strong association between charism and prophecy. Although it can be perilous to divide too neatly hierarchy from charisms, prophecy from priesthood, or sacraments from special graces,[21] *Lumen Gentium* 12 can be read as identifying two distinct dimensions of the church: "the hierarchical-ministerial-sacramental-authoritative" and the "prophetic-charismatic." In the last fifty years it has become some-

19. *LG* 43.

20. Philips explains: "The distinctions between hierarchy and faithful, between religious and non-religious, are not both valid on the same level. The first distinction is based on the divine institution of consecrated offices; the second on a special and charismatic type of call which is answered by those who promise to follow the three classical counsels.... There is no difficulty here, because the distinctions are on two different levels, that of the structure of the ecclesiastical community, and that of the particular ways along which the real end of the Church, holiness, is pursued"; Philips, "Dogmatic Constitution on the Church: The History of the Constitution," *Commentary* 1:123–4.

21. See Ratzinger, *Pilgrim Fellowship of Faith*, 178–87. Ratzinger emphasizes that the hierarchy is also charismatically ordered and that charisms are bestowed and nurtured through sacraments. Hans Küng says one would better speak of a "charismatic structure of the Church which embraces and goes beyond the structure of its government"; Küng, "The Charismatic Structure of the Church," *Concilium* 4 (1965): 30–31. On the perils of setting hierarchy and charism in opposition, see also Congar, *Called to Life*, 68; Congar, *Un Peuple Messianique: L'Église, sacrement du salut; Salut et libération* (Paris: Cerf, 1975), 81; and Congar, *I Believe in the Holy Spirit*, trans. David Smith (New York: Crossroad, 1983), 2:11.

what standard in magisterial teaching to associate religious life with the latter.[22]

Depending upon how the relationship between the charismatic and hierarchical dimensions is envisioned, different questions or problems emerge for religious priests. Basil Cole and Paul Conner represent one approach. They see the clergy as characterized by a "specific mission to govern the whole Church with order and discipline, to teach it with Jesus' authority and to sanctify it through his sacramental ministry."[23] Religious are characterized as prophetic (they have a duty to inspire the rest of the church to holiness) and charismatic, which they say attributes to religious life five characteristics:

> Religious life is a gift of the Spirit for the building up of the entire Church through inspiration and apostolic works (*PC* 1, *LG* 43). It manifests the Spirit of Christ as a powerful sign or witness (*LG* 44). It is not restricted to the hierarchy but is freely given outside it (*LG* 43). It is a stable grace, evidenced by the total dedication of those who receive it. And, finally, it continues to have special effectiveness among the People of God, as shown by its history.[24]

Drawing from the reflections of Ladislas Orsy, Cole and Conner see the hierarchical and charismatic dimensions of the church as reflecting different aspects of God's glory. The hierarchy "reveals his traits of order and discipline"; The charismatic dimension, typified by religious, "reveals those of beauty and spontaneous art."[25] Cole and Conner therefore see the two dimensions living in a kind of complementarity that is analogous to that of "husband and wife."[26]

For religious priests, this way of envisaging things presents a slight difficulty in that it starts with the presupposition that priesthood (as a hierarchical element) is exterior to religious life. Cole and Conner's

22. Cole and Conner, *Christian Totality*, 49. See Pope Paul VI, *Evangelica Testificatio* (June 29, 1971), 11 and 32; John Paul II, *Redemptionis Donum* (March, 25, 1984), 11 and 15; and John Paul II, *Vita Consecrata*, where charism is mentioned in almost every article.

23. Cole and Conner, *Christian Totality*, 47.

24. Cole and Conner, *Christian Totality*, 49.

25. Cole and Conner, *Christian Totality*, 47. See also Ladislas Orsy, *Open to the Spirit: Religious Life after Vatican II* (Washington, D.C.: Corpus, 1968).

26. Cole and Conner, *Christian Totality*, 47.

approach here reflects that of the Council itself. Although the Council clearly expresses in *Lumen Gentium* 43 that some clerics belong to religious life, the Council says nothing more about the meaning of priesthood in a religious context, such as how religious life and priesthood might condition each other in the vocation of a religious priest. Significantly, the longest discussion of the hierarchical ministry in Chapter VI of *Lumen Gentium* takes place in article 45, which describes how the hierarchy holds religious accountable and helps them to flourish. The only real image, therefore, of the relationship between priesthood and religious life portrayed in Chapter VI is one where the priesthood is envisioned as standing outside looking in on religious life. The vocations may be complementary, but what does that mean when the same person participates in both?

A second issue stems from the subordination of the charismatic dimension to the hierarchical one. Cole and Conner emphasize that "since God will never work at odds with himself, the prophetic or charismatic side of the Church must work in living harmony with the hierarchical side. Christ guarantees that he will be with the hierarchy 'until the end of time.' By divine authority the hierarchy must govern the prophetic side of the Church."[27] Cole and Conner's subordination of the charismatic to the hierarchical is fully in line with John Paul II, who said, "No charism dispenses a person from reference and submission to the *Pastors of the Church*,"[28] and with *Lumen Gentium*, which ascribes "judgment" of charisms' authenticity and "proper use" to "those who are appointed leaders in the Church."[29]

However true, this ordering inevitably introduces a tension for religious priests belonging to mixed communities where some are ordained (and thus belong to the governing hierarchy) and some are not. Chapter 4 explained that Benedictines seem to have had an early practice of subjecting priests to the authority of nonordained but charismatically gifted abbots. Francis similarly supported a series of lay superiors of his mixed community. If the charismatic pole is clearly subordinate to the hierarchical, can the "original design" of founders such as Benedict

27. Cole and Conner, *Christian Totality*, 47.

28. John Paul II, *Christifideles Laici* (December 30, 1988), 24; hereafter *CL*.

29. *LG* 12.

and Francis, who "envisaged a brotherhood in which all the members, priests and those who were not priests, were considered equal among themselves," be recovered?[30] Although some institutes have been given permission to have nonordained superiors governing clerical members, the justification for doing so remains a major theological debate.[31]

Sandra Schneiders represents a second approach to ordering the hierarchical and charismatic dimensions of the church. Rather than subordinating the latter to the former, she places them in a Hegelian tension. According to Schneiders, the church requires both "agents who will preserve and implement the current arrangements for the good of the people" and those who can call the church "beyond what is currently understood into the desert journey that leads toward the Reign of God."[32] The hierarchy, responsible for the church's stability and unity, occupies the former place: They have the "basic task" to "serve and preserve the Church as institution."[33] Religious occupy the latter place. They are prophetic persons who advance the "development of doctrine and the evolution of moral practice" by "[raising] questions, [suggesting] alternatives, and [standing] in solidarity with the outcast as the Church struggles toward a deeper unity than what now seems possible."[34] The charismatic freedom of religious,[35] their contemplative dedication, and their liberty from familial and material responsibilities ideally situate them to carry out the prophetic task.[36]

Schneiders's framework presents a different dilemma for religious priests. Religious have a charismatic call to be prophetic. She sees "the primary, although not exclusive addressee of prophecy" as "the Church

30. *VC* 61.

31. See R. Kevin Seasoltz, "Institutes of Consecrated Life and Ordained Ministry," in *A Concert of Charisms: Ordained Ministry in Religious Life*, ed. Paul K. Hennessy (New York: Paulist Press, 1997), 149–53.

32. Schneiders, *Finding the Treasure* (vol. 1 of *Religious Life in a New Millennium*), 271.

33. Schneiders, *Finding the Treasure*, 270.

34. Schneiders, *Finding the Treasure*, 271–22.

35. Schneiders emphatically describes the charismatic freedom of religious: because the religious life is a "gift of God to the Church," "independent in its origin of the Church as hierarchical institution," "the institution that did not invent that life cannot impose it, and must not impede it"; Schneiders, *Finding the Treasure*, 285.

36. Schneiders, *Finding the Treasure*, 272.

itself, including and even especially its institutional embodiment."[37] Schneiders believes that it is difficult for priests to take the prophetic stances that religious should take. Priests have a ministry of unity, and, when they attempt to take prophetic stances, they risk alienating those in the church who are "sincerely convinced that only in obedience to current church teaching can the gospel be lived and preached."[38] Simply put, priests are persons "charged with the pastoral care of the parish congregation as a whole and its relation to the wider institutional church"; therefore, "it may not be possible or desirable" for them "to explicitly and publicly take on official persons or positions with which" priests "might seriously disagree in private."[39]

Although I must disagree with Schneiders's perception that the primary addressee of prophecy is the church itself, and with some of the specific prophetic stances she has in mind,[40] she does effectively highlight the tension that can exist between the hierarchical and prophetic vocations. As Brian Daley notes, religious life has been historically characterized by "Spirit-filled criticism" of society, and sometimes of the church.[41] For Schneiders, priesthood and religious life can be combined only at the risk of great compromise: the priest must preserve unity, sometimes by "insuring or enforcing institutional conformity," and the religious must prophetically challenge the status quo.[42] This is one reason Schneiders concludes against religious priesthood: "There may not be an intrinsic theological incompatibility between the two vocations," she says, "but there is a serious question about whether, in practice, a particular individual or congregation in the present moment of the Church history can live both of them integrally at the same time."[43] In part I of this book, we saw that religious priests have always had to navigate a tension between the ideals of religious life and min-

37. Schneiders, *Finding the Treasure*, 270.

38. Schneiders, *Finding the Treasure*, 270–71.

39. Schneiders, *Finding the Treasure*, 271.

40. For the kind of prophetic stances she has in mind, see Schneiders, *Finding the Treasure*, 271.

41. Daley, "Ministry of Disciples," 622.

42. Schneiders, *Finding the Treasure*, 271.

43. Schneiders, *Finding the Treasure*, 273.

isterial duties and that they have stood as a bridge between institution and movements of reform. Schneiders is skeptical about how successful that navigation and bridging can really be.

Religious Life Defined by the Evangelical Counsels

Returning to the structure of *Lumen Gentium*, Philips implies that the Council's coupling of Chapter VI, on religious, with Chapter V, on the universal call to holiness, is as important as its distancing of Chapter VI from chapters III and IV on the hierarchical structure of the church. This coupling of chapters V and VI contextually frames religious life as, above all, a way of pursuing sanctity. At the end of the Chapter V, which acknowledges that all Christians are "called to holiness" and "the perfection of charity," the evangelical counsels are acknowledged as a "special way" of responding to the general call to holiness.[44] Chapter VI begins by identifying religious as those persons in the church who are vowed to the counsels: "The faithful of Christ bind themselves to the three aforesaid counsels either by vows, or by other sacred bonds, which are like vows in their purpose."[45] In this way religious, like clerics and laity before them in chapters III and IV, have been given a definition in the church; this definition consists of their avowal to the counsels that are a way of responding to the general call to holiness.

Some commentators believe that *Lumen Gentium*'s distancing of the discussion of religious life from the two chapters on the church's structure, chapters that also include considerable reflection on the unique ministerial and missiological tasks of clerics and laity, and placement of the discussion of religious within a treatment of the call to holiness, fostered an incomplete vision of religious life. According to its critics, Chapter VI inadequately presents the public missiological significance of religious life and instead portrays it too much as a private spiritual option, somewhat accidental to the church. For Jean Beyer, "confining [religious] to a single chapter on the vocation to holiness meant that their identity and the importance of their state of life were lost,

44. *LG* 39, 42.
45. *LG* 44.

and their role in the Church was downplayed."[46] Gabriel O'Donnell agrees. The place and content of Chapter VI, he argues, "effected a certain 'muting' of [religious life's] central role and importance within the Church.... As a consequence, the Council might be judged somewhat ambivalent about the religious life, its role in the Church's mission and its witness to the mystery of the transcendent."[47]

Council *peritus* Wulf offers the most constructive critique: according to him, the religious life, constituted by communities of persons publicly vowed to the evangelical counsels, because it is "intelligible only in terms of the mystery of redemption," "refers men to the inmost mystery of the Church" and is an "indispensable" public sign in the Church's mission to the nations.[48] The charism of religious life is always "given for the sake of the Church and her redemptive mission."[49] He sees this truth best reflected in article 44 of Chapter VI, which describes religious life as a special sign of the Kingdom, of the incarnate life of the Son of God, and of the relativity of earthly things that should inspire all Christians onward toward greater holiness. Wulf thinks the public-sign quality of religious life should have framed the entire discussion of religious. Unfortunately, he says, the "affirmations" of the missiological importance of religious as signs "seem rather feeble compared with what they ought to be"; the reason is that the "theological

46. Beyer, "Life Consecrated by the Evangelical Counsels," 3:71.

47. O'Donnell, "Renewal of Religious Life," 205; For another critique, see Elizabeth McDonough, "*De Accommodate Renovatione*: Between the Idea and the Reality; Occasion and Intent and Consequences of Vatican Council II," in *Apostolic Religious Life in America Today: A Response to the Crisis*, ed. Richard Gribble (Washington, D.C.: The Catholic University of America Press, 2011), 67–90. A notable exception to these critiques comes from Joseph Cardinal Tobin, former Archbishop Secretary of the Congregation for Institutes of Consecrated Life and Societies of Apostolic Life, who argued that the distancing of Chapter VI from chapters III and IV did not diminish religious life's significance but highlighted it precisely by indicating that the life of holiness transcends the hierarchical categories of clergy and laity; see Tobin, "A Great History Still to Be Accomplished?: Prospects for Consecrated Life in the Church-Communio," in *God Has Begun a Great Work in Us: Embodied Love in Consecrated Life and Ecclesial Movements*, ed. Jason King and Susan Schrein (Maryknoll, N.Y.: Orbis, 2014), 91.

48. Wulf, "Dogmatic Constitution on the Church," Chapter VI, "Religious," in *Commentary* 1:274.

49. Wulf, "Dogmatic Constitution on the Church," Chapter VI, "Religious," in *Commentary* 1:274.

setting" of the chapter, which has been determined by the context of the personal pursuit of holiness rather than the intrinsic public missiological significance of this life of holiness, was wrong from the onset.[50]

Wulf notes that the public missiological significance of religious life was "controversial" at the Council, with several fathers warning that it should not "obscure the importance of the counsels as admirable means to personal sanctification."[51] This bias, along with the fact that the chapter follows the one on the universal call to holiness, explains why the chapter on religious begins not with the discussion of the public missiological significance of religious but with a discussion of the counsels in terms of personal spirituality. Religious communities, rather than being corporate eschatological signs with collective missiological purposes, are primarily portrayed as supports to individuals in their pursuit of perfection. According to Wulf, the opening article sets the tone for the rest of the chapter, and, despite a more complete treatment of missiology in article 44, "the editors of the chapter did not quite succeed in ... tying in the individual aspect of a religious vocation—personal sanctification—with its apostolic aspect—service of one's brethren—in the mystery of the Church."[52]

For the purposes of this study, a final point should be made about *Lumen Gentium*, Chapter VI. As John O'Malley and other commentators have pointed out, although the chapter defines religious as those committed to the evangelical counsels, the chapter neglects to distinguish religious life from other vocations in the church that also commit in some way to the evangelical counsels (for instance, consecrated virgins, hermits, diocesan priests, members of secular institutes, and societies of apostolic life).[53] It is true that the evangelical counsels are

50. Wulf, "Dogmatic Constitution on the Church," Chapter VI, "Religious," in *Commentary* 1:277.

51. Wulf, "Dogmatic Constitution on the Church," Chapter VI, "Religious," in *Commentary* 1:277.

52. Wulf, "Dogmatic Constitution on the Church," Chapter VI, "Religious," in *Commentary* 1:274.

53. O'Malley, "Priesthood, Ministry, and Religious Life," 223; Beyer, "Life Consecrated by the Evangelical Counsels," 3:66; McDonough, "*De Accommodate Renovatione,*" 78; O'Brien and Schaumber, conclusion to *The Foundations of Religious Life*, 181; O'Donnell, "Renewal of Religious Life," 204.

central to religious identity and that religious life cannot be understood without them. It is also true that just because a central point of one's identity overlaps with the identity of others, this should not deter one from accepting it as a central component of one's own identity.[54] Nonetheless, there still must be a point of distinction between religious and these other vocations if religious life is to make any sense or have any appeal. *Lumen Gentium* does not clarify this difference.

Religious Life as Apostolic

The Council fathers had a second opportunity to unveil the meaning of religious life in the decree *Perfectae Caritatis*.[55] Although some figures considered the decree "superfluous" because *Lumen Gentium* had already treated religious, others, "who were or had been religious, regarded it as almost a point of honor that the Council should promulgate a document pertaining to their state."[56] *Perfectae Caritatis* allowed for continued discussion of some points left ambiguous in *Lumen Gentium* and therefore "represents" a continued "search for identity" for religious within the renewal of the church.[57]

Perfectae Caritatis continues the general framework of *Lumen Gentium*. Article 2 defines religious by the practice of the evangelical counsels. The authors have taken more care than in *Lumen Gentium* to defend the counsels as not just one possible spiritual option among many, but as a particularly esteemed and privileged form of life. The counsels are located at the very origins of the church with Christ and his closest disciples. The life of the counsels is said to be a closer imitation of Christ, a fuller expression of baptismal consecration, and a "special" bond with the Lord.[58]

More than in *Lumen Gentium*, the intrinsic missiological orien-

54. Philosopher Charles Taylor has commented on the unfortunate modern, and particularly American, tendency to need to locate personal identity exclusively in unique characteristics unshared by others. See his *Sources of the Self: The Making of Modern Identity* (Cambridge, Mass.: Harvard University Press, 1989), 32–52, esp. 39–40.

55. Vatican Council II, *Perfectae Caritatis* (October 28, 1965); hereafter *PC*.

56. Norman Tanner, Chapter V, "The Church in the World," in Alberigo and Komonchak, *History of Vatican II*, 4:364–65.

57. Beyer, "Life Consecrated by the Evangelical Counsels," 3:73.

58. *PC* 1 and 5.

tation of the life of the counsels is acknowledged throughout the text. Commitment to the counsels is commitment to live for both Christ and the church.[59] Commitment to the counsels makes religious available for good works and prepares them spiritually for official ministry, and advancement in holiness by those in the counsels contributes to the grace and apostolic efficacy of the whole church.[60] Poverty, chastity, and the common life are each discussed as incarnational and eschatological signs to the church and the world; obedience is ordered to service after the pattern of Christ.[61]

O'Malley, preferring a description of religious that characterizes them more explicitly according to the kinds of ministry they have performed in the church, laments that only two of the twenty-five articles of *Perfectae Caritatis* directly concern ministry.[62] He is correct that the decree does not provide a portrait of the specific ministries undertaken by religious. It says only that "apostolic religious life takes on many forms."[63] However, it should be noted that the document acknowledges in almost every article that religious life is not exhausted by commitment to poverty, chastity, and obedience, but includes apostolic works of service. This is true not only for institutes founded for particular apostolic works, but also for monastic communities that "have legitimately undertaken some apostolate or work of Christian charity" and for mendicants who "join the apostolic life to choir duty and monastic observances."[64] Even the hidden life of strictly cloistered contemplative religious is apostolically efficacious: They "offer to God a sacrifice of praise which is outstanding. Moreover the manifold results of their holiness lends luster to the people of God which is inspired by their example and which gains new members by their apostolate which is as effective as it is hidden."[65] Still, a more detailed depiction of what religious apostolic work looks like in practice would have been helpful. Inasmuch as specialized ministry could be included as an identifying mark of religious

59. *PC* 1 and 5.
60. *PC* 1.
61. *PC* 12–15.
62. These are *PC* 8 and 20; O'Malley, "Priesthood, Ministry, and Religious Life," 249.
63. *PC* 8.
64. *PC* 9.
65. *PC* 7.

life, this lacuna contributes to the truth that *Perfectae Caritatis,* like *Lumen Gentium,* neglects to establish a good distinction between religious and others committed to the counsels.

As for religious priesthood, *Perfectae Caritatis* certainly does not preclude it. Religious life is acknowledged as having preparatory value for ministry,[66] and there is a certain acknowledgment of the existence of religious priests.[67] On the other hand, the text is more interested in affirming the value of the religious life in its own right "without sacerdotal associations."[68] For this reason, and perhaps because there is little in the way of elaborating upon the unique types of ministry engaged by religious, the questions of how religious life informs priesthood or how priesthood is expressed in a religious modality go unanswered.

Religious Life as Faithful to the Charisms of Founders

A final important feature of Vatican II's teaching on religious life is *Perfectae Caritatis'* appeal to religious to "return to the sources" and recover the "original spirit" of their institutes.[69] Even before Vatican II, some scholars had already begun the process of *ressourcement* and were raising questions about the place of priesthood in religious life. Perhaps more than any other Vatican II current,[70] *ressourcement* had consequences for religious priesthood.

Benedictines of the first half of the twentieth century had learned about monasticism from figures such as Columba Marmion and Paul DeLatte, who had raised no doubts about the harmony of monasticism and priesthood. Marmion was convinced that the center of priestly work was "praise and intercession" "in the highest degree efficacious for the salvation of the world."[71] Therefore, a priest who had dedicated

66. *PC* 1.

67. *PC* 10 and 15.

68. Irwin, "On Monastic Priesthood," 244.

69. *PC* 2.

70. O'Malley holds that of the three principles of change evoked at Vatican II—*ressourcement,* development, and *aggiornamento*—"*ressourcement* was the most traditional yet potentially the most radical"; O'Malley, *What Happened at Vatican II,* 301.

71. Columba Marmion, *Christ the Ideal of the Priest,* trans. Matthew Dillon (San Francisco: Ignatius Press, 2005), 259.

his life to prayer in a monastery had not abandoned anything essential to the priesthood, but had chosen to focus on what was most essential. Delatte even taught that because ordination brought a further consecration and a particular conformity to Christ, "a choir composed of priests and clerics is able to offer more perfect praise to the Lord than would a choir of lay religious."[72]

Starting in the 1940s, the works of Pachomius, Cassian, and the *Apophthegmata* (the sayings of the desert fathers) began to be made widely available through the Sources Chrétiennes project. Scholars of monasticism discovered a more negative attitude among the ancients toward ordained monks. In the 1950s, Oratorian Louis Bouyer published books on *The Life of St Anthony* and *The Meaning of Monastic Life* in which he argued for a monasticism that was more faithful to the desert tradition, a monasticism that was centered on a personal quest for God by way of asceticism and contemplative prayer.[73] Bouyer took a very cautious view toward monastic priesthood, saying that no monk should be ordained who had not "reached perfection in the essential of his monastic task."[74] Bouyer's works were highly influential, especially in France, and belonged to a wave of contemplative reform in Western monasticism during the postwar period.

In subsequent years, a number of other prominent scholars of monasticism echoed Bouyer and "spoke negatively about the relationship between priesthood and monasticism."[75] Strong biases among the ancients against ordination, coupled with Vatican II's portrayal of priests as actively engaged in pastoral work, led these scholars to see medieval clericalization as a violation of the monastic spirit. Some argued for a reduction in the number of monastic priests to the minimum necessary for a community's own liturgical needs. Others, more radically, placed monasticism and priesthood in fundamental opposition.[76] There were,

72. Quoted in Lescher, "Laybrothers," 84.

73. See Bouyer, *The Meaning of the Monastic Life*, trans. Kathleen Pond (New York: P. J. Kenedy, 1955); Bouyer, *La Vie de S. Antoine: Essai sur la Spiritualité de Monachisme Primitif* (Abbaye S. Wandrille: Editions de Fontenelle, 1950).

74. Bouyer, *Meaning of the Monastic Life*, 166.

75. Irwin, "On Monastic Priesthood," 248.

76. Irwin, "On Monastic Priesthood," 248n62. Jean LeClercq has catalogued these voices; they include Jacques LeClercq, J.-M. R. Tillard, A. Fernandes, J. C. Guy, A.

of course, some scholars who took a more positive approach and sought to defend the importance of monastic priesthood. They pointed out that the opponents of monastic priesthood somewhat inexplicably prioritized the desert fathers over Benedict and Basil, the early medieval period of missionary monasticism, and the founding visions of most monasteries established within the last millennium.[77]

Franciscans also wrestled with the findings introduced by *ressourcement*. In 1968, Laureito Landini published his doctoral dissertation on the clericalization of the Franciscan order. He showed that at the beginnings of the movement Francis had desired to "create a community of equals" and that the nonordained friars enjoyed numerical primacy. Landini demonstrated a "discrepancy" between Francis' original vision and the face of Franciscanism by the 1260s. By then, the order was constituted primarily by "educated clerics with a 'useful' mission (i.e., preaching and hearing confessions)" requiring orders. The 1260 *Constitutions of Narbonne* legislated against the "acceptance of the unlettered" and excluded the nonordained "from office and governance in the fraternity." Landini showed that clericalization had "touched issues of recruitment, formation, education, prayer, fraternity, mission and the interpretation of poverty"; therefore, "it impacted the integrity of the fraternity's witness to the vision of Francis of Assisi." Landini himself took a moderate view of the clericalization of the Franciscans, arguing that, despite some negative effects, the phenomenon was important for the "friars becoming pastorally useful" to the church; furthermore, it was "a partial consequence of Francis's own commitment, for himself and his successors," to obedience before the demands of the hierarchy, particularly the papacy. In the wake of Landini, however, some scholars of Franciscanism argued that clericalization of the Franciscans had been a true "betrayal of the charism," bringing "the loss of a distinctive

Guillaumont, G. Huyghe, E. von Ivànka, H. I. Marrou, G. Ramsey, M. Schmaus, L. J. M. Verheijen, H. Vogrimler, and H. R. Weber; see LeClercq, "Témoinages contemporains sur la théologie du monachisme," *Gregorianum* 48 (1967): 65–66. For a report on the most radical position, see Daniel Rees, *Consider Your Call: A Theology of Monastic Life Today* (Kalamazoo, Mich.: Cistercian Press, 1978), 323–24.

77. See Irwin, "On Monastic Priesthood"; McGregor, "Monastic Life and the Priesthood," 112–13; Rees, *Consider Your Call*, 335–41.

mission" both in "the practice of poverty" and in the "witness to a communal understanding and practice of Church."[78]

The majority of Franciscan and Benedictine communities neither prohibited nor significantly restricted the ordination of their members after the Council. Nonetheless, for them and for others, *ressourcement* opened questions about the meaning of priesthood in religious life. One issue was the navigation of the divisions that priesthood appeared to create in the community. *Ressourcement* involved confronting the fact that over the centuries, membership had become too strongly divided between those who were ordained and those who were not, and that that state of things was not in conformity with their founders' visions of mixed communities of equals.

Before the Council, it was common for ordained and nonordained to have separate formation tracks, to eat and socialize separately, and to engage in very different types of work, with the former often involved in preaching and teaching and the latter often performing manual labor. In most communities, nonordained religious did not hold chapter rights, could not vote, and could not hold offices of governance within the order.[79] In the years following Vatican II, "the notion of common 'brotherhood'" became increasingly important; communities deemed it necessary to emphasize the "equal status" of brothers and priests.[80] Restoring the commonality and equality envisioned by the founders and Vatican II was interpreted as a need to minimize distinctions between ordained and nonordained.[81] Communities were socially inte-

78. Joseph Chinnici, "The Impact of Clericalization on Franciscan Evangelization," in Saggau, *Franciscan Evangelization*, 82–87. For examples of those who argued strongly that clericalization violated the integrity of the Franciscan charism, see Théophile Desbonnets, *From Institution to Institution: The Franciscans* (Chicago: Franciscan Herald Press,1988); David Flood, *Francis of Assisi and the Franciscan Movement* (Philippines: Quezon, 1989). Chinnici attempts a more constructive, positive approach at 88–122, esp. 103ff.

79. See Cyprian Davis, "The Liturgy, Inculturation, and the Renewal of Religious Life," in *Vatican II: Fifty Personal Stories*, ed. William Madges and Michael J. Daley (Maryknoll, N.Y.: Orbis, 2003), 78–79; Roland J. Faley, "An American Experience of Religious Life," in Hennessey, *Concert of Charisms*, 111–18; Rosen, "Fostering the Patrimony of the Order of Friars Minor Capuchin," 283–86.

80. Faley, "An American Experience of Religious Life," 111.

81. As Elizabeth McDonough points out, the sociological zeitgeist of the 1960s was

grated. Formation, apart from the exception of the seminary, would be the same for those preparing for ordination and those who were not. It became more acceptable for ordained members to engage in manual work and for nonordained members to preach and teach. Nonordained brothers received chapter rights and could vote in community elections. Precedence within the community was no longer based on ordination but upon date of entry.

Nonetheless, it was impossible to erase every distinction. *Perfectae Caritatis* 15 stated that mixed communities could include both nonordained and ordained members "on an equal footing and with equal rights and obligations, excepting those which flow from sacred orders." The difficulty was in identifying just how much arose out of sacred orders. Could, for example, the nonordained be elected or appointed as superiors over clerics? Most Franciscan and all male Benedictine communities are considered clerical institutes by canon law, due to their history and present reality of having many ordained members. As such, their major superiors are considered ordinaries and must be ordained. Some institutes received the privilege, by way of "indults or exception," for nonordained to "serve as local superiors, councilors, or vicars,"[82] but not as major superiors. Also, there remain theological and canonical debates about how to understand placing nonordained persons in positions of authority over ordained ones. Sandra Schneiders notes that while religious sisters were able to overcome quickly the class distinctions between their choir and extern members (as the Council challenged them to do),[83] mixed male communities were unable to achieve quite the same success. This was due in part, says Schneiders, to the difficulty of accepting nonordained members as superiors over ordained ones.[84]

St. Benedict presented the priestly distinction as coming into play

---

also important in inspiring this equalizing movement, especially in light of Vatican II's request for "adaptation" of religious life "to the changed conditions of our time"; see McDonough, *De Accommodate Renovatione*, 70–74.

82. Schneiders, *Finding the Treasure*, 274.

83. "Unless conditions really suggest something else, care should be taken that there be only one class of Sisters in communities of women." The aim is "to arrive at but one category of sisters in women's institutes"; *PC* 15.

84. Schneiders, *Finding the Treasure*, 273.

primarily in liturgical settings (*RB* 60 and 62). But even here, some religious after the Council felt that holy orders too strongly divided the community. Concelebration, for example, "which was initially welcomed as a liturgical expression of a common priesthood, frequently became seen as divisive in separating brothers and priests."[85] Many religious priests, under the pressure of others or by their own choice, began to take a place at liturgy among the nonordained.[86]

A second question *ressourcement* raised for religious was parochialization. During the nineteenth century, in North America and other mission territories, Benedictines, Franciscans, and many other religious orders had taken on an increased involvement in parochial work. This gravitation was due mainly to episcopal pressures stemming from pastoral needs in mission territories.[87] As a result of *ressourcement*, twentieth-century religious questioned whether parish work truly corresponded to their original charism. Many concluded that it did not, and, moreover, that it seemed to have a negative effect on their orders. It distracted them from community life and specialized ministry and led to a disproportionate number of priests in mixed communities. All of this seemed incongruous with the original charism. Others opined that parish work should be embraced as an authentic historical development of their charism. Some held that, after the Council, priesthood only made sense in a parochial context and that religious, rather than restricting priesthood, should embrace parish ministry as a new way of realizing their charism. Debates over the degree to which religious should continue in parish work have been fervent since the Second Vatican Council.[88]

By contrast, for Dominicans, Jesuits, and other mainly clerical institutes, priesthood had been present from the beginning and was too central to the identity of their orders for the question of whether they

85. Faley, "An American Experience of Religious Life," 111.

86. Faley, "An American Experience of Religious Life," 111; Irwin, "On Monastic Priesthood," 256.

87. Mertens, "Franciscans in Parochial Ministry," 528–45; LeClercq, "Monachisme, sacerdoce et missions au Moyen Age," 322–23. As Mertens points out, a second contributing factor was enlightenment emphasis on the utility of orders.

88. Mertens, "Franciscans in Parochial Ministry," 523–26, 549–54; Rees, *Consider Your Call*, 322–25, 336–41.

should restrict ordination to arise in any substantial way. Although they also had to navigate the questions of parochialization and the integration of nonordained members, for them the more immediate concern after Vatican II was that the images of priesthood and religious life provided by the conciliar documents did not seem to correspond well with their own traditions. A number of Jesuits and Dominicans published works drawing attention to this problem.[89] The next section includes a review of the arguments of one of their most important spokespersons, John O'Malley.

Is Religious Priesthood a Compromise of the Religious Life or the Priesthood?

Most discussions about the compatibility of priesthood and religious life have been carried out within the context of particular religious families. Therefore, the debates have centered on the question of how priesthood relates to particular charisms—for instance, the Benedictine or Franciscan. Exceptions are Sandra Schneiders, who argues that priesthood violates the integrity of religious life, and John O'Malley, who laments that Vatican II's teachings on priesthood make it appear that the typically religious ways of being a priest no longer fit the church's vision of ordained ministry.

On the basis of the fourth-century origins of religious life, Vatican II teaching, and the often-contentious experience of male religious after the Council, Schneiders concludes against the desirability of combining the priestly and religious vocations. She offers several reasons. First, "ordination introduces into religious life a fundamental tension between an intrinsically hierarchical vocation and a prophetic one."[90] This objection has been discussed previously. Schneiders sees priests as responsible for

89. See Jesuits: H. J. Lauter, "De Ordenpriester," in *Ordenkorrespondenz* 13 (1973): 134–38; Harmless, "Jesuits as Priests: Crisis and Charism," 25–28; Daley, "In Ten Thousand Places," 15–29; F. Taborda, "Il Religioso presbitero: una questione discussa," in *Vita Consecrata* 38 (2002): 626–40. Dominicans: Paul J. Philibert, "Priesthood within the Context of Religious Life," in *Being a Priest Today*, ed. Donald J. Goergen (Collegeville, Minn.: Liturgical Press, 1992), 73–96; Anthony Fisher, "Reflections on Priesthood in the Dominican Order," *New Blackfriars* 92 (November 2011): 651–63.

90. Schneiders, *Finding the Treasure*, 269.

maintaining institutional unity and religious as being charged with prophetic ecclesial reform. She argues that it is difficult for the same person to respond to both callings. Schneiders's second reason is the one voiced by Pachomius in the fourth century: ordination introduces class structures into an otherwise egalitarian form of life. As Schneiders puts it, "There is some kind of intrinsic and ontological superiority associated with ordination."[91] Although she is not entirely satisfied with this theology of priesthood, she believes that as long as it stands, ordination will remain "the principle of class in the church."[92] Schneiders says the presence of ordained members compromises the evangelical calling of religious to reflect the eschatological equality and unity portrayed in the Acts of the Apostles. Even in those communities that are most sensitive to the equality of their members, the fact that some are ordained creates liturgical inequalities: "Only certain members ... always lead ... in liturgy." They are "the only lawful liturgical preachers, regardless of their gifts." This results in "a two-tiered worshipping community, which could well be more divisive" than the "situation" of communities who depend on "non-members" for the sacraments.[93]

Schneiders's third reason for opposing ordination of religious is that linking religious life to the priesthood introduces a double set of allegiances "to the authority and community structures of the religious order on the one hand and to the diocesan authority and presbyteral structure on the other."[94] Although Schneiders accepts that there is a need to integrate "the ministries of religious into the diocesan structure," she fears that the canonical relationship between priest and the bishop, whereby the former promises obedience to and receives faculties from the latter, cannot help but compromise the principle of religious "exemption" that has historically allowed religious communities to "enjoy not only legitimate autonomy in regard to their internal life but a certain trans-diocesan type of ministry."[95]

91. Schneiders, *Finding the Treasure*, 273

92. Schneiders, *Finding the Treasure*, 273.

93. Schneiders, *Finding the Treasure*, 276.

94. Schneiders, *Finding the Treasure*, 276.

95. Schneiders, *Finding the Treasure*, 276. Schneiders perceives that ordained religious have less protection than nonordained religious from overreaching bishops. Should the religious priest "deviate in any way from official Church policy or practice,"

Schneiders perceives that in the contest of allegiances that sometimes arises between duties and involvement with one's community and pastoral commitment to the local church, it is the latter that usually emerges victorious. Despite the negative effects parochial commitment can have on religious common life,[96] religious priests are influenced by the needs of the church to embrace it. According to Schneiders, the tension between parish and diocese on the one hand, and religious life on the other, unfortunately

> tends to be handled by simply allowing the ordained to be assimilated to whatever degree seems necessary or desirable to him into the diocesan presbyteral structure with a corresponding suspension of whatever aspects of community life are incompatible with that assimilation. Many ordained religious are, in effect, diocesan ordained ministers with congregational letters after their names.[97]

Schneiders's fourth reason for resisting the ordination of religious concerns the identity bestowed by seminary formation. Those on track for ordination are set apart from those who are not. Schneiders fears the emergence of inequalities within the community that results from this scenario and the possible effect such inequalities will have on group unity. Furthermore, religious seminarians, especially those from com-

---

he faces "suspension of faculties to preach or preside sacramentally, administrative leave from pastoral responsibilities," and "refusal of assignment to ordained ministry in the diocese" (277). Recalling what Schneiders said earlier about the fundamentally prophetic orientation of religious life, it is clear why she thinks every possible effort should be made to protect the principle of exemption.

96. Magisterial teaching has recognized this. According to the 1994 Vatican document "Fraternal Life in Community," it is true that "in some regions, the difficulties of living in community while being active in parish ministry create considerable tension for religious priests. At times, the heavy commitment to pastoral work in the parish is carried out to the detriment of the institute's charism and to community life, to the point that parishioners, secular clergy and even religious themselves lose sight of the particular nature of religious life. Urgent pastoral needs must never lead us to forget that the best service a religious community can give to the Church is that of being faithful to its charism. This is also reflected in accepting responsibility for parishes and running them. Preference should be given to parishes which allow a community to live as community and where the religious can express their charism"; Congregation for Institutes of Consecrated Life and Societies of Apostolic Life, "Fraternal Life in Community," *Origins* 23, no. 40 (March 24, 1994): 708–9 (no. 61); hereafter *FLC*.

97. Schneiders, *Finding the Treasure*, 277.

munities in which only a few are ordained, may spend years in seminaries, among mostly diocesan seminarians, away from their community. Complicating the situation, contemporary seminary formation "is largely structured by the provisions for the formation of diocesan clergy": It assumes parochial ministry and provides little training for ministries more typical of those in religious life such as "university teaching, work in publication, or in foreign missions."[98] This formation results in the religious priest being distanced from his community and his core identity as religious.

Coming from a different vantage point, O'Malley has argued that Vatican II makes it appear that the historical ministry and lifestyle of religious priests are a compromise of the church's vision for priestly life and ministry today. In a 1988 essay, he argued that the image of priesthood provided by Vatican II was "inadequate to the historical reality" of religious priesthood in at least three ways.[99] The Council, he says, portrays priesthood as (1) a "ministry by and large to the faithful"; (2) a "ministry conceived as taking place in a stable community of faith"; and (3) a ministry done by clergy in "hierarchical union with the order of bishops."[100]

O'Malley argued that this portrayal of priesthood was inadequate because, in the tradition of religious priesthood, "ministry was not

98. Schneiders, *Finding the Treasure*, 277.

99. O'Malley, "Priesthood, Ministry, and Religious Life," 223. O'Malley's essay has been very influential. After its publication, the United States Conference of Major Superiors of Men conducted an inquiry of its members and discovered that the religious priests were indeed unsure about how to understand their vocation in light of Vatican II's presentation of priesthood. The CMSM established a taskforce for the further study of religious priesthood that resulted in a 1998 volume for which O'Malley wrote the introductory essay; Paul K. Hennessey, "Introduction: The Parochialization of the Church," in Hennessey, *A Concert of Charisms*, 4.The CMSM followed this volume by instituting "The Gift of Religious Priesthood Project," the first initiative of which was to produce a supplement to the *Program for Priestly Formation* (*PPF*) with suggestions for how seminaries can better form religious priests for their distinct ministry in the church. This document has been well received by the USCCB and several Vatican offices, and its historical background section incorporates the main lines of O'Malley's research. The document is "Formation for Presbyteral Ministry in Institutes of Religious Life: A Statement of the Members of the Conference of Major Superiors of Men," Conference of Major Superiors of Men, 2011.

100. O'Malley, "Priesthood, Ministry, and Religious Life," 224.

structured with an eye to a local and stable community, as symbolized by the parish, but transcended diocese and even nation." And, "although all the orders ministered to the faithful, they had a special interest in heretics, schismatics, [and] infidels." When they did minister to the faithful, they "tended to have a special interest in those whom the ordinary ministry of the Church for one reason or another failed to reach ... or, on the other hand, those laity seeking to devote themselves to God and their neighbor in more challenging and unconventional ways." This means religious priests were not pastors of stable flocks of the faithful; their "flocks" consisted of this or that person whom they sought out or who came to them at a given time. Last, their ministry was not conceived primarily in terms of "hierarchical relationship with the ordinary of the place," the bishop, or with the diocesan presbyterate, but in terms of their ministerial cooperation with one another, under the direction of their own superior, who was himself accountable only to the church's law and to the pope.[101]

In 1997, O'Malley wrote a follow-up essay in which he clarified a fourth problematic element he perceives in Vatican II's teaching: "The warrant for ministry, including preaching, is *ordination* to the diaconate or presbyterate."[102] In other words, there does not seem to be a ministerial dimension to religious life *qua* religious life for Vatican II. Religious life is described in the "framework of the three vows" to follow the evangelical counsels; "it is the framework of the personal search for spiritual perfection."[103] O'Malley argues that this view is inadequate for religious because ministry has been at the "center of the self-understanding" of the "majority of orders and congregations founded since the 13th century."[104] "Ministry," he says, "is not something one adds to one's vocation as a Franciscan or Jesuit upon ordination to the priesthood, but something that was central and intrinsic from one's very first moment in the order."[105] For O'Malley, the image of priesthood at Vatican II is the im-

101. O'Malley, "Priesthood, Ministry, and Religious Life," 251.

102. O'Malley, "One Priesthood: Two Traditions," in Hennessey, *Concert of Charisms*, 13.

103. O'Malley, "Priesthood, Ministry, and Religious Life," 249.

104. O'Malley, "Priesthood, Ministry, and Religious Life," 255.

105. O'Malley, "Priesthood, Ministry, and Religious Life," 256–57.

age of the diocesan parochial priest. The image of religious life is limited to spirituality. Neither portrait captures the essence of the apostolic religious vocation, particularly that of the religious priest.

This chapter has shown that O'Malley has overstated things by claiming that Vatican II is indifferent to the missiological/ministerial orientation of religious life. On the other hand, he seems to be right on target when he says that the Council's image of priesthood is that of the diocesan parish priest. As such, religious priesthood, inasmuch as it has been a ministry conducted independently of typical parochial and diocesan frameworks, appears to be a compromise of the Conciliar vision of priesthood.

Conclusion to Part II

Chapters 4 and 5 have attended mainly to lines of thought that maximize the problem of religious priesthood. They have attempted to show that the question of religious priesthood is anything but a "false dilemma."[106] The teachings of Vatican II and postconciliar theological reflection pose numerous challenges to religious priesthood. First, Vatican II does not provide an image of religious priesthood. The figure of the priest is mostly absent in the Council's discussions of religious life. Similarly, there is little discussion of religious priests where the theology of ordained ministry is presented. This lacuna is itself an issue: Religious priests appear to be, at best, a hybrid of two vocations discussed separately by the Council.

Second, Vatican II's teaching on priesthood reflects a diocesan-parochial model. It presents priests as attached to a local church, its bishop, and its presbytery; as exercising all three *munera*; and as pastors, presumably of a "stable flock of the faithful." As O'Malley points out, religious priests do not appear to fit the Council's vision of priesthood. This has led a number of thinkers to argue implicitly or explicitly against religious priesthood.

Third, Vatican II's teaching on religious life also poses challenges for religious priests. Religious are no longer considered a hierarchical

106. Cole and Conner argue that the problem of religious priesthood is a "false dilemma." For their argument, see Cole and Conner, *Christian Totality*, 349.

element in the church but are associated with its charismatic dimension. The charismatic and hierarchical sides of the church are in some kind of complementary relationship, but religious priests occupy both poles. This dual position invites questions regarding the identity and role of religious priests in ecclesial life and about the exercise of authority in mixed communities of religious. Also, religious life is defined in relationship to the evangelical counsels. However, this definition does not help religious understand how they differ from diocesan priests and others whom the Council also encourages to embrace the evangelical counsels. Next, the Council portrays religious life as inherently apostolic, but does not make explicit how the mission of religious institutes conditions the priesthood or how priesthood might condition the religious life. Last, Vatican II called upon religious to recover the original charism of their founders. This invitation has led both scholars and communities to reconsider the place of priesthood in religious life. Questions have been raised about the divisions and inequalities introduced by priesthood, about the appropriateness of parish work, and about the correspondence of religious identity with the identity bestowed by seminary formation.

Pope Paul VI encouraged religious priests not to see their ordinations as a deviation from their religious ideals,[107] and John Paul II once stated that religious priests ought to be able to find a "dynamic unity" between their religious and priestly vocations.[108] The question is how to do so. Is there a way to understand the identity and mission of the religious priest that honors both what he shares with the diocesan priest and nonordained religious and what differentiates him? Is there a way to do this that does not appear to compromise either the religious or priestly vocations? Is religious priesthood worth the tensions it introduces? Fresh perspectives are needed, and to these we now turn.

107. Paul VI, "Ai Superiori Maggiori degli Ordini e Congregazione Religiose," in *Insegnamenti di Paolo VI* (Vatican City: Tipographia Poliglotta Vaticana, 1966), 4:574–75.

108. *VC* 30.

PART 3

HANS URS VON BALTHASAR'S THEOLOGY OF VOCATIONS AND STATES OF LIFE

CHAPTER 6

Key Concepts in Balthasar's Theology of Vocations

We've just seen how Vatican II's teaching on priesthood and religious life posed some challenges for understanding religious priesthood. The Council did not provide a portrait of religious priesthood. Its presentation of priesthood was built on a diocesan/parochial paradigm, and its presentation of religious life was mostly without reference to ordained religious. Not surprisingly, after the Council, a number of thinkers interpreted and developed Vatican II's theology in such a way that presented priesthood and religious life as incompatible. We now turn to Hans Urs von Balthasar's theology of vocations as a helpful resource for understanding religious priesthood more positively—that is, as an authentic expression of both priesthood and religious life.

This chapter lays the foundation for the next two chapters by introducing three key concepts of Balthasar's framework—namely, mission, constellation, and state. Balthasar's language is nuanced, and his scheme is complex. While I will try to state things as simply as possible, what comes next will likely be the most difficult chapter of this book. I hope, however, that it will also be illuminating for our subject.

Mission

Balthasar acknowledged the concept of mission as the "quickest way" into his theology of states of life and vocations.[1] Thus, it is a natu-

1. *CSL*, 82.

ral place to begin. Mission, for Balthasar, has both the most universal and most specific possible meanings. Universally, all specific Christian missions (i.e., vocations, charisms, callings) are participations in the one mission and person of Christ. Through the sacramentality of the church, Christians are incorporated into Christ's person and mission, thus forming part of his body, which continues to make Christ present and visible to the world. Each specific mission contributes to Christ's singular redemptive task, and each has the common form of "two-fold transcendent" love of God and neighbor.[2] Every specific Christian mission will thus contain the common elements of prayer, sacrificial service, fellowship, and proclamation found in the one mission of Christ.

When considering a unique personal "mission," Balthasar uses the term somewhat interchangeably with "charism."[3] It is a special task allotted to someone by the Holy Spirit for the building up of the ecclesial body and for service to the world. Though one's personal mission always involves a participation in Christological love of God and neighbor, it is particularized in each individual's life.[4] For Balthasar, personal mission lies at the core of personal identity. The particular mission one receives from God serves as the human person's "center of gravity"; it is singularly capable of integrating one's otherwise disparate parts.[5] Balthasar's original imagery for one's mission/identity is that of a role one is elected to perform in a divine drama, or that of an instrument one plays in an ecclesial symphony.[6] Although the various roles are united in a common performance expressing love of God and neighbor, love will be incarnated in as many ways as there are persons in the world. The purpose of life is to discern and embrace one's true name, role, or

2. Dermot Power, *Spiritual Theology of the Priesthood*, 2.

3. On the identity of mission and charism, see Balthasar, *Theo-Drama: Theological Dramatic Theory*, vol. 3, *Dramatis Personae: Persons in Christ* (hereafter *TD* 3), trans. Graham Harrison (San Francisco: Ignatius Press, 1992), 231; *Explorations in Theology*, vol. 2, *Spouse of the Word* (hereafter *ET* 2) (San Francisco: Ignatius Press, 1991), 301–15.

4. *CSL*, 392.

5. *CSL*, 74.

6. On the allotment of dramatic roles, see *TD* 3:263–81. On the orchestral analogy, see Balthasar, *Truth Is Symphonic: Aspects of Christian Pluralism*, trans. Graham Harrison (San Francisco: Ignatius Press, 1987), esp. 14.

instrument. Christians discover their personal missions through prayer and contemplation. They are incorporated into their specific missions through sacramental participation.

Each specific mission will contain aesthetic and dramatic elements. That is to say, it will reveal or signify something unique about Christ's person (the aesthetic element) and contribute something specific to Christ's ongoing mission through conscientious Christian action (the dramatic element). For example, a mission as a contemplative religious signifies Christ's poverty, virginity, and obedience and actualizes Christ's redemptive work through prayer and asceticism. An ordained priest reveals the continued presence of Christ as head and bridegroom in the church and actualizes Christ's mediation of grace through the sacraments.

Constellation

A second important term in Balthasar's theology of vocations is "constellation." It refers to the group of biblical figures who surround Christ in the New Testament (e.g., Mary, the twelve apostles, Paul).[7] The members of the constellation are important to Balthasar's theology of vocations in three ways. First, personal missions are not only imitations of Christ and participations in the life of Christ, but also missions in relation to Christ *as other*, whose own unique mission is ultimately unrepeatable, and upon whom every personal mission depends for its strength and example.[8] The members of the constellation serve as scriptural paradigms for the ways in which Christians of every age can relate to Christ as other and be invited to join him in his mission. In short, we learn who we are in relation to Christ and receive inspiration for our missions by contemplating the way his friends related to him in the gospel stories.

Second, reference to the constellation is a way for Balthasar to as-

7. For Balthasar's most extensive treatment of the "Christological Constellation," see his *The Office of Peter and the Structure of the Church*, trans. Andrée Emery (San Francisco: Ignatius Press, 2007), esp. 137–242, 335–60; hereafter *OPSC*.

8. On the relation of Christ's unique unrepeatable mission to all Christian missions, see *TD* 3:154–282.

semble the church's exponentially varied personal missions into broad categories that correspond to scriptural types. For example, Balthasar recognizes the ordinary lay vocation as typologically present in the crowds who listened to Christ and came to believe in him, but who did not, for all that, leave their position in the world of family and secular work. The religious life and priesthood are both typologically present in the twelve who were called to leave all things behind and then anointed by the Holy Spirit to provide an enduring apostolic ministry to the church. The contemplative life is typologically present in John, who laid his head on the savior's breast. The missionary life is typologically present in Paul, who brought the gospel to the gentiles. A more localized ministry is typologically present in James, the brother of the Lord, who defended the Jewish Christian position at the Council of Jerusalem portrayed in Acts. Authoritative office in the church is typologically present in Peter, the chief of the apostles. John the Baptist, the virgin-prophet of the desert, anticipates religious brothers and lay prophetic witness. Mary Magdalene and the women of Christ's traveling company provide a grounding for similar women's missions. Martha and Mary of Bethany "stand for the tasks and dignity of the domestic church," just as the Holy Family does; Joseph stands for fatherhood and secular labor.[9]

Balthasar does not mean that these persons are literally the founders of these ecclesial categories, but that the "post-paschal" structure of the church, with its recognizable vocational categories such as laity, religious, and clergy, can be perceived in an anticipatory way in the original constellation.[10] Through the church's continued engagement with

9. For these associations, see Balthasar, *Explorations in Theology*, vol. 4, *Spirit and Institution* (hereafter *ET* 4), trans. Edward T. Oakes (San Francisco: Ignatius Press, 1995), 393; *CSL*, 372; McDade, "John Paul II and His Ecclesiology," 55–61; Nichols, *Divine Fruitfulness*, 208. For Balthasar on the Holy Family as a model for family life, see also Balthasar, *Two Sisters in the Spirit: Thérèse of Lisieux and Elizabeth of the Trinity*, trans. Donald Nichols, Anne Englund Nash, and Dennis Martin (San Francisco: Ignatius Press, 1992), 119 (hereafter *TSS*).

10. On the relation of the "post-paschal" structure of the church to the ministry of Jesus, see Servais, "Yves Congar and Hans Urs Von Balthasar on the Theological Status of the Laity," 19 (hereafter "Congar and Balthasar"). This is an unpublished English translation of an essay made available to me by the editors of *Communio*. The French original is "Le statut théologique du laic en debat: Yves Congar et Hans Urs von Balthasar," in *Chrétiens dans la société actuelle: L'apport de Hans Urs von Balthasar*, ed. Dideier Gonneaud

scripture, the church's contemporary missions are inspired and conditioned by the original constellational group.[11] Furthermore, given the Eucharistic unity of the church across time, we can recognize the same charism that animated a Paul, Peter, or John now animating Christian missions today.

Third, Balthasar uses the constellation to display how the church's members should relate not only to Christ but to one another in Christ. He argues that the interplay of the constellation's missions continues in those polarities we often find in ecclesiology: clergy (Peter) and laity (Mary); papacy (Peter) and collegiality (the Twelve); institution (Peter) and charism (Paul/John/Mary); objective office (Peter) and subjective discipleship (John and Mary); tradition (James) and innovation (Paul); universality (Paul) and localism (James).[12] As Dermot Power explains, because the church grows "not by moving away from its [scriptural] origin but by allowing that origin to be present each moment in the power of the Holy Spirit," the missions revealed in the constellation should continue to "sustain ecclesial relations with the dynamic that at its beginnings rose from the unfathomable experience of Jesus Christ."[13] For Balthasar, the constellation is indispensable to ecclesiology. It "precedes us and one cannot make it more or less than what it is. We cannot manipulate it."[14]

---

and Philippe Charpentier de Beauvillé (Magny-les-Hameaux: Soceval, 2006), 131–58. On Balthasar's "hermeneutic of recognition," see Dermot Power, *Spiritual Theology of the Priesthood*, 16–17. According to Power, the "hermeneutic of recognition" discerns contemporary ecclesial structures as authentically developed from roots in the "historical pattern of relationship, intimacy, and mission which characterized Jesus' formation of the Twelve." Power contrasts Balthasar's hermeneutic with theological approaches that present contemporary ecclesial structures, especially hierarchical ministry, as sociologically conditioned and eliminable or, at least, radically changeable.

11. For summaries of Balthasar's view of the Marian, Johannine, Petrine, and Pauline relations to ecclesial vocations, see Leahy, *Marian Profile*, 64–66; Nichols, *Divine Fruitfulness*, 200–208; and Robert Barron, *The Strangest Way: Walking the Christian Path* (Maryknoll, N.Y.: Orbis, 2002), 119–22.

12. See *OPSC*, 137–242, 335–60.

13. Power, *Spiritual Theology of the Priesthood*, 54

14. *OPSC*, 19

States of Life and Their Relationships to One Another

A third important concept is state. Most readers will be familiar with the language of "state of life" as one of the ways the church speaks about vocation. While we sometimes speak of works like teaching, medicine, the arts, or public service as vocations, "state of life" is usually reserved for describing something very stable to which one makes a lifetime commitment. While it is possible for someone to commit him- or herself so fully to being an artist that we say that person is "married" to his or her work, it is not the case that professions require this by their very nature.

Any theology of vocations must sooner or later come up against the problematic of naming and numbering the various states of life. In the common parlance of today's church, we most often speak of a lay state, a clerical state, and a religious state, and this seems to correspond to the overarching framework of *Lumen gentium*. However, when we think about the hierarchical structure of the church we might speak of there only being two states, clergy and laity, and this is supported by the 1983 Code of Canon Law.[15] John Paul II, in *Familiaris Consortio*, meanwhile, implied that the two basic states were marriage and consecrated celibacy,[16] though he also spoke elsewhere of three "paradigmatic vocations" with reference to lay life, consecrated life, and ministerial priesthood.[17] Reaching back further into the tradition, we find in scholastic theology the language of a "state of the commandments" and a "state of the counsels" that corresponds more or less to lay life and religious life.[18]

At the time he was writing, Balthasar inherited from tradition the difficulty that the term "state" had already been being used in this myriad of ways, not all of them consistent with each other. Rather than rejecting any of the ways the term had been used in the past, Balthasar, wanting to think with tradition, attempted to integrate them all into his scheme.

15. See *CIC* 207.

16. John Paul II, Apostolic Exhortation *Familiaris Consortio* (November 22, 1981), 11; hereafter *FC*.

17. VC 31.

18. See, for example, *ST* II-II, q. 184, a. 3, and *ST* II-II, q. 181, a. 1.

His approach is less than straightforward, and there are times when Balthasar himself does not seem consistent, such as when he argues in his magnum opus on the subject, *The Christian State of Life*, that there are only two states (the evangelical state and the general state), but, then, only a few chapters later, diagrams the interrelationship of three states (lay state, evangelical state, and priestly state). As for naming states, he speaks of so many that it can quickly become confusing. There is a "lay state," a "secular state," a "general state," a "state of the commandments," a "married state," and a "state of the counsels, a "religious state," an "evangelical state," and a "priestly state," which is sometimes viewed as a subset of the "evangelical state" and sometimes not. To complicate matters further, and for reasons I hope to make apparent, there is a near, but not total, identification between the state of marriage, the state of the commandments, and the lay-secular state. There is similarly a near, but not total, identification of the evangelical state with the religious state and the priestly state.[19]

What Balthasar's approach lacks in simplicity, however, is made up for by the advantage of honoring in a more complete way the complexity

19. In all but a few places in *CSL*, Balthasar prefers the term *Ratestand* (state of the counsels) to *Ordenstand* (religious state). At the same time, he seems to juxtapose the *whole* evangelical state [*Ratestand*] with the lay state according to their eschatological vs. secular characteristics; see *CSL*, 142, 167–71, 197, 203, 329–30. Thus, Balthasar appears to identify the evangelical and religious states. This has likely contributed to some interpreters identifying Balthasar's *Ratestand* with the religious life without qualification; e.g., Gerard O'Hanlon, "Von Balthasar on Ecclesial States of Life," *Milltown Studies* 22 (1988): 113 and 114; Power, *Spiritual Theology of the Priesthood*, 91–98; Nichols, *Divine Fruitfulness*, 217–22. The conflation of the evangelical state with religious life poses certain problems because the nonidentity of evangelical and religious, as well as the nonidentity of the lay-secular state and the state of the commandments with marriage as its paradigm, is what allows for the possibility of secular institutes. Balthasar does clarify in *CSL* that secular institutes are an instantiation of the evangelical state located more within the incarnational/lay/secular pole, while the religious vocation [*Ordenstand*] has a more eschatological stance; see *CSL*, 359–61; *ET* 2:421–57, esp. 437, and *OT*, 48–49. However, this clarification is somewhat lost in *CSL* among the more consistent contrast between the secular state and the state of the counsels. Hence, evangelical and eschatological/religious draw very, very near to each other in *CSL*, and there is very little alternative in discussing *CSL* but to follow Balthasar in this near conflation. It can be justified, however, based on the idea that marriage is paradigmatic of the lay state, and religious life is paradigmatic of the evangelical state, whereas vocations to secular institutes are somewhat exceptional, as even Balthasar thinks they are; see *CSL*, 361–62.

of ecclesial vocational categories and their interrelationships. The key to his scheme is a dialectical approach. Instead of describing states in isolation, he shows that their meaning is best apprehended in how they relate to each other. In what follows, I will try to get to the heart of four key distinctions made by Balthasar that can help us recognize what the basic states are and how they contrast with each other.

Moral Distinction

From the perspective of moral theology, Balthasar defines "state" as a "form of life" to which an individual commits through vows or promises and that forms the existential context in which he or she carries out his or her personal mission/vocation.[20] According to Balthasar, every Christian is "enstated" in the "general Christian [i.e., lay] state" by baptismal commitment, which is already a permanent commitment. However, most Christians further specify their state by committing to marriage, priesthood, or religious life with a total, stable, irrevocable self-gift expressed in promises or vows.

For Balthasar, the paradigmatic vows are the religious vows of poverty, chastity, and obedience, since these represent the totality of what the human person can pledge in love—namely, one's possessions, one's body, and one's will. The "state of the counsels" or "evangelical state" is thus characterized by vowed commitment to the evangelical counsels,[21] and to it belong religious, clergy, consecrated virgins, and members of secular institutes to varying degrees. Vocations to the "state of the counsels" are relatively exceptional and indicate a certain set-apartness from the general state. Those who are not called to the evangelical state remain in the "state of the commandments," though they should, as explained by St. Paul, adopt the spirit of the counsels.[22] In order to do this

20. Cautioning that the word "state" has become "heavily 'burdened'" by its association with outdated medieval sociology, Balthasar suggests the term "form of life" as an alternative in *LLC*, 182–83.

21. See *CSL*, 12, 41–65.

22. *CSL*, 170. With St. Paul, Balthasar says that the Christian in the state of the commandments must live "as if" he had no wife, buy "as though not possessing," and make use of the world "as though" not using it (1 Cor 7:39–31). Such a person, as Paul says, is "divided" (1 Cor 7:33), but, according to Balthasar, this means simply that they have a different way of taking up the cross through which they will know true freedom.

well, they need the concrete witness of those in the evangelical state so that they can imitate it in spirit.

From within the "state of the commandments," one can be further "en-stated" in marriage, which approaches the totality, stability, and permanence of religious vows but does not indicate a similar departure from the general [lay] state.[23] Among the special tasks of the married is to continue to fulfill the Lord's never nullified commandment from Genesis to "be fruitful and multiply" and to use personal freedom and property toward righteous ends that glorify God. In Balthasar's later work he dropped the language of the "state of the commandments" and spoke only of the "state of marriage" and "state of the counsels" as further moral specifications taking place after baptism.

Distinction according to Sacred Geography

From the perspective of the church-world relationship, there is a distinction between a lay state, characterized by remaining embedded in created secularity, and a religious state, characterized by an eschatological renunciation of the world (*fuga mundi*).[24] To be lay, from this perspective, is not simply to lack ordination or religious profession, but to be positively called to engage the world as Christians and to bring grace and the gospel to bear upon the world from within the world's own structures, especially those of family life, secular work, culture, and politics. To be "religious" is to have made a formal departure from these structures, not because they are evil, but in order to positively signify to the world and draw the world to its eschatological finality.

Balthasar appeals to a wide range of scriptural evidence to "prove" a dominically instituted distinction between two groups in the original ecclesial community: "the people" and "the apostles," whom the Lord called forth from among the larger numbers of those who had begun to believe.[25] Characteristic of the Twelve is that they were invited to remain with Jesus and share his life and ministry. To the apostles, the

23. Marriage is "the hidden and often buried core of the secular state"; *LLC*, 185.

24. *CSL*, 379; *ET* 2:421–57, esp. 437.

25. *CSL*, 143. "He called to him men of his own choosing, and they came to him" (Mk 3:13). "He *summoned* his disciples and from these he *chose* twelve (whom he also called apostles)" (Lk 6:13).

Lord said, "Come, follow me" (Mt 4:19). He called them "away from their fishing nets or, like Levi, from their tax collecting (Mt 9:9)."[26] They were to "leave all things" (Lk 5:28) and live exclusively for the Lord's service.

Just as characteristic, but perhaps overlooked, is that the people, in contrast, were dismissed by Jesus. To them, the Lord consistently says "'*vade*'—'go now,'" indicating his intention that they not remain part of his wandering ministerial party but return to their "*milieu*."[27] As Balthasar notes, to this group the Lord "bestows ... his graces of body and soul.... He reveals himself as their Savior, their Redeemer, their source of comfort and courage, as the true light of the world. But once this grace has been given and they stand in his light, he sends them back among the people."[28]

According to Balthasar, the Twelve, and probably others such as the seventy-two and the women who traveled in Jesus' company,[29] but not the wider masses, constituted the original group set apart to live the evangelical counsels. It would be anachronistic to call them "religious," but their way of life constitutes the core of what became religious life. They were called to a radical, formal, and material renunciation of the world. They were directed "not only out of the 'world' that lies outside the Church, but also out of the world within the Church" (i.e., the lay state).[30] They were called to leave all things behind, their fishing nets, the places where they might lay their heads, their families, and their secular futures. This call to renunciation implies a total dispossession of all things. Balthasar writes, "They take their stand with the world's

26. *CSL*, 144.

27. *CSL*, 145. Balthasar provides ample examples. This group includes the man at the pool by the Sheep gate (Jn 5:2–9); the lame man (Mk 2:11); the woman with the hemorrhage (Mk 5:34); the Canaanite woman (Mk 7:29); the sinful woman (Lk 7:50); the blind man of Bethsaida (Mk 8:26); the blind man of Jericho (Mk 10:52); the woman caught in adultery (Jn 8:11); the centurion (Mt 8:13); the tenth leper (Lk 17:19); the royal official (Jn 4:50); and the crowds after feeding them (Mk 8:38–9). "The most notable of these dismissals is that of the possessed man of Gerasa, who, after, he had been healed, 'began to entreat [the Lord] that he might remain with him. And he did not allow him, but said to him, 'Go home to thy relatives, and tell them all that the Lord has done for thee, and how he has had mercy on thee" (Mk 5:18–19; Lk 8:38–39).

28. *CSL*, 144–45.

29. *CSL*, 372.

30. *CSL*, 148.

all behind them and before them only the following of him who calls himself the way."[31] It is also a call to stable, irrevocable commitment. "The renunciation of this world must be determinative for all time"; the apostles "were not to return home."[32]

Balthasar supports the dignity of both states in various ways. He notes, for example, that Jesus and Mary participated at one point or another in both states, giving each therefore the highest dignity.[33] He also makes a trinitarian argument. As we have noted, the two groups relate to Jesus in the gospel in complementary ways. There is a movement of the apostolic group that remains with Jesus, shares his life, and descends with him down the mountain to exercise ministry, only to retreat again. There is a corresponding movement of those who are situated in the world who come to Jesus and then return to the world. Balthasar observes:

> The two forms of encounter, the two modes of approach, are in sharp contrast. The people's way to the Lord is to search for him in their necessity; their dismissal is attended with healing and grace for their subsequent existence in the world. The sending of the apostles into the world occurs only by the Lord's commission and for his purposes; their return to him is a return to the place where they belong.[34]

The sharp contrast, however is simply a reverse image. Both groups are participating in an "oscillation" between God and the world, an oscillation that is based on Christ's perpetually oscillating *exitus/reditus* between the world and the Father.[35] In Balthasar's highly Johannine perspective,

> [His] coming and his going constitute the whole essence of the Son.... His Incarnation and his reality as man are the result of his mandate as one sent from above, from the Father, and the proof for this will be found in the "Spirit," *that is to say* in his return to the Father.... As coming from the Father, he is always caught up in the

31. *CSL*, 149.
32. *CSL*, 172.
33. *CSL*, 183–210.
34. *CSL*, 146.
35. *LLC* 183; see also *CSL*, 147, 193–94.

> act of the Word's incarnation. . . . As returning to the Father, he forever *is* an act of handing man over to God.[36]

Both states then are "forms of personal following of the Lord,"[37] because each state participates, albeit in juxtaposed ways, in Christ's single undivided "stand" in the will of the Father,[38] a stance that is really a dynamic movement.

This Christological oscillation, says Balthasar, is movement within a "field of tension between incarnation and eschatology."[39] He states that the church is a "new aeon within the old."[40] When either half of this phrase is emphasized, it highlights an aspect of the church's identity. Seen as a "new aeon *within the old*," the church reflects the mystery of the Incarnation where "the seed of the definitive kingdom was planted in the kingdom of the world."[41] As such, the church is inserted into secularity. It journeys with and alongside the world, facilitating its transformation, moving toward eschatological finality. This aspect of ecclesial existence corresponds most directly to the lay reality. At the same time the church is a "*new aeon* within the old"; it participates in the already-ness of the resurrection where "the Kingdom of God has become so powerful that the entire kingdom of the world appears implanted within *it*."[42] Here, the church appears as a supernatural society set apart from the world, but because the church is constructed, in part, from the world's material, it is a sign to the world of creation's eschatological finality. This aspect corresponds most directly to religious life.

Nonetheless, Balthasar emphasizes that the whole church participates in the incarnational and eschatological dynamics. For instance, ordinary lay "Christians, have, by the power of baptism, died to the world, been buried with Christ, risen with him, and thereby been incorporated into the heavenly, eschatological kingdom. As citizens of the

36. *GL* 1:322–30.
37. *CSL*, 147.
38. *CSL*, 185.
39. *ET* 2:431.
40. *ET* 2:433.
41. *ET* 2:433, 432. Emphasis original.
42. *ET* 2:433, 432. Emphasis original.

approaching Kingdom of heaven, they are foreigners on earth."[43] No follower of Jesus, therefore, can be exempt from the "withdrawal from the world" in the contemplation and asceticism that are necessary for discipleship.[44] On the other hand, those in religious life depart from the world only so that they can reenter it in a transformative way. In imitation of the Lord, they pass through the Cross (not only by baptism and faith but by the further step of material commitment to the counsels). Rising again, they turn back to the world, either through an active mission or in an apostolate of prayer.[45] Ultimately, all Christians are "in the world, but not of the world."[46] The enduring distinction between the two groups (lay and religious) is a matter of where they *primarily* stand *in comparison with each other* in the "oscillation" between God and world, eschatology and incarnation.[47] The religious takes his or her stand primarily in an eschatological pole. He or she moves toward the world in apostolic service and then retreats again to a home set apart from the world. The laity take their stand primarily in an Incarnational pole. They stand in the world, helping order the world to the Kingdom. They move, liturgically, toward the real presence of the eschatological kingdom, but then go back to their primary stance in the world.[48] Together, the two states make known the mystery of the church as a "new aeon within the old." The religious represents the "newness" of the aeon, its eschatological uprootedness from and achieved transformation of the old. The laity represent the church's presence "within the old," its incarnate stance as "yoked to the world and its total destiny."[49]

Readers may notice that there is a connection between the religious state, here described, and the evangelical state mentioned in the moral distinction. The two are close but not totally identified. Members of secular institutes, consecrated virgins, and consecrated members of ec-

43. ET 2:431. This explains why Balthasar sees the call of the Twelve as a type not only for religious life but, analogously, for the church as a whole: See *CSL*, 147.

44. *TSS* 211.

45. *TSS* 150.

46. *ET* 2:437.

47. *LLC* 183–85.

48. *CSL*, 146; *LLC* 182.

49. *ET* 2:433.

clesial movements like Communion and Liberation and Focalare commit to one or more of the evangelical counsels but do not embrace the same kind of eschatological *fuga mundi* as religious.[50] Their primary stance remains, by design, in the lay-secular field of mission. They also do not usually live in common or wear habits.[51] Conversely, religious life, with its common life set apart and distinctive dress, becomes the church's most visible public sign of eschatological finality. Canon law acknowledges, "The public witness to be rendered by religious to Christ and the Church entails a separation from the world."[52] Balthasar would read this as being right on target. The sacred geographical distinction, then, is how Balthasar resolves a question left open by Vatican II, which is how to differentiate religious from others committed to the evangelical counsels.[53]

Readers may also wonder whether the religious state described here is not in fact the clerical state. The calling of the Twelve, of course, is also a founding moment for the priestly state. However, according to Balthasar, diocesan clergy have only a qualified participation in the eschatological *fuga mundi*. This is because (1) they do not commit to evangelical poverty; and (2) they are rightly called "secular clergy," which connotes their closer approximation than religious to the world. Their ministry is exercised in accompanying ordinary lay faithful through the life cycle and by helping the laity navigate the world in a Christian way.[54]

Distinction according to Ecclesial Representation

The previous two distinctions have highlighted especially the contrast between laity and religious. We now turn our attention to how Balthasar distinguishes the clerical state on the one hand from the laity (which here includes religious) on the other. For Balthasar, the clergy

50. See Balthasar, "Toward a Theology of the Secular Institute," *ET* 2: 421–57, esp. 437.

51. See *LLC* 104 (habits), *LLC* 109–10 (common life), *OT* 146 (inconspicuous nature of secular institutes).

52. *CIC* 607, §3.

53. For more on the distinction between secular institutes and religious life, see Balthasar, "Le Paradoxe des instituts séculiers," *Vie Consacrée* 46 (1974): 199–203.

54. See *CSL*, 367.

signify and exercise an objective priesthood, while the laity signify and exercise a subjective one.[55]

Balthasar explains that the Holy Spirit gives to the church both objective and subjective gifts. The objective elements are those sacred gifts that typically direct, shape, and mold the church and that the Christian generally experiences as coming to him or her from outside. This set of elements includes the church's official proclamation (*fides quae*), hierarchical ministry/office, liturgy, sacraments, scripture, tradition, and canon law. The subjective set of elements includes those gifts to the church by which she receives the objective ones and brings them to fruition and that the Christian generally experiences more as coming up from within the self or the community. This set includes the church's faith (*fides qua*), freedom in the Spirit, prophetic witness and life (including the evangelical counsels), charisms, and the subjective union of the ecclesial body, which is itself a participation in trinitarian communion.[56] This side is also holy because it is the life of graced communion with God, which is the very goal and purpose of the objective gifts.

It goes without saying that ordained priests also participate in the subjective priesthood (if they did not, they would not be disciples). However, Balthasar emphasizes that the clergy cannot be the primary symbols of the subjective priesthood. We need to have an ideal of subjective holiness different from what the clergy represent so that we do not equate holiness with ministry and conclude that the only or best way to be Christian is to be ordained. Hence, constellationally, St. Joseph, John the Baptist, and especially Mary stand as ideal types of the subjective priesthood unjoined to sacramental ministry. Their missions are continued in lay persons and nonordained religious. We also need to have a sense of the objective priesthood as independent of the subjective priesthood in order to stave off Donatist heresies that would make the efficacy of ministry depend on a ministerial priest's subjective holiness. Constellationally, Peter is the primary signifier of the objective priesthood (though of course he still has a subjective discipleship). His mission is continued by priests. Thus, the objective clerical state is also

55. See *ET* 2:319–21.

56. See Balthasar, *Theo-Logic*, vol. 3, *The Spirit of Truth* (hereafter *TL* 3), trans. Adrian J. Walker (San Francisco: Ignatius Press, 2005), 319–412.

called by Balthasar, the Petrine "pole" or "profile" in honor of St. Peter, its constellational referent. Laity and religious, in contrast, constitute the Marian "pole" or "profile" of the church.

By describing the ministerial priesthood as objective, Balthasar highlights that the priest stands over and against the church. As one who represents Christ in preaching and teaching and who mediates the grace of the transcendent head to the body, the priest is a symbolic reminder to the church that it is not self-generating or "self-actualizing," but depends on something above and beyond it for its holiness and fruitfulness.[57] The objectivity of priestly office also highlights that the efficacy of the sanctifying function can be trusted despite any weakness or personal flaws of the office bearer.[58] The subjective priesthood, meanwhile, depends entirely on one's personal response to God.

To demonstrate the right relation between the objective and subjective priesthoods, Balthasar portrays the life of the church according to a nuptial analogy. The church is a marriage between God and the world. It was founded in the nuptial moments of the Incarnation in which humanity was wedded to the divine Second Person of the Trinity, as well as in the Passion, in which the body of Christ was offered to and for the bride. Through the Eucharist, the church celebrates and renews its nuptial covenant with God as it recapitulates these moments.[59] The

57. Dermot Power, *Spiritual Theology of the Priesthood*, 117. See also *LLC* 17; *OPSC*, 196. Mark O'Keefe has argued that postconciliar theologies of priesthood can be roughly divided into two models. There is a "Ministerial Model" that describes the priest as deriving authority from the church itself, which has commissioned him to function *in persona ecclesiae*. On the other hand, there is a "Representational Model" that describes the priest as deriving his authority more directly from God, who has chosen the priest to stand over and against the church to represent Christ as head and bridegroom and to function *in persona Christi capitis*. Although these models are somewhat artificial, they are helpful for positioning Balthasar in relation to other contemporary theologies of priesthood. Balthasar seems to fit better within the second model; Mark O'Keefe, *In Persona Christi: Reflections on Priestly Identity and Holiness* (St. Meinrad, Ind.: Abbey Press, 1998), 1–7.

58. *GL* 1:569.

59. *ET* 2:171, 318; *LLC* 197. See also Angelo Scola, "The Theological Foundation of the Petrine Dimension of the Church: A Working Hypothesis," *Ecclesiology* 4 (2007): 12–37, esp. 24–31; Nicholas J. Healy and David L. Schindler, "For the Life of the World: Hans Urs von Balthasar on the Church as Eucharist," in Oakes and Moss, *Cambridge Companion to Hans Urs von Balthasar*, 51–63.

Lord and the world/church are each represented within the liturgy by different figures. The laity represent the Marian world-body-bride in the event of communion that is the Eucharist. Through their presence, consent, and offering, the lay faithful bring the goods of the world into communion with God, just as Mary did at the Annunciation and at the foot of the Cross.[60] If the ordinary laity represent the various secular fields and created goods coming into this union, the religious among them represent the radical obedience, poverty, and virginal availability the world must have to receive God most fruitfully. Hence for Balthasar, the religious "existentially represents ... the innermost heart of the Church," the receptive bride and cooperative body of the Lord.[61] While priests must be "anchored" in the Marian church, for they are Christians before they are priests, they represent liturgically, and within the life of the church, Christ as bridegroom.[62] Balthasar states, "Though they belong to the overall feminine modality of the Church, [priests] are selected from her and remain in her to exercise their office; their function is to embody Christ, who comes to the Church to make her fruitful."[63]

The nuptial context of the liturgy highlights the interdependence of the Petrine and Marian profiles. According to Balthasar, "the male priesthood is, as it were, crystallized divine love—for the sake of the female community, which, through this form of love, is able to come into direct contact with the Lord and with the triune God."[64] The whole raison d'être of the priesthood is to "nurture, safeguard, and make transparent, the spousal love of Christ for the Marian Church."[65] Through the priest's sacramental mediation, Christ's life-giving love flows forth

60. *ET* 2:320–21.

61. Servais, "Congar and Balthasar," 24.

62. For more on the priest's representation of the bridegroom, see Balthasar's essays "How Weighty Is the Argument from 'Uninterrupted Tradition' to Justify the Male Priesthood?," trans. Lothar Krauth, in *The Church and Women: A Compendium*, ed. Helmut Moll (San Francisco: Ignatius Press, 1988), 153–60; "Thoughts on the Priesthood of Women," *Communio* 23 (Winter 1996): 701–9; and "Women Priests? A Marian Church in a Fatherless and Motherless Culture" *Communio* 22 (Spring 1995): 164–70.

63. *TD* 3:354.

64. Balthasar, *Priestly Spirituality* (hereafter *PS*), trans. Frank Davidson (San Francisco: Ignatius Press, 2013), 61.

65. Dermot Power, *Spiritual Theology of the Priesthood*, 50.

to the church and through the church reaches out to the world. The layperson, representing the natural, worldly element but standing in Marian subjective grace and holiness, actively receives the objective gift and brings to bear the trinitarian form of life into the world.[66] There is, therefore, a cooperative interdependence between the two. The layperson needs what the priest can offer—objective, transcendent grace. The priest needs the layperson to actualize this grace and to complete the church's mission, which is nothing other than the "salvation and rescuing of the world."[67] As Balthasar states, "The layman looks up with reverence to the ministry, for without its mediation he would have no access to the source of salvation. But the priest looks up with reverence to the layman, in whom he sees the purpose and the goal of his servant function."[68]

Distinction according to Office and Charism

The fourth distinction builds upon the objective/subjective polarity. It associates clergy, in the Petrine pole, with institutional stability and religious, in the Marian pole, with charismatic movements of ecclesial reform. Priests are holders of objective offices who safeguard institutional stability. Religious life and other similar movements are God's way of renewing and reforming the church.[69]

Balthasar argues that whenever the church tries to reform itself, it ends up with bureaucratic top-down solutions; when God wants to renew the church, he raises up saints.[70] While it is true that some saints live rather inconspicuously, others receive an outstanding prophetic mission of reform and renewal. Balthasar colorfully describes such

66. Accordingly, Balthasar notes that the *opus operatum* of the sacraments "is possible . . . only in the simultaneous positing of the receiving community, which is present, joins in the celebration of the sacrifice, gives its consent, and gives the work of salvation its fullness and rounds it off"; *ET* 2:321.

67. *ET* 2:316.

68. *ET* 2:325.

69. Balthasar upholds the prophetic-charismatic aspect of religious life, meanwhile, as its second most definitive feature, right after commitment to the evangelical counsels: see *LLC* 66–68; Balthasar, *Die Grossen Ordensregeln* (hereafter *DGO*) (Einsiedeln: Johannes, 1974), 25–26.

70. *OPSC*, 40.

saints as like "lightning ... that ignites a blaze," "volcanoes pouring forth molten fire from the inmost depths of Revelation," and "meteors" that fall into the pristine "garden of the Church," disturbing the status quo and calling the church back to its Christological center.[71] Saints like Benedict, Francis, Bernard, Ignatius, and Teresa of Avila demonstrate the potentiality of new in-breakings of the Holy Spirit to renew the church in every age. According to Balthasar, they are "irrefutable proof, all horizontal tradition notwithstanding, of the vertical presence of the living *Kyrios* here, now and today."[72]

These reforming saints often attract disciples and inaugurate corporate movements. Hence, authentic ecclesial renewal almost always "coincides" with "major religious foundations."[73] Commonly, there is an initial tension between the newness of orders (and other similar movements) and the stable institutional hierarchy. Just as Paul struggled for recognition from Peter, James, and John (see Gal 2:9; Acts 15:2), new foundations often have to struggle to prove to ecclesial authorities that their inspiration comes from God.[74] Through their success, the orders remind the church of God's continued freedom vis-à-vis the church and of his constant creativity within the church.[75]

According to Balthasar, religious of subsequent generations receive a participation in the prophetic-charismatic mission of their founders. The founder is like a "consecrated seed" of the whole future of the order.[76] So, for example, the Order of Preachers can be thought of as "the charity of St. Dominic spread out in time and space."[77] As noted previously in our reflection on the constellation, charisms can be shared across time. The charism that was displayed in the founder's incarnate life can be shared through the Holy Spirit with those who follow in their

71. *OPSC*, 40; *LLC* 67–68.

72. Balthasar, *A Theology of History* (hereafter *TH*) (San Francisco: Ignatius Press, 1994), 110.

73. *DGO* 26.

74. *CSL*, 379–80.

75. *LLC* 17 and 67.

76. Balthasar, *Prayer*, trans. Graham Harrison (San Francisco: Ignatius Press, 1986), 106.

77. Balthasar, *Prayer*, 106. Balthasar is quoting George Bernanos. Original source not provided.

wake. Religious receive a share in the charism of their founder through baptism, confirmation, and religious consecration and are henceforth subjectively animated by it. Moreover, the charism of the founder is objectified in the rule of the order so that future religious will be externally guided by it.[78] The rule, therefore, functions analogously to scripture in the lives of religious; it stands over and against them as a form that impresses itself upon them and continues to shape the order long after the founder's death.[79]

Balthasar, in conformity with Vatican II, encourages religious to be faithful to the inspiration of their founders. Even if their founding charism was initially bestowed in response to the needs of the church during a different epoch, these charisms remain relevant. Their role does not simply disappear in the midst of new historical conditions. Benedictines continued after the dawn of the mendicant orders, and the mendicants continued after the advent of the Jesuits. That they did so proves all the more the supernatural origin of these orders and their enduring place in the ecclesial symphony.[80] Their continued presence and witness continues to remind the church of timeless truths. For example, Benedictines continue to display for the church the primacy of worship; Franciscans perhaps best represent the ideal of evangelical poverty; Jesuits hold up an example of radical obedience;[81] the missionary orders recall the church to the Great Commission to go forth and make disciples of all nations (see Mt 28:19–20). Those who follow in the founder's wake bear the "stamp" of their founders who were but the original pulse of the order that ripples "through the ages."[82] In the case of the major orders, the "stamp" of the founder may become, in fact, a new profile in the church—not independent of the original constellational profiles, but a further specification of them—so much so that, in some cases, if the charism were to disappear from the church, the church's face would be altered, and it would be "hardly recognizable."[83]

78. *TSS* 149–170.
79. *DGO* 8.
80. *DGO* 27.
81. *LLC* 142–43.
82. *DGO* 7.
83. *DGO* 8.

Religious of the great traditional orders, however, are not mere museum pieces. Although they may not be called to start something new in the church, as were Benedict, Dominic, Francis, and Ignatius, they are called to continue the renewing prophetic energy displayed in their founders' lives and teachings. The eschatological position of religious makes them a prophetic sign and liberates them to take prophetic stances in the church and in the world. Balthasar calls the religious "an element of Christian unrest," a "disturber of the peace," and a "disrupter of plans."[84] This does not mean that religious stand in fundamental opposition to the church's stable institutions or that they constitute an alternative hierarchy to the ministerial one. As Balthasar notes, "All the great founders were distinguished by their unfathomable humility before the hierarchical church," and so their spiritual descendants should also be.[85] Nonetheless, religious should continue to call the church, both laity and clergy, to the radical ideals of discipleship and to the renewing movement of the Holy Spirit.[86] Balthasar appeals to constellational referents to explain the way religious and office will ideally relate. Since religious priests play an essential role in this relation, discussion of it is deferred to a later chapter.

Conclusion

According to Balthasar, the various ecclesial states show themselves in a series of "mysteriously dialectic" relationships.[87] There is a moral distinction between the general state, married state, and evangelical state that concerns the kind of total, stable, and permanent self-gift one makes. Next, Balthasar recognizes an ecclesial oscillation between creational/secular/incarnate and eschatological poles that provides him with his primary means of distinguishing between laity and religious. The former represent Christian life in the world. The latter represent

84. *CSL*, 379.

85. *DGO* 26.

86. As Balthasar states of the religious, "It is his function in the Church to open all closed ideals and pastoral goals to the always limitless demand of Christ"; *CSL*, 379.

87. *ET* 2:430.

Christian life as being not of this world.[88] There is also a dialectical relation between the church's objective (Petrine) and subjective (Marian) priesthoods, and this is the primary way Balthasar distinguishes between clergy and laity (of whom religious would be a subset in this instance).[89] Finally, there is a dialectical relation between the church's stable, hierarchical, institutional framework (also called the "determining-institutionalizing" principle) and the forces of charismatic renewal (also called the church's "liberating-universalizing" principle).[90] Balthasar draws attention to this last dialectical relationship when he wishes to distinguish between clergy (determining-institutionalizing) and ecclesial movements (liberating-universalizing), the most notable of which are religious.

Because "state" is probably the most difficult of Balthasar's terms to grasp and keep straight, I will mostly avoid using the word going forward. Instead, I will simplify matters and, following John Paul II, refer to the "paradigmatic vocations" of laity, consecrated religious life, and ministerial priesthood, the meanings of which, I hope, have been somewhat illumined by this excursus.[91] The moral, geographical, representational, and charismatic distinctions, however, that Balthasar recognizes between the states are imperative to the coming discussion and should be kept in view.

To conclude, in Balthasar's theology of vocations, all the members of the church are united in the singular task of building up communion between God and the world through sacrificial love. The one life of Christ is the ultimate inspiration, ground, and summation of all possible missions. At the same time, Christ wills to be the firstborn of many brethren with their own unique missions, and so he sends the gifts and charisms of the Holy Spirit for this purpose. Accordingly, there is room

88. See *TH* 119–32.

89. *CSL*, 254–55.

90. Dermot Power, *Spiritual Theology of the Priesthood*, 149. Power attributes this phrasing to Balthasar but does not provide a source. For the identification of religious with charismatic renewal, see *LLC* 66–68; *CSL*, 379–80.

91. "The vocations to the lay life, to the ordained ministry and to the consecrated life can be considered paradigmatic, inasmuch as all particular vocations, considered separately or as a whole, are in one way or another derived from them or lead back to them, in accordance with the richness of God's gift"; *VC* 31.

for an exponential diversity of missions in his one body. Missioned persons each uniquely incarnate Christ depending on their particular inspirations, divinely bestowed gifts, and historical life circumstances.

In between the one mission of Christ and the exponential diversity of particular missions, Balthasar recognizes two mediating categories: constellational profiles and states of life. One's personal mission is expressed in, finalized, and made possible by a choice of a state of life, and each of the states has constellational types or referents. States of life and constellational profiles indicate that, in Balthasar's ecclesial symphony, there are instrumental sections. In the *Theo-Drama*, there are recurring characters.

States of life and constellational profiles are Balthasar's way of acknowledging and discussing the paradigmatic vocations familiar to Catholicism—namely, the laity, religious life, and priesthood. It is now possible to investigate how Balthasar presents their interrelationship in such a way that opens up new vistas for understanding religious priesthood.

CHAPTER 7

Balthasar's Christological and Trinitarian Ana-Logic of Vocations

Having introduced some key concepts in Balthasar's theology of vocations, it is now possible to turn more explicitly to two significant contributions he makes to a theology of religious priesthood. First, Balthasar's theology of vocations is presented within an analogical framework that gives it a flexibility and intrinsic openness to religious priesthood lacking in other ecclesiological approaches that imagine the church's vocations (e.g., laity, religious life, and priesthood) as rigid, mutually exclusive categories. Second, where the Council did not provide any guiding images of religious priesthood that might illuminate its specific function in the church, Balthasar points to the apostles John and Paul as scriptural types for this vocation. In this chapter, we'll explore how and why Balthasar's analogical approach to the theology of vocations is helpful to the theology of religious priesthood. Chapter 8 will attend to Balthasar's portrayal of John and Paul.

Analogy

Given the density of Balthasar's key concepts, it is perhaps not so surprising when he contends that all attempts to describe the church's various vocations and their relations to each other will always be somewhat imprecise. However, he is not arguing this based simply on his own theology. He argues that the placement of *Lumen Gentium*'s first chapter on the church as *mystery* before the more "sociological" second chapter on the church as people of God, and before the subsequent chapters on clergy, laity and religious, is an important reminder that the church's divine-human structure and life can never be fully grasped or exhaustively comprehended.[1] Ecclesiology must be carried out with a humility and sensitivity that respects the church's ultimately mysterious, divine nature.[2] *Lumen Gentium* described the mystery of the church as the body of Christ (*LG* 7) and the temple of the Holy Spirit (*LG* 4). For Balthasar, these titles serve as warnings against overly sociological approaches to ecclesiology that foolhardily assume a "comprehensive view" of the church "from the outside" could be attained, whereby the church's internal dynamics could be exhaustively demarcated and final definitions of her various vocations could be pronounced.[3]

It is not necessary, however, to abandon all attempts to understand and describe ecclesial vocations and their relations. The church still has a revealed, discernible, and stable constitution, even if she remains open to new developments inspired by the Holy Spirit. The proper way forward, according to Balthasar, is through dialectics and analogy. Dialectics do not define so much as observe phenomena in relation. We have already witnessed Balthasar's use of them in our discussion of state. What, then, is analogy?

Analogy is an important tool in theology. It stands midway between univocity (where we say the same thing about two things in an identical way—for instance, both the tablecloth and the bride's dress are white) and equivocity (where we may use the same word for two very different realities—for instance, the word "bear" can mean either "to carry" or a large animal at the zoo). Analogous relations include both similarity and difference.

We can further distinguish between different types of analogy. First, there is analogy of proportionality (*analogia proportionalitatis*). Here, the same middle term (analogon) can be applied to two outer terms without establishing one or the other outer terms as the primary referent (*analogatum princeps*) for the meaning of the middle term (analogon). John Knasas provides an example of analogy of proportion-

1. *ET* 4:139n1.
2. *LLC* 178.
3. *LLC* 206.

ality from sports. The term "great baseball player" applies to both Willie Mays and Sandy Koufax. Both men were great baseball players, but they were so differently. Willie Mays was known for his hitting and fielding. Sandy Koufax was known for his pitching. Mays and Koufax have an analogous relation to each other as great baseball players, but neither Mays nor Koufax is the primary referent for the meaning of "great baseball player." Rather, the term applies equally to both but in different ways.[4] To offer another example, golden retrievers and poodles are both equally dogs, but are so differently.[5] Second, there is analogy of attribution (*analogia attributionis*). It differs from analogy of proportionality because in analogy of attribution one of two terms serves as *analogatum princeps*, representing the full meaning of, and thereby serves as a referent for, a concept that then can be also applied to another term in a secondary, dependent way.[6] To use a classic example, "health" as it is used to refer to "healthy complexion" derives from the primary predication of health to the body (the *analogatum princeps*).[7] To confuse matters, analogy of attribution is sometimes also called by theologians and philosophers "the analogy of proportion," which unfortunately sounds very close to "analogy of proportionality."[8]

4. John Knasas, "Whither the Neo-Thomist Revival?," *Logos: A Journal of Catholic Thought and Culture* 3, no. 4 (2000): 127.

5. Oakes, *Pattern of Redemption*, 16.

6. *TD* 3:221n52.

7. Oakes, *Pattern of Redemption*, 16.

8. Thomas Aquinas makes a further distinction within the analogy of attribution between *multa ad unum* analogy of attribution and an *ad alterum* analogy of attribution. Aquinas makes this distinction to account for the difference between "intra-creaturely" analogies (*multa ad unum*) and the analogy between the being of God and the being of the world (*ad alterum*). Only the former are true analogies of proportion, where a second term participates in the same way but to a lesser degree than the first term does in the reality in question. When one recognizes, for instance, the proportional analogical relation between "red" and "reddish," one is making a *multa ad unum* analogy. Between the being of God and the being of the world, however, there is a difference in kind and not only degree. As the Fourth Lateran Council taught, for every similarity between God and the world, there is ever greater dissimilarity. God's essence and existence are identifiable, whereas creaturely being is contingent, ontologically dependent on God's being, and not merely a proportional or degreed participation in God's being (though it is also that). Accepting this distinction, Balthasar reserves the language of analogy of proportion for *multa ad unum* analogies and uses *analogia attributionis* for *ad alterum* analogy (see *TD* 3:221n52). On Aquinas's distinction between analogies of attribution, see Thomas

The Christ/church and Trinity/church relations involve analogy of attribution.[9] In Balthasar's vision of the church, Christ's mission is the ultimate *analogatum princeps* for the church's mission as a whole (since she is ontologically dependent on Christ), and for every particular human mission.[10] Trinitarian communion is the ultimate *analogatum princeps* for the communion of personal missions in the church.[11] Within the church, different vocations have attributed to them different aspects of the single mission of Christ. They participate in, reveal, and communicate Christ in a secondary, dependent way. Collectively, vocations represent Christ, but only by operating in a communion with one another, which is understood by way of analogy with the trinitarian relations.

There are also important analogous relationships between the particular vocations themselves.[12] Sometimes these are analogies of proportionality. "Priesthood," taken in its most general sense, applies equally to both the lay and ordained, the "priesthood of the faithful" and "the ministerial priesthood," but in different ways. More often, there are analogies of attribution in the relations among the vocations. Without diminishing Christ's role as *analogatum princeps*, Balthasar frequently uses one paradigmatic vocation as a referent,[13] or archetype, for an

---

Joseph White, *Wisdom in the Face of Modernity: A Study in Thomistic Natural Theology* (Ave Maria, Fla.: Sapientia, 2009), 90–92. For the language of "intra-creaturely" analogies, see Erich Przywara, *Anologia Entis: Metaphysics; Original Structure and Universal Rhythm*, trans. John R. Betz and David Bentley Hart (Grand Rapids, Mich.: Eerdmans, 2014), 231. For more on the importance of analogy in Balthasar and Przywara's influence on his concept of analogy, see Oakes, *Pattern of Redemption*, 15–44.

9. For more on the analogy of attribution in ecclesiology, see Servais, "Congar and Balthasar," 4.

10. See Larry S. Chapp, "Who Is the Church? The Personalistic Categories of Balthasar's Ecclesiology," *Communio* 23 (Summer 1996): 323–38.

11. Constellational missions provide secondary referents for specific vocations, and the interrelations of the constellation provide a secondary referent for how the vocations relate, but in neither case are they the *analogatum princeps.*

12. For example, see *CSL*, 379, for the analogy between the evangelical state and the laity (or "general state") of the church; *CSL*, 299, for the analogical relation between priesthood and religious life; *ET* 2:431, 445 for the analogical relation between religious life and secular institutes; *LLC* 17–18, for the analogical relation between clergy and laity; and *LLC* 189, for the analogical relation between vowed virginity and marriage.

13. Tertiary if one counts the constellational missions as the secondary referent.

aspect of Christ's mission in which the other vocations participate in a less pronounced way. For example, religious serve as the primary referent for Christian existence as "not of this world"; the laity serve as a referent for Christian existence "in the world"; and the hierarchical priesthood serves as the referent for ministry in which lay ministers analogously participate.[14] In this way, Balthasar's *ana*-logic allows both overlap and distinctiveness between vocations.

Sacramental Ecclesiology

Balthasar's Christological and trinitarian *ana*-logic unfolds in a fully sacramental ecclesiology. The church, as the opening paragraph of *Lumen Gentium* states, is a "sacrament," a "sign and instrument" through which Christ, the true "light of nations," continues to carry out the work of drawing humankind into union with the Triune God and with one another.[15] Balthasar agrees[16] and emphasizes that no individual, acting alone, can represent the totality of Christ's person and work to the world. Only as the corporate body of Christ can the church accomplish its task of communicating the saving mystery of Jesus to men and women through the ages. Hence, a "specialization of the members" is "necessary precisely so they can together give expression, by their inward interdependence, to the fullness of the 'Mystical Body of Christ.'"[17] The church's paradigmatic vocations must therefore cooperate if the church is to be the sacrament that reflects and mediates the person of Jesus and the Triune love he came to share.[18]

In order to cooperate with others, the Christian must have a sense of his or her place in the sacramental body. In Balthasar's framework, each paradigmatic vocation has aesthetic and dramatic elements. To use more traditional language, each vocation is *sacramental* insofar as

14. *CSL*, 364–87.

15. *LG* 1.

16. "The Church, and with it the states of life, must be, in the midst of the secular world, a sacrament that not only reflects this true and absolute love in the midst of the secular world, an outward sign, but also possesses it interiorly and pours it out upon the world, so that, in loving, it is, in its totality, both an end and a means to an end"; *CSL*, 387.

17. *OT* 122.

18. *CSL*, 385–87.

it is a specific "sign" (the aesthetic element) and "cause" (the dramatic element) in the work of redemption. The laity signify the incarnation of Christ in the world and cause the ordering of secular structures from within to God's will. Religious signify the evangelical counsels as well as the resurrection, and they affect the consecration of the world by their example, prayers, sacrifices, and apostolates. Clergy signify the objective presence of Jesus Christ as head and bridegroom of the church, and they teach, lead, and sanctify the people of God through their ministerial activities. When cooperating together, the vocations approach a more complete and more efficacious sign of Christ's salvific person and work.

The three paradigmatic vocations relate, in Balthasar's framework, according to a trinitarian *ana*-logic. Ecclesial communion is based on and is a participation in trinitarian communion. Hence, to appreciate the internal dynamics of the relations between vocations, one must look ultimately at trinitarian relations.[19] The trinitarian relations are marked by "union-coincident-with-distinction,"[20] interdependent complementarity, and *perichoresis*.

In the Trinity, union is coincident with distinction. There is one God and three persons. The three persons share in the one divine nature. As such, they are coeternal, coequal, and consubstantial. To each can be attributed the name of the almighty, all knowing, all loving God. Balthasar, however, does not prefer to reflect on the one divine nature in abstraction from the communion of the three distinct persons.[21] In Balthasar's view, distinction, like unity, is a perfection, one that has per-

19. *CSL*, 385–87. Elsewhere Balthasar states that the first basis of ecclesial communion is "God himself, who could not bestow personal communion with himself and among men if he were not already in a profound sense a community in himself: loving mutual inherence, loving exchange"; Balthasar, "Communio—A Program," *Communio* 33 (Spring 2006): 157–58.

20. According to David Schindler, "Union is coincident-with-distinct-integrity.... The deeper and truer the union, the more the partners grow in the distinct integrity proper to each.... I become more myself not by first pulling away from the other, but by serving the other, subordinating myself to the other, indeed obeying the other: in short, by receiving the other and in turn giving myself completely to the other"; David L. Schindler, *Heart of the World, Center of the Church: "Communio" Ecclesiology, Liberalism, and Liberation* (Grand Rapids, Mich.: Eerdmans, 1996), 18–19.

21. See Anne Hunt, *The Trinity and the Paschal Mystery: A Development in Recent Catholic Theology* (Collegeville, Minn.: Liturgical Press, 1997), 83.

haps been not sufficiently reflected upon by the theological tradition. The distinction between the persons is so perfect that every distinction and difference among creatures is but a reflection of the eternal, infinite distinction between the trinitarian persons.[22] Distinction, moreover, is a condition of any authentic union (lest unity be conflated with identity).[23]

The three distinct persons relate in a complementary, interdependent way. In the immanent life of God, the divine nature, which is love, is fulfilled in kenotic outpouring and receiving among the trinitarian persons. Hence, in God, there must be a communion of interdependent persons for all eternity. The Father needs the Son to be the Son (and different from the Father by virtue of the latter's Son-ship) if He is to be the Father in a love relationship, and vice versa.[24] Economically, there is also an interdependent complementarity. Tradition, most notably the great creeds, recognizes an appropriation of salvation-historical tasks to the different persons of the Trinity. Creation is appropriated to the Father. Redemption is appropriated to the Son. Sanctification is appropriated to the Spirit.[25] This appropriation does not mean that the other divine persons are excluded from or somehow inoperative in these works, but that the glory of a particular person is on display in a special way in certain moments of salvation history. From this display it can be deduced that this person is in some way at the forefront of this divine action. These economic missions, moreover, reveal certain features of immanent trinitarian life. Hence the economic tasks are "appropriate" to the eternal processions. The Father who creates is also the one who eternally begets the Son. The Christ who redeems by returning the world to the Godhead is the only-begotten Son who eternally turns back in love toward

22. "In the Trinitarian dogma, God is one, good, true, and beautiful because he is essentially love, and love supposes the one, the other and their unity. And if it is necessary to suppose the Other, the Word, the Son, in God, then the otherness of the creation is not a fall, a disgrace, but an image of God, even as it is not God"; Balthasar, "A Résume of My Thought," *Communio* 15 (Winter 1988): 473.

23. *ET* 2:184–85.

24. "This person [the Son], in order to preserve his identity, must be Trinitarian. In order to be himself, he needs the Father and the Spirit"; *TD* 3:162.

25. On appropriation, see Gilles Emery, *The Trinity*, trans. Matthew Levering (Washington, D.C.: The Catholic University of America Press, 2011), 164–68; Walter Kasper, *The God of Jesus Christ*, trans. Matthew J. O'Connell (New York: Crossroad, 1984), 282–83.

the Father.[26] The Spirit sanctifies by creating a bond between creatures and God that reflects his personhood as the bond between the Father and the Son.[27] The economic missions are interdependent in the sense that salvation history is carried out through their cooperative action.

In addition to distinction and interdependence, there is *perichoresis* in the Trinity. The self-gifting and reception among the trinitarian persons is so profound that the persons "circumincess" or indwell one another.[28] Hence, trinitarian union is more than the sharing of an abstract nature. Rather, the divine nature *is* love, and the Godhead is united in an eternal sharing of interpersonal love so complete that each of the persons is truly present in the others. The closest analogy in human experience to the *perichoretic* unity of trinitarian love is the one-flesh union of husband and wife where, in a good marriage, the husband and wife not only join together corporally but dwell spiritually by the power of love in one another's hearts while still remaining distinct. Another related example is the fruit of their union, a child who shares the flesh and blood, and something of the personality, of both of them, yet is his own person.[29] Through *perichoretic* exchange, the trinitarian persons are truly present in one another, so much so that Balthasar states, "Christ is at the same time not only Himself—Savior, Judge, Logos—but also the representative of the Father. He makes the Father tangible, visible: in seeing the Son, we have access to the Father's heart. Christ is, moreover, *the* spiritual man, the Presence of the *Pneuma* (Spirit) in the world."[30]

The trinitarian relations condition ecclesial relations that are a sacramental "representation of the love of the blessed Trinity."[31] Accordingly, the church's vocations' relations to one another resemble the re-

26. *TD* 3:230n68 and *FG* 59.

27. *ET* 3:127–28.

28. Balthasar, *Explorations in Theology*, vol. 1, *The Word Made Flesh* (San Francisco: Ignatius Press, 1989), 222; hereafter *ET* 1.

29. See Schindler, "Institution and Charism: The Missions of the Son and Spirit in Church and World," *Communio: International Catholic Review* 25 (Summer 1998): 253–73, esp. 258.

30. Balthasar, "Johannine Themes in the Rule and their Meaning Today" (hereafter JT), *Monastic Studies* 11 (1975): 69–70.

31. *CSL*, 386.

lations of the trinitarian persons. They are marked by unity, distinction, complementary interdependence, and *perichoresis*.

The unity of the church has been guaranteed by the prayer of Christ himself that "they may be one just as we are one. I in them, and thou in me, that they may be perfectly one" (Jn 17:22–23). Ecclesial unity is generated by and reflected in the church's members' sharing "one faith" and "one baptism" (Eph 4:5) and the Eucharistic "one bread and one body" (1 Cor 10:17).[32] In the *one* body of Christ, there is, then, an essential unity underlying every distinction among vocations. It is the unity of the Christ-form animating the church through the Spirit in whom every Christian participates. In all cases, the Christian vocation will involve the twofold love of God and neighbor that is at the heart of Christ's own mission. It will be expressed by every Christian through prayer, worship, sacrifice, service, and witness of word and deed. Whatever specific vocational form this love takes is ultimately secondary.

As with the Trinity, union is coincident with distinction in the church.[33] This, of course, is underlined by the teaching of Paul that "the body, though one, has many parts" (see 1 Cor 12:12). As we have seen, Balthasar distinguishes the church's vocations according to their aesthetic (what they signify) and dramatic (what they perform or do) elements. We can now establish how the distinct vocations are interdependent and complementary in their aesthetic and dramatic features. For example, the layperson needs the concrete public witness of religious life to understand the *spirit* of the evangelical counsels according to which all Christians are, in fact, called to live (1 Cor 7: 29–31). He or she also depends on religious for their prayers and sacrifices that bear fruit for the whole church. The layperson similarly needs the gift of the ministerial priesthood so that he or she might hear the gospel authoritatively preached and doctrine taught and so that he or she might receive the sacramental grace that will animate his or her own vocation in the world.

32. Balthasar, *Love Alone Is Credible* (hereafter *LAIC*), trans. D. C. Schindler (San Francisco: Ignatius Press, 2004), 122–23.

33. On the trinitarian relations as the basis for the unity and distinction of persons in the church, see Balthasar, *Theo-Drama: Theological Dramatic Theory*, vol. 5, *The Final Act*, trans. Graham Harrison (San Francisco: Ignatius Press, 1998), 485–86.

Conversely, the clergy are dependent on the laity insofar as the very purpose of the former is to support the Christian life and mission of the latter. Objective ecclesiastical office is justified by its making possible the subjective sanctification of the faithful and to support the baptized in missiological engagement with the world.[34] As we said in chapter 6, Balthasar often compares the relation of clergy and laity to that between a husband and wife. The masculine priesthood seeds the feminine church with word and sacrament and depends on the faithful to bring that gift to fruition. Clergy are also dependent on religious. The priest looks to the religious to be a public sign of the bride of Christ radically responding to grace with obedience and total availability and to provide charismatic reform and prophetic wisdom that can complement official teaching.

Like the laity, religious depend on the clergy for objective official teaching, the grace of the sacraments, and special solicitude for ecclesial unity. Also with the laity, religious look to the threefold ministerial office as a visible point of reference for understanding their own participation in the analogous prophetic-royal-priesthood of the faithful.[35] Like the clergy, religious depend on the ordinary faithful to bring to fruition the gift they offer; the layperson translates the material witness of the counsels into spirit. Furthermore, laypersons in families model the meaning of authentic espousal, fraternity, sorority, paternity, maternity, sonship and daughterhood that conversely, analogously serve as the relational categories of both clerical and religious life.[36]

Finally, in the church as in the Trinity, there is *perichoresis*. Just as the Father indwells the Son and the Son reveals the Father, there is, among the paradigmatic vocations, "a reciprocal indwelling that lies beyond all imagination."[37] Balthasar laments that too many ecclesiological treatises, in an attempt to delineate sharply the roles of the various vocations, ignore the mystery of *perichoresis*: "The ecclesiastical states are treated as though they were separate departments of a secular as-

34. According to Balthasar, the priest stands like an "armor bearer" behind the lay "battling knight" as the latter engages the world; *ET* 2:327.

35. *CSL*, 365–87.

36. See *FC* 16.

37. *LAIC*, 123.

sociation, without due attention to the profound mysteries of the ontology of the Church and the resultant circumincession of the various states."[38] The church should be regarded as a living body where "everything is interrelated with everything" and that cannot be dissected into separate, isolated parts without violence being done to its integral union.[39] The mystery of *perichoresis* means that each paradigmatic vocation is, in fact, "a specific representation of something that is present" in the others.[40] Hence, there is a fluidity between and among them. Just as it is impossible to pinpoint where Christ ends and the church begins, where the human nature of Christ ends and the divine nature begins, or where the person of the Father ends and the person of the Son begins, even though they are all nonetheless distinct, it is rarely possible to draw definitively the boundaries of the states and vocations that flow from the Christological and trinitarian mysteries.[41]

The *perichoretic* unity of the church means that even though certain tasks are appropriated to particular vocations, the same tasks are participated in—either vicariously or directly—by the other vocations. Vicarious participation is possible because the vocations of specific persons are drawn Eucharistically into the *perichoresis* of the Trinity itself "and given a 'collective' reality" that mirrors the trinitarian *analogatum princeps*.[42] As the Father is present in the Son through the Spirit, the vocations of ecclesial persons, when "rooted in the realm of grace ... can be said to be present to one another in the Spirit in a manner that is truly real. The 'mission' of the most obscure and hidden person is, therefore, 'present' in the mission of a more 'public' person and vice-versa."[43]

Concrete examples of vicarious *perichoretic* participation are helpful here. When, for instance, the priest acts *in persona Christi* in the liturgy, he also acts *in persona ecclesiae*, which means that the whole church is involved through him in his action. The whole church is present, mysteriously, *perichoretically*, in the deeds performed by the priest

38 *ET* 1:222.
39. *OPSC*, 138–39.
40. CSL, 385.
41. *LLC* 16–17, 178, 256.
42. Chapp, "Who Is the Church?," 330.
43. Chapp, "Who Is the Church?," 330.

in the name of the church.[44] When a young person enters religious life, he or she represents and includes in himself or herself the home and family from which he or she came and thus brings those who shaped his or her background to a vicarious representational eschatological finality.[45] When the lay person acts in the church or in the world, he or she really brings the spirit of those in the vowed life of the counsels, and the graces won by their prayers, to his or her work. If the priest has truly made a gift of his own person when he shared the gospel and the sacraments, then he, too, is vicariously present in the layperson's activity. These instances of vicarious participation are all possible only in the Eucharistic church, where the body of Christ is shared and the members of the church through loving union pneumatically indwell one another after the model of trinitarian *perichoresis.*

Furthermore, because of the analogy to the Trinity's *perichoretic* unity, it is possible for the various vocations to be involved not only vicariously but also directly in what is primarily appropriated to the other vocations without doing violence to the integrity and distinction of each. Analogous to the way Son and Spirit played a role in creation without losing their distinction from the Father, the various vocations may and do directly participate to varying degrees in the roles that are primarily signified by and tasked to other vocations.

The asceticism and contemplation typified by religious are activities in which the other vocations can and must participate. Everyone has an "inner monk" that he or she can cultivate. It is also true that each one has an "inner priest" or "inner minister." Balthasar notes several ways in which laypeople share in "ministeriality itself ... performing acts that either pertain to them by right as a Christian or else are specifically entrusted to him by the hierarchy."[46] Laypeople may baptize in an emergency and act as extraordinary ministers of communion. Man and woman are the official ministers of the sacrament of marriage and act as priests within their home. Balthasar is even sympathetic to Thomas's speculation that a layperson can offer a "quasi-sacramental" forgive-

44. *ET* 2:154.

45. See *TSS* 118, where Balthasar compares the completion of family life in religious life to the transition from the Old to the New Testaments.

46. *ET* 2:322.

ness to his brothers and sisters.[47] There are also the many instances of nonordained persons delegated to exercise ecclesial offices with official authority such as religious superiors and, in another way, lay administrators of ecclesial institutions such as hospitals and schools. Finally, there has been a long tradition of lay teaching and preaching, not just in terms of the informal sharing of faith that is the duty of every Christian, but as an "explicit sharing in the preaching of the hierarchy," such as is carried out by official catechists, institutionally backed lay evangelists, licensed theologians, and canonical judges who have some authorization to act "in the name of the Church."[48] These actions reveal the interpenetration of the lay and ministerial priesthoods and the potentiality of the former to even cross over into some actions usually performed by the latter. On the other side, Balthasar readily acknowledges that religious and clergy may engage in secular occupations and discussions, otherwise appropriated to the laity, such as when the medieval monks developed the arts and sciences. While it would be "dillentantism," he says, for priests and religious to assume authority over secular fields in which they have no expertise,[49] it is nonetheless permissible for clergy and religious to develop secular interests and avocations.[50] "In the last analysis," clergy and religious, like laity, "are in the world."[51] Although they represent eschatological mysteries, they are still in history and have not yet reached the lasting city, so therefore they can and even must engage the secular.

There are limits, of course, to direct participation in what is appropriated to the others. In the natural order, a male can be motherly, but he can never bear a child. Theologically, the Son is everything the Father is, but he is not the Father. Against the ancient heresy of Patripassianism, only the Second Person underwent bodily death on the Cross. Ecclesiologically, a layperson's priesthood differs in "essence" and not only "degree" from that of the clergy;[52] hence the layperson can never

47. *ET* 2:323.

48. *ET* 2:324.

49. *CSL*, 357.

50. See Balthasar's celebration of medieval monastic contributions to secular fields in *LLC* 76–81. See also his interest in encouraging contemporary priests to develop an interest in psychology in *CSL*, 374.

51. *CSL*, 213.

52. *LG* 10.

confect the Eucharist or ordain a priest. It is, meanwhile, canonically illegal for clergy and religious to hold secular political authority, and monks and nuns cannot marry and remain monks and nuns. Hence, however great *perichoresis* may be, it does not imply that one vocation may simply become the other.

Near the end of *The Christian State of Life*, Balthasar offers a framework by which he carefully respects the vocations' interdependence and distinctiveness. The laity, he says, stand at the forefront of the church's incarnate movement, its penetration into creation with its secular structures of family life, secular work, and culture; but they are followed by clergy and religious who also participate in this work, either vicariously or directly. Religious take the first place in the eschatological movement of ascetic withdrawal from the world and the subjective imitation of Christ's way of life in the evangelical counsels, but they are followed, second, by clergy (who commit to obedience and celibacy, though not poverty) and, third, by the ordinary faithful (who must still interiorize the spirit of the counsels). Clergy hold first place in exercising official public ministry, but they are followed in second place by religious who share with them in representing the public face of the church to the world. Nonordained religious, notes Balthasar, rather often perform apostolic services "in the name of the Church," and in cooperation with the hierarchy.[53] The ordinary faithful rank third here, but they, too, must be conscious that they represent the church in their actions and may even be formally commissioned to exercise office on its behalf.

The principle of *perichoresis* is what makes Balthasar's system open to religious priesthood. Since each paradigmatic vocation represents something that is also present in the others, it is only a short leap to consider it possible for there to be vocations that are capable of representing two paradigms at once. This may even be helpful for the church so that the underlying unity of the states is embodied and borne witness to. This need not violate the integrity of either paradigm. Just as a human child represents the communion of his two parents whose nonidentity with each other made love possible between them, but then embodies their objective fruit in the one flesh, which is distinctly his

53. *ET* 2:455.

own, so too there can be vocations in the church that embody juxtaposed vocations and emerge as something new without violating the distinction of the "parent" vocations. In a way, Balthasar's beloved secular institutes, which unite the life of the counsels (typified by religious) with life in the world (typified by the lay-married state) are one such vocation. So, too, is religious priesthood, which unites the paradigmatic vocations of religious life and hierarchical ministry. The religious priest is not a hybrid or a compromise. He has his own distinct mission in the church. As the Holy Spirit is both the bond of communion of the Father and the Son and the objective fruit of their mutual spiration,[54] so, too, the religious priesthood is both the union of the vocations to religious life and priesthood and a particular vocation in its own right. That Balthasar embraced such a vision of religious priesthood, and that he saw a specific function for it in the church, is best demonstrated by his descriptions of the figures of John and Paul, to which we now turn.

54. *ET* 3:126–28.

CHAPTER 8

The Apostles John and Paul as Images of Religious Priesthood

In addition to his analogical ecclesiology, Balthasar made a second major contribution to a theology of religious priesthood by identifying the apostles John and Paul as representative types of this vocation. Balthasar provides a great service here because Vatican II did not provide any guiding images for religious priesthood. As scriptural images of religious priesthood, John and Paul model the integration of the vocations of religious life and priesthood into a single personal mission. Also, because contemporary ecclesial relations ought to recapitulate the original constellational relations, John and Paul illuminate how religious priesthood ideally functions within the *communio* of today's church. To put things in a Balthasarian way, in John and Paul we are able to "see the form" of religious priesthood.

Why does Balthasar identify John and Paul as types of religious priesthood and not, for example, James, Andrew, or Peter? Like all the apostles, John and Paul are ministerial priests called to radical renunciation of the world. However, in contrast to the other original apostles, both are associated, either by scripture or tradition, with explicit virginity, and thus they depict more completely and less ambiguously than the other apostles the fullness of the life of the counsels.[1] Furthermore,

1. *CSL*, 155 and 281. Aidan Nichols explains that in the New Testament descriptions of the apostolic life, poverty is emphasized more than virginity, with the latter seeming like "a subset of poverty (abandoning one's partner is part and parcel of becoming poor). Eventually, it [virginity] will acquire a primacy but, to begin with, the Redeemer

both have a special association in Balthasar's system with charismatic reform/renewal and eschatological witness, which are characteristic features of religious life.

In this chapter, we will examine Balthasar's presentation of John and Paul as types of religious priesthood. Specifically, we'll discuss his vision of religious priesthood, as revealed by John and Paul, as a vocation that both signifies subjective holiness and objective ministry and mediates between charism and institution. Then, we will note John and Paul's eschatological stance and explain how this stance conditions their ministries. Finally, we will show how Balthasar associates John and Paul with different trajectories in the tradition of religious priesthood. For Balthasar, John is especially a type of contemplative/monastic religious priesthood, and Paul is especially a type of itinerant/active religious priesthood.

John's Mediating and Unifying Mission

Balthasar takes it for granted that the John mentioned in the synoptic gospels is the author of the Fourth Gospel and the "beloved disciple" mentioned therein; he also accepts that John is the author of the Johannine epistles and the book of Revelation.[2] His position conflicts with that of many contemporary scripture scholars, but it accords with ancient tradition and serves Balthasar's purpose of providing the fullest possible portrait of John.[3]

---

made his choice from the faithful of the House of Israel for whom marriage was itself a state of promise"; Nichols, *Divine Fruitfulness*, 216. Balthasar highlights that the Apostle John already seemed to have taken poverty to its ultimate conclusion in this regard by remaining a virgin, as will Paul. Hence, virginity is latent in the original group living the counsels and only fully realized in some of them.

2. *OPSC*, 238–42 and 318–19.

3. Most contemporary Catholic scripture scholars follow the ancient tradition insofar as they admit a relationship between the Fourth Gospel and the Johannine epistles, noting that these share similar language and themes. The majority view is that these works emerged from the same community, though perhaps from different individual authors. Despite the use of the name "John" by the author of Revelation (Rv 1:1), this book's relation to the Johannine community is more controversial, though there are important literary parallels between Revelation, the Fourth Gospel, and the epistles. Raymond E. Brown, for example, argues for a substantial degree of contact between the author

According to Balthasar, this apostle's specific mission is to mediate between the church's charismatic/subjective and official/objective poles. As a mediator, John represents and communicates charismatic wisdom and subjective holiness to Peter, the symbol of objective office, and represents and communicates official objective authority to Mary, the symbol of the church's charismatic/subjective pole. In addition to this interpersonal mediating role, John "unites in his own person" the charismatic/subjective and official/objective poles, which is to say that Mary and Peter are both *perichoretically* present in John.[4]

In portraying John, Balthasar often stresses the apostle's subjective holiness and charismatic wisdom. John has profound knowledge of the Lord and the Lord's will. This is knowledge born from deep personal intimacy with Christ. Balthasar highlights that it was John who was called "beloved"; John who was allowed to lay his head on the savior's breast; John who faithfully remained by Jesus at the Cross; and John who was entrusted by Jesus to care for Mary.[5] In Balthasar's writings, he often

of Revelation and the Johannine community, but stops short of identifying the author of Revelation as a member of the Johannine community; see Brown, *An Introduction to the New Testament* (New York: Doubleday, 1997), 802–5. Among contemporary Catholic scripture scholars, Luke T. Johnson is a reputable figure willing to entertain Johannine authorship of Revelation or at least authorship by a figure in the Johannine community; see Johnson, *The Writings of the New Testament: An Interpretation* (Philadelphia: Fortress, 1986), 518–20. Johnson also provides references to the ancient fathers, who attributed Revelation to John the Apostle. Balthasar never mounts a defense of his identification of John the Apostle with the author(s) of the Fourth Gospel, the epistles, and Revelation. It is not an easy task to defend Balthasar on this point. One would have to recognize the importance that reading each text in light of tradition and of the whole canon—an approach endorsed by the church itself (see *CCC* 112 and 113)—has for the Swiss theologian (see Bramwell, "Hans Urs von Balthasar's Theology of Scripture," 319–22), and then show that such a reading invites this identification. It may be easier to just note that in Balthasar's ecclesiology, constellational missions are taken up into the church and shared with later figures. Hence, one could argue that even if these figures were in fact different people, they shared in the same basic Johannine mission. If accepted, this approach would harmonize Balthasar with those who see the Fourth Gospel, Johannine epistles, and Revelation as under the same basic influence (such as Johnson and, to some degree, Brown). For a negative critique of Balthasar's scriptural methodology, see Steffen Lösel, "Conciliar, Not Conciliatory: Hans Urs von Balthasar's Ecclesiological Synthesis of Vatican II," *Modern Theology* 24, no. 1 (2008): 23–49, esp. 40–42.

4. *CSL*, 289.

5. See *CSL*, 287–88, 369.

emphasizes the necessity of prayer and sanctity to theology.[6] It is not surprising, then, that Balthasar sees in John one who is simultaneously the "beloved disciple," who is a symbol of "Christian life well lived,"[7] and the apostle who "from the earliest time ... was called 'the Theologian,' which shows that what he has to say comes from the inner realm between Father and Son, inspired by the Spirit like no other writer."[8] According to Balthasar, John is the evangelist most able to articulate the soteriological significance of Christ's obedience, the dynamics of the Father and Son's love, and the ecclesial requirement of self-sacrifice for one's brothers and sisters in imitation of the Lord's laying down of his life for his friends.[9] John was able to know and communicate these things, says Balthasar, because he was the Lord's greatest friend. Although John is a priest, his authority as a prophetic teacher comes not only from his office, but from his sanctity, his subjective communion with the Lord. As Balthasar puts it, "One cannot understand anything in the realm of love unless one loves."[10] John's charismatic wisdom is a Christian *gnosis* born from the contemplative intimacy and faithful discipleship Balthasar also associates with the Marian profile.[11]

As a charismatic-prophetic wisdom figure, John is described by Balthasar as charged with "conveying and interpreting the presence and the will of the Lord" to Peter, the chief of the apostles.[12] For example, at the Last Supper, Peter asks John, who was "reclining at Jesus' side" (Jn 13:23), to discover which of the apostles would betray the Lord. "The Lord answered [John] openly and clearly," writes Balthasar, "for he would leave unanswered no question put to him by love."[13] Also, at the resurrection scene by the Sea of Tiberias, John quickly recognizes the

6. See Balthasar, *Convergences: To the Source of Christian Mystery*, trans. E. A. Nelson (San Francisco: Ignatius Press, 1983), 17–45.

7. Nichols, *Say It Is Pentecost: A Guide through Balthasar's Logic* (Washington, D.C.: The Catholic University of America Press, 2001), 185.

8. *TL* 3:78.

9. *LLC* 64; *CSL*, 254–55.

10. *CSL*, 284.

11. As Brendan Leahy points out, "Balthasar closely links John with Mary to a degree that in his writings the Marian and Johannine principles are not always easy to distinguish"; *Marian Profile*, 65.

12. *LLC* 68.

13. *CSL*, 283.

Lord and informs Peter, inspiring the latter to go out and meet Christ (see Jn 21:7). As Robert Barron states, "These stories evoke the mystical intuition that 'sees' before office, and more clearly."[14] John's mediating mission requires him to share what he sees and knows with Peter, who does not yet see.

Peter must learn not only from John's charismatic wisdom, but from his moral example. For Balthasar, the conversation between Christ and Peter by the Sea of Tiberias carries tremendous import (see Jn 21:15–19). Peter, who has betrayed Christ three times, is now asked to affirm his love for Christ three times. Balthasar highlights that each time Peter is asked to affirm his love, he is addressed as "son of John." Balthasar sees great significance in this appellation. By calling Peter "son of John," the Lord, Balthasar surmises, intended to emphasize that Peter must ground himself in the same subjective love typified by the beloved disciple who faithfully followed Christ to the Cross. Peter must follow John's example. "He must also become the embodiment of love," incarnating what John has incarnated, even "more than" John (Jn 21:15).[15]

According to Balthasar, the relational pattern between Peter, the symbol of office, and John, the symbol of the charismatic wisdom that flows from subjective discipleship, serves as a model for relations between clergy and religious. The scenes just mentioned illustrate that the hierarchy must be open to learning from the charismatic wisdom of religious and must strive to attain the subjective holiness for which religious life serves as a public sign. Additionally, Balthasar uses the Petrine-Johannine relation to demonstrate that the clergy should recognize and protect religious life as a "region of mystery" with a relative autonomy.[16] Balthasar sees the scene at the foot of the Cross in which John is given to Mary with the words, "Woman, behold your son," and Mary is given to John, with the words, "Behold your mother" (Jn 19: 26–7), as an anticipation of religious life, for it instituted for the first time a "community of virgins."[17] The scene suggests the charismatic nature of religious life's origins. Balthasar notes that John and Mary's

14. Barron, *Strangest Way*, 121.

15. *CSL*, 284.

16. *CSL*, 285–87.

17. *CSL*, 210.

community is founded "during Peter's absence and without consulting him."[18] This scene anticipates the way religious life will most often unfold as a charismatic gift to the church inspired directly by the Lord rather than being a product of any initiative by the hierarchy. Accordingly, the hierarchy must respect the mystery of religious life as a divine gift to the church. The hierarchy "does not possess the right to reject or suppress such a mission once it is recognized as divine."[19]

On the other hand, Balthasar notes that John willingly subordinates himself to Peter. Although John's special relationship to the Lord is highlighted in the Fourth Gospel, Balthasar notes that the same Gospel is in harmony with the synoptic emphasis on Peter's preeminence among the Twelve.[20] At the beginning of Acts, John is always present with Peter, but John is largely silent, and then disappears.[21] At the Last Supper, John inquires of the Lord about the betrayal only at the request of Peter, thus indicating John's obedience to Peter.[22] On Easter morning, John arrives before Peter at the empty tomb but then pauses and allows Peter to enter before him. Balthasar concludes, "Love ... arrived more quickly at the goal, but did not use the nearness thus afforded it to take precedence over office. On the contrary, John waited for Peter to come up, let him enter the tomb first, and went in himself only after Peter had concluded his official inspection."[23] John recognized that it was Peter's job to "officially verify the facts."[24] The pattern repeats by

18. "During Peter's absence and without consulting him, the Lord bound the virgin souls at the foot of the Cross into a new community conferred directly from above, which Peter had later to acknowledge as coming from the Lord. This is also the way in which true religious orders were later established. Apostolates conferred directly by the Holy Spirit filled the founders, as it were, with a new 'spirit,' a new 'spirituality,' and, after their genuineness had been properly tested, were acknowledged by the official Church and incorporated into its innermost life"; *CSL*, 289.

In another place, Balthasar notes that "the [religious] Orders, the strongest bulwark of the Christian life in the Church, are perhaps the only thing in the Church that she herself has never founded: each time, she has received them anew from above, from the Holy Spirit"; *LLC*, 66–67.

19. *LLC* 67.

20. *OPSC*, 240.

21. *OPSC*, 351–52.

22. "John's greater love is placed at Peter's disposal. He may use it"; *CSL*, 284.

23. *CSL*, 283.

24. *OPSC*, 351.

the Sea of Tiberias. John is first to recognize the Lord standing on the shore, but allows Peter "in his official capacity to take charge of the situation."[25] Balthasar even implies that John and Mary, having been joined by the Lord at the foot of the Cross, would have sought Peter's recognition and blessing of their new community once Peter's faith had been strengthened after the resurrection.[26]

In Balthasar's view, these scenes provide a pattern of mutual respect as the way in which office and charism, hierarchy and religious life should ideally relate. Although the hierarchy depends on religious for mystical insights, charismatic wisdom, and moral example, religious life must allow the hierarchy to put questions to it, to test and investigate its claims and authenticity. Religious life cannot withdraw from "Peter's ken"; rather, it must "reveal and subject" itself to the hierarchy so that, if affirmed, its life may be a source of renewal for the whole church.[27] All of the great religious founders, claims Balthasar, were "distinguished by their unfathomable humility before the hierarchical church," entrusting their new structures to the latter's discernment.[28] In doing so, they followed John's example. The hierarchy, for its part, has a duty to investigate and test charismatic renewal in order to discern its validity for the church.[29]

John's role involves him not only in mediating charismatic wisdom and example of subjective holiness to Peter, but also in mediating the church's official and objective office to Mary. Balthasar observes that the figures of Peter (the masculine type of office) and Mary (the feminine type of the church as well as of much that is associated with religious life—that is, charismatic renewal, and signification of subjective holiness) barely ever encounter one another in the gospels. In Balthasar's estimation, John's "express task is to link these two *Real symbols* of the Church," to "mediate between Peter and Mary,"[30] so that the church does not fall into "two separate parts" (perhaps a cold, dog-

25. *CSL*, 283.
26. *CSL*, 289 and 386.
27. *CSL*, 286.
28. *DGO* 26.
29. *CSL*, 286 and 369.
30. *OPSC*, 239, and *CSL*, 289.

matic institution on the one hand and an affectively warm but chaotic charismatic community on the other).[31] John receives and represents this unifying-mediating task during the scene at the foot of the Cross where John and Mary are entrusted to each other (see Jn 19:26–27). John is an apostle, a priest, who represents the Petrine pole.[32] In receiving Mary, John thus receives her for the official church. In receiving her, he receives the church's subjective heart. In being received by John, who represents office, Mary's availability and wisdom will be "channeled" through John to Peter and the other apostles and thus made available to the whole church.[33] At the same time, the Marian church receives a guardian and protector in the form of John, who guarantees apostolic stewardship of her and will communicate authoritative teaching to her. Meanwhile, John is identified as her "son" in the church, which places the ministry in the context of service and implies the unofficial authority present in the Marian pole.[34]

In the scene at the foot of the Cross, Mary represents not only herself, but the entire laity of the church and the state of the counsels (for she too is a virgin).[35] Hence, the event has implications far beyond the relation between religious life and priesthood. Nonetheless, because Balthasar specifically identifies this moment as an inaugural event for religious life and points to John's identity as a priest in this moment, it suggests a special role for religious priests.[36] The religious priest will represent religious life to the hierarchy of the church, thus bringing the witness of subjective discipleship and charismatic wisdom into dialogue with the ecclesiastical institution. At the same time, the religious priest must represent the hierarchical pole of the church to and within the religious family, thus affirming a community's union with the rest of the church and providing a medium for official authority and teaching within it.

Undoubtedly, nonordained religious engage directly with diocesan

31. *OPSC*, 241.

32. "John is under Peter's jurisdiction"; *CSL*, 289.

33. *OPSC*, 222.

34. *OPSC*, 153. See also Leahy, *Marian Profile*, 134–36.

35. *CSL*, 288–89.

36. *CSL*, 210 and 287–89.

clergy, and diocesan clergy certainly benefit from the witness of nonordained religious without the mediation of religious priests. In this sense, the role assigned by Balthasar to John and religious priesthood can seem superfluous. Perhaps a line from the Second Vatican Council can shed light, however, on how the mediating presence of religious priests benefits the church: *Apostolicam Actuositatem* highlights the efficacy of an "apostolate of like towards like" (*AA* 13). Religious may be more open to the official teaching and governance of the Petrine pole if one of their own is seen as exercising these functions.[37] In the fourth century, for example, Athanasius advocated the ordination of monks as a way to advance orthodoxy among the desert ascetics. The clergy, meanwhile, may be more receptive to the witness and wisdom of religious if one of their own introduces these gifts to them. Accordingly, in the thirteenth century, one reason popes defended the mendicant orders and advanced their clericalization was because they sensed it would have a reforming effect on the entire clergy. While all religious and clergy need to foster unity and reciprocal influence between them, the Johannine religious priest, who "is intimately linked" to both religious life and priesthood, has the special task of safeguarding their reciprocal influence and communion.[38] Balthasar takes the scene at the foot of the Cross quite seriously as indicating this special role for religious priests.

John not only mediates, in an interpersonal way, between the charismatic/subjective and official/objective poles, he also "unites in his own person both the personal [subjective] and official [objective] priesthood of the Church."[39] Thus, he is a sign of the potential of two paradigmatic vocations—namely, religious life and priesthood—to be integrated in a singular personal mission. John's association with the charismatic and subjective elements of religious life has already been well established. John's ministerial identity is emphasized a bit less in Balthasar's writings (mainly because he is usually discussed in contrast to Peter), but it is neither ignored nor denied. Balthasar notes that just as Peter "bore John

37. Women's communities are not necessarily excluded from this equation if one considers that a male chaplain from their "religious family" may be more readily considered one of their own.

38. *OPSC*, 241.

39. *CSL*, 289.

in himself" with his threefold affirmation of love by the Sea of Tiberias, so too "John bore Peter in himself."[40] John's assumption of (Petrine) pastoral leadership is most evident in his care of Mary and at Ephesus, where the Johannine epistles show him acting as an official teacher defining doctrine for the community he governs, and where he exercises shepherding authority by confronting Diotrephes (3 Jn 9–10).[41]

Priests must be Christians before they are ordained ministers, and every priest continues to practice subjective discipleship in addition to holding objective ministerial office. Nonetheless, in Balthasar's estimation, there is a subtle difference between John and Peter in how they balance these two aspects (discipleship and ministry) of their respective vocations. Noting the difference in the way they relate to the Lord in the gospels, where John is consistently portrayed as Christ's friend and Peter is mainly characterized by the charge he receives to lead, Balthasar concludes that for John, subjective personal discipleship always has an existential priority: "John was, from the beginning, the epitome of love. . . . He received the office of priest by reason of his personal dedication."[42] For Peter, in contrast, the objective ministry of priesthood has a priority: "Peter received an office and love was then bestowed upon him for the sake of the office—that he might accomplish it more perfectly."[43] Balthasar thus uses John and Peter to illustrate the difference "between a primarily participatory state of the counsels," which may unfold into a priestly vocation, and "the primarily functional priesthood," which requires a secondary subjective conformity.[44]

In sum, Balthasar uses the figure of John to illuminate the vocation of religious priesthood. John interpersonally mediates between the charismatic/subjective (Marian) and official/objective (Petrine) poles of the church and serves as a type for double signification of religious life and priesthood in a single personal mission. Balthasar uses the figure of Paul in a similar way.

40. *CSL*, 287.
41. *OPSC*, 240.
42. *CSL*, 287.
43. *CSL*, 287.
44. *CSL*, 282.

Paul's Mediating and Unifying Mission

Even more than John, Paul is a symbol of charismatic renewal. Paul is the apostle "born abnormally" (1 Cor 15:8), a description that underlines his surprising emergence as a leader within the early church. His conversion on the road to Damascus and subsequent rise as an apostle whose authority was coequal to the Twelve, and whose mission was more extensive, was a shocking development. Paul had not only been an enemy of Christ and persecutor of Christians, but he had never known the Lord before the resurrection. Furthermore, the place among the Twelve that had opened upon the betrayal and death of Judas had already been filled by Matthias, and, as Balthasar points out, "no provision is made for a thirteenth gate" (Rv 21:14).[45] Nonetheless, Paul emerges, is recognized as legitimate, and accomplishes the "lion's share" of the apostolic work.[46]

In Balthasar's view, Paul's biography makes him a particularly apt type for the charismatic pole of the church and of religious life in particular. He anticipates all the great charismatic movements and religious foundations that will "fall into the garden of the Church like a meteor," thus proving for the church the Holy Spirit's freedom and continued creative presence in her life.[47] "The case of Paul shows that there are new callings, new designations through the Holy Spirit" in every age.[48] These missions serve the dual purpose of reminding the church that it depends on the Lord, who grants it "spontaneous, free vocations" that it cannot "manipulate" or "institute,"[49] and of providing for the specific missiological needs that arise within history.[50]

As with John, Balthasar perceives Paul's pattern of relating to official authority as instructive for religious in their dealings with the hierarchy. In contrast to John, however, Paul's biography points more to the real tension that can exist between the charismatic and official ecclesial

45. *OPSC*, 151.
46. *OPSC*, 151.
47. *LLC* 67.
48. *LLC* 16.
49. *LLC* 17.
50. *TH* 109–10.

elements.[51] Paul "has to fight" for recognition of his mission by Peter, John, and James.[52] His struggle for legitimization by the official ecclesial authorities has been repeated through the ages in the drama of religious life:

> New religious communities ... have always been called into existence directly by God and have frequently been founded against strong opposition from the Church—have often even had to prove by this very opposition that they were willed by God. When one of these orders succeeds in opening the closed mind of the Church—as a tender seed, a small root, can split a stone—then the Church recognizes the finger of God ex post facto in this world, lets it prosper and in the end praises and approves it.[53]

For Balthasar, however, Paul's struggle for recognition should not be read simply as evidence that religious are often ahead of the "closed mind of the Church." It is just as important that Paul perceives the need to attain official legitimization of his mission and is willing to suffer for it. Only by succeeding in his quest for recognition can Paul's mission, and by implication religious missions, be validated in their authenticity and incorporated as a gift for the good of the church.[54]

Paul possesses a prophetic teaching charism. With John, he provides "those two great theologies which conclude the New Testament."[55] One of Paul's most important teachings is the expansion of the covenant to include the Gentiles and the subsequent relativization of the Old Testament law. This puts him into conflict with a Judaizing party for whom Peter, and even more so James, appear to have had sympathies. Paul is in the right, and is willing to "oppose" Peter "to his face" (Gal 2:11), a scene that highlights how conflictual the relation between the charismatic-prophetic and official-institutional principles in the church can sometimes be. It also shows, however, the need that office sometimes has to be influenced by prophetic-charism toward the right course. At the same time, Paul's subsequent behavior exemplifies the humility and

51. For more on this tension, see *TD* 3:353–60.

52. *OPSC*, 151.

53. *CSL*, 379–80.

54. *CSL*, 380; Leahy, *Marian Profile*, 65.

55. *GL* 1:131.

spirit of cooperation that charismatic figures must show in their relations to office: "For the sake of peace and unity, and to avoid schism in the Church, [Paul] yielded on the advice of James to a Jewish temple custom to show that he was still loyal to the law (Acts 21:24)."[56] Paul undertook this humbling act for the sake of ecclesial unity.

Balthasar observes that Peter seems to lack the intellectual acumen of Paul, "the brilliant convert."[57] The contrast between Peter and Paul typifies the "distance" that sometimes exists between "ecclesial office and the gifted theological writer,"[58] a distance Balthasar was well familiar with as one whose own insights were suspect through much of the twentieth century. Nonetheless, Balthasar lauds Peter for fulfilling his official pastoral obligation of testing and discerning Paul's thought and interpreting Paul's teaching with the good of the *ecclesia* in mind. "The nod that 'Peter' gives, at the end of his second Letter," writes Balthasar, "to the 'wisdom given' to Paul, is accompanied by a reservation that, of course in Paul's letters 'there are some things ... hard to understand, which the ignorant and unstable twist to their own destruction' (2 Pt 3:15–16)."[59] According to Balthasar, Peter's words about Paul are the

> heartfelt sigh of the bishop over a dear brother's gifted writings, which are too deep for the ordinary member of the flock but which Peter supports with his authority, praising their wisdom and conformity with the teaching handed down, of which he is the guardian, while also warning the flock against reading them with immature faith or unbalanced judgment. Lovingly he situates Paul's writings within the total context of the "other Scriptures"—all of which are susceptible of being twisted. Such censorship is necessary within the Church's communion of love if Peter is to fulfill his ministry, just as it was necessary for him to overcome the waiting John on the way to the empty tomb, so that, alone, he could "officially" verify the facts.[60]

56. *OPSC*, 350.
57. *OPSC*, 352.
58. *OPSC*, 171.
59. *OPSC*, 171.
60. *OPSC*, 350–51.

The Petrine-Pauline relation, therefore, like the Petrine-Johannine relation, displays the dynamic of interdependent creative tension that exists between charismatic wisdom and official authority.

Like John, Paul also has the task of embodying in his own self the ideals of both religious life and priestly existence. As has been established, Paul is a type of the charismatic prophetic-teacher. He is also a radical disciple. Immediately after his conversion, Paul spent three years in the Arabian desert where he learned to "listen," "empty" himself, be "still," and obey.[61] This action corroborates Balthasar's view that contemplation and ascesis must precede an active apostolate.[62] It is also a pattern that is carried on by the canonical requirement for a period of prayer and spiritual deepening in the novitiate at the start of religious life.

In his writings, Paul illuminates the great themes of subjective discipleship. He articulates the importance of dying to the world and becoming a new man in Christ. Like John, he perceives Christian sacrificial service as a participation in Christ's redemptive suffering and therefore as missiologically significant. He teaches the attainment of Christian perfection through the evangelical state and makes a pivotal contribution to the theology of religious life by delineating between commandment and counsel.[63] Furthermore, Paul often points to his own life as one set apart in order to be a sign of right conduct for the church to imitate.[64] Paul thus participates in the public signifying of subjective holiness that typifies religious life.

On the other hand, Paul is an official authority, a pastor. Balthasar argues that the outlines of ministerial priesthood—that is, the Petrine office—are given their greatest scriptural articulation by Paul. All the great themes are there, claims Balthasar: the "naked" objective authority that demands obedience,[65] the exercise of the *tria munera*, and the burden of office undertaken as a sacrifice of love for the community.[66] Just as John takes Peter into himself, so too Peter "is immanent in

61. *LLC* 54.
62. *CSL*, 349–51; *LLC* 54.
63. *LLC* 143, 186, 237.
64. *OPSC*, 384–85; *TSS* 108.
65. *OPSC*, 152. See also *OPSC*, 320.
66. *ET* 4:353–81; *OPSC*, 384–85.

Paul."[67] Balthasar has challenging words for those who reduce "Paulinism" to charismatic freedom and subjective faith and neglect Paul's teachings on church governance; Balthasar observes that in the letters to the Corinthians, for example, Paul often "sounds more authoritarian than any successor of Peter."[68]

Like John and Peter, Paul must also unite objective priesthood and subjective discipleship within himself. In his dealings with the church in Corinth, he points to both apostolic commission and his holy life as credentials for his authority. According to Balthasar, both elements are equally important to Paul's ministry.

> [The] objective factor relieves him of any dependence on the opinions and demands of the congregation.... This factor is so objective, that Paul views it as actually having been forced on him by the Lord, and denies that it owes anything to his merit.... But to prove that his calling as an apostle is authentic, he rests his case entirely on the second factor, his life, whose every aspect bears consistent witness that his claim is genuine.[69]

Thus, Paul stands somewhere between John and Peter. In John's uniting of office and discipleship, the subjective maintains an existential priority. In Peter, the objective does. In Paul, the objective and subjective are equally balanced.

In order to deflect Donatistic heresies, it is necessary for the church to distinguish well between objective office and subjective discipleship. Nonetheless, it is just as important to show their harmony. As Balthasar states in *The Christian State of Life*, their combined signification in apostolic figures like John and Paul reveals that the objective priesthood will be aided by the subjective (that is, the holy priest will have more grace to sustain him and enrich his leadership),[70] and vice versa (the priest's subjective discipleship will be conditioned by and find

67. *OPSC*, 171.

68. *OPSC*, 152.

69. Balthasar, *Paul Struggles with His Congregation: The Pastoral Message of the Letters to the Corinthians* (hereafter *PSC*), trans. Brigitte L. Bojarska (San Francisco: Ignatius Press, 1992), 36.

70. *CSL*, 277.

an expression in apostolic ministry).[71] The truth of the complementary union of objective and subjective, however, is important not only for the priest's own personal spirituality, but also as a sign for the whole church. Subjective discipleship depends on the objective gifts of official proclamation, shepherding, and sacramental grace and therefore cannot set itself against office. At the same time, subjective holiness is not just a matter of individual "moral striving for perfection" but bears missiological fruit in partnership with apostolic ministry.[72] Thérèse of Lisieux, for example, conceived of her entire vocation as a partnership with priests in winning souls, and the church has recognized the efficacy of her prayers by naming her patron of missions. Objective office, then, cannot be divided from the support and partnership of subjective discipleship.

In the religious priest, the interdependence of office and discipleship has an embodied sign. He incarnates the "reciprocal immanence" of objective and subjective and shows that these are not "separate and entirely unrelated."[73] Although Paul is "a lasting example to all who serve as priests,"[74] he is a special model for religious priests who must combine public signification of total radical discipleship with an official apostolate.

John and Paul's Eschatological Stances

For Balthasar, John and Paul are eschatological figures, which further connects them to religious life. As noted in chapter 7, every vocation has incarnate and eschatological elements; every Christian is in the world but not of the world. Religious life, however, in comparison to lay-married life and life in secular institutes, is more set apart from the world as an eschatological sign. Religious are even more set apart than diocesan clergy, who are also rightly called secular clergy. John and Paul are priests characterized by an eschatological stance more typical of religious. This stance, in turn, conditions their ministry.

71. *CSL*, 372–73.
72. *CSL*, 372.
73. *CSL*, 372.
74. *PSC*, 36.

John's Eschatological Stance

Near the end of the Fourth Gospel, it is foretold that the beloved disciple will "remain," whereas Peter will be led into active ministry and martyrdom. In Balthasar's speculation, John's "remaining" took the form of life of a stable community with Mary, as is suggested by the Fourth Gospel's report that "from that hour the disciple took her into his home" (Jn 19:27). Accepting the ancient traditions that John is the beloved disciple and the author of the book of Revelation, Balthasar deduces that John and Mary eventually "fled to the desert" (Rv 12:6) and lived a common life characterized by asceticism and contemplation.[75]

The Johannine-Marian community is eschatological in three senses. First, it is a contemplative community. John has been "'transported' to another place," where he is to "anticipate the bliss of the future Church in the beatific vision."[76] Thus, following Augustine, Balthasar says that John's position contrasts with Peter (the diocesan priest), who is more deeply inserted in the world with its "dangers and temporal evils."[77] John's "abiding," which continues to be "expressed in the 'religious state' in the Church by all who "withdraw to the heights to fast and pray in silence," is an "eschatological perseverance," a focus on the "presence of the one thing necessary" that can "justify and redeem this condition which we are fated to be in—our distraction amongst the 'many things.'"[78] It is the contemplative existence typified by the beloved disciple who laid his head on the savior's breast, who reported favorably of the woman who would waste her resources in love (Jn 12:1–8), and who would end his days in adoration of the Lamb's eternal marriage banquet (see Rv 21–22). Quoting Mechtild of Magdeburg, Balthasar writes of John, "Between his body and the creation of heaven, there is merely a thin partition."[79]

Second, although this contemplative existence appears serene, it is an ascetical life marked by spiritual combat, for "the dragon, in his great

75. Balthasar, "Our Lady in Monasticism," *Word and Spirit* 10 (1988): 52–56.

76. *OPSC*, 318, 191.

77. *OPSC*, 191.

78. *TH* 125.

79. *OPSC*, 319.

wrath, opposes her [the Marian-Johannine community]" (see Rv 12:4).[80] The ascetical life of the Johannine-Marian community is eschatological insofar as it is a life deliberately withdrawn and uprooted from the world and located in the spiritual wilderness. Balthasar notes that "the biblical desert has a double face: intimacy with God, but intimacy in dereliction, in a place haunted by ghosts and demons."[81] Where Peter may contend more with temporal evils, John faces the unveiled contest between primordial light and darkness (see Jn 1:5; 1 Jn 5–10).[82] Furthermore, John and Mary constitute a "community of virgins," and, according to Balthasar, the asceticism of virginity is a hallmark of the eschatological stance.[83] Since prayer and asceticism are missiological acts, the Johannine-Marian "community of virgins" is also an apostolically fruitful community: "She continues to give birth, and that to which she gives birth is fruit for eternal life."[84]

A third eschatological feature of the Johannine-Marian community is its common life. In John and Mary's "community of virgins," the communal aspect is at least as important as the ascetical-virginal to the eschatological character of the community. Citing the church father Ephrem, Balthasar posits that John and Mary discover "the 'sacramentality' of the presence of God in each neighbor and the 'sacramentality' of the presence of Christ in the 'two or more gathered in his name' (Mt 18:20)."[85] Reciprocally recognizing Christ in one another, John and Mary are the first to experience the reality that through Christ's "death and resurrection, the visible presence of Christ on earth is now to be found invisibly among those who are gathered" in the church.[86] John's letters are a pedagogy in the truth that, through *koinonia*, God is revealed and can be known.[87] For example, John writes, "Let us love one another because love is of God; everyone who loves is begotten by

80. Leahy, *Marian Profile*, 99.

81. JT 64.

82. JT 64–65.

83. *CSL*, 210; *ET* 4:392.

84. Leahy, *Marian Profile*, 99; see *TD* 3:334–35.

85. Leahy, *Marian Profile*, 140; Balthasar, *Mary for Today* (Middlegreen, UK: St. Paul's, 1987), 50.

86. Leahy, *Marian Profile*, 140.

87. *LAIC*, 117–18.

God and knows God. Whoever is without love does not know God" (1 Jn 4:7–8). The sacramental encounter with Christ is possible in *koinonia* because the "future consummation is already present in seed here and now. Christian life is 'eschatological existence.'"[88] Thus, the common life of religious, anticipated by the Johannine-Marian community, is a "realized eschatology."[89]

John's eschatological stance conditions his ministry. Balthasar observes that in Acts, John is conspicuously absent from the controversy regarding the inclusion of the gentiles in the nascent church, and that ultimately John "disappears ... to the sidelines."[90] For Balthasar, this scenario typifies John's position in the constellation as one withdrawn from and above disputation and argument. Balthasar surmises that instead of becoming entangled in ecclesiastical disputes that will pass, John has gone off to the desert to set up a "school of love" and "school of obedience" that he will quietly teach and govern.[91] Nonetheless, here John becomes all the more "the direct voice of the Lord to his Church."[92] A prophet and teacher, he produces the great literature that will conclude the gospels and the New Testament as a whole. For Balthasar, John is the figure chosen by God to provide the summative texts of scripture, the final culmination of everything God wants to say.[93] Hence, John is evidence of Balthasar's contention that those who are most ascetically committed are also often the most missiologically fruitful.[94]

Paul's Eschatological Stance

Paul, who was "caught up into the third heaven ... caught up into Paradise and heard ineffable things, which no one may utter" (2 Cor 12:2, 12:4), also serves as a type for Balthasar of the eschatological stance. Balthasar contrasts Paul with James, who was a member of the local leadership of the church in Jerusalem and who defended the Torah in

88. Nichols, *Word Has Been Abroad*, 250.
89. JT 70.
90. *OPSC*, 351–52.
91. *OPSC*, 352.
92. *OPSC*, 318.
93. *ET* 1:115; Nichols, *Word Has Been Abroad*, 249.
94. See *LLC*, 190.

contest with Paul in Acts. James "represents continuity between the Old and New Covenants, tradition, the legitimacy of the letter of the law as against the mere spirit, yet in harmony with the incarnate spirit."[95] Paul, on the other hand, "who became a Christian by pure grace, without words and merits, and relentlessly broke with his past," typifies the discontinuous aspect of eschatological existence with the old order.[96] To incorporate language Balthasar uses elsewhere, Paul exemplifies the "new"-ness of the "aeon" that has entered the old, and James serves as a reminder that the "new aeon" is present in and fulfills "the old."[97]

In the book of Revelation, John describes a moment when "all the nations will come and worship" the Lord (Rv 15:4). This scene, which builds on the Old Testament theme of the gathering of nations in Jerusalem, implies a close association between eschatology and the universal expansion of the covenant.[98] As Aidan Nichols explains, the integral relation between eschatology and universalism indicates that the church's "eschatological existence" can be seen "in the very nature of the *Catholica*, the Catholic Church, as she abandons the 'protection' offered by restriction to one (the Jewish) people and opens herself in an 'unprotected' way to the universality of the world."[99] The universalist theme is especially evident in Paul, whose great missionary charism was given for the sake of drawing the nations into a Christian communion that anticipates the final kingdom.[100]

Ultimately, it was Paul's universalistic emphasis that placed him in conflict with the Judaizing party with whom James and Peter had sympathies. James, a local figure whose episcopal authority derived

95. *OPSC*, 336.

96. *OPSC*, 336.

97. *ET* 2:432–33.

98. This Old Testament theme is most clearly and beautifully given expression in Isaiah 2:2: "In days to come, the mountain of the Lord's house shall be established as the highest mountain and raised above the hills. All nations shall stream toward it." See also Ps 86:9; Jer 10:6–7, 16:19; Mi 4:1–4. For more on the internationalist motif in Revelation's eschatology, see Frank J. Matera, *New Testament Theology* (Louisville, Ky.: Westminster John Knox, 2007), 419.

99. Nichols, *Word Has Been Abroad*, 250.

100. N. T. Wright has demonstrated the centrality of the universalist theme in Paul's writings. For example, see Wright, *Paul: In Fresh Perspective* (Minneapolis: Fortress, 2005).

from his position "as a blood relative of Jesus" (see Mk 6:3),[101] ultimately sided with Paul at the Council of Jerusalem. But he was, in Balthasar's estimation, "a party man" who insisted on Paul's honoring of local custom so as to not upset the "traditionalist upholders of the letter of the law."[102] Peter, incidentally, stands between James and Paul. His "sense of Catholic universalism, firmly founded on his vision at Joppa and openly announced at the 'Council of the Apostles' (Acts 15:7–11), places him spiritually close to Paul's outlook."[103] On the other hand, Balthasar surmises that "being one of the Twelve," Peter "was much closer to Jerusalem than Paul, and therefore he must have felt a greater inner conflict over the delicate, and at the time not tidily manageable problems that arose between Jewish and Gentile Christians."[104] According to Balthasar, Peter's place between local and universal anticipates the papal position of one who is both bishop of a local church and shepherd to the whole church. Paul's role in the early church controversy was to advocate for catholicity and universalism.

For Balthasar, Paul's ministry embodies the great commission that is labor for the eschatological gathering of nations. Unlike James, Paul is not rooted in any particular place. He never remains tied for long to the administration of a single community. Rather, he focuses on an itinerant, universal preaching and teaching mission. He goes in and out of places, adopting their customs for a time so as to be better heard in his witness: so that God may be "all in all" (1 Cor 15:28), he seeks to "become all things to all" (1 Cor 9:22). "'To the Jews' he 'became *as* a Jew,' and 'to those who are without law, *as* without law'" (1 Cor 9:21).[105] Then Paul uproots himself again in order to move on to another place. This approach, which has served as the inspiration for the great apostolates of foreign missionaries, reveals to the church its international charac-

101. *OPSC*, 336. Balthasar recognizes that the James of Acts is not the same as the James of the synoptics. However, he does recognize a typological relation between them. For example, Balthasar claims that the synoptic "represents his later namesake" at Mt Tabor; Balthasar, *Prayer*, 195.

102. *OPSC*, 336.

103. *OPSC*, 163.

104. *OPSC*, 164.

105. See *PSC*, 32.

ter and the universal relevance of its gospel.[106] Paul will "embody the Catholic unity in the midst of diversity," and the people may "learn what Catholic universality is" by observing his life.[107] On the other hand, Paul's mission has a downside in that it can never fully penetrate a culture unless it is balanced by a complementary stable presence within a community that is better typified by James, Peter, and even John.[108] The newness of the aeon must ultimately take root *in the old.*

John and Paul as Types of Different Religious Priesthoods

John and Paul have much in common. Both mediate between the charismatic and institutional poles. Both represent the unity of objective office and subjective discipleship. Both are eschatological men. Despite the tremendous degree of overlap between their missions, however, they actually represent for Balthasar two different kinds of religious life and priesthood. John signifies a contemplative, monastic form of religious life of which Benedictines are the most representative. Paul signifies more the active-itinerant-apostolic form of life that is found most notably among mendicants, Jesuits, and missionary congregations.

John as a Type of Monastic Priesthood

Balthasar's most prolonged attention to John as a type of Benedictine religious life occurs in his essay "Johannine Themes in the Rule of St. Benedict." He highlights four aspects of the *Rule of St. Benedict* that give Benedictine life a Johannine stamp. These are stability, spiritual combat, obedience, and a sacramental sense of the common life.

Balthasar notes the frequent use in Johannine literature of the verb *menein,* which is translated as "stay," "remain," and "abide." John's initial call is to come stay with Jesus: "They came and saw where he was staying, and they stayed with him" (Jn 1:39); and his final destiny is to "remain" (Jn 21:22). John's special mission is to stay "at Jesus' side" (Jn

106. *LLC* 151.
107. *OPSC,* 320.
108. *LLC* 151–55.

13:23), planted like "a tree."[109] The Johannine *ethos* of staying, remaining by the Lord, has an ecclesial expression in Benedictine life where *stabilitas loci* is perhaps the most distinguishing characteristic. Concretely, stability involves commitment to a particular community and particular geographic space, but there is a spiritual meaning. "One stays in the monastery because one stays with Christ."[110] In the seventh chapter of the *Rule*, St. Benedict identifies the first step of humility as remaining "fixed as Christ was under the gaze of the Father,"[111] and Balthasar notes the similarity between this teaching and John's understanding of Christ as one who "can do nothing of himself, but only what he sees the Father doing.... For the Father loves the Son and shows him all things" (Jn 5:19). According to the fourth step of humility, the monk will remain stable "under difficult, unfavorable, and even unjust conditions, his heart quietly embracing suffering" (*RB* 7.35), like John at the foot of the Cross.

Balthasar perceives an eschatological dimension to Benedictine stability. At first this seems contradictory, because Balthasar usually associates eschatological existence with uprootedness. To be sure, stability implies grounded presence "in an earthly (and thereby historical) place."[112] Nonetheless, monastic stability is also a participation in "the mystery of the forty days that Christ spent in the desert" immediately after Jesus uprooted himself from the world, leaving behind his family and secular occupation, and was baptized by John in the Jordan.[113] It similarly reflects the ecclesial experience in the desert described in the twelfth chapter of John's apocalypse, which is characterized by withdrawal into "existence in solitude and the stability of that existence."[114] The desert is "a place prepared by God," and the community is "to be nourished there during the time of tribulation ... 'away from the face of the dragon,' although the dragon tries to destroy her."[115]

The monastic desert is at once representative of "trusting and tran-

109. *OPSC*, 318.
110. JT 63. See also *RB* 7:10–11.
111. JT 63.
112. *LLC* 153.
113. JT 63.
114. JT 63.
115. JT 63.

quil solitude of mind" and a place of testing, "vigilance and penance."[116] Thus, the second correlation Balthasar identifies between Benedictine life and Johannine themes is "combat, or more exactly, the judgment (*krisis*) of darkness by the light."[117] The dramatic context of light and darkness is a uniting motif between the Fourth Gospel, the Johannine epistles, and the book of Revelation (for instance, Jn 1:5; 1 Jn 1:5–10; Rv 21:23–24; Rv 22:5).[118] Spiritual combat is similarly "the most ancient and most traditional of monastic theological themes, from Antony and Pachomian sources, through Evagrius ... Origen ... then Jerome, the Macarian homilies, Cassian and the Master."[119] Christian monasticism is most fundamentally an ascetical movement, but, in contrast to Platonic and Asiatic precursors, is also an explicit "effort to recover the peace of God and of Christ."[120] Benedict writes, "Let peace be your quest and your aim" (*RB Prol.* 17; see *PS* 34:15). In Balthasar's view, Benedict surpasses the monastic fathers before him by bringing ascetical practice in line with a sense of dependence on grace in conformity with Christ that is itself a Johannine emphasis.[121]

The third link that Balthasar makes between Benedictine life and Johannine themes is the emphasis placed by each on obedience as the manifestation of "perfect love."[122] For Benedict, obedience is Christological. The Christological character of obedience is seen in two ways: "On the one hand, the abbot could not demand an absolute obedience if he was not authorized by Christ.... The abbot represents Christ through his function as teacher and pastor, and he is held to represent him by giving an example of the Word incarnate." [123] The Christological basis of abbatial authority is encoded by Benedict's teaching that the "abbot is believed to hold the place of Christ in the monastery" (*RB* 2.2). "On the other hand," states Balthasar, "the obedience which is due him is no less Christological since it must be absolute, without reserve, prac-

116. JT 64, 63.
117. JT 64.
118. Brown, *Introduction to the New Testament*, 803–4.
119. JT 64.
120. JT 64.
121. JT 65. This advance is, of course, evidence of Augustinian influence on Benedict.
122. JT 65.
123. JT 66.

ticed out of love for Christ ... and practiced in imitation of Christ."[124] Both aspects of obedience are Johannine: "The one who has seen me has seen the Father" (Jn 14:9); and "I have not come to do my own will, but the will of the one who sent me" (Jn:5:13). Balthasar summarizes that, in Benedictine life, "Christ is manifested ... in the master as well as in the disciple. He himself is, in fact, inseparably both the Logos, the lawgiver, and also the humble servant."[125] By placing obedience in a Johannine Christological context, Benedict has ensured that his disciples will never see obedience as "merely a pedagogical measure and for that reason limited in time," but as something "which possesses an absolute value, unsurpassable in itself."[126]

The fourth link flows from the third. For both John and Benedict, there is a sacramental concretization of the presence of God in the community that makes loving obedience plausible and sensible. For John, Christ can be trusted because he represents the Father. For Benedict, the abbot can similarly be trusted and loved because he represents Christ. Thus, monastic life can recapitulate trinitarian life just as John indicates ecclesial common life must do.[127] Furthermore, although Balthasar does not elaborate upon it, the sacramental concretization of divine presence that takes place most notably in the abbot extends analogously for Benedict to the whole community (see *RB* 72), to the sick in particular (see *RB* 36.1), and to the guest (see *RB* 53.1). Hence Benedict teaches his monks to exercise love in *koinonia* out of reverence for the presence of Christ in the other in much the same way that John does in his epistles (see *RB* 72).

For Balthasar, then, Benedictine monastic life, with its emphases on stability, spiritual-ascetical combat, obedience, and a sacramental vision of common life appears to have a particularly Johannine stamp. In "Johannine Themes," there is no mention of monastic or Benedictine priesthood per se, but elsewhere Balthasar supports monastic priesthood for the sake of both liturgical functions within the community and pastoral outreach.[128]

124. JT 66.
125. JT 66.
126. JT 66.
127. JT 69–70.
128. See *LLC* 68–72. He supports monastic priesthood but recognizes the distractions and divisions it sometimes introduces to the community.

Paul as a Type of Itinerant Religious Priesthood

Balthasar explicitly links Paul with the tradition of itinerant preachers, teachers, and missionaries in what he identifies as a "Pauline-Ignatian" trajectory that contrasts with the more stable existence of Benedictines and diocesan clergy.[129] In the Pauline-Ignatian line, there is no geographical desert where the religious makes his home. Rather, the eschatological stance is expressed by imitating the geographical "uprootedness" first practiced by the Twelve in their itinerant ministry and by Paul in his travels. In this trajectory, the link between eschatological "uprootedness" and universal ministry is very important: "Giving up one's 'unique situation' in the material context of the world results in the ecclesial universalization of the apostle."[130]

The asceticism of uprootedness expands the missionary's scope in three ways. First, there is his availability for work: "It is only because the Jesuit is detached from the world" in this way "that he can be totally available to the pope and to his religious superiors, who are in principle unrestricted in the use they may make of him."[131] Second, detachment from the trappings of his past allows him to wander in and out of various missionary fields. Balthasar notes how "Peter di Nobili takes on all the mannerisms of an Indian monk, Schall of a Chinese Mandarin."[132] They are like Paul, who strives to "become all things to all men."[133] Finally, this uprootedness extends to liberation from responsibilities in-

129. *LLC* 150. It should also be noted that most of Balthasar's comments here occur within a polemical argument against Karl Rahner. Defending secular institutes, Balthasar is critiquing Rahner for too closely identifying the evangelical state with this Pauline-Ignatian perspective. Hence, much of what he says in this section of *LLC* appears in its original context as somewhat disparaging toward vocations to itinerant missions. Nonetheless, as long as room is made for the expression of the counsels in Benedictine stability and secular institutes, he acknowledges the validity of this perspective and a correspondence of uprootedness from the secular, expressed by itinerancy, with a universal apostolate in many traditional religious orders. As indicated later, his respect for itinerant religious priesthood is apparent. For Rahner's position, see his "Notes on the Lay Apostolate," in *Theological Investigations*, vol. 2, *Man in the Church*, trans. Karl H. Kruger (Baltimore: Helicon, 1963), 319–52.

130. *LLC* 150.

131. *LLC* 151.

132. *LLC* 151.

133. *LLC* 54.

volved in particular pastorates and thus allows him to concentrate on a more universal preaching and teaching mission. According to Balthasar, there is a difference

> between priestly ordination for the secular priest and that for the religious priest. Whereas the secular priest is primarily the pastor of a specific, delimited flock, to whom he mediates the Word of God and the sacraments, the religious priest is primarily an apostle who scatters the seed of God in the world across all the boundaries of parishes and dioceses.[134]

Balthasar notes that Paul "thanks God that he did not baptize anyone in Corinth, 'for Christ did not send me to baptize but to preach the gospel' (1 Cor 1:14–17 [at 17])."[135] Thus, Paul anticipates the mendicant, Jesuitical, and missionary tradition of refusing posts as parochial pastors for the sake of availability to a wider mission.

It should be emphasized that, for Balthasar, the diocesan clergy are essential. In his vision, they serve primarily as pastors within stable communities where they live closer to the people and share in many of the secular features of human existence (hence, it is called the "secular" priesthood). The diocesan priest's responsibility is "to work first and foremost for the interior edification of his congregation." He must be solicitous toward the lapsed and nonbelievers, but he accomplishes this not

> by leaving his congregation or local church in order to bring his missionary endeavors to others, but by drawing those outside the Church into the congregation.... He is the shepherd of the already existing flock entrusted to him by Christ. His primary obligation is, therefore, to preach the Gospel in the place where his congregation is located.[136]

Balthasar lauds those who accept this pastoral role. Christ's shepherding function is most fully inherited "when an individual, sent and consecrated, takes up the task of 'pasturing' a (more or less) Christian community.... Courage has always been needed for this task, and today it

134. *LLC* 117.
135. *LLC* 117.
136. *CSL*, 353.

is needed more than ever."[137] Still, the church's mission *ad extra* will be accomplished primarily by the laity, nonordained religious, and religious priests,[138] especially those who, like Paul, are not burdened with the responsibility of "administering single communities."[139]

With the Pauline example in mind, Balthasar has challenging words for those who would limit priesthood to a parochial expression. He criticizes bishops who "see religious priests as an important and welcome help for regular parochial parish work" but imagine a time when enough vocations to diocesan priesthood would make religious clergy "superfluous."[140] Such a view—all too clearly, in his view—indicates that such bishops misunderstand the mission of religious priests, which is not primarily a parochial task. Moreover, such a view suggests a faulty ecclesiology that identifies the church exclusively with parochial and diocesan structures and, by implication, priesthood with its exercise within these structures. It is helpful to quote Balthasar's observations on this point at length:

> Of its very nature, the clergy tends to picture to itself the Church under the image of a parish or a district, as a flock that can somehow be taken in at a glance, as a flock on which it can carry out its functions. This mutual relationship of pastor and those who receive his pastoral care, something saturated in itself, appears as the ideal and perhaps already as the real prefiguration of the "one Shepherd and one flock," although this overlooks the fact that the "one Shepherd" is Christ, not the Pope, and the "one flock" is humanity as a whole, not the few sheep within the realm of the Church. This reductive image can have unhealthy effects in various directions, above all by obliterating the openness of the Church to the world, the missionary character of the Church wherever she is, so that, for example, the aim in missionary countries is to transform the missionary territory (with its own forms and methods) as quickly as possible into a Church territory divided up into districts and parishes, while either postponing decisive missionary tasks consciously 'till later on' (e.g., the intellectual and also practical problems of

137. *OT* 155.
138. *CSL*, 353.
139. *OPSC*, 163.
140. *LLC* 59.

> the mission to Islam) or simply forgetting them. This fantasy, which goes only as far as the parochial structure and somehow lets the diocesan priest who administers his parish always unconsciously see the missionary religious priest who works in a freer manner as a marginal phenomenon of the ordinary pastoral care, not seldom affects even missionary congregations today, although the opposite ought really to be true. A Church that is not open to the world in her totality would have ceased to be the Church of Christ.[141]

According to Balthasar, an awareness of the eschatological unity of the church and of the human race should prevent a provincial mentality that would reduce priestly ministry to a function within a stable flock of the faithful. For Balthasar, the ministry of Paul is scriptural evidence that the priesthood cannot be confined to a parochial context.[142] It can have an itinerant, missionary expression.

Conclusion

Balthasar points to the apostles John and Paul as images of religious priesthood. In their teachings and lives, the specific mission of religious priesthood can be discerned, and the form of religious priesthood can be seen. Like John and Paul, religious priesthood mediates between charism and institution. It unites public signification of subjective holiness with objective ministry. It is expressed eschatologically, either in a withdrawn ascetical lifestyle or in itinerant evangelization and teaching. Finally, the stamp of John is identifiable in monastic, Benedictine life. The stamp of Paul is identifiable in the itinerant religious priesthood of mendicants, Jesuits, and missionary congregations. We are now ready to evaluate the potential of Balthasar's theology to meet the challenges to religious priesthood examined in chapters 4 and 5 and attempt to develop an illuminating sketch of the charism of religious priesthood through a Balthasarian lens.

141. *ET* 2:413–14.
142. *LLC* 117.

PART 4

MARKS OF RELIGIOUS PRIESTHOOD

Having investigated the historical development of religious priesthood in part I, the state of the question in part II, and some Balthasarian insights on religious priesthood in part III, it is now time to provide a portrait of the identity and mission of religious priesthood. In doing so, I hope to offer theological support for the historical characteristics of religious priesthood described in part I and open some new horizons for understanding religious priesthood. Methodologically, I'll bring Balthasar's analogical theology of vocations into dialogue with the many questions and concerns that have been raised regarding religious priesthood since the Second Vatican Council and demonstrate that Balthasar's framework, when corroborated, buttressed, and extended by the contributions of other scholars and theologians, is able to meet many of the explicit and implicit objections to religious priesthood. I also hope to show the basic harmony of Balthasar's theology of religious priesthood with Vatican II's ecclesiology, postconciliar magisterial teaching, especially that of Pope St. John Paul II,[1] the 1983 Code of

1. John Paul II is a particularly important magisterial voice on

Canon Law, which John Paul referred to as the final document of Vatican II,[2] and the approved liturgical rites of the Roman Catholic Church.

This final part proceeds by establishing and discussing four characteristics of religious priesthood that I hope can be agreed upon as universal (that is, they can be ascribed to nearly all religious priests and not just Benedictines or Franciscans or Jesuits or Dominicans). These traits pertain to: (1) Signification (the religious priest is a sign, liturgically set apart, of both radical discipleship and official apostolic ministry); (2) Mediation (the religious priest unites office and charism in himself and mediates ecclesiologically between the stable institutional elements of the church and charismatic movements of reform and renewal); (3) Mission (the religious priest exercises primarily an extraparochial and transdiocesan apostolate); and (4) Ministerial Identity (the religious priest is primarily identified with, and concentrates on, the preaching/teaching and sanctifying *munera*, though not in a

---

the subject of vocations and states of life. During his pontificate, five ordinary general synods of bishops met to discuss and clarify the ecclesial roles of families, the laity, priests, consecrated persons, and bishops. After each synod, John Paul issued a treatise on the vocation under discussion. Apostolic Exhortation *Familiaris Consortio* (November 22, 1981) followed the 1980 synod on the topic of "The Christian Family." *Christifideles Laici* (December 30, 1988) followed the 1987 synod on "The Vocation and Mission of the Lay Faithful in the Church and World." *Pastores Dabo Vobis* (March 15, 1992) followed the 1990 synod on "The Formation of Priests in the Circumstances of the Present Day." *Vita Consecrata* (March 25, 1996) followed the 1994 synod on "The Consecrated Life and Its Role in the Church and in the World." *Pastores Gregis* (October 16, 2003) followed the 2001 synod on "The Bishop: Servant of the Gospel of Jesus Christ for the Hope of the World." Outside of relation to an episcopal synod, John Paul issued Apostolic Exhortation *Redemptionis Donum* to men and women in religious life on March 25, 1984.

2. Cole and Conner, *Christian Totality*, 14.

way that separates him from the shepherding function). Under each heading, pertinent questions raised about religious priesthood are reintroduced and the Balthasarian framework is brought into dialogue with magisterial teaching and with other theologians in order to propose an illuminating, defensible vision of religious priesthood.

CHAPTER 9

Religious Priesthood and Signification

The first mark of religious priesthood is that the religious priest signifies both radical subjective discipleship and official apostolic ministry, as well as the unity of the two. It would be difficult to overstate the importance of signification to contemporary theology and magisterial teaching. So far in this book, we have established that Vatican II was a Council of images and that it employed images to direct the imagination, intellect, and will of the church's members toward important ideals. Before and after the Council, a number of twentieth-century theologians made signification central to their theology.[1] Among them, Balthasar's theology is a particularly brilliant recovery of theological aesthetics. In the field of ecclesiology, he identifies specific vocations as referents or signs of mysteries that all of the church's members participate in. The idea of vocations as signs was a major motif in the teaching of John Paul II, and it has continued to appear in more recent magisterial teaching, such as the 2015 document "Identity and Mission of the Religious Brother in the Church" authored by the Congregation for Institutes of Consecrated Life and Societies of Apostolic Life.[2]

1. See Hans Boersma, *Nouvelle Théologie and Sacramental Ontology: A Return to Mystery* (Oxford: Oxford University Press, 2009).

2. Congregation for Institutes of Consecrated Life and Societies of Apostolic Life, "Identity and Mission of the Religious Brother in the Church, "October 4, 2015, http://files.ctctcdn.com/8c97a3ce301/1827e765–8669–44f0-aaa5–5040c9dea164.pdf (accessed August 17, 2018).

Signification is liturgically based. Through the rites of the church, its members are consecrated and become public signs. Baptism, for example, signifies conversion from sin, adoption by God, incorporation into the body of Christ, and initial participation in the priesthood of the faithful. Christians attending a baptism are reminded by the public celebration of their own participation in these mysteries and are even invited by the rite to renew their baptismal commitment. Through the sacrament of matrimony, the couple is set apart as a sign of the union of Christ and the church. Witnesses to a wedding are drawn into a deeper appreciation of Christ's free, faithful, full, and fruitful covenant with his bride, the church, of which they are members.

Religious as Signs of Radical Subjective Discipleship

Religious life is a sign of radical discipleship, a following of Christ into his own lifestyle. We say "radical" because religious profession transcends baptismal commitment by entailing a public renunciation not only of sin, but even of created goods out of love for and in imitation of Christ through religious vows: one's spouse (evangelical chastity); one's property (evangelical poverty); and one's will (obedience). The professed religious renounces all things to seek the one thing necessary.

We can deepen this concept of radical discipleship and say that religious profession is particularly a sign of a radicalized subjective priesthood. Thomas Aquinas taught that the evangelical counsels were not only a means of sanctification (that is, a renunciation of goods so as to give the religious freedom to pursue higher goods); they were also the content of a personal holocaust.[3] Through profession of them, the religious offered the totality of himself to God. He offered his goods in poverty, his body in chastity, and his will in obedience. This aspect of religious commitment is illustrated well by the rite of profession used by my own community, the Benedictine monks of St. Meinrad Archab-

3. *ST* II-II, q. 186, a. 1; see also *CSL*, 50–53. An excellent summary of Balthasar's reading of Thomas on this point can be found in David S. Crawford, *Marriage and the "Sequela Christi": A Study of Marriage as a "State of Perfection" in the Light of Henri De Lubac's Theology of Nature and Grace* (Rome: Lateran University Press, 2004), 41n47.

bey. The monk professes his vows by reading from a vow chart, which he then places on the altar and signs. It will remain there through the Mass. Next, he lies prostrate before the altar and is covered by a funeral pall in a symbolic death as the community prays over him, a prayer that is concluded by the abbot entreating the Lord to accept this man's commitment as an "offering." This is followed by the prayer that consecrates the man as a religious/monk that then flows into the liturgy of the Eucharist. In these striking ways, the rite highlights that the monk's vows are a participation in the call of the faithful to join the sacrifices of their lives to the Eucharistic sacrifice, which the monk does here with a certain totality and permanence.

By making religious profession, the religious priest thus signifies radical discipleship and subjective priesthood. John O'Malley, however, objects to the notion that commitment to the evangelical counsels meaningfully distinguishes religious priestly identity from diocesan identity, because the latter also make commitments to the evangelical counsels. He notes that in the West, celibacy is the norm for all priests, diocesan and religious. Furthermore, all priests make a promise of episcopal obedience, and nearly every substantial magisterial treatment of priesthood since at least the pontificate of Pius XI has strongly encouraged priests to embrace some expression of poverty.[4] Accordingly, all priests, religious or not, would seem to signify radical discipleship in the life of the evangelical counsels. According to O'Malley, the idea that religious priests have a special call to link the counsels and ministry is not particularly helpful in distinguishing them from their diocesan counterparts.[5]

Priesthood and the Counsels

To answer O'Malley, we must show that the religious priest's relationship to the evangelical counsels is special enough that it does, in fact,

4. See *CSL*, 316–21, for discussions of the evangelical counsels in Pius XI's, John XIII's, Vatican II's, Paul VI's, and the 1971 Synod of Bishops' documents on priesthood. See also John Paul II, Apostolic Exhortation *Pastores Dabo Vobis* (*PDV*) (March 25, 1992), 27–30.

5. O'Malley, "Priesthood, Ministry, and Religious Life," 223.

differentiate him from others (especially the diocesan priest), who commit in some ways to the evangelical counsels. The first thing to note (as we did in chapter 6) is that while other vocations in the church participate in the evangelical counsels, religious life is their most public, visible expression. Religious habits and a common life set apart make it far more recognizable, for example, than the vocations of consecrated virgins or members of secular institutes.[6] Consecrated virgins and members of secular institutes, while they make commitments to one or more of the counsels, wear ordinary clothes, very often keep their secular occupations, and typically live alone or with their families of origin. Religious make solemn vows in the context of public liturgy, whereas members of secular institutes do not. Religious thus stand out, and are meant to, as a sign to the world of the inauguration of the kingdom of God that relativizes the value of temporal goods.[7] While others may live the evangelical counsels, religious are consecrated and commissioned to be a special public sign of them for the rest of the church.

Priests also stand out by their clerical dress and by their ministerial profession. They are highly visible, and many people rightly associate them with the evangelical counsels, especially celibacy. Nonetheless, there is a difference between religious and diocesan clergy in their relationship to the counsels. Reflection on history, liturgy, and magisterial teaching supports Balthasar's claim that diocesan clergy have a more indirect and analogous relationship to the counsels than religious life does, which is why signification of radical discipleship is considered only a secondary signification of diocesan priesthood. For religious, it is primary.

History

Historically, there is a long-established ecclesial discipline in the West requiring diocesan priests to promise celibacy in an unmarried state. For a long time, the reigning narrative among historians has been that celibacy was not mandated for Western clergy until the Second Lateran

6. The way canon law expresses it, the set-apart-ness of religious life is intrinsic to its signification. "The public witness to be rendered by religious to Christ and the Church entails a separation from the world"; *CIC* 607, §3.

7. *VC* 87.

Council in 1139 as a result of Gregorian reforms attempting to eliminate nepotism and concubinage among the clergy by forcing them to adopt a more monastic lifestyle.[8] Hence, the requirement of diocesan priestly celibacy has been seen as historically contingent and reversible. It seems that if the discipline were lifted, the specific identity of religious priests would be clearer.[9] In the East, for example, there is still a large presence of married priests, and celibate priests unattached to monasteries are rare. Furthermore, the Western variety of religious institutes, secular institutes, societies of apostolic life, and ecclesial movements has not appeared in the East, and, thus, there are fewer vocational options for the person called to the life of the counsels.[10] The relationship between nuptial commitment and vocation in the Eastern Church therefore remains mainly a choice between marriage and monasticism.[11] In the Eastern context, the specific identity of a religious priest as an ordained figure committed to virginity stands in a higher relief.

Scholarship conducted in the last thirty years or so, however, has revealed that the historical relation between diocesan clergy and celibacy is more complicated than the reigning narrative has implied.[12] Writers such as Alfons Maria Stickler, Stefan Heid, and Christian Cochini have demonstrated, "clearly and persuasively," in the opinion of Joseph Ratzinger, [13] that in the early church, during the patristic age, and through the first millennium there were strong biases in East and West against ordaining married men to higher orders (priesthood and

8. Alfons Maria Stickler, *The Case for Celibacy: Its Historical Development and Theological Foundations*, trans. Brian Ferme (San Francisco: Ignatius Press, 1995), 45.

9. See Faley, "An American Experience of Religious Life," in *A Concert of Charisms: Ordained Ministry in Religious Life*, ed. Paul K. Hennessy (New York: Paulist Press, 1997), 123, and Michael Najim, "Two Ways in the East: The Marital Status of Clergy," in *Vested in Grace: Priesthood and Marriage in the Christian East*, ed. Joseph J. Allen (Brookline, Mass.: Holy Cross, 2001), 236–46.

10. Roberson, "Profile of Eastern Monasticism Today," 118.

11. Najim, "Two Ways in the East," 234.

12. For what follows, see Stickler, *Case for Celibacy*; Stefan Heid, *Celibacy in the Early Church: The Beginnings of a Discipline of Obligatory Continence for Clerics in East and West*, trans. Michael J. Miller (San Francisco: Ignatius Press, 2000); and Christian Cochini, *Apostolic Origins of Priestly Celibacy*, trans. Nelly Marans (San Franciso: Ignatius Press, 1990).

13. Ratzinger, *Pilgrim Fellowship of Faith*, 180n2.

episcopacy) and definitive prohibitions, which remain today in both East and West, of clerical remarriage in the event of a wife's death. In most places, from at least the fourth century, bishops were chosen only from among celibates. More significantly for our purposes, there was an almost universal expectation, through the first two-thirds of the first millennium, of perpetual continence of higher clergy (bishops, priests, and possibly deacons) who were married.[14] That is to say, a married man could be ordained a priest and even remain living with his wife, but the two were no longer to engage in conjugal relations. For Stickler, Heid, and Cochini, the medieval mandate requiring celibacy of all priests and bishops unfolded naturally from the final realization that continence within marriage was much more difficult on the practical level than chaste unmarried virginity was. Where the East, at the Second Council of Trullo (691), moved in the direction of allowing married priests to resume or continue conjugal relations after ordination, the West strived to maintain the older tradition of asking for continence from its married clergy until it finally arrived at the wisdom that continence was more achievable if the priest remained unmarried. According to this revisionist history, East and West settled the same problem of the difficulty of continence in marriage in different ways.

If Stickler, Heid, and Cochini are correct, then there is a longer and stronger historical correlation between priesthood and continence than has sometimes been thought, which in turn suggests some kind of intrinsic bond between the evangelical state and official ministry. The Western Church's intuition for a celibate clergy would not be an "invention of the Middle Ages" but rather would be patristic, maybe even apostolic in its roots.[15] The Western practice of requiring unmarried chastity of diocesan priests could not be reduced to either a late "clericalization of celibacy" or a monasticization of the clergy.[16] Such history, in fact, supports Balthasar's claim that the evangelical state is and has always

14. To clarify terms: continence, also sometimes called "perfect chastity," refers to total abstinence from conjugal relations. Since it can be practiced within a marriage, it differs from consecrated virginity, which is a renunciation, not only of the conjugal act, but of the married state; Augustine Roberts, *Centered on Christ: A Guide to Monastic Profession* (Kalamazoo, Mich.: Cistercian Press, 2005), 105–8.

15. Ratzinger, *Pilgrim Fellowship of Faith*, 180n2.

16. Najim, "Two Ways in the East," 237.

been wider than religious life and that priesthood has always belonged in some way to it.[17] At the same time, the fact that first-millennial priests often *were married*, even though perpetually continent (or at least expected to be), supports the difference between religious and clergy that is also implied by the latter's analogous relation to the evangelical state. The priesthood's relation to the evangelical state is less direct and more ambiguous than religious life's relation to the counsels.

The diocesan priest's analogical relation to the counsels is most evident with regard to the counsel of virginity/celibacy/chastity. "Monk" comes from *monos*, "alone"; the "monk" is never married.[18] The continent married priest has a wife, which makes him more like the ordinary lay-married person; but, since the two abstain from conjugal relations, the continent married priest draws nearer to the virginal state, which includes a renunciation of marriage in its totality. A married priest, however, would seem to also need a more qualified relationship to the other counsels than his religious counterpart. Because the monk is not married, he can also be more radically poor and completely available to an ecclesiastical superior in obedience. The degree to which married-continent priests were expected to live poverty and ecclesial obedience needs further study. Nonetheless, it would seem that first-millennial priests, if they maintained a household, would have had to practice more of a poverty of spirit than the radical renunciation that characterizes monks. Their obedience, if it was anything like that of contemporary married deacons, would also seem to necessarily make provision for family needs. All this is to say that even if there was an integral relationship between priesthood and celibacy in the first millennium, there would likely remain dissimilarity and disparity between the lifestyles of religious and diocesan clergy insofar as they related to the counsels.

Liturgy

In addition to history, liturgy is another area where the priesthood's indirect but real (that is, analogous) relation to the counsels is expressed. In marriage, religious consecration, and priestly ordination, Christians

17. *CSL*, 292–99.

18. As Eoin de Bhaldraithe points out, an early usage of the word "monk" was "simply the male counterpart of 'virgin'"; de Bhaldraithe, "Daily Eucharist," 400.

make public commitments in a liturgical setting. There is a difference, however, between religious vows and marital promises on the one hand, and priestly promises on the other. For marriage and religious life, the subjective commitment of the persons involved is constitutive of and at the climax of what is taking place. Since at least the twelfth century, marriage promises have been understood as the very form of the sacrament in the West.[19] Although religious vows are not a sacrament, they are the "form" of the monk-making moment[20]; that is, in religious consecration, one's promises of chastity, poverty, and obedience before God formally constitute the act after which the man or woman is now a religious. It is called, appropriately, the "rite of profession." By way of contrast, in the priestly "rite of ordination," "there is no promise that enters into the very making of the priest ... as there is in the making of both married people and the religious life."[21] It is true that priests promise obedience and, in the West, celibacy, but these are made prior to the actual part of the rite that makes the man a priest. They are not at the climax of the priest-making action, and they are never considered solemn. Hence, the priestly promise "is rather a requirement of the legal than the sacramental order.... It is a requirement of great pastoral and spiritual fittingness, but not one built into the structure of the sacrament just as such."[22]

According to Guy Mansini, the "indirect" and "laconic" expression of priestly promises in the ordination rite is appropriate.[23] It is appropriate because rather than highlighting the ordinand's subjective willingness, the rite intends to emphasize the ordinand's being selected by the church and given the necessary graces to henceforth represent the objective presence of Christ, the head of and for the church.[24] Furthermore, the priesthood can exist in men who do not imitate Christ's lifestyle of the counsels and can even still be efficacious, at least in terms of valid sacramental ministry, in a man who fails to keep his subjective

19. Edward Schillebeeckx, *Marriage: Human Reality and Saving Mystery*, trans. N. D. Smith (New York: Sheed and Ward, 1965), 294–95.

20. Beyer, "Life Consecrated by the Evangelical Counsels," 67 and 69.

21. Mansini, *Promising and the Good* (Ann Arbor, Mich.: Sapientia, 2005), 159.

22. Mansini, *Promising and the Good*, 159.

23. Mansini, *Promising and the Good*, 162.

24. Mansini, *Promising and the Good*, 162.

commitments.[25] Religious life, conversely, cannot be enjoined by a subject who does not promise himself to it, for vows form the basis of the vocation he or she intends to live.[26] Also, since the primary signification of the religious vocation is subjective radical discipleship, failure on the part of a religious to live the vows well will be a more direct and complete destruction of the meaning of the vocation itself than the subjective failings of diocesan clergy would be. As Aidan Nichols explains, "The priest is an instrument through which God can work even when the man resists. But the gift given a religious is a reciprocal love which will not move forward unless the recipient is willing."[27] The disparity in the rites regarding the respective prominence each gives to subjective commitment, such that religious vows are seen as the apex of the rite of profession and priestly promises are somewhat underplayed in the rite of ordination, therefore makes sense, and this disparity is, then, liturgical evidence that religious are a sign of the subjective radical discipleship in ways that diocesan clergy are not.

Magisterial Teaching and Canon Law

The structure and content of contemporary magisterial documents are a final place where we see a difference between religious and clergy's relationship to the counsels. The former is the more pivotal sign of subjective discipleship, while the latter's signification is primarily one of objective apostolic ministry and only secondarily of subjective discipleship. It is significant that Chapter VI of *Lumen Gentium* on religious, *Perfectae Caritatis*, and John Paul II's treatises on religious/consecrated life, *Redemptionis Donum* and *Vita Consecrata*, begin immediately with a discussion of the evangelical counsels and a definition of religious life as those who are committed to the counsels. Commitment to the counsels is intrinsically related to religious signification of Christ's way of life and death, trinitarian communion, eschatological existence, and the

25. As Mansini puts it, "Valid ordination permanently makes a man radically capable of acting as a priest, whether or not the priest intends or has promised to live as a priest until death"; Mansini, *Promising and the Good*, 159.

26. Beyer, "Life Consecrated by the Evangelical Counsels," 67.

27. Nichols, *Divine Fruitfulness*, 224.

Marian-bridal church.[28] Notably, *Vita consecrata* describes the active apostolates of religious only after it has substantially described the life and meaning of the evangelical counsels.[29]

In contrast, *Lumen Gentium*, Chapter III, on the hierarchy, mentions the counsels only briefly in the very last article.[30] *Presbyterorum Ordinis* waits until article 15 to discuss the counsels only after a substantial description of the priest's sacramental identity and ministry has been given. The same pattern of deferring discussion of the counsels until after discussions of the priest's sacramental identity and ministry is repeated in John Paul II's apostolic exhortations on priesthood and episcopacy, *Pastores Dabo Vobis* and *Pastores Gregis*.[31] The priestly vocation undoubtedly involves a call to personal holiness,[32] but the primary signification of priests, according to the Vatican II documents, is the threefold apostolic preaching/teaching, sanctifying, and ruling office of Christ.[33] John Paul II emphasizes, along with the signification of Christ's threefold office, the priest's representation of Christ as head and bridegroom.[34]

There are also differences, both small and great, in how magisterial

28. For signification of Christ's lifestyle and death, see *LG* 44; *RD* 9, 15; *VC* 1, 24; of trinitarian communion, see *RD* 13; *VC* 21, 41–42; of eschatological existence, see: *PC* 1; *LG* 44; *RD* 8; *VC* 26; of the Marian/Bridal Church, see *RD* 8; *VC* 28, 34.

29. See *VC* 72–103. Basil Cole and Paul Conner, who have conducted a close analysis of *Vita consecrata*, conclude that the document supports the following order of priority in religious mission: (1) the conversion of oneself (which is indeed the first mission of every believer); (2) signification of the church's holiness "by giving *public witness* to human union with God" through material and formal commitment to the evangelical counsels; (3) sanctification of the church through moral and spiritual example; (4) specific apostolic works; Cole and Conner, *Christian Totality*, 51.

30. *Lumen Gentium* 29 mentions celibacy very briefly in light of its teaching that married men might be ordained as permanent deacons.

31. *Pastores Dabo Vobis* describes the sacramental identity and mission of priests in a chapter subtitled "The Nature and Mission of the Ministerial Priesthood," nos. 11–18. Significantly, it describes the role of the counsels in the life of priests in articles 27–30, after and outside of the chapter on the "nature" of the priesthood. *Pastores Gregis* describes the sacramental identity and ministry of the bishop in a chapter entitled, "The Mystery and Ministry of the Bishop," nos. 6–10. The counsels are described outside and after this chapter in one entitled "The Spiritual Life of the Bishop," nos. 18–21.

32. *PDV* 20, 33.

33. *LG* 28; *PO* 2.

34. *PG* 13, 21; *PDV* 3, 16, 22, 25, 29, 50.

teaching and canon law present the relationship of the priestly and religious vocations to each of the counsels. These differences again illustrate the more indirect nature of the priesthood's relation to the counsels. John Paul proposes little difference in the area of celibate chastity. This counsel admits no range of degrees; it is what Michael Root calls a "non-scalar" concept.[35] Unless perpetually continent married clergy were reintroduced, one would seem to belong quite clearly to either the married or the virginal state. In magisterial descriptions of the chastity of religious and clergy, the primary difference is that celibacy is definitive of the former, belonging to its essence, and only highly fitting for the latter. There is another difference with respect to the signification of the celibacy of each. In terms of signification, the priest's celibacy is described as befitting his role in representing Christ the bridegroom, who is married only to the church,[36] whereas the religious signifies by her virginity the meaning of the church as bride.[37] There is an important theological truth underlying this difference in the signification of priestly and religious celibacy. The priest represents Christ the bridegroom who lays down his life in service to the bride, sanctifies the body, and makes it fruitful through the imparting of word and sacrament; the religious primarily represents the fruitfulness of the body, the unfolding of grace in the life of cooperative discipleship. This portrayal could be misleading, however, if one concluded from it that priestly celibacy had only, or even mainly, the object of the church as spouse, and religious celibacy had only, or even mainly, the object of Christ as spouse. The priest is married to Christ first, and then to the church.[38] When the

35. See Michael Root, "Bishops, Ministry and the Unity of the Church in Ecumenical Dialogue: Deadlock, Breakthrough, or Both?," *CTSA Proceedings* 62 (2007): 19–35.

36. *PDV* 29.

37. *RD* 8; *VC* 28, 34. See also Congregation for Institutes of Consecrated Life and for Societies of Apostolic Life, "'*Verbi Sponsa*,' 'Instruction on the Contemplative Life and on the Enclosure of Nuns,'" 1 and 4, *Origins* 29, no. 10 (August 12, 1999): 155–64.

38. Mk 3:13–14, states, "He called those whom he desired ... and he appointed twelve to be with him, and to be sent out to preach and have authority to cast out demons." On the basis of this text, Mansini writes, "The priest is first to be with Christ and then to be sent out. He is sent from Christ and to the Church, and he is therefore engaged to both, though to the Church on the basis of his engagement to Christ"; Mansini, *Promising and the Good*, 139. John Paul II states, "The priest's fundamental relationship is to Jesus Christ, head and shepherd ... but intimately linked to this relationship is the priest's

religious marries Christ, he or she, too, makes a self-gift to the ecclesial body[39] and to Christ's mission of service.[40]

The differences are greater in the areas of obedience and poverty. In order to understand these differences it is helpful to keep in mind two principles as they are being discussed. First, there is a distinction between the spirit of the counsels, a virtue that is in fact encouraged of all the faithful,[41] and the actual canonical obligations to obedience and poverty, which are different for laity, clergy, and religious. Our concern is with the latter two groups. As will be shown, the canonical obligations of the clergy to observe obedience and poverty are a bit different than they are for religious. This is due mainly to the second principle, which is that, for the clergy, the life of the counsels is subordinated to a ministerial end.[42] The church's expectation for clerical participation in the counsels is governed by the advantage of the counsels for the ministry that itself exists for the good of the church. At the risk of overstatement, religious embrace the counsels for their own sake, whereas clergy embrace them more instrumentally. This is true especially for poverty and obedience.[43] While the spirit of these two counsels always sup-

relationship with the Church"; *PDV* 16. In his apostolic letter *Mulieris Dignitatem*, John Paul says the priest's nuptial gift to Christ is to be "understood analogously" through what is expressed physically in the consecrated woman, who more visibly expresses the church as bride; *MD* 20.

39. See Jean-Marie Roger Tillard, *The Mystery of Religious Life*, ed. R. F. Smith (St. Louis, Mo.: Herder, 1967), 6–8.

40. John Paul II states that by commitment to the counsels, one comes to share in the mission of Christ; *VC* 18. As such, religious "make his mission their own"; *VC* 19. "Consecrated persons are enabled to take up the mission of Christ, working and suffering with him in the spreading of his Kingdom"; *VC* 36.

41. *VC* 30; *PDV* 1; *CL* 30, 33.

42. John Paul II states that, for the clergy, the counsels always have "specific 'pastoral' connotations"; *PDV* 30.

43. Priestly obedience, writes John Paul II, "has a particular 'pastoral' character. It is lived in an atmosphere of constant readiness to allow oneself to be taken up, as it were, 'consumed,' by the needs and demands of the flock"; *PDV* 28. Priestly poverty manifests in a "simple and austere lifestyle" that allows the priest better to "stand beside the underprivileged; to practice solidarity with their efforts to create a more just society; to be more sensitive and capable of understanding and discerning realities involving the economic and social aspects of life; and to promote a preferential option for the poor"; *PDV* 30. Priestly celibacy arguably has a less instrumental quality insofar as it is itself "the

ports ministerial goals, their radical material expression could impede those goals. As Balthasar points out, a priest serving in a parish needs a greater degree of autonomy than a cloistered nun,[44] and, as the Council points out, he needs "equitable remuneration" in order to support his relatively autonomous life amidst the faithful.[45]

Concretely, there is a difference between the canonical obligations of obedience for diocesan clergy and religious. The "obligation of obedience" for diocesan priests, writes canonist Brendan Daly, "is limited to areas of pastoral work under the governance of the diocesan bishop."[46] Priests are bound by obligation to "undertake and fulfill faithfully" those ministerial tasks entrusted to them.[47] If a priest is requested by the bishop to take up, modify, or cease a ministry, he should agree. The priest "has been ordained for the spiritual necessities of the people and should obey the bishop in those things concerning the good of souls in the governance of the diocese."[48]

When it comes to the priest's personal and spiritual life, however, the bishop has a more limited reach than a religious superior. According to Daly, "A bishop cannot interfere in the private life of a diocesan priest unless it affects ministry."[49] Now, one could certainly argue that most of a priest's life affects his ministry, since he is a public person, but Daly contends that a bishop cannot generally dictate where a priest spends his holidays, with whom the priest chooses to socialize, or in which spiritual or ascetical practices the priest engages, unless he can show a direct correlation to ministry. For certain, John Paul encouraged bishops to exercise paternal solicitude for the personal life of the priest,[50] but the bishop's legal right to command in this area is more limited than that of a religious superior. A priest may, in the spirit of obedience—that

---

gift of self in and with Christ to his Church" and corresponds to the priest's sacramental configurement to "Jesus Christ the head and spouse of the Church"; *PDV* 29.

44. *ET* 2:446–47.

45. *PO* 20.

46. Brendan Daly, "The Promise of Obedience of Diocesan Priests: What Does It Mean?," *Australian Catholic Record* 90, no. 3 (July 2013): 343.

47. *CIC* 274, §2.

48. Daly, "Promise of Obedience of Diocesan Priests," 335.

49. Daly, "Promise of Obedience of Diocesan Priests," 338.

50. See, for example, *PG* 47.

is, as a matter of personal virtue—respond to the bishop's encouragement of him to spend more time in prayer and less time watching television, but is not canonically obligated to obey in such matters unless it can be shown to impact his ministry.[51]

It is difficult to generalize about religious obedience because the proper law of particular institutes determines the mode in which obedience is lived in each. Nonetheless, in most institutes religious superiors have an extensive reach such that religious obedience "covers all areas" of life and, thus, much of what might fall only under the spirit of obedience for the diocesan.[52] A religious superior can, for instance, require all the members of the institute, province, or house to engage in a certain set of prayers or ascetical practices. He or she can command individuals to lose weight or stop smoking. He or she can deny a vacation request "because it impacts on the vow of poverty. The diocesan priest could only be required to give a mobile phone number or email address so that he be contactable in an emergency."[53]

In terms of work, religious are assigned at the liberty of the superior. Today most assignments are worked out in cooperation with the individual religious, but, in principle, the superior has full authority to determine the assignment. If the assignment is an external apostolate involving an office in the church, the religious is accountable to both the local bishop and one's major superior, in a situation of "dual authority."[54] In relation to both bishop and superior, the religious priest has fewer rights than a diocesan one does in his ministry. The religious, even if he is a canonical pastor, can be removed at any time by either the bishop or the major superior irrespective of term, provided that the bishop or major superior informs the other authority. If the diocesan priest is a pastor, however, and the bishop wishes to transfer him, the diocesan priest has a canonically recognized right to remain in place insofar as particular law allows (for instance, some local churches have

51. Francis J. Schneider, "Obedience to the Bishop by the Diocesan Priest in the 1983 Code of Canon Law" (JCD diss., The Catholic University of America, 1990), 288 and 324.

52. Daly, "Promise of Obedience of Diocesan Priests," 338.

53. Daly, "Promise of Obedience of Diocesan Priests," 338.

54. On the dynamics of "dual authority," see Rose McDermott, *The Consecrated Life: Cases, Commentary, Documents, Readings* (Alexandria, Va.: Canon Law Society of America, 2006), 161–64. See also *CIC* 682, §2.

set terms). If the bishop wishes to transfer a pastor, the bishop "is to propose the transfer to him in writing and persuade him to consent to it for the love of God and of souls."[55] If the pastor's term in his current placement has not expired, or if no term limits are in place, however, "the pastor is not bound to obey the bishop," though he may choose to do so in the spirit of obedience.[56]

There are also differences between the canonical obligations toward poverty for clergy and religious. According to canon law, religious should be poor "in fact" and "in spirit."[57] In ancient orders such as the Benedictines, Franciscans, Dominicans, and Jesuits, evangelical poverty has meant and still means "radical renunciation" of all goods held at the time of final vows, full handing over of all future earnings to one's religious community, and renunciation of the right to use common property without permission of one's superiors.[58] The 1983 Code of Canon Law protects this custom and maintains it as the general norm for religious life.[59] The code makes provision for the proper law of institutes where radical renunciation of all goods held at the time of final vows is not required (goods may, for instance, be held in trust by a family member),[60] but even in these institutes religious are still unable to use these goods unless given permission by their legitimate superiors.[61] Moreover, if a

55. *CIC* 1748.

56. Schneider, "Obedience to the Bishop by the Diocesan Priest in the 1983 Code of Canon Law," 261.

57. *CIC* 600.

58. Yūji Sugawara, *Religious Poverty: From Vatican Council II to the 1994 Synod of Bishops* (Rome: Editrice Pontifica Università Gregoriana, 1997), 302.

59. "Whatever accrues to a religious in any way by reason of pension, subsidy, or insurance is acquired for the institute unless proper law states otherwise"; *CIC* 668, §1. "A professed religious who has renounced his or her goods fully due to the nature of the institute loses the capacity of acquiring and possessing and therefore invalidly places acts contrary to the vow of poverty. Moreover, whatever accrues to the professed after renunciation belongs to the institute according to the norm of proper law"; *CIC* 668, §5.

60. "Almost all the canons which concern poverty have reference to proper law. Considerable numbers of norms in the universal law are simplified and leave practical applications to each institute. The Code leaves ample space for freedom, avoiding the making of laws in what can be entrusted to the initiative and responsibility of the institute. The Code has chosen this way so that the institutes may live and express their charism more fully"; Sugawara, *Religious Poverty,* 353.

61. McDermott, *Consecrated Life,* 153–56.

religious comes into possession of any new monies or properties after profession, these "belong to the institute according to the norm of proper law."[62]

Diocesan clergy are instead only "*invited* to embrace voluntary poverty."[63] At the time of the Council, Cardinal Florit, archbishop of Florence, wanted "a promise of poverty to be included in the Rite of Ordination along with the promises of celibacy and obedience," but this request was denied.[64] *Presbyterorum Ordinis* recommends but does not require, to all priests, the sharing of goods in a common life "as an excellent means of pastoral charity."[65] John Paul encouraged priests to adopt a simple lifestyle in solidarity with the poor, which he framed as responsible stewardship rather than as radical renunciation.[66] The 1983 Code of Canon Law similarly does not require radical renunciation from diocesan clergy. Rather, it requires them to "foster simplicity of life" and "refrain from all things that have a semblance of vanity" and encourages them "to give to the poor and needy what is over and above what is necessary for their worthy upkeep."[67] Furthermore, in a relaxation of the norms of the 1917 Code, which forbade diocesan clergy from conducting commerce or trade, the 1983 code allows diocesan priests to engage in "*negotio economica* or the stable investing of funds to make a profit,"[68] provided this is not done in a way "unbecoming to their state."[69]

The church, then, does not require radical renunciation, sharing of goods in a common life, or foreswearing of profit-making activities from its clergy as it does for religious. In fact, it seems that the church's expectation for priestly poverty is rather close to the spirit of poverty that is also recommended to the ordinary faithful. John Paul II stated,

62. *CIC* 668, §5.

63. *PO* 17, emphasis mine.

64. Daly, "The Lifestyle of the Diocesan Priest in Relation to Poverty," *Australian Catholic Record* 91, no. 1 (Jan. 2014): 79.

65. *PO* 17.

66. *PDV* 30.

67. *CIC* 285; Daly, "Lifestyle of the Diocesan Priest in Relation to Poverty," 81. See also *CIC* 282, §2.

68. Daly, "Lifestyle of the Diocesan Priest in Relation to Poverty," 83.

69. *CIC* 285, §1.

> [The] spirit of poverty [that] should inspire the priest's behavior, characterizing his attitude, life and very image as a pastor and man of God ... [is] expressed in disinterest and detachment toward money, in renunciation of all greed for possessing earthly goods, in a simple lifestyle, in the choice of a modest dwelling accessible to all, and in rejecting everything that is or appears to be luxurious, while striving to give himself more and more freely to the service of God and the faithful.[70]

It would be difficult to show that the simplicity and detachment recommended here are substantially different from the spirit of poverty recommended to all the faithful.

In the magisterium's framework, then, religious have the primary signification of subjective discipleship, especially the evangelical counsels. Diocesan clergy's signification of subjective discipleship is secondary to its primary signification of the objective presence of Christ as head and bridegroom and his ministerial office of prophet, priest, and king. Signification depends on praxis. Canon law is the church's theology practically applied. As the canons indicate, there is, in fact, a difference on the practical level between religious poverty and obedience and priestly poverty and obedience.

To sum up, John O'Malley argues that identifying the religious priest as a special sign of the life of the counsels does not adequately differentiate him from secular priests. I've tried to show that religious priests are a greater signification of the life of the counsels than their diocesan counterparts, whose relation to the counsels is more indirect and analogous. This point of view is supported by history, liturgy, and magisterial teaching/canon law. With religious life recognized as the more visible, and in some sense more radical, commitment to material poverty and obedience, it is evident that the religious priest is an objectively clearer sign of radical discipleship and subjective priesthood than his diocesan counterpart.

70. John Paul II, *General Audience*, July 21, 1993, quoted in Daly, "Lifestyle of the Diocesan Priest in Relation to Poverty," 84.

Religious Apostolates and Ministries

If we look more deeply into the rite of religious profession, we discover that religious are set apart not only to signify the evangelical counsels, but also for various forms of horizontal service, apostolates, and ministries. This makes sense. Discipleship includes the love of neighbor, and since religious are set apart to signify radical discipleship, we would expect this aspect of the commitment to be reflected in the rites.

The 1970 Rite of Religious Profession was offered by the Sacred Congregation for Divine Worship as a recommended model for religious communities who were, in turn, instructed to adapt it "in such a way that the ritual clearly brings out the institute's special character."[71] Its prayer of consecration establishes connections between religious life and ecclesial service. It reads, "The voice of the Spirit has drawn countless numbers of your children to follow in the footsteps of your Son. They leave all things to be one with you in the bonds of love and give themselves wholly to your service *and the service of all your people*." It then states, "May they *build up the Church* by the holiness of their lives, *advance the salvation of the world*, and stand as a sign of the blessings that are to come."[72] In addition to the prayer of consecration, there are other moments within the Rite of Profession that highlight the relation between religious life and horizontal outreach. For instance, the standard Rite begins with a petition to make vows and includes the statement "we now ask to be allowed to make perpetual profession in this religious community of N. for the glory of God *and the service of the Church*."[73] During the litany of the saints it is prayed, "By the self-offering of your servants *and their apostolic work*, make the life of your Church ever more fruitful."[74]

Connotations of ecclesial service are also present in some of the Rite's approved adaptions. In the Rite of First Profession of the Dominican Sisters of Mary Mother of the Eucharist, for example, the novice is

71. International Commission on English in the Liturgy, ed., *The Rites of the Catholic Church* (hereafter *RCC* 2) (Collegeville, Minn.: Liturgical Press, 1991), 2:204.

72. *RCC* 2:228; emphasis mine.

73. *RCC* 2:221–2; emphasis mine.

74. *RCC* 2:225; emphasis mine.

instructed, "Sister, receive this veil, by which you are to show that you are totally given to Christ the Lord, *and dedicated to the service of the Church*."[75] In the examination before final profession, the sisters are asked by the bishop, "Are you resolved with the help of the Holy Spirit to spend your whole life *in the generous service of God's people*?" After the prayer of consecration, the bishop states, "*Be faithful to the ministry the Church entrusts to you to be carried out in its name*."[76] These liturgies clearly indicate an intention to identify the religious not only as one committed to God in prayer and through the counsels, but as one who is being set aside for apostolic outreach, public ecclesial service, and even "ministry" in the church's "name" as the Dominican Rite portrays.

It is important to again note that recognition of religious life as missiological, apostolic, or publicly ministerial is a long-overdue development. As we saw in parts I and II, religious life has always had a missiological dimension, but it was often described by the church's official teaching and law as an endeavor undertaken mainly for the sake of one's personal salvation and moral perfection, despite the countless evangelical and charitable works exercised by men's and women's religious communities through the ages. This seemed to overlook the importance of religious in the church's mission through their prayer, asceticism, proclamation, teaching, and works of charity. Like the rites, contemporary magisterial teaching confirms an understanding of religious life that takes better account of its historical reality. *Vita Consecrata*, for example, uses the term "mission" one hundred and fifty times and provides extensive descriptions of the various forms of services, apostolates, and ministries provided by religious and other consecrated persons to the church and the world.[77] Today we understand that religious are set apart for apostolic mission and not only to practice the evangelical counsels.

At this point, however, we can reintroduce a question from chap-

75. Dominican Sisters of Mary, Mother of the Eucharist, "Mass for First Religious Profession" (program, Christ the King Catholic Church, Ann Arbor, Mich., August 6, 2004), 4; emphasis mine.

76. Dominican Sisters of Mary, Mother of the Eucharist, "Mass of Perpetual Religious Profession" (program, Christ the King Catholic Church, Ann Arbor, Mich., July 31, 2013), 7, 13; emphases mine.

77. *VC* 72–103.

ter 5 raised by Ghislain Lafont. Similar to the way O'Malley asked how commitment to the life of the counsels adequately differentiates the religious from the diocesan priest, Lafont asks how ordination meaningfully differentiates the religious priest from his nonordained confrères. Lafont notes that many religious ministries such as retreat preaching, teaching, and spiritual direction are already carried out by nonordained religious. According to Lafont, the perceived need to be ordained for these ministries belongs to a clericalist past.[78] In order to best respond to Lafont, we must consider first how religious life's relationship to horizontal service differs from that of the laity and then consider how the ministry of religious priests differs from that of their nonordained religious.

Distinction of Religious and Laity in Relation to Ecclesial Service

As we saw in chapter 4 of this book, Vatican II taught that the entire church was a subject of mission and that the laity were called and given graces for participation in services, apostolates, and ministries. It is natural to ask whether religious differ in any meaningful way from other laity in their relation to these activities. By attending a little bit to the meaning of service, apostolate, and ministry, we hope to show that while there is much overlap between laity and religious in these activities, there remains some difference.

Every Christian vocation involves horizontal *service* to one's fellow men and women, such as informal witnessing or other acts of charity. In religious life, there is plenty of mutual service that goes on between the members of the community, much as there would be in a family. *Apostolate* comes from the term "apostle," which means "one sent," and so seems to connote that kind of service that extends outward beyond one's home or religious community to the wider public. When magisterial teaching discusses the lay apostolate, it is referring primarily to action by lay persons to evangelize, sanctify, and order the secular world to right relationship with God.[79] For religious too, apostolates must involve some kind of outreach beyond themselves to the wider church

78. Lafont, *Imagining the Catholic Church*, 162.

79. *LG* 33. See also *LG* 31.

and world. I would argue that every religious institute is engaged in an apostolate insofar as each one, even the most cloistered, exercises, at the very least, an apostolate of prayer when it intercedes for the church and world in its liturgy.

Among forms of service and apostolate, some, such as hospitals and soup kitchens, are oriented mainly toward corporeal goods. Others are more specifically oriented toward spiritual goods insofar as they advance salvation by evangelization, catechesis, or prayer. Both kinds are engaged by clergy, religious, and laity according to their mode of participation in the office of Christ as prophet, priest, and king.[80]

Of the spiritually oriented services, however, some, such as preaching or teaching in the name of Christ and his church, administering sacraments, and pastoring ecclesiastical institutions, are duties proper to the clergy. The Congregation for the Doctrine of the Faith calls these "sacred ministry" or "pastoral ministry."[81] According to the CDF, religious and laity may be called upon to assist with these functions, such as in the "teaching of Christian doctrine," "certain liturgical actions," and "the care of souls."[82] When they do, they may be called ministers in an analogous way, with the sacred ministry of clergy serving as the primary referent for the full meaning of ministry.[83] These terminological distinctions will be helpful for highlighting religious life's close cooperation with the hierarchy, as will soon become clear.

The difference we wish to highlight between laity and religious with respect to their missiological activity is that the religious services, apostolate, and ministries have an *official* quality. This is true in three ways. First, such activity is public. Religious exercise their missiological activity as visible, public, ecclesial persons. The religious is no longer a private Christian citizen. He or she, as the rites of profession indicate, is

80. Congregation for the Doctrine of the Faith, "Some Questions Regarding Collaboration of Non-ordained Faithful and Priests' Sacred Ministry," *Origins* 27, no. 1 (November 27, 1997): 397–410; hereafter "Some Questions." For a critique of the magisterial document, see Richard Gaillardetz, "Shifting Meanings in the Lay-Clergy Distinction," *Irish Theological Quarterly* 64 (1999): 115–39. For a defense, see Robert A. Connor, "Why Laity Are Not Ministers," *Communio* 29 (Summer 2002): 258–85.

81. CDF, "Some Questions," Art. 1, §§2 and 3.

82. CDF, "Some Questions," intro.

83. CDF, "Some Questions," Art.1, §2.

set apart permanently for a life of public ecclesial witness and service. Whatever he or she does now is done as part of the public face of the church. Even the quotidian acts of kindness between religious members are incorporated into the public sign of the religious community, which is held up in a special way as a collective corporate witness to the church and world of Christian *koinonia*.[84] When religious act in service, then, they represent not only themselves but the church. Though as religious, they do not represent Christ the head or bridegroom, they are an enduring public sign of his body and bride. Corporately, they reveal the missiological nature of that part of the church that is not the head, though it works in close cooperation with the head.

Second, not only is religious service always publicly ecclesial, much of it is a participation in what we earlier called "sacred ministry" that has a "connection with the function of the hierarchy."[85] Nonordained religious are frequently involved in activities like formal catechesis, spiritual direction, retreat preaching, and public liturgical roles. This is often enough the case that Balthasar says religious have a secondary signification of objective office in the church, much as clergy have a secondary signification of subjective discipleship.

John Paul reminded us, in *Christifideles Laici*, that "only the sacrament of Orders gives the ordained minister a particular participation in the office of Christ, the Shepherd and Head, and in his eternal priesthood." Hence, formal teaching, sacramental administration, and official ecclesiastical leadership (that is, the ministerial *munera*) are proper duties of the clergy. However, there are public ministerial "tasks," such as official catechesis, distribution of Holy Communion, and administration of ecclesial institutions, that can be engaged by the nonordained. These take their "legitimacy ... from the official deputation given by the Pastors," and must be exercised "under the guidance of ecclesial authority."[86] Lay participation in official ministries is thus possible, and certainly common, in the North American context. While such ministries may be delegated, according to ecclesial need, to any layperson in good standing, the Dominican rite we reviewed suggests that the religious

84. See *VC* 41.
85. *ET* 2:455.
86. *CL* 23.

sister is being commissioned to carry out a ministry in the church's name in a stable way that will continue through her life. This stability is the third aspect of the official quality of religious apostolates and ministry.

John Paul's writings evidence the official (public, stable, often ministerial) dimension of religious missiological activity. In *Redemptionis Donum,* he stated that religious are engaged in "direct apostolic action" that is a "sharing in the Church's apostolate" that is "linked to the mission of the hierarchical order"; this participation, he says, is "proper" to the religious vocation.[87] *Vita Consecrata* acknowledges that some religious institutes have been founded precisely for the purpose of "carrying out different forms of apostolic service to the People of God." These include not only "Clerical Institutes," such as the Benedictines, Dominicans, and Jesuits, but also many communities of nonordained religious brothers who practice authentic "ecclesial ministries, granted by legitimate authority." John Paul adds that because of their official participation in ecclesial ministries, there are valid reasons for ceasing to call communities of nonordained religious men "Lay Institutes," as they are currently named by canon law, and rather to call them "Religious Institutes of Brothers."[88] This terminological shift echoes a view expressed by Karl Rahner that when a Christian is stably exercising official, public, ecclesial ministries, he or she is doing something exceptional rather than normative for laity.[89]

Does the official (public, stable, often ministerial) quality of religious apostolic activity signify a retreat, then, to the position of Pius XII that religious constitute "a state between" clergy and laity?[90] Vatican II made the well-known assertion that religious life does not constitute such a middle way between the hierarchical structure of the church between clergy and laity. The distinction between clergy and laity made in *Lumen Gentium,* however, is best viewed as a sacramental one between the ordained and the nonordained. It is tempting to impose upon this distinction a hard division between ministerial (priestly) and nonmin-

87. *RD* 15.

88. *VC* 9, 60.

89. See Rahner, "Notes on the Lay Apostolate," 320–21.

90. Pius XII, *Provida Mater Ecclesia* 9.

isterial (lay) ecclesial poles and envision official ecclesial ministry as the exclusive domain of clergy. As noted in chapter 7, Balthasar does not make a hard division between vocations. He recognizes the potential of nonordained persons to participate in official ministerial acts even if these are most directly appropriated to clergy. His view, as has been shown, is supported by John Paul II, who portrays lay participation in ministry as delegated in specific instances and religious participation in official apostolates as proper to membership in a religious institute.

According to canonist Jean Beyer, *Lumen Gentium*'s claim that religious do not occupy a middle tier and its implicit distancing of religious from the hierarchical structure of the church represent only a "partial" view that does not consider the church as a "harmonized and unified organic whole" in which every member, clergy, religious, and laity, is hierarchically arranged.[91] Beyer's words evoke the image of the church as body of Christ. While it is possible to imagine the head of the body (the clergy) in a simplistic, dualistic relationship with the body (laity and religious) where only the former is ministerial, it is better, thinks Beyer, to conceive of the ecclesial body in such a way that the terminology of "hierarchy" could apply to the whole of it, harmoniously arranged, with certain parts, perhaps religious or professional lay ministers, functioning in closer relation to the clerical head and its mission.

Beyer states that the "solution" to religious life's relation to hierarchical ministry will "be found" only when "the correct place is again given to the 'orders' of persons," laity, clergy, and religious, "that liturgical tradition has recognized within the Eucharistic assembly, and thus also within the concrete life of the Church."[92] Hence, it is imperative to examine the liturgical texts for evidence of the relationship between religious life, apostolates, and ministries. We have done that and concluded that religious are set apart not only to signify the life of the counsels but for ecclesiastical services, apostolates, and ministries, which entails a public signification of the church as body and bride in cooperative mission the head and bridegroom.

91. Beyer, "Life Consecrated by the Evangelical Counsels," 71–72.
92. Beyer, "Life Consecrated by the Evangelical Counsels," 72.

Distinction of Religious Priests from Religious in Relation to Ministry

Is nothing really added to the religious priest, then, by his ordination, since already, as religious, he has an acknowledged public representation of official apostolates and ministries? Not quite. Most evidently, the religious priest can do certain things, by virtue of his ordination, that the nonordained cannot do. He can, for instance, confect the Eucharist, absolve sins in the sacrament of reconciliation, anoint the sick, preach a Eucharistic homily, and serve as the ordinary minister of communion and baptism. Hence, a religious priest is able to minister in ways that his nonordained confrère is unable.

More subtly, but also perhaps more importantly, there is something important about *who the priest is*, not just about what he can do. Francis George has argued that the people of the church rightly sense that there is something "qualitatively different" about a priest stemming from the "sacramental distinctiveness" of his reception of holy orders.[93] It is a participation in the threefold ministerial office of Christ, which, as the Council explains, differs in kind and not only degree from the priesthood of the faithful.[94] Balthasar would agree. For him, the priest is the "guarantee" of Christ's "presence and of the sacramental existence of grace in the whole life of the Church."[95] As a representative of the good shepherd, the priest displays the establishment "at the heart of the New Covenant of love" an authority of service.[96] As a representative of Christ's prophetic office, he represents "the wisdom of another,"[97] "the power to proclaim the word of God 'not as a human word, but as that which it is in truth, the word of God' (1 Thes 2:13)."[98] As a representation of the sanctifying function, he recalls to the church that it is not self-generating, but depends on one who is above and beyond it for its holiness and fruitfulness.[99]

93. Francis George, *The Difference God Makes: A Catholic Vision of Faith, Communion, and Culture* (New York: Crossroad, 2009), 201 and 196.

94. *LG* 10.

95. *CSL*, 385.

96. *CSL*, 257.

97. Dermot Power, *Spiritual Theology of the Priesthood*, 121.

98. *ET* 2:400.

99. *LLC*, 17; *OPSC*, 196.

John Paul brings further clarity to the distinctiveness of priesthood. As a sharer in the ministerial *munera*, the priest has a different relationship with Christ and the church than does any nonordained person. The priest, he says, is the "visible continuation and sacramental sign of Christ in his own position before the Church and world, as the enduring and ever new source of salvation, he 'who is head of the Church, his body, and is himself its savior' (Eph 5:23)."[100] Where a religious can represent the church as body and bride and can perform public acts in the church's name,[101] the priest represents and can act "in the name and person of Christ the head and shepherd," and of the "bridegroom" himself.[102]

The signification of Christ as head and bridegroom, explains Lawrence Welch, is essential for the discipleship of Christians. As a sign of Christ the head, the priest's presence reminds against "ecclesial Pelagianism," a belief that the body and its members are self-sufficient, able to act independently of the head who stands above them. As a sign of Christ the bridegroom, the priest's presence contests "ecclesial monophysitism," a belief that the identity of the church is undifferentiated from Christ who in fact stands distinct from it. The presence of the priest is a living reminder to the church and its members to relate to Christ as other.[103]

As for the religious priest himself, identity with Christ the head and bridegroom can condition the whole range of his ministry, even when

100. *PDV* 16.

101. For more on ministry in the church's name by nonordained persons, see Susan K. Wood, "A Theology of Authorization of Lay Ecclesial Ministers," in *In the Name of the Church: Vocation and Authorization of Lay Ecclesial Ministry*, ed. William J. Cahoy, 99–116 (Collegeville, Minn.: Liturgical Press, 2012).

102. *PDV* 15. See also *Mulieris Dignitatem*, 26 and 27, for the representation of Christ as bridegroom. The 2015 document "Identity and Mission of the Religious Brother in the Church" identifies the religious brother as a special sign of Jesus the brother (at no. 15). More work needs to be done on the understanding of the specifically *spousal* signification of celibate male religious. Perhaps he can be understood analogously through the spousal relationship the priest has with the church, much as the priest understands his own spousal gift to Christ the bridegroom through the spousal relationship represented in the consecrated woman. Surely there is a constellational referent in St. Joseph for nonordained espousal to the church.

103. Lawrence J. Welch, "Priestly Identity Reconsidered: A Reply to Susan Wood," *Worship* 70 (July 1996): 307–19.

his actions sometimes overlap with those carried out by nonordained persons. When religious priests and nonordained religious are engaged side by side in ministries such as retreat preaching, teaching in schools, works of charity, and spiritual direction, their activities may be, for all intents and purposes, identical and do not require ordination for their exercise. Since he is the representative of Christ head, shepherd, and bridegroom, however, when the priest teaches and preaches, he will carry a different kind of authority (and responsibility) than the nonordained religious. His word will be the word of a shepherd with special accountability for the souls of the faithful and to the bishops and superiors under whom he serves.[104] When he distributes the Eucharist alongside a nonordained extraordinary minister, he will visibly represent the bridegroom whose gift of embodied grace is being offered to the bridal church. When he runs a school or practices spiritual direction, he will not only imitate the good shepherd, but be a sacramental sign of the good shepherd's presence. Even when he is not actively ministering, his sacramental presence is a reminder to both the church and to his own community, of their continual dependence on the head and bridegroom.

To conclude, I agree with Lafont that religious *qua* religious already have a strong association with ecclesial apostolates and ministry. Religious missiological activity unfolds naturally from the imitation of Christ's lifestyle, which religious life is all about. On the other hand, insofar as that activity is official and public it is subject to the hierarchy, and insofar as it is also ministerial it is understood as analogous to the hierarchical ministry. Since the religious priest is ordained, he has a more direct relation to sacred ministry than his nonordained counterparts, represents apostolic office to a higher degree than they do, and bears the responsibility such representation entails. A religious priest can certainly do some things that a religious brother cannot, but the

104. John Paul II states that the preaching and teaching of a bishop is more than words of personal witness. It is "the word of a pastor who strengthens the community in faith, gathers it around the mystery of God and gives it life. The faithful need the word of their Bishop, they need to have their faith confirmed and purified"; *PG* 29. The priest, of course, has lesser authority in his word than a bishop, but this statement could be similarly applied to priests.

priest's ministerial identity cannot be reduced to functions. There is a qualitative difference to his being that pertains to his sacramental representation of, and configuration to, Christ the head and bridegroom. This qualitative difference cannot help but condition even those ministries he may share with his nonordained brothers.

Three Signs

With much overlap between vocations, it is helpful to pause and reflect some more why it is important to have the three distinct signs of nonordained religious life, diocesan priesthood, and religious priesthood. The nonordained religious is the clearest, least ambiguous expression of the value of the evangelical counsels in the church. There is a tendency, perhaps a very unfair one, among those both inside and outside the church to look at the priest, even the religious priest, and to assume that the man wanted to be a priest, wanted the status or power that came with it, and only accepted celibacy because the church's law required it. He may have decided it was worth it, but if the church had not required it, he would not have taken this step. To the religious priest a further assumption is sometimes made that, since he was required to be celibate in order to be a priest, and since he wanted so much to be a priest, he entered a religious community in order to avoid loneliness. Against this assumption, the nonordained religious offers the clearest countertestimony that the evangelical counsels are worth embracing not as a means toward office or power, but because Christ is worth renouncing everything else for.[105]

The diocesan priest, by not being the primary sign of the evangelical counsels, signifies that ministry has an objective efficacy that does not depend on the quality or degree of one's subjective discipleship. This is especially true with respect to the sanctifying function, even if

105. Regarding the evangelical counsel of poverty, George Goethals, one of the chief engineers of the Panama Canal, is reported to have said, "I remember once visiting a monastery of Jesuit Fathers. I saw the wretched cells they lived in, the little rude cots they slept in, the rough tables at which they had their meals. And then I remembered the vast power that the men who lived like that had once exercised. It was worth living simply in order to have that"; David McCullough, *The Path between the Seas: The Creation of the Panama Canal 1870–1914* (New York: Simon and Schuster, 1977), 572.

it is obvious that one's teaching, preaching, and leadership are greatly complemented and aided by one's subjective witness. The faithful need the distinction of this sign so that they know they can fully and always trust the sacramental ministry offered by the priest. Otherwise, we end up in the heresies of Donatism and Montanism. Furthermore, in practical terms, the mitigated relationship that the diocesan priest has with the evangelical counsels of obedience and poverty allows him to share in some ways more concretely with the lives of the ordinary faithful. A strict adherence to religious obedience and evangelical poverty would be rather difficult for a diocesan priest, especially one living alone in a rectory, to maintain.

The religious priest has a double signification of radical discipleship and objective, official, apostolic ministry. John Paul stated rather dramatically that "he reproduces in his life the fullness of the mystery of Christ"—that is, both Jesus' subjective lifestyle and his objective office with the saving grace it brings.[106] By signifying both mysteries, the religious priest also shows their union. According to Balthasar, the unity of this dual signification is beneficial to the church because it shows: (1) that it is extremely fitting for the one who represents Christ as head and bridegroom in the Eucharist to be himself totally, instrumentally, available to God and the church through subjective poverty, chastity, and obedience;[107] (2) that radical discipleship and official ministry cannot, ultimately, be in opposition if they can in fact be embodied in the same person; (3) that subjective holiness is fruitful of grace that supports official ministry; and (4) that all subjective discipleship is oriented toward a missiological end.[108]

Having covered so much ground in the chapter, it is helpful to summarize. The signification of religious, clergy, and religious priests, according to our Balthasarian framework is:

106. *VC* 30.

107. Balthasar states, "In light of Jesus' self-offering, the life of self-giving, in the ecclesial form of an explicit, lifelong commitment to the three evangelical counsels, can be seen as the most appropriate response on the part of a man called to pastoral office in the Church"; Balthasar, *Our Task*, 155.

108. For points two through four, see *CSL*, 372, and 277, and *PS*, 27.

TABLE 9-1.

	Religious Life	*Priesthood*	*Religious Priesthood*
Primary Signification	Subjective Priesthood/Radical Discipleship	(Objective) Apostolic Office of Christ as Prophet, Priest, and King; Christ as Head and Bridegroom	(Objective) Apostolic Office/Christ as Head and Bridegroom; Radical Discipleship/ Subjective Priesthood
Secondary Signification	Objective Office	Subjective Discipleship	The Unity of the Objective and Subjective

The religious priest is a double sign in the church of radical subjective discipleship and official apostolic ministry. As we shall see in chapter 10, this double signification enables the religious priesthood to exercise a vocation of mediation between the hierarchical institution of the church and movements of charismatic prophetic renewal.

CHAPTER 10

Religious Priesthood and Mediation between Charism and Institution

Back in chapter 5, we pointed out that Vatican II makes a distinction between "prophetic-charismatic" elements in the church and "hierarchical-ministerial-sacramental-authoritative" ones.[1] Because Balthasar prefers to use personal categories rather than abstract principles, he describes these elements as the Marian and Petrine poles or profiles, respectively.[2] Peter represents the objective hierarchical priesthood and the church's institutional stability. Mary represents the subjective priesthood and charismatic-prophetic renewal. According to Balthasar, John mediates between the Petrine and Marian poles. Hence, John's is a unifying/mediating mission, and it is continued in the church by religious priests.

In chapter 5, we also showed that, depending on how the relational dynamics between the church's objective/hierarchical/institutional (Petrine) and subjective/prophetic/charismatic (Marian) poles are envisioned, different questions or problems emerge for religious priests, such as: (1) how to personally integrate charism and hierarchical office into a single vocational identity; (2) how to integrate priests and non-ordained brothers in a single religious community; and (3) how to personally, practically navigate between the duties and ideals of religious life and ministerial priesthood in a way that benefits the religious priest

1. Cole and Conner, *Christian Totality*, 49. See also *LG* 12.
2. See Leahy, *Marian Profile*, 129–30.

himself and the wider church. This chapter shows that Balthasar's thought helps meet many of these challenges. When Balthasar's thought is developed with the help of postconciliar magisterial teaching and the insights of other theologians, it can be demonstrated that the religious priest's mediation between the objective/institutional and subjective/charismatic poles is a characteristic and important mission of religious priests.

Vocational Identity

A first issue for religious priests arises from the mere juxtaposition of these two poles and therefore of the categories of religious life and priesthood. Priesthood was presented paradigmatically by Vatican II under a diocesan type. Religious life was presented paradigmatically without sacerdotal associations. The juxtaposition of clergy and religious is nowhere clearer than in *Lumen Gentium*, Chapter VI. This chapter on the topic of religious life, when it describes clergy, primarily describes them as figures outside of and external to the religious community.[3] In neither *Lumen Gentium* nor *Perfectae Caritatis* is there provided much description of or imagery for the identity and mission of clergy who are *also* religious. Roland Faley, TOR, former major superior of his order and former executive director of the Conference of Major Superiors of Men, argues that this lacuna leads the religious priest to imagine his singular vocation in a bifurcated way that can result in an identity crisis. In order to resolve this crisis, the religious priest may feel forced to choose whether his religious or his priestly identity has pride of place. He will either make priesthood an "appendage" to his religious vocation or "the overriding and determining factor" in his vocation rather than finding his priesthood "situated squarely within" his religious vocation as an authentic expression of his religious charism.[4]

As discussed in chapter 8 of this book, Balthasar provides images for the identity and mission of religious priests in the figures of the apostles John and Paul. John, the beloved disciple and one of the Twelve—who

3. *LG* 45.

4. Faley, "American Experience of Religious Life," 123.

remains lovingly by Jesus' side from the Last Supper to the Cross, who withdraws into a common life with Mary, and who authors a mystical-existential theology—is an image, for Balthasar, of monastic priesthood. Paul, the church's first great missionary and teacher—who founded and ministered to many churches in many places but avoided settling in anyone of them, and who unabashedly held himself up as a model of radical discipleship—is an image, for Balthasar, of itinerant religious priesthood. Certainly, for Balthasar, John and Paul's example is instructive for diocesan clergy and nonordained religious as well. He uses John, for example, to signify the prayer life in general, and he uses Paul to clarify the contours of all pastoral office. The fullness of their missions, however, which involves mediating between charism and office and embodying both the objective and subjective priesthoods in their own persons, is continued most manifestly by religious priests. In John and Paul, religious clergy can thus find biblical affirmations for, and images of, their callings. These images can help religious priests integrate their two paradigmatic vocations into a single personal mission in imitation of the great apostles. Had Balthasar provided nothing else for a theology of religious priesthood, his identification of John and Paul as types of religious priesthood would have still been a tremendous contribution.

Religious Priests in Community

A second issue arises for religious priests from the subordination of the charismatic pole to the hierarchical, institutional pole. This approach, taken by Cole and Conner and also typical in contemporary magisterial teaching,[5] invites a question about the integration of clergy into mixed communities of religious brothers and priests. If the charismatic religious pole is situated firmly under the authority of the hierarchical pole, what does this mean for the concrete, living relation between religious priests and their nonordained brothers? Here, one of Sandra Schneiders's objections to religious priesthood can be recalled. As she sees it, ordination introduces an unwelcome element of "class" into religious

5. Cole and Conner, *Christian Totality*, 46–47; see also *LG* 45; *PG* 44, 50; *VC* 46, 48, 49, 50; *CL* 24; *MR* 8, 9, 13, 22, 44, 45.

life, which, according to great founders such as Pachomius, Benedict, and Francis, should be an essentially egalitarian community.[6] The presence of religious priests, Schneiders fears, works against the religious ideals of unity and equality.

When dealing with the question of priesthood's effect on the corporate dynamics of religious common life, Balthasar shows some sympathy toward the concerns Schneiders raises. He is, for example, somewhat negative regarding the extent to which male religious life was clericalized during the Middle Ages, with the consequent marginalization of religious brothers.[7] Nonetheless, he is not opposed to religious priesthood *in esse*, and he provides at least three ideas for a priesthood that would fit more harmoniously into religious community than it sometimes did in previous centuries. We'll discuss these ideas in the order of what we find least to most helpful in his writings.

First, Balthasar is open to the idea that priesthood in religious life may operate somewhat differently than it does in the wider church. He implies that if the religious priest belongs to a religious family such as the Benedictines or Franciscans in which the charism has been associated more with radical subjective discipleship than with priestly ministry, then religious priesthood will be lived in that context in a more functional way that recognizes its occasional and necessary activity without emphasizing any distinctive priestly identity or spirituality.[8] Since religious families like the Benedictines and Franciscans are also more likely to be mixed communities of brothers and priests, the downplaying of clerical uniqueness can help minimize any divisive or class-conscious effects introduced by the presence of priests. These "class" distinctions, of course, would be much less felt in communities like the Dominicans and Jesuits, where the vast majority of members are ordained. Balthasar's suggestion here, however, seems to trigger the concern of Faley that religious priests of the Benedictine or Franciscan variety are forced to choose one vocational identity over the other rather than fully embracing and integrating both.

Second, Balthasar entertains the notion of Ildefons Herwegen that

6. Schneiders, *Religious Life in a New Millennium*, vol. 1, *Finding the Treasure*, 273.

7. See *LLC*, 68–76.

8. *LLC*, 68–74, esp. 69–70n4; *CSL*, 374.

within religious communities, clerics might be placed sometimes under the authority of nonordained superiors deemed to have a charism for leadership. Balthasar does not recommend this approach outside the context of religious life, but he thinks it may work within a "monastic ordering," where the exercise of priesthood is better understood by all as "subordinate" to "the total form of life"[9] and "bound to the limits . . . drawn" by the religious community according to its self-understanding and mission.[10] In such a context, which was surely the aspiration of Benedict and Francis, apparent inequalities arising from the presence of the ordained would be significantly lessened by the official recognition of nonordained charismatic authority. At the same time, the religious priest could fully embrace his ministerial identity, provided he does so within the context of an obedience that accepts his religious commitment as conditioning his priesthood. In other words, he would not exert the clerical authority or clerical prerogatives of ministry unless his legitimate superiors, ordained or nonordained, authorized him to do so.

Although the church is still wrestling with the exercise of authority in "Mixed Institutes" like the Benedictines and Franciscans,[11] a few communities have been granted permission to have nonordained superiors exercising some authority over clerics. While this is a promising development in my estimation, a caution is probably in order. Religious priests spend many years in priestly formation. A strong emphasis in today's seminaries is preparing men for leadership in the church. Priesthood is an office, and seminaries are officer-training schools. Overenthusiasm toward elevating nonordained to positions of leadership in the name of equality could end up preventing the very men who have been best prepared to assume this leadership from doing so.

9. *LLC*, 69–70n4.

10. Abbot Leodegar Hunkeler, quoted in *LLC*, 70n4.

11. John Paul II, in *Vita Consecrata*, 61, uses the term "Mixed Institutes" to refer to groups like the Benedictines and Franciscans. Contemporary canon law, however, recognizes only the existence of "Lay Institutes," and "Clerical Institutes" such as the Dominicans and Jesuits, but to whom Benedictines and most Franciscans also technically belong (see *CIC* 588, §§2 and 3). For further discussion of how the canonical designation as "Clerical Institute" contributes to the difficulty of Benedictines and Franciscans in their attempts to have nonordained superiors approved, see Seasoltz, "Institutes of Consecrated Life and Ordained Ministry," 149–53.

Balthasar's third and best idea calls for the conversion of both religious priests and their nonordained confreres. Balthasar agrees with Schneiders that priesthood is associated with hierarchical authority and hence introduces an asymmetry with other members of the community.[12] On the other hand, he states that authority should always be exercised in a spirit of humble service, which should, at least ideally, balance any authoritarian distortions. For Balthasar, the great lesson of the end of the Fourth Gospel is that Peter's commission to leadership will forever take the form of service and sacrifice.[13] Also, the priest must remember that he is himself, first, a disciple, first, a son of Mary, set apart from the Marian church only to provide a service for the community; the priest's existence as a representative of Christ's objective priesthood is for the sake of fostering and nourishing the subjective discipleship of others.[14] Meanwhile, all Christians, in order to grow in holiness, need the priesthood's leadership, preaching, teaching, and mediation of sacramental grace. The nonordained should thus be open and receptive to the presence and functions of the ordained.[15] Indeed, religious should be distinguished among the faithful by their reverence for the church's ministers.[16]

To illustrate the kind of conversion Balthasar is calling for, it is helpful to appeal to the ethos of the two saints for whose families this has been such an issue. The religious priest would do well to recognize with St. Benedict that his ordination is no entitlement to authority. The mere fact of ordination does not include a canonical mandate to be this or that person's canonical pastor. One's being a priest does not give one automatic authority over any of one's brothers in religious life. The reli-

12. "The priest and the layman stand over against one another as the man with the ministry and the man without the ministry. For although there exist in the membership of the Church manifold functions, charisms, and missions that pertain to the laity, these can never be set in comparison and rivalry to the hierarchical ministry, nor can one relativize the hierarchical ministry in favor of these"; *ET* 2:319.

13. "Peter's singular participation in Jesus' authority and responsibility obliges him also to participate especially in Jesus' spirit of service and his readiness to suffer"; *OPSC*, 149–50.

14. *TD* 3:353–54.

15. *ET* 2:320–21.

16. *DGO*, 26.

gious priest's obedience must be exercised in an ascesis that renounces any status over others that has not been given him by his superiors. As Benedict wrote of the priest in the monastery:

> He must recognize that he is subject to the discipline of the rule, and not make any exceptions for himself.... Whenever there is a question of an appointment or of any other business in the monastery, he takes the place that corresponds to the date of his entry into the community, and not that granted him out of respect for his priesthood.[17]

At the same time, nonordained religious would do well to recall the ethos of St. Francis, stripped perhaps of its extremes, that that dignity and calling of the priesthood should at all times be respected. What is most needed for the integration of religious priests into religious communities is conversion of hearts.

Interecclesial Mediation

A third and final issue arises for religious priests when the relationship between institutional and charismatic poles is framed in such a way that highlights a sociological and existential tension between them. For some scholars, such as Schneiders, this tension is enough to make the combining of religious life, a primarily charismatic-prophetic phenomenon, with priesthood, a hierarchical-institutional one, existentially undesirable. As discussed in chapter 4, Schneiders describes clergy as institutional men whose task is to "preserve and implement the current arrangements for the good of the people" and whose preeminent concern is ecclesial unity.[18] Religious are charismatic prophets who call the church "beyond what is currently understood into the desert journey that leads toward the Reign of God."[19] They advance the "development of doctrine and the evolution of moral practice" through their questions and proposed alternatives.[20] They are primarily charged with challeng-

17. *RB* 60.5 and 60.7.
18. Schneiders, *Finding the Treasure*, 271.
19. Schneiders, *Finding the Treasure*, 271.
20. Schneiders, *Finding the Treasure*, 271–72.

ing the status quo and only secondarily concerned with ecclesial unity. As noted in chapter 5, Schneiders objects to religious priesthood on the grounds that a single individual cannot easily live out both these callings, so different in their nature, and maintain personal integrity.

Schneiders takes the framework of tension between the motives of religious and clergy to an extreme in my view. With that said, this framework does appear in more moderate form in the reflections of a number of notable, credible theologians. There is something to it. According to Brian Daley, the religious is the idealist in the church, committed to radical discipleship and its promotion. Hence, he or she will be "critical, prophetic, and challenging to stable institutions."[21] The priest, on the other hand, is commissioned to work for the unity of the church, promote institutional stability, and look out for the good of the whole flock, even the most mediocre members. Clergy, therefore, must remain realists, and their interest will be "conciliatory, preservative, moderate, oriented to institutional survival."[22] For Jean-Marie Tillard, the tension between religious and clergy is the tension John Henry Newman acknowledged between the "prophetic" and "royal" poles of the church.[23] The religious "prophet" will be marked primarily by the "comportment of conviction," and the cleric "king" will be marked by the "comportment of responsibility."[24] Ideally, their functions are interdependent, but the complementary union of their roles "risks becoming torn" by mutual suspicion; the religious fears the cleric being oppressive, and the cleric fears the religious being disruptive.[25] Daley and Tillard do not follow Schneiders in recommending against religious priesthood, but Daley, at least, admits that the religious priest will be uniquely challenged to navigate between his two roles.[26]

Joseph Ratzinger warns against imagining that the church's charismatic and institutional dimensions are inherently at odds. First, it risks

21. Daley, "Ministry of Disciples," 628.

22. Daley, "Ministry of Disciples," 628.

23. Tillard, *Devant Dieu et Pour Le Monde: Le projet de religieux* (Paris: Cerf, 1974), 344.

24. Tillard, *Devant Dieu et Pour Le Monde*, 327.

25. Tillard, *Devant Dieu et Pour Le Monde*, 327.

26. Daley, "Ministry of Disciples," 629.

devaluing the charismatic-prophetic potential of the clergy. Holy Orders, Ratzinger reminds, is a sacrament. Sacraments involve epiclesis, the invocation and bestowal of the Holy Spirit. Thus, the priesthood itself has a charismatic dimension, and it should be lived as an authentic charism by spiritual men.[27] Moreover, the charism of priesthood can involve authentic elements of prophetic renewal. Ratzinger states, "God, again and again arouses prophetic individuals—these may be laymen, religious or even bishops and priests—who call out to her the right message, which does not in the ordinary workings of the 'institution' attain sufficient strength."[28] Second, Ratzinger warns that too strongly juxtaposing the charismatic-prophetic and institutional-hierarchical poles of the church can lead to factionalism. In political society, positions are divided into left and right wings, and camps become hardened in their views and at odds with one another. Should the church operate like a political society, with religious and clergy pitted against each other, it will be divisive and destructive for her.[29]

Nonetheless, Ratzinger admits of a distinction, though not a division, between the "enduring forms of Church order" and "charismatic upsurges,"[30] and he acknowledges that there can be some tension between them at the level of the moral life. They clash not because of any inherent incompatibility, but because of human failures. He notes that charismatic movements like religious life have characteristic temptations to overemphasize their own "specific task" or "charismatic gift," to "attribute an absolute value" to their own group,[31] and to want to remake the Church in their "own likeness."[32] "Movements," he writes, "even if they have found the whole gospel on their path and are sharing it with others—must be warned that they are a gift made to the Church

27. Ratzinger, *Pilgrim Fellowship of Faith*, 182.

28. Ratzinger, *Pilgrim Fellowship of Faith*, 186.

29. See Ratzinger, *Pilgrim Fellowship of Faith*, 186. Ratzinger adds that when God raises up prophets for specific reforming purposes, he usually calls individuals rather than groups. In the Old Testament, groups of prophets are almost always false prophets, whereas authentic prophets act alone.

30. Ratzinger, *Pilgrim Fellowship of Faith*, 181.

31. Ratzinger, *Pilgrim Fellowship of Faith*, 206.

32. Ratzinger, *Pilgrim Fellowship of Faith*, 177.

as a whole and that they need to submit to the demands of the whole in order to remain true to their own nature."[33] The institutional pole has its own characteristic temptation. It has a tendency to "harden into an armor that stifles [the church's] actual spiritual life."[34]

Balthasar, for his part, emphasizes the interdependent relation between charism and institution, between religious and clergy. For Balthasar, religious discipleship requires the guarantee of authority present in the hierarchy to practice authentic obedience and confirm the communion of religious with the wider church. Clergy depend on religious for charismatic wisdom and an example of radical discipleship. Ideally, when guided by love, religious and clergy see the other's necessity and cooperate with a mutually respectful reciprocity. Furthermore, Balthasar teaches that objective office and subjective charisma are both expressions of the Holy Spirit's presence in the church. Although their interrelation on this earthly plane may be marked by tensions, the pneumatological origin of both poles insures that they cannot ultimately be at odds with one another.[35]

Balthasar is not naïve, however. He is well aware of the historical conflicts between religious and clergy, and he admits of an enduring "tension" between the institutional and charismatic poles.[36] In *The Office of Peter and the Structure of the Church*, Balthasar refers to his constellational ecclesiology to illuminate these tensions. Peter and Mary represent the institutional and charismatic poles. Balthasar notes that Peter and Mary rarely meet in the New Testament. They require the

33. Ratzinger, *Pilgrim Fellowship of Faith*, 206–7.

34. Ratzinger, *Pilgrim Fellowship of Faith*, 181.

35. See *TL* 3:291–411.

36. See *TD* 3:353–60. Balthasar would have witnessed some of these tensions unfolding in his own life. In the twentieth century, Benedictines pioneered liturgical renewal while Dominicans and Jesuits spearheaded the ecumenical movement and interreligious dialogue before these things became official concerns at Vatican II. As Tillard writes, in many cases, religious pioneers who "had foresight on questions" that had yet to "hit the general conscience" suffered initial resistance and suspicion from clergy and from the Holy See; Tillard, *Devant Dieu et Pour Le Monde*, 348. For a recounting of some confrontations between religious thinkers and Rome during the preconciliar era, see Robert Nugent, *Silence Speaks: Teilhard de Chardin, Yves Congar, John Courtney Murray, and Thomas Merton* (Mahwah, N.J.: Paulist Press, 2011).

mediation of John to "prevent the Church from falling into two separate parts."[37]

Later, in a far richer description, he extends his usual binary scheme (the Petrine and Marian poles) to a quaternary one (involving the Johannine, Petrine, Pauline, and Jacobian principles).[38] He envisions the church as a "concert" where each member has a specific part to play.[39] The Johannine part resounds in contemplatives and mystics (very often religious). The Pauline part is played by missionaries and speculative theologians (also often religious). The Petrine role of official authority is played by clergy, especially the bishops, and ultimately by the pope. There is also a Jacobian part, whose players give consistent voice to the value of tradition. Balthasar sees scripture scholars, canon lawyers, and positive theologians as playing the Jacobian role. When this communion operates in kenotic love, with each part influencing and receiving the others, it is a harmonious "contrapuntal symphony."[40] However, Balthasar notes that because the church is made up of human members, who during the time of pilgrimage suffer the effects of sin, the harmonious relation between the church's sections sometimes falls out of balance. When this happens, one or more of the parts becomes muted while another becomes inflated and overbearing. The connection be-

37. *OPSC*, 241.

38. For what follows, see *OPSC*, 335–91. It is difficult, but possible, to correlate Balthasar's binary and quaternary schemes. Peter and James would occupy the Petrine pole of the binary scheme, since Peter represents office and James represents canon law and sacred tradition, which, in the *Theo-Logic*, Balthasar places in the church's objective pole; *TL* 3:319, 352. John and Paul occupy the Marian pole, because in the quaternary scheme John represents mysticism and Paul represents "freedom in the Holy Spirit" (*OPSC*, 337), both of which are identified by Balthasar in the *Theo-Logic* with the subjective pole of the binary scheme (*TL* 3:369, 379). A complication arises because John, and to some extent Paul, is used in the binary scheme as a mediator between the Petrine and Marian Poles, but in the quaternary scheme John and Paul are portrayed as parties in the symphony. It may be that Balthasar opts for the quaternary scheme to explain the effects of sin in the church not only because it provides a richer description of the various interests involved, but also because it allows him to avoid the attribution of ecclesial discord to the *Immaculata* who is replaced here by John and Paul.

39. *OPSC*, 342.

40. Danielle Nussberger, "Saint as Theological Wellspring: Hans Urs von Balthasar's Hermeneutic of the Saint in a Christological and Trinitarian Key" (PhD diss., University of Notre Dame, 2007), 46.

tween the parts weakens, and the parts collapse into themselves, suffering what Balthasar calls "involutions."[41] Disassociated from the others, the Petrine emerges as tyrannical and despotic; the Johannine part becomes fideistic and chaotically enthusiastic; the Pauline part becomes coldly rationalistic (the theologians) or relativistic (the missionaries who will be "all things to all people"); the Jacobian part devolves into fundamentalist, ossified traditionalism.

Where Schneiders argues that the tension between charism and institution is a reason not to have religious priests, Balthasar perceives the tension between the church's parts precisely as a reason *to* have religious priests. The important thing, in Balthasar's framework, is for the various parts of the church to remain in communion and reciprocal dialogue with one another. History shows that they often fall out of contact and mutual balance. The religious priest will be in a unique position to mediate between them.[42] As a member of both the clergy and of the religious family, he can carry out, in the words of Vatican II, an "apostolate of like towards like,"[43] representing the concerns of clergy to religious and of religious to clergy. To the clergy, for example, he can communicate the church's spiritual and mystical tradition and be an example of radical discipleship. To religious, he can voice concern for ecclesial unity and the following of proper norms. Importantly, he does not have to be a superior in the community to communicate hierarchical values to the religious community. If he has been well formed as a priest and remains in fraternal contact with other clergy, he will do this informally and humbly.

Although magisterial teaching does not often articulate a specific role for religious priests, religious priesthood's mediating function can be inferred from other statements. In *Pastores Dabo Vobis*, John Paul teaches that "each priest, whether diocesan or religious, is united to the other members of this presbyterate on the basis of the sacrament of holy orders and by particular bonds of apostolic charity, ministry

41. *OPSC*, 354. See also Barron, *Strangest Way*, 118–23. Barron refers to the typical negative tendency of each principle as its "shadow-side," at 121.

42. See *CSL*, 287; *OPSC*, 241–42.

43. *AA* 13.

and fraternity."[44] Since the priesthood has a "radically communitarian form," with every priest acting in communion with the bishops and presbyterate, the priest belongs to and represents the priestly fraternity in whichever context he finds himself.[45] His presence reminds others of their connection to the wider church and their lack of self-sufficiency. Furthermore, every priest is particularly charged with fostering and preserving ecclesial unity.[46] If a diocesan cleric represents these things to the parish, the religious would also seem to represent them to his own community.[47] Such a function is important. Although great religious founders have been distinguished by their "lively sense of church, and obedience to bishops, and especially the pope," there are also, notes John Paul, "centrifugal and disruptive forces" operative in religious life that subvert communion with the hierarchy.[48] The 1978 "Directives for the Mutual Relations between Bishops and Religious in the Church" (*Mutuae Relationes*), issued jointly by the Sacred Congregation for Bishops and the Sacred Congregation for Religious and for Secular Institutes, makes explicit the mediating potential of religious priests. Since religious priests belong to both the religious family and the presbyterate, they "can and should serve to unite and coordinate religious men and women with the local clergy and bishop."[49]

Religious life, meanwhile, is a poignant prophetic sign, a "special source of spiritual and supernatural energy" for renewal of the church and the world.[50] Through their common life, religious point to the value of fraternal relations in a world of isolation, and, through the practice of the counsels, religious bear witness to the primacy of God and of eschatological mysteries.[51] They are, writes John Paul, "spiritual thera-

44. *PDV* 17.

45. *PDV* 17.

46. See *PDV* 12.

47. Along these lines, it is interesting to note that *Mutaue Relationes* states that the pastoral care of religious should be "entrusted to prudently chosen religious priests"; *MR* 30. According to *Verbi Sponsa*, when possible, religious women will be ministered to by religious priests of their same religious family; *VS* 26. These statements affirm the principle of "like to like."

48. *VC* 46.

49. *MR* 36.

50. *RD* 7.

51. *VC* 87–92.

py" for a world marked by hedonism, materialism, and false notions of freedom.[52] Magisterial teaching does not make explicit that religious clergy, by belonging at once to a religious family and to the priestly fraternity, have a special opportunity to represent charismatic renewal and the values of radical discipleship specifically to their brother priests. Nonetheless, given Vatican II's affirmation of the efficacy of an apostolate of "like to like," it follows that religious priests can serve in a special way to do so.

Benefits of a Unifying and Mediating Religious Priesthood

Nothing of what has been stated negates the existential tensions that religious priests may encounter as they attempt to embody both religious and priestly identities and practically navigate between religious and priestly ideals. Some conflicts are probably inevitable. Early monks resisted ordination because they regarded clerical obligations as distractions from the contemplative life and/or the common life. Balthasar points out that a person dedicated to contemplation, who must however frequently prepare homilies, may be impeded from entering the deeper realms of the spiritual life if he is constantly focusing in his scriptural meditation on what will be useful for others to hear.[53] The egalitarian dimensions of common life, as well as the virtue of humility, will probably always be challenged by clerical status, even if inordinate focus is not placed upon it. The value of religious fraternity can be challenged by the practical realities of ministerial duties that require one to be sometimes or often absent from community life and common prayer. The unity of the community, as Schneiders points out, can be further compromised by dual tracks of formation.[54] Finally, communities that have placed strong value on corporate and not only personal poverty inevitably come up against the fact that priesthood requires education and education requires considerable financial resources.

Ultimately, religious institutes will have to decide for themselves if

52. *VC* 87.

53. Balthasar, *Prayer*, 116–17, 257.

54. Schneiders, *Finding the Treasure*, 277–88.

the challenges associated with religious priesthood are worth the trouble. I have argued that the vocation to religious priesthood is a unique charism that is a gift to both the religious priest himself and to the church. Brian Daley summarizes how the religious and priestly sides of one's vocation are mutually corrective for the religious priest himself.[55] In my view, his words are helpful. Both callings, he says, have characteristic temptations or occupational hazards. Priests are tempted by clericalism and institutional ambition; religious are tempted toward fanaticism, anticlericalism, and withdrawal from the public into sectarianism. A religious priest's membership and formation in a religious community benefit him because religious life typically "relativizes clerical status" and is "critical of clerical privilege" and "sensitive to the danger of clerical ambition." Instead, it emphasizes "self-effacing service, communitarian equality, and intense spiritual commitment." A religious priest's formation for orders and membership in the presbyteral order benefit him because the clerical community promotes concern for the good of the whole church, "not just for that of the radically committed," and a healthy suspicion of sectarian tendencies "that charisms can spawn."

The religious priest's mediating vocation also benefits the religious community and the wider church. To his brother priests, he will be an example of one who does not make his "position a means of personal power, wealth or comfort," of one who has learned through common life how to be a "colleague and follower" and not just a leader. To his religious confrères he will be an example of embracing union with the ecclesial hierarchy, of not "shrinking from being identified with the Church as it is, or of accepting his share of responsibility for it." Additionally, the religious priest, "by virtue of his ordination and profession," is a public sign to the whole Church of what every Christian is called to live in his or her own way—responsible leadership and humble service.

Daley wisely notes that "results" are not "guaranteed"; if the religious priest withdraws from the ethos of religious life, he will simply be a cleric with a "retirement plan" and a community to fall back on. Daley does not state it, but one can also note the converse: If the religious priest withdraws from the hierarchical allegiances of his priestly

55. For what follows, see Daley, "Ministry of Disciples," 629.

commitment, he will simply be assisting his community—who can depend on him for sacramental functions—to avoid interaction with and oversight by external clergy and thus to become more sectarian.

Schneiders argues that religious priests will be compromised by their dual commitment to institutional priesthood and prophetic religious life. Daley admits that the life can be marked by tension, but argues that any potential compromise is balanced by the potential value of this unique vocation for both the priest and the church. Daley's is the position of Balthasar as well, and, as I have shown, it harmonizes with magisterial teaching.

CHAPTER 11

Religious Priesthood's Extraparochial and Transdiocesan Mission

The third mark of religious priesthood is that it typically exercises an extraparochial and transdiocesan mission. Part II demonstrated that the image of priesthood provided by Vatican II was that of a member of a local presbyterate, subordinate to a local bishop, ministering to a stable community of the faithful. This type is most evident in the resident pastor of a parish. Although this image resulted from the welcome reemergence of Eucharistic ecclesiology, it had the disadvantage for religious priests of making them seem to compromise the church's intention for the priesthood. This was pointed out presciently by John O'Malley, who desired a broader description of priesthood that would account for its various expressions in religious life.[1] Other theologians took a different approach. On the basis of a certain reading of the Council's teaching, Castellucci, Osborne, and Streider more or less implied that all priesthood should now be conceived of within the localized diocesan, parochial framework.[2] Schneiders and Lafont, more radically, argued for greatly restricting, even eliminating, religious priesthood.[3] For Schneiders, the contemporary model of priesthood involves absorption into diocesan structures and parochial obligations, and these commit-

1. O'Malley, "Priesthood, Ministry and Religious Life," 224.

2. See Castellucci, "I Religiosi Presbiteri Nella Chiesa: *Excursus 'Storico,'*" 106; Osborne, *Priesthood*, 322–23; Streider, *Promise of Obedience*, 110–21.

3. See Schneiders, *Finding the Treasure*, 276; Lafont, *Imagining the Catholic Church*, 162.

ments too greatly compromise the integrity of religious life. For Lafont, the decisive point is that priesthood is a coordinating leadership role within a Eucharistic community. Few such persons are needed. Most religious ministries do not really require ordination.

Balthasar's position, which this book adopts, is that while the diocesan priest typically exercises a localized ministry in a parish, where his "primary obligation" is to "shepherd ... the already existing flock entrusted to him by Christ" and to "preach the gospel in the place where his congregation is located," outreach to those outside the congregation is "predominantly the task of religious priests and of other men and women in the evangelical state together with laypersons in the world."[4] Balthasar criticizes those who would identify all ministry with parochial contexts or who would, in the words of the Gianfranco Agostino Gardin, "consider not ecclesial everything that is not rigidly 'diocesan.'"[5] According to Balthasar, the tendency to envision the church solely as it is expressed in parishes and geographical "districts," with each one headed by its particular shepherd, risks veiling the unity of the church, the unity of ministry, and the mission to those still remaining outside the fold. He notes that this "reductive image" tends especially to marginalize religious priests whose tasks have typically been transdiocesan and extraparochial.[6]

Balthasar's view of religious priests in this regard is quite traditional. Part I noted that most religious institutes have historically exercised nongeographic apostolates. Religious have, for example, typically focused their ministry on outreach to nonbelievers and those with special needs, such as the imprisoned, the sick and homebound, soldiers, youth, students, and those seeking out deeper spiritual commitment. This means that the audience of religious ministries has transcended diocesan and parochial borders. One reason the mendicants and the Jesuits did not generally accept resident pastorates was, precisely, to make themselves more available for specialized ministry. Moreover,

4. *CSL*, 353.

5. Gianfranco Agostino Gardin, "Vescovo, Clero Diocesano, Vita Consecrata: Istanze Nel Cammino Di Communione Nella Chiesa Locale," *Sequela Christi* 2 (2009): 182. Gardin is the Franciscan archbishop of Treviso, Italy.

6. *ET* 2:413.

many religious institutes have had an international, itinerant membership that moves in and out of local churches.[7] Accordingly, members of such institutes could not be considered ministers of the local church without significant qualification. With the possible exception of stable Benedictines, religious themselves, according to their itinerant apostolic charism, have had an apostolic lifestyle that transcended parish and even diocese.

Several of Balthasar's insights are helpful for meeting the concerns raised by theologians after Vatican II and thus supporting religious-priestly involvement in extraparochial and transdiocesan ministry in a postconciliar church. These are: (1) his constellational ecclesiology; (2) his analogical approach to the theology of vocations; (3) his identification of religious as continuing the charismatic mission of their founders; and (4) his strong sense of the unity of the church and of the ministry.

Constellational Ecclesiology

Balthasar's first important contribution to the discussion is his constellational ecclesiology, which affirms that within the present life of the church should be found recapitulations of the vocational patterns of the New Testament. Balthasar observes that Paul never settled into a localized ministerial post among a stable community of the faithful, but rather exercised an itinerant ministry with an almost global scope. As Ratzinger states, "Paul was never the bishop of any particular place and never wanted to be," his "sphere of action" was "the world."[8] But Paul was a priest, at least in a prototypical sense,[9] which means that there is or should be room in the church for a priestly ministry that is not parochially centered and oriented exclusively, or even mainly, to the needs

7. Herbert Workman has tracked the development of religious life as an international itinerant phenomenon. See his *The Evolution of the Monastic Ideal* (Boston: Beacon Press, 1962). Workman refers to the "connexional spirit" of religious life as something that already characterized Cluniac and Cistercian monks but that reached its height in the mendicant movement (243).

8. Ratzinger, *Pilgrim Fellowship of Faith*, 188.

9. For a discussion of the appropriateness of applying the titles priest and bishop to the New Testament apostles, see Brown, *Priest and Bishop*, 47–86, and Sullivan, *Church We Believe In*, 152–84.

of a local church. For Balthasar, Paul is a model for transparochial and transdiocesan priesthood and scriptural proof of its authenticity. Religious priests are his heirs.

Analogical Relationship of Vocations

Balthasar's second contribution is his analogical approach to the theology of vocations, which supports authentic variations within priestly ministry. We have seen how, for Balthasar, the paradigmatic vocations (laity, religious, clergy) serve as primary signs for realities that in fact extend, with variances in degree and kind, *perichoretically* to the other vocations. Thus, what one represents the others participate in analogously.

For Balthasar, there is also an analogical relationship between types of priesthood. Balthasar seems to indicate that if one wants to understand most clearly what a priest is, one should look at a diocesan priest rather than a religious priest as the primary referent for priesthood because the former is the clearest expression (after that of a bishop) of the priesthood as service to the Eucharistic assembly, of the way in which the official priesthood exists to unite, support, and nurture the priesthood of the faithful, and of one who acts in union with his fellow presbyters in subordination to the episcopacy.[10] Above all, the diocesan priest has the honor, in Balthasar's system, of being linked with Peter, the chief of the apostles, whose name Balthasar applies to the essential hierarchical pole of the church.[11] Accordingly, Balthasar acknowledges the indispensable and central role that the diocesan, parochial pastor plays in the church, and he exhorts able, service-minded men to embrace this role. He even laments that certain men enter religious orders in order to avoid pastoral responsibility.[12]

However, what the diocesan parish priest represents, the religious priest also participates in. For Balthasar, the Petrine office is clearest in Peter, but it is also *perichoretically* present in John and Paul. This has already been described in chapter 8, and even more shall be said on it lat-

10. See *CSL*, 352–53; *OT*, 155–56.

11. *CSL*, 287.

12. *OT*, 155n2.

er. The important thing to establish here is that, for Balthasar, John and Paul can participate in the office of Peter without serving as its main type or referent.

Jacques Servais has argued that the Council's teaching on vocations involves an analogical presentation similar to Balthasar's.[13] It is evident in the way the Council acknowledges that all people are called to holiness, but religious life involves a "special," closer imitation of Christ.[14] It is evident in the way the whole church is acknowledged as having a secular mission, but laity are given particular responsibility for it.[15] It is evident in the way that the framework of prophet, priest, and king is used for both the discussion of clergy and of the laity with the acknowledgment that participation in the priesthood of Christ differs "in essence and not only in degree" between the hierarchy and the laity.[16] These descriptions suggest that one or another vocation serves as a sign for realities participated in by the others.

The Council's language suggests that such an analogical hermeneutic also be used for its teaching on the relation between diocesan and religious priesthood. *Presbyterorum Ordinis* states, "What is said here applies to all priests, especially those devoted to the care of souls, with suitable adaptations being made for priests who are religious."[17] *Optatum Totius*, the decree on the training of priests, states in its opening paragraph, "While these prescriptions directly concern the diocesan clergy, they are to be appropriately adapted to all." Applied to the present discussion, an analogical hermeneutic of vocations allows the Council's image of priesthood to be a helpful image but not an exclusive one. It allows diocesan priesthood to be the primary referent for our understanding of priesthood without eliminating possibilities for other expressions. In the absence of an analogical hermeneutic, one is forced to follow those thinkers who conclude that the Council's guiding image, admittedly highly diocesan and parochial, is normative for priesthood. With an analogical framework, one can follow O'Malley and conclude

13. See Servais, "Congar and Balthasar," 4.

14. *LG* 39 and *PC* 1.

15. Vatican Council II, *Gaudium et Spes* (December 7, 1965), 43, and *LG* 31.

16. *LG* 10.

17. *PO* 1.

that the lack of a of description of religious priests does not mean that the church has no room for them, only that it has not yet given a full account of them.

Fidelity to Charism

A third insight of Balthasar's, also supportive of religious extraparochial ministry, is his conviction, shared by Vatican II, that religious should be faithful to the charisms of their founders. According to Balthasar, the founder is like a "consecrated seed" of the whole future of the order.[18] As we described in chapter 6, the founder's mission is universalized through the Holy Spirit, and his life and writings continue to form and inspire all subsequent members of his religious family. Applied to religious priesthood, fidelity to the founder means religious priests will typically minister in extraparochial contexts. While there are and have long been religious priests involved in parish ministry, few institutes were founded for this purpose. When it comes to ancient orders such as the Benedictines and Dominicans, writes Tillard, parochial involvement is arguably an "aberration."[19]

Neither Balthasar nor Vatican II provided much in the way of detailed descriptions of specific religious ministries and apostolates and the connection of these to religious founders. John Paul II's *Vita Consecrata,* however, laid some groundwork in this direction. It is helpful to summarize what he says in some detail.

Early in the document, John Paul differentiates among various forms of consecrated life (for instance, monastic, exclusively contemplative, and apostolic).[20] The mission of exclusively contemplative religious life, such as one might find in cloistered Carmelite monasteries (inspired by Sts. John of the Cross and Teresa of Avila) or among the Carthusians (founded by St. Bruno), is concentrated on prayer and asceticism, the

18. Balthasar, *Prayer,* 106.

19. Tillard, *Mystery of Religious Life,* 75.

20. Using the wider category of consecrated life, rather than religious life, John Paul II also describes hermits and widows, secular institutes, societies of apostolic life, and consecrated members of new movements. Since this book is focused on religious ministry, the discussion here is limited to monastic, exclusively contemplative, and apostolic religious life; see *VC* 6–12.

life of the counsels, the common life, and the mission of eschatological signification to the church and to the world.[21] Because other forms of religious life also share these characteristics but add to them specific apostolates, the exclusively contemplative life might be considered religious life *sine additio*. As Balthasar poignantly observes, there is such a thing as exclusively contemplative life and such a thing as a mixed life of contemplation and action, but there is no exclusively active life.[22] According to John Paul, exclusively contemplative religious forswear external apostolates (beyond, of course, the apostolate of prayer) in order to "direct the whole of their lives and all their activities to the contemplation of God" and "provide singular testimony of the Church's love for her Lord."[23] This form of religious life, though hidden, is apostolically fruitful.

Under "apostolic religious life," John Paul considers canons regular, mendicants, clerics regular (for instance, Jesuits), and "religious congregations of men and women devoted to apostolic ministry and missionary activity."[24] These also are dedicated to common life, prayer, asceticism, and the life of the counsels. They may be distinguished from contemplative life insofar as, because they were founded precisely "for the sake of carrying out different forms of apostolic service," they always involve external apostolates.[25] They may be further distinguished from each other according to their particular spiritualities and apostolates.

Very interestingly, and appropriately, John Paul distinguishes monastic life from both exclusively contemplative life and apostolic religious life. The Western form of monastic life, which John Paul notes has been inspired above all by St. Benedict, involves typically contemplative elements such as "evangelical commitment to conversion of life, obedience and stability, and in persevering dedication to meditation on God's word (*lectio divina*), the celebration of the liturgy and prayer."[26] While monastic stability and strong orientation to prayer make Benedictine

21. See *VC* 8.
22. *CSL*, 352.
23. *VC* 8.
24. *VC* 9.
25. *VC* 9.
26. *VC* 6.

life like the exclusively contemplative life, it is, nonetheless, a more visible form of life than the cloistered Carmelite and more publicly engaged through hospitality and other apostolates. John Paul notes that monasteries are "eloquent signs of communion, welcoming abodes for those seeking God and the things of the Spirit, schools of faith and true places of study, dialogue and culture."[27]

In later chapters, John Paul describes a variety of apostolates typically exercised by religious without assigning them to any specific groups. He names spiritual direction and formation, retreats, evangelization, interreligious dialogue, outreach to the poor, ministry to the sick, education and schools, social communication, and ecumenism.[28] Striking a particularly Balthasarian note, John Paul claims that the apostolates are charismatically differentiated and that each is a pneumatic way of not only continuing their founder's mission but of incarnating particular scenes in the life of Christ, giving "witness to some aspect of his mystery."[29] In this sense, Christ is the first founder. The contemplative is Christ at prayer on the mountain; the apostolic religious is Christ teaching, preaching, or ministering to the sick.[30] John Paul does not specify the place of the Benedictine monk (which is of special interest to the present author) in the recapitulation of Christ. Perhaps, through the ministry of hospitality, the monk represents that moment when Christ "remained outside in deserted places *and* people kept coming to him from everywhere" (Mk 1:45). Notably, pastoring parishes does not make John Paul's list of apostolates typical of religious life.

Lafont, of course, objects that the majority of these specialized ministries exercised by religious do not require ordination. Chapter 9 argued to the contrary that the religious priest will be able to offer sacramental ministry in extraparochial settings and that there will also be a qualitative difference to his personal presence in the ministries he carries out alongside nonordained religious. An argument from "fidelity to the founders" can also be made to support extraparochial priestly ministry. Chapter 3 described how, in the centuries following the Jesu-

27. *VC* 6.

28. At VC 38 and 103, 38, 77–78, 81, 79 and 102, 82, 83, 96–97, 99, 101.

29. *VC* 36.

30. *VC* 32.

its, more and more orders were founded with a specific ministry and ministerial audience in mind. Fabio Ciardi has shown that a number of founders during the modern era envisioned the priests of their orders as being ordained not for service to the diocese or parish and not for service to the other members of their own community, but precisely for service of the charismatically differentiated mission of the particular institute. That is to say, they were ordained for the service of the sick, of youth, of the poor, or of the immigrant, depending upon the specific mission willed by the founder.[31]

The One Priesthood

A fourth and final helpful insight of Balthasar's is his strong sense of the unity of the universal church and of the priesthood, which can be used to support a transdiocesan ministry. Like Ratzinger, whose views were articulated in chapter 4, Balthasar is critical of those Eastern Orthodox theologians whose versions of Eucharistic ecclesiology so prioritize the authenticity and autonomy of the local church that they see neither urgency for concrete ecclesial unity nor a manifestation of it in Catholicism.[32]

According to Balthasar, the universal unity of the church is displayed in both its Marian and Petrine poles. The "Marian all-embracing universality" is the church's "truly *unlimited* availability," which makes her "bridal womb, *matrix* and mater," the "*fiat*" through which Christ "forms the truly universal Church."[33] Insofar as the church has a Marian subjectivity, "it follows night as day," writes Aidan Nichols, that there cannot be

31. See Ciardi, "Il Ministero Presbitale a Servizio del Carisma," 235–55. Ciardi states, "At the origin of every community is the initiative of the Spirit, mediated by the founder or foundress.... The Spirit always shows new ways to fulfill the Gospel, always opening new paths to proclaim the Gospel and to serve humanity, above all where many are suffering and in need. The instruments that the Spirit gives are diverse—from prayer to asceticism, from confession to contemplation, from education to social work. The priestly mystery can re-enter the charismatic project as 'ministry,' as a path, as concrete service" (252).

32. See *OPSC*, 288–305 and 327. Quoting the theologian Vladimir Soloviev, a convert from Russian Orthodoxy, Balthasar states that unity in the East "remains a 'fiction'"; in reality, "there are only isolated national churches"; *OPSC*, 302.

33. *OPSC*, 221–22; emphasis original.

"a multiplicity of churches," for there can be only one "Bride of Christ."[34]

The Petrine universality expresses itself in the hierarchical ministry. Insofar as the church has a Christological subjectivity (for the church is the body and not just bride), there can only be one head.[35] Of course, this head is Christ, but his vicar is the Roman pontiff, and all ministry must be carried out in union with him. Just as there is only one church, there is also ultimately only one ministry. Balthasar writes, "The good shepherds ... are bound in a particular manner to the One Shepherd who is the Head of the Church.... When Jesus entrusts his flock to Peter, he stresses the unity; because there were many apostles, but only to one is it said, 'Feed my lambs.' There are many good shepherds, but they are all in the One, they are one."[36] Balthasar does not believe that subordination of all ministry to Peter needs to be understood in an ultramontane way. Balthasar believes that "Vatican II basically fulfilled the demands and longings" for the pope's office to be integrated into episcopal collegiality and ecclesial communion.[37] Nevertheless, the pope maintains a ministry of unity in the church, and this ministry requires more than "an honorary authority, an office of teaching, supervision, and leadership"; to be effective, it must involve "real, universal, jurisdictional primacy."[38]

Castellucci claims that it is difficult, "after Vatican II, to conceive of the ministry of a priest divorced from the actual path of a particular Church."[39] Osborne states that all priesthood must be conceptualized today as "belonging to a regional presbyterium, under the leadership of a very definite, regional bishop."[40] He also contends that the only way to conceive of ministry otherwise is to locate ministry within an "undifferentiated," "spiritual," "a-temporal," "a-spatial" context.[41] Balthasar's reminder that both the church and ministry are *one* provides an open-

34. Nichols, *No Bloodless Myth: A Guide through Balthasar's Dramatics* (Washington, D.C.: The Catholic University of America Press, 2000), 126. See also Nichols, *Word Has Been Abroad*, 117.

35. See *OPSC*, 220.

36. *OPSC*, 189.

37. *OPSC*, 76. See *OPSC*, 9, 236–37.

38. *OPSC*, 72.

39. Castellucci, "I Religiosi Presbiteri Nella Chiesa: *Excursus 'Storico,'*" 106.

40. Osborne, *Priesthood*, 332–33.

41. Osborne, *Priesthood*, 333.

ing to a different approach. Although he does not explicitly make all the necessary connections, it shall be argued here that: (a) priesthood can be conceived of not only as membership in a local presbyterate, under a specific regional bishop, and oriented to the service of a particular church, but also as membership in the universal order of presbyters, subordinated to the college of bishops and to the Roman pontiff;[42] and (b) religious priesthood can be understood as *highlighting* the one ministry's universal, transdiocesan character that complements the diocesan priesthood's highlighting of the one priesthood's commitment to and expression in particular churches. Again, there is an analogous relationship between the priesthoods. Diocesan clergy serve as the primary referent for localized ministry; religious clergy serve as the primary referent for extraparochial and transdiocesan outreach.

A few points in contemporary magisterial teaching show openness to this way of envisioning religious priesthood. *Presbyterorum Ordinis* and *Pastores Dabo Vobis* emphasize the essential unity of the priesthood and note that priesthood is ordered "not only to the particular Church, but also to the universal Church."[43] "Ordination does not prepare [priests] merely for a limited and circumscribed mission, but for the fullest, in fact, the universal mission of salvation to end of the earth."[44] Vatican II and John Paul II both encourage diocesan priests to generously avail themselves of the possibility of ministering in other dioceses in order to provide for a "fair distribution of clergy."[45] All priesthood is then, in some sense, transdiocesan in identity and mission. Although David Power has argued that this encouragement of diocesan priests to volunteer for missionary work outside their dioceses further obscures the distinction between diocesan and religious clergy,[46] it is just as important to note that the magisterial acknowledgment of the transdiocesan nature of all priesthood can be used to safeguard the existence of a transdiocesan priesthood against whatever objections some theologians may have to the contrary.

42. See Brian Daley, "In Ten Thousand Places," 14–15, 23–26.

43. *PDV* 16. See also *PO* 10.

44. *PO* 10; *PDV* 18.

45. *PDV* 74. See also *PO* 10.

46. David N. Power, "Theologies of Religious Life and Priesthood," 62.

Furthermore, magisterial teaching and canon law do imply that ministry to the local church is appropriated, within the one ministry, especially to the diocesan clergy, and transdiocesan ministry is appropriated especially to religious clergy. Two key canonical concepts insure this distinction and appropriation of roles: incardination and exemption.

Incardination

Canon 265 makes clear that a priest must be incardinated "either in a particular church or personal prelature, or in an institute of consecrated life or society endowed with this faculty." Incardination in a particular church means that one has been "advanced" to ordination for the sake of service to that church.[47] It is reasonable to think that a religious priest, who is not incardinated into a particular church but rather into an institute of consecrated life, has not been advanced to ordination primarily for the sake of service to the particular church where he happens to be ordained or presently serving, but for the sake of service to his institute and its charismatic mission. While Vatican II says that religious priests belong "in a real sense" to the local presbyterate where they are serving at a given moment in time, it must be admitted that there is a difference between the relationships religious and diocesan priests have to the particular church.[48]

The juridical difference is that diocesan clergy are incardinated in a particular diocese, whereas religious are not. The difference, however, is not merely juridical but pertains to the spirituality and pastoral identity and mission of each type of priesthood. John Paul teaches that incardination in a particular church "cannot be confined to a purely juridical bond, but also involves a set of attitudes."[49] The incardinated priest will share "in the bishop's ecclesial concern and his devotion to the evangelical care of the People of God in the specific historical and contextual conditions of a particular Church."[50] Incardination "presupposes a particular love" on the part of the priest "for his own church."[51] The incar-

47. *CIC* 266, §3.
48. *CD* 34.
49. *PDV* 31.
50. *PDV* 31.
51. *PDV* 74.

dinated priest will love his particular church in such a way that it will "lead him to share in the history or life experience of this same particular Church, in its riches and in its weaknesses, in its difficulties and in its hopes, working in it for its growth. And thus to feel himself both enriched by the particular Church and actively involved in building it up."[52] John Paul does not excuse religious priests serving in dioceses from cultivating these attitudes,[53] but his words are directed at those who are incardinated into the particular church—namely, diocesan priests.

The diocesan priest, therefore, has an inherently territorial element to his spirituality, identity, and mission. As one book on diocesan priestly spirituality puts it, "The diocesan priest is centered in a specific diocese and at home with a particular parochial people. An availability for any and all dioceses is not, and should not be expected to be, the ideal for the diocesan priest."[54] This "territorial dimension" is rooted and expressed in incardination and the diocesan priest's "special relationship" with the "ordinary of the diocese."[55] As John Paul notes, when a priest is ordained for a particular church and becomes a member of a local presbyterate under a local bishop, "the young presbyter chooses to entrust himself to the Bishop and the Bishop for his part obliges himself to look after [the] hands" of the young presbyter.[56] It is important to emphasize that John Paul is speaking specifically here of the bond between the bishop and the diocesan priests of his presbyterate. He does not go into similar detail about the specifics of a religious priest's bond with the bishop.

Itinerant religious do not have and should not be expected to have the same kind of bond with the local church and its bishop. It would not be unusual, for example, for a Jesuit to be ordained in the Archdiocese of Chicago and to be sent the next year to serve in Detroit and the following year to Milwaukee. Even stable Benedictines, who, given their vow of stability, undoubtedly also have a "territorial" aspect to their spirituality, may, as a matter of course, be sent out for weekend as-

52. *PDV* 74.

53. *PDV* 31.

54. George A. Aschenbrenner, *Quickening the Fire in Our Midst: The Challenge of Diocesan Priestly Spirituality* (Chicago: Loyola University Press, 2002), 38.

55. Aschenbrenner, *Quickening the Fire in Our Midst*, 39.

56. *PG* 47.

sistance to several neighboring dioceses. Also, the retreatants, oblates, and students to whom they will minister at their abbey will likely come from several dioceses. The primary ministerial commitment of the religious priest is thus best framed as being to his institute and its mission, and he will be held accountable primarily through the superiors of his institute (who themselves are accountable to the Congregation for Institutes of Consecrated Life and Societies of Apostolic Life). This fact is expressed juridically in that the religious priest is incardinated not in the particular church but in the religious institute. Spiritually, it means that his pastoral heart will be oriented less toward the "specific historical and contextual conditions" of the local diocese and more toward the religious institute and its ministerial audiences, local or not.

Exemption

The second important canonical concept for appropriating transdiocesan ministry to religious is exemption. The tradition of exemption, which dates at least to the seventh century, developed as a way to protect the internal life of monasteries from the interference of local bishops by attaching these communities to the supervision of the Holy See. Later, the same link to the Holy See established through exemption was used to legitimize the transdiocesan "apostolates of the mendicant orders."[57] Hence, exemption involved three important things: *freedom from* interference, *freedom for* a wide, even international, transdiocesan ministry, and a special *bond with the pope*. These three realities are still reflected in Canon 591 of the Code of Canon Law, which states:

> In order to provide better for the good of institutes and the needs of the apostolate, the Supreme Pontiff, by reason of his primacy in the universal Church and with a view to common advantage, can exempt institutes of consecrated life from the governance of local ordinaries and subject them to himself alone or to another ecclesiastical authority.

Although the Code continues to acknowledge exemption, some interpreters have argued, not without reason, that its force, especially with

57. Seasoltz, "Institutes of Consecrated Life and Ordained Ministry," 143.

respect to ministry, has been somewhat dimmed by the Council. *Christus Dominus* reframed exemption as relating "primarily to the internal organization of institutes. Its purpose is to ensure that everything is suitably and harmoniously arranged within them, and the perfection of the religious life promoted."[58] In their external ministries and apostolates, religious are accountable to the ordinaries of the dioceses in which they operate:

> All Religious, exempt and non-exempt, are subject to the authority of the local Ordinaries in those things which pertain to the public exercise of divine worship—except where differences in rites are concerned—the care of souls, the sacred preaching intended for the people, the religious and moral education of the Christian faithful, especially of the children, catechetical instruction and liturgical formation.[59]

This teaching seems to continue the freedom *from* interference, but significantly weakens the freedom *for* extraparochial and transdiocesan ministry.

On the other hand, *Mutuae Relationes* clarifies that the main purpose of this episcopal oversight is to ensure that religious and local ministerial initiatives are not working at cross purposes.[60] It does not mean that bishops can deploy religious clergy wherever they wish.[61] Although the dynamics of "dual authority" are not always clear, it does not seem that a bishop can commission a particular religious priest to a specific ministry without the consent of that priest's religious superior.[62] This caveat implies that religious are still to be left free *for* specialized ministry.

58. *CD* 35.

59. *CD* 35. Rose M. McDermott explains that exemption's importance has lessened not only because of Vatican II's better regard for episcopal authority, but also because "many of the provisions once reserved to exempt institutes are now applicable to all clerical institutes of pontifical rite"; McDermott, Part III, "Institutes of Consecrated Life and Societies of Apostolic Life (cc. 573–746)," in *New Commentary on the Code of Canon Law*, ed. John P. Beal, James A. Coriden, and Thomas A. Green (New York: Paulist Press, 2000), 759.

60. See *MR* 39.

61. See *CIC* 671.

62. *CIC* 682; McDermott, "Institutes of Consecrated Life," 163–64.

Indeed, in the same article in which it defines exemption, *Christus Dominus* describes what might be called a broader "spirit of exemption" that should govern the relations between religious and local ordinaries in their approach to ministry. It states that bishops should give "due respect for the character of their institute" and "its constitutions" before requesting religious to engage in particular ministries; religious, meanwhile, should take care to focus on apostolates that are "imbued with the spirit of their religious community."[63] Exemption, then, is understood today as referring primarily to religious common life, but its spirit has ministerial consequences. It requires respect for the specific nature of religious charismatic mission and recognizes the continuance of religious freedom *for* their traditional apostolates.

Tillard argues that the idea of exemption is still a substantial basis upon which to understand religious extraparochial and transdiocesan ministry. He describes exemption as the setting aside of religious from the "proximate needs of each diocese" in order to concentrate on ministries and activities that may otherwise be overlooked.[64] Since, through exemption, religious stand somewhat apart from "proximate needs," they are uniquely able to attend to needs that the pressing pastoral concerns of the parish and the diocese tend to overwhelm—needs such as the development of theology, preservation of the church's spiritual treasures, and ministry to those who are out of the immediate purview of otherwise preoccupied pastors. Tillard writes:

> The superior general who has, from the vantage point of his community a global view of the needs of the Church, and who is not (as the bishop may sometimes be) too exclusively involved in the problems of a particular part of the Church or of a particular era, is able to see farther than the present moment. In his prudence as superior, he may exercise a boldness that the bishop in his pastoral prudence cannot have because of circumstances. Hence the superior general helps keep alive essential values in spite of crises in which these are almost relegated to oblivion by pastors engaged in problems of the moment.... Exemption redounds to the good of the Church.[65]

63. *CD* 35.
64. Tillard, *Mystery of Religious Life*, 28.
65. Tillard, *Mystery of Religious Life*, 28.

Tillard's idea of exemption is that it is not just about freedom *from* episcopal interference, but freedom *for* ministries that the church needs in order to be fully itself.

Of great pertinence to the issue of transdiocesan ministry is the fact that exemption, even after the Council, still establishes a special bond between religious and the pope. According to *Christus Dominus*, the privilege of exemption ensures also that the pope can employ religious "for the good of the universal Church."[66] Thus *Christus Dominus* continues to reflect the historically close relationship that religious institutes have had with the pope. This relationship is fitting. Religious institutes are often international bodies with global-scale missions. It makes sense, then, that their governance and apostolates fall ultimately under the oversight of the bishop of Rome, who, in the words of Ratzinger, is a "bishop for the whole Church and in the whole Church."[67]

Without using the language of exemption, John Paul refers in *Vita Consecrata* 47 to the three realities it has historically signified. He acknowledges the "particular bond of communion which the different Institutes of Consecrated Life and the Societies of Apostolic Life have with the Successor of Peter in his ministry of unity and missionary universality." He says of this bond that it has had a "providential function both in safeguarding the specific identity of consecrated life and in advancing the missionary expansion of the Gospel." He acknowledges that religious have cooperated with popes through the centuries and that the "successors of Peter" have found in religious "a generous readiness to devote themselves to the Church's missionary activity." He states that institutes of consecrated life have a "supra-diocesan character grounded in their special relation to the Petrine ministry."

In highlighting the connection between religious life's "supra-diocesan character" and the successor of Peter and his ministry, John Paul makes a very interesting point about an important, but insufficiently acknowledged contribution that religious make to the church. According to John Paul, religious support the pope not only in his global evangelization, but also in his work of fostering union between par-

66. *CD* 35.

67. Ratzinger, *Pilgrim Fellowship of Faith*, 201.

ticular churches.[68] According to John Paul, there is a "'*perichoresis*' between the universal Church and the particular Churches."[69] The "supradiocesan character" of religious life and the back-and-forth movement of religious between particular churches "effectively promotes an 'exchange of gifts'" among these churches.[70] Accordingly, he says that "the Church entrusts to communities of consecrated life the particular task of spreading the spirituality of communion"; this task, he writes, has great urgency today when a "return of the idols of nationalism" is occurring.[71] "Those gathered together in religious communities" are "women and men 'from every nation, from all tribes and peoples and tongues' (Rv 7:9)."[72] As such, religious are "called to uphold and to bear witness to the sense of communion between peoples, races and cultures."[73]

Applied to religious priests, exemption—insofar as it is freedom from interference, freedom for specialized extraparochial and transdiocesan ministry, and establishes a special bond with the pope—appears to be in tension with Vatican II's portrait of the priest as a member of a local presbyterate subordinate to a regionally defined bishop who heads the Eucharistic community of a diocese. A small step forward in resolving this tension is to recall that ordination introduces one into the universal order of presbyters that is collectively subordinate to the universal order of bishops and that, technically, only incardination makes one a full member of a local presbyterate.[74] As a member of the universal order of presbyters, the priest is commissioned to "the universal mission of salvation" that extends "to the ends of the earth."[75] Rather than incardination in a local church, religious are incardinated

68. John Paul II, Encyclical Letter *Ut Unum Sint* (May 25, 1995), 94.

69. *PG* 57.

70. *VC* 47. Along these lines, Tillard writes, "When the book of a theologian of Warsaw is placed in the whole world, the Church of Warsaw serves catholicity; when a missionary community … sends a religious envoy to work in a country to evangelize," the diocese "from which the religious comes, serves the entire Church"; *Devant Dieu et Pour Le Monde*, 349.

71. *VC* 51.

72. *FLC* 1.

73. *VC* 51.

74. See Lécuyer, "Decree on the Ministry and Life of Priests: History of the Decree," *Commentary* 4:199.

75. *PO* 10.

in their institutes that have a "supra-diocesan" character and exercise a transdiocesan ministry. As such, religious priests will be especially dedicated to the universal quality of the one priesthood rather than to a territorial ministry. They will not have the same bond with the local church or its ordinary as their diocesan counterparts will. They are exempt in order to focus on other things.

The special attachment to the pope involved with exemption can be harmonized with a strong theology of the local church and of the bishop if the papacy itself is understood within the context of collegiality.[76] The bishops constitute a universal order of service to the church, and the pope functions in union with, and as head of, the episcopal college.[77] Therefore, when the religious priest operates in a transdiocesan way, he will be serving under not only the Roman pontiff, but also the college of bishops and the communion of churches that the Roman pontiff represents. A "healthy exemption," according to Tillard simply "depends on the vision of church in which it is inserted."[78] As a contributor to *Perfectate caritatis*[79] and as a major exponent of the twentieth-century theology of the local church,[80] Tillard's comments on this matter ought to carry special weight.

The Promise of Obedience

As something of a side note, perhaps the principle of episcopal collegiality might also be used to reimagine the promise of obedience that religious *ordinandi* make before the bishop at the time of ordination. Streider seems to assume this promise is made to the particular bishop in the same way diocesan priests make it.[81] But, if so, how can such a promise be meaningful when a religious priest could very easily be operating in another diocese within six months? What happens to the promise? However, if the promise were understood as being made not so much to the particular bishop but to him as a representative of the

76. See Tillard, *Devant Dieu et Pour Le Monde*, 350. See also *Mystery of Religious Life*, 25–27.

77. See *LG* 22 and 23.

78. Tillard, *Devant Dieu et Pour Le Monde*, 350.

79. See Alberigo and Komonchak, *History of Vatican II*, 2:477.

80. See Ruddy, *Local Church*.

81. Streider, *Promise of Obedience*, 110–14.

college, then it would be easier to see what happens to this promise when the religious priest operates in another diocese. It would go with him and remain applicable to the bishop in whichever diocese he was serving. This reimagining is supportable by the difference in phrasing used for diocesan and religious candidates for orders. For the diocesan candidate for orders, the phrasing of the inquiry before the promise is, "Do you promise me and my successors respect and obedience?" But, "if the elect is a religious, the bishop says: Do you promise the diocesan Bishop and also your legitimate Superior respect and obedience?"[82] The use of the more generic term "diocesan bishop" as opposed to "me and my successors" supports a reimagination of the promise along the lines of a more general promise to the college.

To sum up, some postconciliar Catholic theologians have argued that priesthood makes most sense as parochial ministry in a diocesan context, as ministry to a local church, and as membership in a local presbyterate under a regional bishop. This chapter has attempted to show how Balthasar's insights can be developed toward a different vision of priesthood that incorporates the extraparochial and transdiocesan ministry of religious priests and to show that this vision is in basic harmony with magisterial teaching.

Tillard and Yves Congar have noted that a sound theology of religious priesthood, which authenticates extraparochial and transdiocesan ministry, serves not only religious priests but also those diocesan clergy who are involved in specialized ministries.[83] There are, in fact, diocesan clergy whose full-time work is not that of a parochial pastor, but that of teaching, leading of retreats, and service in the chancellery. Some of these may even work outside of the dioceses for which they have been ordained. It is important, then, not only for religious priests, but also for the ministerial priesthood itself, to articulate and defend a wider perspective of priestly ministry that accounts for its variations from the diocesan-parochial-pastor type. In order to complete the sketch of such a priesthood, our discussion must now turn to the *munera*.

82. Streider, *Promise of Obedience*, 110–11.

83. See Tillard, *Mystery of Religious Life*, 28; Congar, *A Gospel Priesthood*, trans. P. J. Hepburne-Scott (New York: Herder and Herder, 1967), 182–200, esp. 189.

CHAPTER 12

Religious Priesthood and Ministerial Identity

The *Munera*

Earlier chapters described how the intelligibility of religious priestly identity was made possible in part by an understanding of the sacrament of holy orders that allowed for a strong theoretical and practical separation of the prophetic (or preaching and teaching), priestly (sanctifying), and royal (leading/ruling/shepherding/pastoring) functions. These are the classic ministerial munera: the *munus docendi, munus sanctificandi,* and *munus regendi,* respectively. Historically, religious priestly identity has demonstrably centered on the *munus docendi* and the *munus sanctificandi.* We've also seen how Vatican II's insistence on the unity of the *munera* has challenged this intelligibility. I am arguing that a fourth mark of religious priesthood remains its special emphasis on the preaching/teaching and sanctifying functions in its ministerial identity and praxis and that there is no reason after Vatican II that this cannot continue to be the case. At the risk of repetition, let us return to the historical argument introduced in earlier chapters by reviewing the main points and adding a few pertinent ones.

Historical Review

Ignatius of Antioch describes presbyters as an advisory council surrounding a bishop. Hence, the earliest image we have of the presbyter is not one of him as a pastor, representing a singular head over a single parochial body, but rather as part of a ministerial team. In the fourth century, however, with the boom in the Christian population, these presbyters were increasingly sent out to serve satellite Eucharistic assemblies as preachers/teachers, shepherds, and administrators of sacraments. They were like "mini-bishops" in the parishes of antiquity.[1] It is important for our purposes to note that, at this time, men were ordained to serve a particular church, and there was no additional legal commissioning to do so beyond the ordination rite itself.

The first ingredient for change came with the Donatist controversy. St. Augustine defended the efficacy of the sacramental ministry of lapsed and schismatic bishops and priests, even if they were no longer authentic teachers and shepherds of the church. With this crisis, the church began to think differently about the sanctifying function than it did about the teaching and ruling functions. The sanctifying function had something more stable about it than the others did, and so it was strongly identified with sacramental character. How the other functions related to character was not clarified, but in antiquity there was no real questioning of the idea that the liturgical rite of ordination provided something for preaching, teaching, and leading, even if what it gave was not quite the same as character.

A second ingredient for change came during the early Middle Ages with the introduction of frequent private and daily masses. Monks were frequently ordained to say these masses without any corresponding expectation that they would also be active preachers, teachers, and pastors. This development led to a much stronger emphasis in presbyteral identity and ministry on the sanctifying function than the preaching/teaching and ruling ones. It is one way we end up with priest, rather than pastor or preacher, as the usual shorthand for the presbyter.

During the high medieval period, two developments solidified the identification of presbyteral ordination with transmission of the sanctifying function only. First, in order to defend itself against the encroachment of secular rulers in ecclesiastical affairs, the church asserted its legal rights to govern itself. In order to achieve this, it described itself as

1. Nichols, *Holy Order*, 134.

a perfect (complete) society, with its own power of jurisdiction, which was akin to the divine right of kings to rule their own realms. This theory provided a way of prohibiting secular rulers from moving bishops and priests around like chess pieces to advance their own political agendas or secure economic benefits for their families. It was common for lords and princes to manipulate the appointment of bishops and pastors. Emerging canon law now made a useful distinction between the bare possession of sacramental power and the right to use it. A priest or bishop needed not only ordination but also a canonical mandate from a higher ecclesial authority (a bishop, if he were a priest; the pope, if he were a bishop) irrespective of what secular rulers wanted. This canonical mandate came through a juridical act rather than ordination all by itself. Second, the mendicant orders began to be ordained for a priesthood that was exercised in a transdiocesan way, and they depended upon juridical authorization from the papacy through a myriad of papal bulls to do so. The question could now be asked, in a way that it couldn't before, "What does ordination all by itself do, what all by itself does it give prior to installation in an office?"[2] The answer was the *potestas ordinis* (the power of orders), which was different from the *potestas iurisdictionis* (the power of jurisdiction).

St. Thomas Aquinas strongly associated the power of orders, received in ordination, with sacramental character and the sanctifying function. Though he seems to have acknowledged that the power of orders still gave habitual grace for the *munera* of preaching, teaching, and ruling (though not the mandate), his later interpreters lost sight of this and made preaching/teaching and ruling entirely a matter of juridical delegation. It was fitting to give this delegation to a cleric, they thought, but the ministries of preaching/teaching and leadership were not sacramentally sourced in any way. Ordination all by itself bestowed only the sanctifying function.

From the late Middle Ages through Trent to the early twentieth century, it was taught that the power to preach, teach, and lead did not pertain directly to the sacrament of orders but was juridically delegated. The pope possessed the power of jurisdiction in full and delegated

2. Mansini, *Word Has Dwelt among Us*, 165.

his power to bishops; bishops passed it on to ordinary priests, and thus authorized them to preach, teach, and lead. Chapter 4 described some problems of this system—namely, its separation of rule over the church from a sacramental source and its marginalization of bishops, who appeared to be ordinary priests with added delegated authority.

Religious priesthood, however, could easily be made sense of within this system, which bifurcated the two powers. By ordination priests participated only in the sanctifying *munus*. The most cloistered contemplative monastic priest could thus easily see himself as fully functioning as a priest simply by offering the Mass, even in private. His priestly identity was centered in the sanctifying *munus*. Also, since the power of jurisdiction could be delegated in part, rather than in total, mendicant clergy and missionary priests could understand their vocations as involving the preaching/teaching functions along with the sanctifying function, but not typically the pastoral *munus*, insofar as the *munus regendi* was identified with the canonical *cura animarum*.[3] Indeed, they often refused pastorates and their attendant *cura animarum*, precisely to focus on a preaching, teaching mission. They would have understood their priesthood *in esse* as the sanctifying *munus*, but their broader ministerial identity included the preaching/teaching *munus*, as is indicated by the official name of the Dominicans, the Order of Preachers.

Vatican II and the 1983 Code of Canon Law

Vatican II did not deny the distinction of sacramental and juridical powers, but it also did not speak much at all about the *potestas iurisdictionis*. Rather, it went back to the ancient rites and recovered their sense that the sacramental ordination communicated a call and bestowed grace for all three *munera*. The Council consistently portrayed the three *munera* as united in both ministerial identity and praxis, and this, inevitably, invited a rethinking of religious priesthood. Based on a certain reading of the Council, it could seem that the *munera* were never to be separated, either theoretically or practically. A contemplative monastic priest offering masses in his monastery and the itinerant Franciscan,

3. See Cole and Conner, *Christian Totality*, 340.

Dominican, and Jesuit who preached, taught, and heard confessions, but did not have stable congregations for which they served as pastors, could appear to compromise the Council's vision of priesthood. Castellucci, for example, noting that every priest is ordained to participate in the whole ministry (prophetic, priestly, pastoral), and pointing out that the Council's aim was bringing "unity to these tasks," cautioned against a delegation of labor whereby diocesan clergy are seen as pastors and religious clergy are seen as prophetic.[4]

In order to respond to this objection, we recall that the Council's teaching, even if it acknowledges that ordination gives grace for all three *munera* and demonstrates their interpenetration, still deals with the *munera* as conceptually distinct. If it did not, *Lumen Gentium* 25–27, *Presbyterorum Ordinis* 4–6, and *Christus Dominus* 12–16 would look very different indeed. Also, the code of canon law, which is the church's theology practically applied, depends on the distinction between the *munera* as well as the distinction between the graced capacity for ministries and the legal mandate to exercise them. A quick examination of the canons indicates not only that the *munera* remain conceptually distinct but that they can be practically separated.

The 1983 code describes the *munus docendi,* or the preaching and teaching function, as "entrusted principally to the Roman Pontiff and the college of bishops,"[5] and states that it is "proper" for ordinary priests to "proclaim the gospel of God" and a "duty" of canonically appointed pastors to do so within their congregations.[6] The ordinary priest has the canonical mandate (faculty) to preach, but this faculty can be either "restricted" or "taken away" by competent higher authority.[7]

The *munus sanctificandi* (the priestly function) pertains "in a particular way" to "the sacred liturgy."[8] It is the bishops who "in the first place exercise the sanctifying function; they are the high priests, the principal dispensers of the mysteries of God, and the directors, promoters, and guardians of the entire liturgical life in the Church entrusted to

4. Castellucci, "I Religiosi Presbiteri Nella Chiesa," 110.

5. *CIC* 756; see also CIC 749.

6. *CIC* 757.

7. *CIC* 764.

8. *CIC* 834, §1.

them."[9] "Presbyters also exercise this function; sharing in the priesthood of Christ and as his ministers under the authority of the bishop, they are consecrated to celebrate divine worship and to sanctify the people."[10] Priests need canonical faculties to administer confirmation validly, to hear confessions, and to preside over marriages.[11] In most cases, a priest can still baptize or celebrate the Eucharist validly without such a mandate.

The 1983 Code does not have a specific book on the *munus regendi* as it does on the *munus docendi* and the *munus sanctificandi*. Book II, part II, on "The Hierarchical Constitution of the Church," explains, however, that the supreme office of authority in the church belongs to the pope and the college of bishops in union with him.[12] The *munus regendi* is exercised on the local level principally by the diocesan bishop in the particular church and by the pastor in the parish.[13] These have, by virtue of their office, *cura animarum* in the specific ecclesial bodies to which they are attached.[14] The office of pastor "can be made either perpetually or for a specific predetermined time."[15] It is not, then, by its nature, permanent. Nor is it conflated with presbyteral ordination, which is what gives a man the sacramentally graced capacity to fulfill the office.[16]

It is obvious then that the church still deals with the *munera* as distinct from each other. If it did not, then the laws regarding the various functions would be unintelligible. It is also true that the church makes a distinction between the grace given capacity to fulfill a ministry and the legal mandate to do so. Instances where a mandate is lacking are helpful for revealing the practical separation of the *munera*. As is evident from the aforementioned canons, not every priest, not even every diocesan priest, has *cura animarum*, the full manifestation of the *munus regendi*. Retired priests, certainly, do not. They have the capacity for it,

9. *CIC* 835, §1.
10. *CIC* 835, §2.
11. *CIC* 882–84, 966–76, 1109–11.
12. *CIC* 331 and 336.
13. *CIC* 369 and 516.
14. *CIC* 519.
15. *CIC* 520.
16. "To become a pastor validly, one must be in the sacred order of the presbyterate"; *CIC* 521, §1.

through ordination, but not the canonical mandate. Many priests who do not have *cura animarum* authentically preach, teach, and offer the sacraments without being canonical pastors. There are also schismatic or otherwise disciplined priests who have lost the faculties to preach or teach in the name of Christ and the church. Yet, the Eucharist offered by these priests may still be considered valid. Hence, from this narrow, canonical vantage point, they exercise only the sanctifying *munus*. It is evident, then, that the church's teaching and law still admit of a certain distinction and even a practical separation of the *munera*. This helps us see that not every priest will always be actualizing all three *munera* with the same amount of emphasis in every instance of ministry and that some priests may exercise a ministry highly concentrated on one or two of the *munera* but not all three, depending on their canonical mission.

When Vatican II and postconciliar magisterial teachings speak of the unity of the *munera* in practice and minister, they must, therefore, be employing a broader, more analogical vantage point. This approach perceives the capacities for all three *munera* present within the ordained minister and the interwovenness of the *munera* in all ministerial acts. This unity and interpenetration are most apparent in the celebration of the Eucharist. One thinks of this act primarily and rightly as an exercise of the sanctifying *munus*, but it is also, in its way, a proclamation of the gospel (thus an exercise of the preaching/teaching *munus*) and a building up of the community (and thus an exercise of the shepherding *munus*),[17] even if the effects are rather hidden—for example, in a private Mass. Less apparently, but still truly, when a priest preaches and teaches, he is also sanctifying and leading. He is pointing people (thus leading) through the ministry of the Word to greater holiness (thus sanctifying). When a priest leads, there is a pedagogical aspect of all his actions and example as a leader, and so he can be thought of as also teaching and preaching; and because the goal to which he is guiding the people through his judgments is holiness, he is also sanctifying.[18] From this broader perspective, when a priest exercises one *munus*,

17. *PO* 4 and 6.

18. Along these lines, John Paul II states, "When the Bishop teaches, he also sanctifies and governs the People of God; when he sanctifies, he also teaches and governs; when he governs, he teaches and sanctifies"; *PG* 9.

the others will still be engaged, at least implicitly, and thus not be isolated from a priest's mission or person.

The canonical distinctions are helpful to the more analogical perspective because they clarify the actions that are primary referents for each of the *munera*. The pastoral office, narrowly defined, involves *cura animarum*, and so, to understand best what the *munus regendi* involves, one should look to someone who occupies such an office and the leadership he exercises. The prophetic office, narrowly defined, is the office of the authoritative teacher, and so, to understand what the *munus docendi* involves, one refers to its display in a person who is preaching and teaching authentically with a mandate to do so. The priestly office, narrowly defined, involves the offering of the sacraments, and so, to understand best what the *munus sanctificandi* involves, one only has to imagine its display in a priest validly offering the Eucharist.

In Vatican II's teaching, the types for priesthood are the diocesan bishop and parochial pastor, who exercise all three *munera* as a matter of course. The Council's typology makes sense. An active diocesan bishop has a more extensive *cura animarum* and teaches with greater authority than an ordinary priest. He is also the high priest, and the Cathedral liturgy is the "pre-eminent manifestation of the Church."[19] Accordingly, the bishop is the "primary analogate" for the minister,[20] and the parish pastor represents in his parish what the bishop is to the diocese.[21] In these persons, the *munera* are, indeed, not only united, but also expressed in the actions that serve as the primary referents for all that might be included more analogously under the headings of preaching/teaching, sanctifying, and ruling. Since these are the primary types of priesthood in the Council's teaching, it can become difficult to imagine priests who do not follow quite the same model—to imagine, that is to say, priests who do not manifest all three *munera* and their unity in the same way that bishops and pastors do in their ministries. But, herein lies a difficulty for religious priests and other clergy who are not functioning as pastors.[22] Even if the teaching of the church allows

19. *SC* 41.

20. Mansini, *Word Has Dwelt among Us*, 169.

21. *LG* 21.

22. As Congar observes, there are many clergy who "have not habitually the concrete

for a charismatically and missiologically differentiated priesthood, the images within Vatican II's teaching point to the pastor standing before his own particular flock exercising all ministerial tasks, with apparently equal amounts of concentration, and in unison, as the paradigm that should seemingly be followed.

Insights from Balthasar and Congar

Balthasar's theology can be of great service here. Balthasar's theology of priesthood accords with the Council's teaching. He acknowledges that ordination bestows grace for all three *munera* and that the *munera* are united in both the minister's person and practice.[23] Also, with the Council, he uses the parish pastor, exercising all three *munera*, as his typical image of priesthood.[24] However, Balthasar's thought opens a way to understand religious priesthood as identified especially with, and concentrated in, the sanctifying and preaching/teaching *munera*, without, for all that, denying its capacity for and participation in the royal *munus*. The keys to his vision are the now familiar terms "appropriation" and "*perichoresis*." Through these trinitarian concepts, illustrated in the figures of Peter, Paul, and John, Balthasar offers a way to understand religious priesthood's traditional ministerial identity in a postconciliar theological context.

Peter, Paul, and John are all images of priesthood for Balthasar, and yet each is different from the others according to a charismatically differentiated mission. Robert Barron has made the provocative, but not unfounded, suggestion that inherent to this missiological distinction, each of the *munera* has a relative priority in the typology of each of the three apostles.[25] In Acts, Peter is an authoritative shepherd who teaches, preaches, and sanctifies, but Peter's distinction from the others, as the

charge of a people: the religious, but also the diocesan 'staff,' the professors, certain chaplains: in short, those whose only [ministerial] connection is with souls or with ideas" rather than with a stable flock over which one has canonical responsibility; Congar, *Gospel Priesthood*, trans. P. J. Hepburne-Scott (New York: Herder and Herder, 1967), 189.

23. On the unity of the *munera*, see *OPSC*, 149, and *CSL*, 261.

24. For an example of Balthasar's use of the parish priest as the image of the typical priest, see *CSL*, 352–53.

25. See Barron, *Strangest Way*, 120–22.

leader of the Twelve and of the original Jewish-Christian community, is his higher authority as chief of the apostles. When Balthasar examines Peter's interactions with Paul and John, for example, he takes Peter to represent hierarchical office in relation to them.[26] It is as if, for Balthasar, when John and Paul are compared to Peter, their representation of authority fades into the background. Peter's association with authority is so complete that the office of Christ as head and shepherd is the *Petrine*, rather than the *Pauline* or *Johannine*, office. For Balthasar, Peter is the primary exemplar of authority in the church and, therefore, of the *munus regendi*.[27]

Paul is also an authoritative shepherd, but he needs to be legitimated by Peter, and thus his authority is somehow less than Peter's and more dependent than Peter's. Furthermore, he is not a resident pastor, but an itinerant preacher and teacher with a special mission to the Gentiles. Although Paul has Peter-like authority, his distinctive charism is evangelical outreach and teaching. Thus, his typology is especially associated with the prophetical preaching/teaching *munus*.[28] John is a shepherd, too, presumably of a community at or near Ephesus,[29] but, relative to Peter, John is unassuming and deferential. Like Paul, John is also a preacher and teacher, but a slightly less prolific one (they are both more prolific than Peter), and John does not appear to have adopted the same level of itinerancy as Paul. John's mission is primarily one of contemplation and prayer, evidenced by his call to "remain" with Christ. Insofar as the sanctifying *munus* concerns prayer and offering, it is most central to the typology of John.[30]

Balthasar's framework, as interpreted by Barron, allows *both* that the three *munera* are operative or at least present in every priest *and* that in particular priests, certain *munera* are at the forefront of identi-

26. See, for example, *CSL*, 283–89 (Peter in relation to John); *OPSC*, 171 (Peter in relation to Paul); *OPSC*, 335–91 (Peter in relation to John, Paul, and James).

27. Barron, *Strangest Way*, 120–21.

28. Barron, *Strangest Way*, 121–22.

29. See Raymond Brown, *The Community of the Beloved Disciple: The Life, Loves and Hates of an Individual Church in New Testament Times* (Mahwah, N.J.: Paulist Press, 1979), 56, 67, 70, 98, 179. According to Brown, the Ephesian location for the Johannine community is unprovable, but "attractive" (67).

30. Barron, *Strangest Way*, 121.

ty and mission. In other words, the trinitarian principles of *perichoresis* and appropriation are at work in the charismatically differentiated priesthood. For example, Paul, the preacher, can and does act as a shepherd, and John, the one who prays, can and does evangelize. Balthasar would express this by saying that Peter is *perichoretically* present in Paul and Paul is *perichoretically* present in John.[31] Nonetheless, authority is clearest in Peter, and so the *munus regendi* can be appropriated to and primarily symbolized by him. It remains most clearly expressed in the Petrine type of pastor who has *cura animarum*.[32] The identity of preacher is clearest in Paul, not because he has greater teaching authority than Peter, but because it is the special focus of his mission, and so the preaching/teaching *munus* can be appropriated to and symbolized by him. It remains clearly expressed in Pauline-type priests, like the Order of Preachers. The sanctifying *munus*, appropriated to and symbolized by John, is most nakedly on display in a Johannine contemplative priest who may be neither a canonical pastor nor an active preacher, but who primarily expresses his priesthood by concelebrating Mass every day in a monastic community. These trinitarian principles of *perichoresis* and appropriation, as explained in chapter 6, govern Balthasar's whole theology of vocations. Of interest here is that these trinitarian principles can also be operative in the relation of the various types of priests, each associated with a different *munus*, and not just in the wider relation between religious, clergy, and laity. Framing the relationship of the *munera* this way allows religious priests to understand themselves as concentrating in the sanctifying and preaching/teaching *munera* and identifying principally with the priestly and prophetic offices without denying their participation in the shepherding *munus* and without artificially dividing the *munera*.

An insight from Yves Congar about the relation of the *munera* to various ministerial audiences further illuminates why this idea of the appropriation of the *munera* is fitting for the ministries of different kinds of priests. Congar describes the church's field of mission as three concentric circles (see figure 12-1). There is an innermost circle of the faithful who accept ministry from all three *munera*. The people

31. See *OPSC*, 153.

32. See *OT*, 155

within this zone are prayed for, receive the sacraments, are taught and preached to, and are willingly obedient to the church's shepherds. Importantly, the inner circle is the only circle in which all three *munera* operate at full force.

In the middle circle, one finds lapsed Catholics, Protestants, people of other faiths, and nonbelievers who are willing to hear what the church has to say but do not yet, or have ceased to, offer full assent. In this second ring, the capacity of all three *munera* to have influence is diminished, but especially the royal *munus*. The people of this circle do not accept the hierarchical ministry's authority to lead them. Therefore, the other two *munera* come into a relative ascendency. More than authoritatively leading, priests must evangelize and pray for the middle circle. The royal *munus* recedes, and the prophetic and priestly *munera* are left primarily to meet the needs of this group.

A final outer circle is constituted by those who are either psychologically or geographically cut off from the influence of the church's teaching and preaching. They cannot be effectively reached by either the prophetic or ruling *munera*. In this sphere, the sanctifying function—the church's prayer—best ministers to them.[33]

It is easy to see that the priest who operates primarily in the inner circle would be the Petrine-type diocesan priest, the resident pastor ministering to the stable flock of the faithful. He shepherds, preaches, teaches, and sanctifies. This priest actuates all three *munera*, but the royal *munus* is clearer here than in the other ministerial contexts, because this is the only context in which it can be fully on display. Religious priests may also minister to this inner circle as teachers, spiritual directors, and retreat preachers, for example. However, unless they are pastors, religious superiors, or chaplains, they will serve this circle mainly through the preaching/teaching and sanctifying *munera*.[34] They will be ministers of word and sacrament and, less often, its official pastors.

33. Congar, *Laypeople in the Church*, 96–98.

34. See *Mutuae Relationes* 13 on religious superiors and the ruling function. See Canon 564 of the 1983 Code on the chaplain as a "priest to whom is entrusted in a stable manner the pastoral care, at least in part, of some community or particular group of the Christian faithful."

The Pauline-type priest—the mendicant, Jesuit, or member of a missionary congregation—is suited to the middle circle. He has the capacity to be a pastor, but he is dedicated especially to reaching people outside the parochial context. In the words of John Paul, the religious missionary is like Paul at the Areopagus, "reaching out to all those who, knowingly or not, are searching for the truth and the life (see Acts 17:27)."[35] He concentrates on the preaching and teaching mission, since that is fitting for those who exist outside the inner circle but can still be reached by the ministry of the Word. The Petrine priest obviously still has obligations to the middle circle, but he will meet these, states Balthasar, not so much by "leaving his congregation or local church in order to bring his missionary endeavors to others, but by drawing those outside the Church into the congregation,"[36] and by standing as an "armor bearer" behind the lay "battling knight" as the latter engages the world.[37] The Johannine priest is also not absent from the middle circle, but his position is in some ways more like Peter's than it is like Paul's. He will evangelize primarily through public liturgies and retreats and depend on people showing up for them. He will also support oblates as they go out into the world.

For the final, outer circle, the Johannine-type priest—especially the most radically contemplative incarnations of the religious priest, such as the Carthusian or the hermit—is the primary minister. Neither an official pastor nor an active preacher, this priest limits himself to offering prayer for the church and the world. If at first he seems the least "apostolic," he actually has the widest field of mission. According to the document *Verbi sponsa,* the contemplative life with its "silent emanation of love" bears the fruit of "superabundant grace" redounding to the good of the whole church and world.[38] John Paul points out that the ordained monk can bring a special sacramental efficacy to the contemplative mission: "The contribution made to the Church's life by religious priests completely devoted to contemplation" is of "immeasurable value," he

35. *VC* 98. On this point, see also Gardin, "Vescovo, Clero Diocesano, Vita Consecrata," 180.

36. *CSL,* 353.

37. *ET* 2:327.

38. *VS* 5.

writes.[39] "Especially in the celebration of the Eucharist, they carry out an act of the Church and for the Church, to which they join the offering of themselves, in communion with Christ who offers himself to the Father for the salvation of the whole world."[40]

Religious priesthood, therefore, has justification for concentrating ministerial identity primarily in the preaching/teaching and sanctifying *munera*. Balthasar, through the figures of Peter, John, and Paul, shows how such an appropriation need not be perceived as artificially separating the *munera*. It is a matter of appropriation and *perichoresis* rather than of division. Congar helps establish why the appropriation is fitting.

Figure 12-1 portrays the field of mission in three images and summarizes these helpful insights from Congar and Balthasar.

The Religious Priest as Shepherd

The discussion thus far has centered on responding to Castellucci's caution that the *munera* not be separated. Other authors, such as Lafont, George, Kasper, and others, argue that the ruling *munus* is foundational for all priesthood and imply that, among the *munera*, it therefore should have the central place in *every* priest's identity.[41] This is an important perspective not only because the shepherd leading his flock was a principal image of priesthood for the Council, but also because the image of shepherd has continued to be paramount in postconciliar magisterial teaching about priesthood. John Paul, in fact, entitled his exhortations on ordained ministry *Pastores Gregis* ("Shepherds of the Flock") and *Pastores Dabo Vobis* ("I Will Give You Shepherds").

Mansini has shown that there are good reasons for not making the *munus regendi* the central one in priestly identity.[42] Nonetheless, given the prominence of the shepherd image in magisterial teaching on priesthood and the deep correspondence this image seems to have with

39. *VC* 30.

40. *VC* 30.

41. Lafont, *Imagining the Catholic Church*, 155–205; Galot, *Theology of Priesthood*, 129–53; George, "Significance of Vatican II," 14–32, esp. 22–24; Walter Kasper, "New Dogmatic Outlook on the Priestly Ministry," 20–33; Osborne, *Priesthood*, 333.

42. Mansini, *Word Has Dwelt among Us*, 159–79.

FIGURE 12-1. THE FIELD OF MISSION

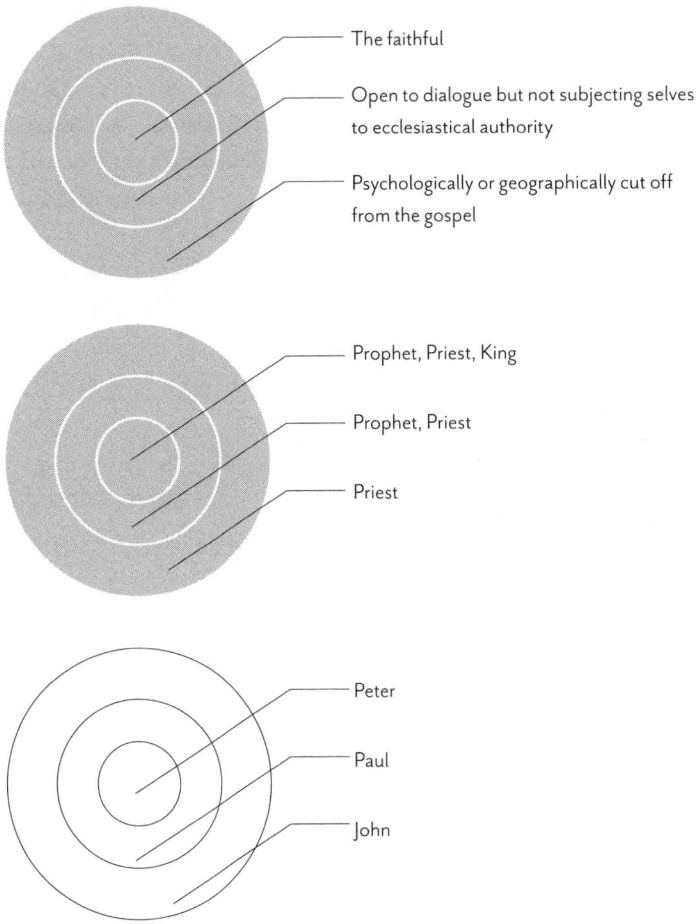

the function of leadership/the *munus regendi,* it remains important to restate that religious priests do exercise this *munus* in a variety of ways.

If the *munus regendi* is interpreted narrowly as the canonical office of pastor with a specific *cura animarum,* then religious superiors, those religious priests who are parochial pastors, and chaplains of various kinds would still be seen to exercise it in the typical way. If the *munus* is interpreted broadly and more analogously, however, as involving more than the strict canonical *cura animarum*, then it can be said to be exercised by others. Pastors, chaplains, and superiors are often surrounded by other religious priests who function as part of a pastoral team ministering to a specific audience. While only one of them may be formally delegated the *cura animarum*, the others can feel themselves to be sharing shepherding responsibility in a way that evokes, in fact, the original identity of the presbyter as a member of a council of elders. Priests, who serve as itinerant preachers, spiritual directors, retreat masters, confessors at shrines, or academic theologians but do not seemingly execute any formal leadership, can recall the analogous and implicit way in which the *munera* are linked and thus the implicit operation of the shepherding *munus* in their ministries of word and sacrament. Finally, as we noted in chapter 9, there is an aspect of ministerial identity that pertains first to the being of the priest and thus transcends any particular ministerial activities. Even if a religious priest does not currently or ever hold the office of pastor or a similar position of formal leadership, he can always comport himself with paternal shepherding care in the way he relates to the church and prays for its members.

Nonetheless, John Paul acknowledged that there are vocations "within" the vocation to priesthood and that priests are formed and ordained for a "specific pastoral end."[43] Basil Cole and Paul Conner have interpreted John Paul to mean that not every priest is formed and ordained with the same specific pastoral end in mind and that religious priests, such as Dominicans, are oriented to "only a portion" of the threefold ministry—namely, sacramental ministry and "teaching sacred doctrine by Word and writing and the other disciplines that promote the spread of the faith."[44] In other words, they are formed and ordained primarily for the sanctifying and preaching and teaching functions that befit their vocation within the vocation to the priesthood. This interpretation is reconcilable with the Council's forthright statement that its own teaching refers "especially" to those priests "devoted to the care of souls—namely, parochial pastors—and that "suitable adaptations" ought to be made for religious priests according to their circumstances.[45] Magiste-

43. *PDV* 70, 57.

44. Cole and Conner, *Christian Totality*, 340.

45. *PO* 1.

rial teaching is more open to a charismatically differentiated priesthood than some theologians have been. With that said, we have tried to show that even if he specializes in preaching, teaching, and sanctifying, the religious priest can still understand himself as a shepherd, enjoying and sometimes revealing the perichoretic presence of Peter in his otherwise Pauline or Johannine charism.

Conclusion to the Book

Near the beginning of *Vita Consecrata*, John Paul II reflected upon the fact that since the Second Vatican Council, which had done so much to emphasize the "profound reality of ecclesial communion," there was still need to "clarify *the specific identity of the various states of life*, their vocation and their particular mission in the Church."[46] This book has been an attempt to reflect specifically on, and to clarify the vocation of, religious priesthood. Drawing upon contemporary magisterial teaching, Balthasar, and other theologians whose thought is constructive for religious priesthood, it has concluded that this vocation involves (1) a public double signification of radical discipleship and apostolic office and of their link; (2) an ecclesial mediation between the church's stable institution and its movements of charismatic renewal; (3) a mission that specializes in extraparochial and transdiocesan ministry; and (4) a ministerial identity primarily associated with the preaching/teaching and sanctifying *munera*.

Religious priesthood has involved and will always involve certain tensions. The religious priest sometimes must navigate between the ideals of radical discipleship and official ministry. The religious commitment to poverty, for example, can be challenged by the considerable resources required for priestly formation. Religious commitment to humility and corporate equality can be challenged by clerical status. Religious commitment to prayer and contemplation can be challenged by pastoral demands. Religious commitment to charismatic renewal sometimes comes into tension with priestly duties of upholding unity and representing institutional authority. It would be wrong, therefore, to say

46. *VC* 4.

that the questions surrounding religious priesthood present a "false dilemma."

This book, however, has argued that the benefits to religious priests themselves and to the wider church are worth the price of navigating these tensions. The religious priest benefits from his dual formations and his membership in both religious life and the order of presbyters. His position between priesthood and religious life can mitigate against the "involutions" to which priesthood and religious life are both tempted. Before the church, he embodies the unity between charism and office, between subjective discipleship and objective ministry, and in so doing reveals to the church their complementarity. Furthermore, he serves as an interpersonal mediator between religious families and the priestly fraternity, thereby reducing potential conflict.

The religious priest is also a boon to the church's mission. Dedicated especially to extraparochial ministry, he can reach those whose needs cannot be easily met by parochial pastors: people in missionary lands, those who do not attend parishes, and even those who are looking for a deeper spiritual commitment than they find opportunity for in parish life. As a transdiocesan figure, the religious priest helps to reveal the *perichoresis* of the universal church and the particular churches, thus fostering their communion.

Raymond Brown has observed that various New Testament figures—the radical disciple, the itinerant apostle, the liturgical presider, and the resident presbyter-bishop—have all played a role in shaping the contemporary image of priesthood. The contemporary priest is effectively expected to fulfill all of the duties that were once carried out by different people. He is called to signify holiness, to show missionary concern for the whole church and world, and to be a resident pastor. This expectation, says Brown, is to "ask of one man, the priest, more than was asked of any man who played one of the New Testament roles."[47]

Balthasar has provided a way, through his constellational ecclesiology, to legitimize a charismatically differentiated priesthood that takes some of the burden off priests to feel they must do and be everything involved in priestly ministry. A diocesan priest can be more like Peter,

47. Brown, *Priest and Bishop*, 44.

indeed a pastor who exercises all three *munera*, but who does not need to travel as far as Paul or publicly signify holiness in the same way that John does through the radical material renunciation involved in the evangelical counsels. The religious priest, I have argued, can find his identity and mission with John and Paul and, thus, primarily with the sanctifying and preaching/teaching *munera* they represent. This approach does not conclude that he is somehow separated from the shepherding *munus*. It is a question of appropriation and *perichoresis*. To the Pauline-type priest is appropriated preaching and teaching. He will be free to move in and out of ministerial contexts as a minister of word and sacrament, but without the duties and obligations of a Petrine-style resident pastor. The Johannine-type of priest, to whom the sanctifying function is appropriated, is more stable than Paul but may not have all the duties of Peter, which will free him for a ministry of prayer and other works of his monastery. Both, however, maintain the capacity to be pastors that they received in ordination. Sometimes they will manifest this capacity explicitly in positions of formal leadership. Other times, it will be present only *perichoretically*—but still truly—in their priestly preaching, teaching, and sanctifying.

BIBLIOGRAPHY

1917 *Catholic Encyclopedia*. "Oblates of Mary Immaculate." New Advent. http://www.newadvent.org/cathen/11184b.htm. Accessed April 19, 2019.

1985 Extraordinary Synod of Bishops. "Final Report." *Origins* 15 (December 19, 1985): 444–50.

Afanasieff, Nicholas. "The Church Which Presides in Love." In *The Primacy of Peter*, edited by John Myendorff, 91–143. Crestwood, N.Y.: St. Vladamir's Seminary Press, 1992.

Alberigo, Guiseppe, ed. *History of Vatican II.* English version edited by Joseph Komonchak. 5 vols. Maryknoll, N.Y.: Orbis, 1995–2006.

Allen, M. Prudence, and M. Judith O'Brien. "The Decree on the Appropriate Renewal of Religious Life: *Perfectae Caritatis*." In *Vatican II: Renewal within Tradition*, edited by Matthew L. Lamb and Matthew L. Levering, 251–70. Oxford: Oxford University Press, 2008.

Anderson, C. Colt. "Clerics, Laity and Preaching the Gospel among the Early Franciscans." In *Franciscan Evangelization: Striving to Preach the Gospel*, Washington Theological Union Symposium Papers 2007, edited by Elise Saggau, 33–54. St. Bonaventure, N.Y.: Franciscan Institute, 2008.

Andrews, Frances. *The Other Friars: The Carmelite, Augustinian, Sack and Pied Friars in the Middle Ages.* Woodbridge, UK: Boydell, 2006.

Armstrong, Regis, J. A. Wayne Hellmann, and William Short, eds. *Francis of Assisi: Early Documents.* Vol. 1. New York: New City Press, 1999.

Aschenbrenner, George A. *Quickening the Fire in Our Midst: The Challenge of Diocesan Priestly Spirituality.* Chicago: Loyola University Press, 2002.

Ashley, Benedict M. *The Dominicans.* Eugene, Ore.: Wipf and Stock, 1990.

Balthasar, Hans Urs von. *Rechenschaft 1965*. Einsiedeln: Johannes, 1965.

———. *Die Grossen Ordensregeln* (*DGO*). Einsiedeln: Johannes, 1974.

———. "Le Paradoxe des instituts séculiers." *Vie Consacrée* 46 (1974): 199–203.

———. "Johannine Themes in the Rule and Their Meaning Today" (JT). *Monastic Studies* 11 (1975): 57–71.

———. *The Christian State of Life* (*CSL*). Translated by Mary Frances McCarthy. San Francisco: Ignatius Press, 1977.

———. *First Glance at Adrienne Von Speyr* (*FG*). Translated by Antje Lawry and Sergia Englund. San Francisco: Ignatius Press, 1981.

———. *The Glory of the Lord: A Theological Aesthetics* (*GL*). Vol. 1, *Seeing the Form*. Translated by Erasmo Leivà Merikakis. Edinburgh: T. and T. Clark, 1982.

———. *Convergences: To the Source of Christian Mystery*. Translated by E. A. Nelson. San Francisco: Ignatius Press, 1983.

———. *The Glory of the Lord: A Theological Aesthetics*. Vol. 2, *Studies in Theological Style: Clerical Styles* (*GL* 2). Translated by Andrew Louth, Francis McDonough, and Brian McNeil. Edinburgh: T. and T. Clark, 1984.

———. *Prayer*. Translated by Graham Harrison. San Francisco: Ignatius Press, 1986.

———. *Mary for Today*. Middlegreen, UK: St. Paul's, 1987.

———. *Truth Is Symphonic: Aspects of Christian Pluralism*. Translated by Graham Harrison. San Francisco: Ignatius Press, 1987.

———. "How Weighty Is the Argument from 'Uninterrupted Tradition' to Justify the Male Priesthood?" Translated by Lothar Krauth. In *The Church and Women: A Compendium*, edited by Helmut Moll, 153–69. San Francisco: Ignatius Press, 1988.

———. "Our Lady in Monasticism." *Word and Spirit* 10 (1988): 52–56.

———. "A Résume of My Thought." *Communio: International Catholic Review* 15 (Winter 1988): 468–73.

———. *Theo-Drama: Theological Dramatic Theory* (*TD*). Vol. 1, *Prolegomena*. Translated by Graham Harrison. San Francisco: Ignatius Press, 1988.

———. *Explorations in Theology*. Vol. 1, *The Word Made Flesh* (*ET* 1). San Francisco: Ignatius Press, 1989.

———. *Explorations in Theology*. Vol. 2, *Spouse of the Word*. (*ET* 2) San Francisco: Ignatius Press, 1991.

———. *Paul Struggles with His Congregation: The Pastoral Message of the Letters to the Corinthians* (*PSC*). Translated by Brigitte L. Bojarska. San Francisco: Ignatius Press, 1992.

———. *Theo-Drama: Theological Dramatic Theory*. Vol. 3, *Dramatis Personae: Persons in Christ* (*TD* 3). Translated by Graham Harrison. San Francisco: Ignatius Press, 1992.

———. *Two Sisters in the Spirit: Thérèse of Lisieux and Elizabeth of the Trinity* (*TSS*). Translated by Donald Nichols, Anne Englund Nash, and Dennis Martin. San Francisco: Ignatius Press, 1992.

———. *The Laity and the Life of the Counsels* (*LLC*). Translated by Brian McNeil, with D. C. Schindler. San Francisco: Ignatius Press, 1993.

———. *My Work: In Retrospect*. Edited by Cornelia Capol. San Francisco: Ignatius Press, 1993.

———. *Our Task: A Report and a Plan* (*OT*). Translated by John Saward. San Francisco: Ignatius Press, 1994.

———. *A Theology of History* (*TH*). San Francisco: Ignatius Press, 1994.

———. *Explorations in Theology*. Vol. 4, *Spirit and Institution* (*ET* 4). Translated by Edward T. Oakes. San Francisco: Ignatius, 1995.

———. "Women Priests? A Marian Church in a Fatherless and Motherless Culture." *Communio* 22 (Spring 1995): 164–70.

———. "Thoughts on the Priesthood of Women." *Communio* 23 (Winter 1996): 701–9.

———. *Theo-Drama: Theological Dramatic Theory*. Vol. 5, *The Final Act*. Translated by Graham Harrison. San Francisco: Ignatius Press, 1998.

———. *Love Alone Is Credible* (*LAIC*). Translated by D. C. Schindler. San Francisco: Ignatius Press, 2004.

———. *Theo-Logic* (*TL*). Vol. 3, *The Spirit of Truth*. Translated by Adrian J. Walker. San Francisco: Ignatius Press, 2005.

———. "Communio—A Program." *Communio: International Catholic Review* 33 (Spring 2006): 153–69.

———. *The Office of Peter and the Structure of the Church* (*OPSC*). Translated by Andrée Emery. San Francisco: Ignatius Press, 2007.

———. *Priestly Spirituality* (*PS*). Translated by Frank Davidson. San Francisco: Ignatius Press, 2013.

Barron, Robert. *The Strangest Way: Walking the Christian Path*. Maryknoll, N.Y.: Orbis, 2002.

Bedouelle, Guy. *Saint Dominic: The Grace of the Word*. Rev. Ed. Translated by Mary Thomas Noble. San Francisco: Ignatius Press, 1987.

Benedict XVI. *Sacramentum Caritatis*. Apostolic Exhortation. February 22, 2007.

Bérulle, Pierre. "Pièce 891: A Letter on the Priesthood." In *Bérulle and the French School*, edited by William M. Thompson, translated by Lowell M. Glendon, 183–85. New York: Paulist Press, 1989.

Beyer, Jean. "Life Consecrated by the Evangelical Counsels." In *Vatican II: Assessment and Perspectives*. Vol. 3, *Twenty-Five Years After (1962–1987)*. Edited by René Latourelle. Translated by Leslie Werne, 64–89. New York: Paulist Press, 1988.

Boersma, Hans. *Nouvelle Théologie and Sacramental Ontology: A Return to Mystery*. Oxford: Oxford University Press, 2009.

Borghesi, Massimo. *The Mind of Pope Francis*. Collegeville, Minn.: Liturgical Press Academic, 2018.

Botte, Bernard. "Collegiate Character of the Presbyterate and Episcopate." In *The Sacrament of Holy Orders: Some Papers and Discussions Concerning Holy Orders at a Session of the Centre de Pastorale Liturgique, 1955*, 75–97. London: Aquin, 1962.

Bouyer, Louis. *La Vie de S. Antoine: Essai sur la Spiritualité de Monachisme Primitif.* Abbaye S. Wandrille: Editions de Fontenelle, 1950.

———. *The Meaning of the Monastic Life*. Translated by Kathleen Pond. New York: P. J. Kennedy, 1955.

Brakke, David. *Athanasius and the Politics of Asceticism*. Oxford: Clarendon Pres, 1995.

Bramwell, Bevil. "Hans Urs von Balthasar's Theology of Scripture." *New Blackfriars* 86, no. 1003 (2005): 308–22.

Brown, Raymond E. *Priest and Bishop: Biblical Reflections*. Eugene, Ore.: Wipf and Stock, 1970.

———. *The Community of the Beloved Disciple: The Life, Loves and Hates of an Individual Church in New Testament Times*. Mahwah, N.J.: Paulist Press, 1979.

———. *An Introduction to the New Testament*. New York: Doubleday, 1997.

Buckley, Michael J. "Jesuit Priesthood: Its Meaning and Commitments." *Studies in the Spirituality of Jesuits* 8, no. 5 (1985): 135–66.

Burrows, William R. "Catholics, Carey's 'Means,' and Twenty-first-Century Mission." *International Bulletin of Missionary Research* 34 (2010): 131–38.

Butler, Sara. "Priestly Identity: 'Sacrament' of Christ the Head." *Worship* 70 (1996): 290–306.

Capol, Cornelia, and Claudia Müller, eds. *Hans Urs von Balthasar: Bibliographie; 1925–2005*. Einsiedeln: Johannes, 2005.

Carr, Ephrem. "Basil and Chrysostom: Apostolic Activities for Monks" (audiocassette). Monastic Institute Tapes: Benedictine Federation of the Americas, n. 7907. Richardton, N.Dak.: Christian Life Center, 1979.

Cassian, John. *The Institutes of the Common Life* 11.18. Translated by Boniface Ramsey. Ancient Christian Writers 58. New York and Mahwah, N.J.: Newman Press, 2000.

Castellucci, Enrico. "I Religiosi Presbiteri Nella Chiesa: *Excursus 'Storico.'*" *Sequela Christi* 2 (2009): 86–119.

Catechism of the Catholic Church (*CCC*). 2nd ed. Washington, D.C.: Libreria Editrice Vaticana and United States Conference of Catholic Bishops, 2000.

Chadwick, Owen, ed. *Western Asceticism*. Philadelphia: Westminster, 1958.

Chapp, Larry S. "Who Is the Church? The Personalistic Categories of Balthasar's Ecclesiology." *Communio: International Catholic Review* 23 (Summer 1996): 322–38.

Chinnici, Joseph. "The Impact of Clericalization on Franciscan Evangelization." In *Franciscan Evangelization: Striving to Preach the Gospel*. Washington Theological Union Symposium Papers 2007, edited by Elise Saggau, 79–122. St. Bonaventure, N.Y.: Franciscan Institute, 2008.

Ciardi, Fabio. "Il Ministero Presbitale a Servizio del Carisma: Approfondimenti e Commento All'Esperienza Carismatica Nella Chiesa." *Sequela Christi* 2 (2009): 235–55.

Clopper, Lawrence M. "Langland and the Franciscans on *Dominium*." In *Defenders and Critics of Franciscan Life: Essays in Honor of John V. Fleming*, edited by Michael F. Cusato and G. Geltner, 85–103. Leiden: Brill, 2009.

Code of Canon Law: Latin-English Edition; New English Translation (*Codex Iuris Canonici* [*CIC*]). Washington, D.C.: Canon Law Society of America, 1998.

Cochini, Christian. *Apostolic Origins of Priestly Celibacy.* Translated by Nelly Marans. San Francisco: Ignatius Press, 1990.

Cole, Basil, and Paul Conner. *Christian Totality: Theology of the Consecrated Life.* Rev. ed. New York: Alba House, 1997.

Congar, Yves. "De la communion des églises a une ecclésiologie de l'église universelle." In *L'Épiscopat et L'Église Universelle,* edited by Y. Congar and B. D. Dupuy, 227–60. Unam Sanctam 39. Paris: Cerf, 1962.

———. *A Gospel Priesthood.* Translated by P. J. Hepburne-Scott. New York: Herder and Herder, 1967.

———. "My Path-Findings in the Theology of Laity and Ministries." *Jurist* 32 (1972): 169–88.

———. *Un Peuple Messianique: L'Église, sacrement du salut; Salut et libération.* Paris: Cerf, 1975.

———. *Études d'ecclésiologie médiévale.* London: Varorium, 1983.

———. *I Believe in the Holy Spirit.* Translated by David Smith. 3 vols. New York: Crossroad, 1983.

———. *Lay People in the Church: A Study for a Theology of the Laity.* Rev. ed. Translated by Donald Attwater. London: Geoffrey Chapman, 1985.

———. "Moving Towards a Pilgrim Church." In *Vatican II Revisited: By Those Who Were There,* edited by Alberic Stacpoole, 129–52. London: Geoffrey Chapman, 1986.

———. *Called to Life.* Translated by William Burridge. New York: Crossroad, 1987.

Congregation for the Doctrine of the Faith (CDF). "Some Aspects of the Church Understood as Communion." *Origins* 22 (June 25, 1992): 108–12.

———. "Some Questions Regarding Collaboration of Non-ordained Faithful and Priests' Sacred Ministry." *Origins* 27, no. 1 (November 27, 1997): 397–410.

Congregation for Institutes of Consecrated Life and Societies of Apostolic Life. "Fraternal Life in Community" (FLC). *Origins* 23, no. 40 (March 24, 1994): 693–712.

———. "'*Verbi Sponsa*': Instruction on the Contemplative Life and the Enclosure of Nuns" (*VS*) *Origins* 29, no. 10 (August 12, 1999): 155–64.

———. "Identity and Mission of the Religious Brother in the Church." October 4, 2015. http://files.ctctcdn.com/8c97a3ce301/1827e765–8669–44f0-aaa5–5040c9dea164.pdf (accessed August 17, 2018).

Conner, Robert A. "Why Laity Are Not Ministers: A Metaphysical Probe." *Communio: International Catholic Review* 29 (Summer, 2002): 258–85.

Cooke, Bernard. *Ministry to Word and Sacraments: History and Theology.* Philadelphia: Fortress, 1976.

Cordes, Paul J. "Decree on the Ministry and Life of Priests: Commentary on the Decree; Priests as Related to Others." In *Commentary on the Documents of the Second Vatican Council,* edited by Herbert Vorgrimler, translated by Hilda Graef, J. O'Hara, and Ronald Walls, 4:236–60. New York: Herder and Herder, 1969.

Council of Major Superiors of Religious Women. *The Foundations of Religious Life: Revisiting the Vision*. Notre Dame, Ind.: Ave Maria, 2009.

Crawford, David S. *Marriage and the "Sequela Christi": A Study of Marriage as a "State of Perfection" in the Light of Henri De Lubac's Theology of Nature and Grace*. Rome: Lateran University Press, 2004.

Cusato, Michael F. "Francis of Assisi, Deacon? An Examination of the Claims of the Earliest Franciscan Sources 1229–1235." In *Defenders and Critics of Franciscan Life: Essays in Honor of John V. Fleming*, edited by Michael F. Cusato and G. Geltner, 9–39. Leiden: Brill, 2009.

———. "The Renunciation of Power as a Foundational Theme in Early Franciscan History." In *The Early Franciscan Movement, 1205–1239: History, Sources, and Hermeneutics*, 29–48. Spoleto: Fondazione Centro Italiano di Studi Sull'alto Medioevo, 2009.

Dalarun, Jacques. *Francis of Assisi and Power*. St. Bonaventure, N.Y.: Franciscan Institute, 2007.

Daley, Brian E. "'In Ten Thousand Places': Christian Universality and the Jesuit Mission." *Studies in the Spirituality of Jesuits* 17, no. 2 (1985): 1–32.

———. "The Ministry of Disciples: Historical Reflections on the Role of Religious Priests." *Theological Studies* 48 (1987): 606–29.

Dallen, James. *The Reconciling Community: The Rite of Penance*. New York: Pueblo, 1986.

Daly, Brendan. "The Promise of Obedience of Diocesan Priests: What Does It Mean?" *Australian Catholic Record* 90, no. 3 (July 2013): 329–43.

———. "The Lifestyle of the Diocesan Priest in Relation to Poverty." *Australian Catholic Record* 91, no. 1 (January 2014): 73–90.

Davis, Cyprian. "Monasticism and Priesthood in the Egyptian Desert" (audiocassette). Monastic Institute Tapes: Benedictine Federation of the Americas, n. 8102. Richardton, N.Dak.: Christian Life Center, 1981.

———. "The Liturgy, Inculturation, and the Renewal of Religious Life." In *Vatican II: Fifty Personal Stories*, edited by William Madges and Michael J. Daley, 75–80. Maryknoll, N.Y.: Orbis, 2003.

———. "Prayer as a Battle: The Monastic Contribution." In *The Tradition of Catholic Prayer*, edited by Christian Raab and Harry Hagan, 51–68. Collegeville, Minn.: Liturgical Press, 2007.

De Bhaldraithe, Eoin. "Daily Eucharist: The Need for an Early Church Paradigm." *American Benedictine Review* 41 (1990): 378–439.

———. "Lay Abbots: Should We Return to the Earlier Church Practice?" *American Benedictine Review* 59 (2008): 316–31.

De Lubac, Henri. *Corpus Mysticum: The Eucharist and the Church in the Middle Ages*. Translated by Gemma Simmonds. Notre Dame, Ind.: University of Notre Dame, 2006.

De Vogüé, Adalbert. "Eucharist and Monastic Life." *Worship* 59 (1985): 498–510.

———. "Priest and Monastic Community in Antiquity." *Cistercian Studies* 22 (1987): 17–24.

Demacopoulos, George E. *Five Models of Spiritual Direction in the Early Church.* Notre Dame, Ind.: University of Notre Dame Press, 2007.

Desbonnets, Théophile. *From Institution to Institution: The Franciscans.* Chicago: Franciscan Herald Press, 1988.

Dominican Sisters of Mary, Mother of the Eucharist. "Mass for First Religious Profession." Program, Christ the King Catholic Church. Ann Arbor, Mich., August 6, 2004.

Dominican Sisters of Mary, Mother of the Eucharist. "Mass of Perpetual Religious Profession." Program, Christ the King Catholic Church. Ann Arbor, Mich., July 31, 2013.

Donnelly, John Patrick. *Ignatius of Loyola: Founder of the Jesuits.* New York: Pearson-Longman, 2004.

Doyle, Dennis. *Communion Ecclesiology: Vision and Versions.* Maryknoll, N.Y.: Orbis, 2000.

Dulles, Avery. *Models of the Church.* Rev. ed. New York: Image, 1987.

———. *The Priestly Office: A Theological Reflection.* New York: Paulist Press, 1997.

———. *The Splendor of Faith: The Theological Vision of Pope John Paul II.* Rev. ed. New York: Crossroad, 2003.

———. "Nature, Mission, and Structure of the Church." In *Vatican II: Renewal within the Tradition*, edited by Matthew L. Lamb and Mathew Levering, 25–36. Oxford: Oxford University Press, 2008.

———. "Trends in Ecclesiology." In *Called to Holiness and Communion: Vatican II on the Church*, edited by Steven Boguslawski and Robert Fastiggi, 1–16. Scranton, Pa.: University of Scranton, 2009.

Eberle, Luke, trans. *The Rule of the Master.* Kalamazoo, Mich.: Cistercian, 1977.

Emery, Gilles. *The Trinity.* Translated by Matthew L. Levering. Washington, D.C.: The Catholic University of America Press, 2011.

Esser, Cajetan. *Origins of the Franciscan Order.* Chicago: Franciscan Herald, 1980.

Faley, Roland J. "An American Experience of Religious Life." In *A Concert of Charisms: Ordained Ministry in Religious Life*, edited by Paul K. Hennessy, 104–26. New York: Paulist Press, 1997.

Faggioli, Massimo. *True Reform: Liturgy and Ecclesiology in "Sacrosanctum Concilium."* Collegeville, Minn.: Liturgical Press, 2012.

Fisher, Anthony. "Reflections on Priesthood in the Dominican Order." *New Blackfriars* 92 (November 2011): 651–63.

Flood, David. *Francis of Assisi and the Franciscan Movement.* Philippines: Quezon, 1989.

Fry, Timothy, ed. *RB1980: THE Rule of St. Benedict in Latin and English with Notes.* Collegeville, Minn.: Liturgical Press, 1981.

Gaillardetz, Richard R. "Shifting Meanings in the Lay-Clergy Distinction." *Irish Theological Quarterly* 64 (1999): 115–39.

———. *Ecclesiology for a Global Church: A People Called and Sent.* Maryknoll, N.Y.: Orbis, 2008.

Galot, Jean. *Theology of Priesthood.* Translated by Roger Balducelli. San Francisco: Ignatius Press, 1984.

Ganoczy, Alexandre. "Splendours and Miseries of the Tridentine Doctrine of Ministries." In *Office and Ministry in the Church,* edited by Bas van Iersel and Roland Murphy, 75–86. New York: Herder and Herder, 1972.

Gardin, Gianfranco Agostino. "Vescovo, Clero Diocesano, Vita Consecrata: Istanze Nel Cammino Di Communione Nella Chiesa Locale." *Sequela Christi* 2 (2009): 172–83.

Gelpi, Donald L. "Theological Reflections on the Priestly Character of our Jesuit Vocation." *Studies in the Spirituality of Jesuits* 19, no. 3 (1987): 49–63.

George, Francis. *The Difference God Makes: A Catholic Vision of Faith, Communion and Culture.* New York: Crossroad, 2009.

———. "The Significance of Vatican II." *Communio: International Catholic Review* 39, no. 1–2 (Spring–Summer 2012): 14–32.

Gottemoeller, Doris. "The Priesthood: Implications in Consecrated Life for Women." In *A Concert of Charisms: Ordained Ministry in Religious Life,* edited by Paul K. Hennessy, 127–38. New York: Paulist Press, 1997.

Gribomont, Jean. "Obéissance et Évangle selon S. Basil Le Grand." *Vie Spirituelle,* suppl. no. 21 (1952): 192–215.

Grillmeier, Aloys. "Dogmatic Constitution on the Church." Chapter I, "The Mystery of the Church." In *Commentary on the Documents of the Second Vatican Council,* edited by Herbert Vorgrimler, translated by Lalit Adolphus, Kevin Smyth, and Richard Strachan, 1:138–52. New York: Herder and Herder, 1967.

———. "Dogmatic Constitution on the Church." Chapter III, "Article 28." In *Commentary on the Documents of the Second Vatican Council,* edited by Hebert Vorgrimler and translated by Lalit Adolphus, Kevin Smyth, and Richard Strachan, 1:218–26. New York: Herder and Herder, 1969.

Grootars, Jan. "The Drama Continues between the Acts: The 'Second Preparation' and Its Opponents." In *History of Vatican II,* edited by Guiseppe Alberigo and Joseph Komonchak, 2:359–514. Maryknoll, N.Y.: Orbis, 1997.

Guerriero, Elio. *Hans Urs von Balthasar.* Milan: Edizione Paoline, 1991.

Hagstrom, Aurelie. *The Concepts of the Vocation and the Mission of the Laity.* San Francisco: Catholic Scholars, 1994.

Harmless, J. William. "Jesuits as Priests: Crisis and Charism." *Studies in the Spirituality of Jesuits* 19, no. 3 (1985): 1–47.

Healy, Nicholas J., and David L. Schindler. "For the Life of the World: Hans Urs von Balthasar on the Church as Eucharist." In *The Cambridge Companion to Hans*

Urs von Balthasar, edited by Edward T. Oakes and David Moss, 51–63. Cambridge: Cambridge University Press, 2004.

Heid, Stefan. *Celibacy in the Early Church: The Beginnings of a Discipline of Obligatory Continence for Clerics in East and West.* Translated by Michael J. Miller. San Francisco: Ignatius Press, 2000.

Hennessy, Paul K., ed. *A Concert of Charisms: Ordained Ministry in Religious Life.* New York: Paulist Press, 1997.

Hennessy, Paul K. "Introduction: The Parochialization of the Church." In *A Concert of Charisms: Ordained Ministry in Religious Life*, edited by Paul K. Hennessy, 1–8. New York: Paulist Press, 1997.

Henrici, Peter. "Hans Urs von Balthasar: A Sketch of His Life." In *Hans Urs von Balthasar: His Life and Work*, edited by David L. Schindler, 7–43. San Francisco: Ignatius Press, 1991.

Hesburgh, Theodore. *The Relation of the Sacramental Characters of Baptism and Confirmation to the Lay Apostolate.* Washington, D.C.: The Catholic University of America Press, 1946.

Hinnebusch, William A. *The History of the Dominican Order.* Vol. 1, *Origins and Growth to 1500.* New York: Alba House, 1965.

Horan, Daniel P. *Franciscan Priesthood: The Possibility of Franciscan Presbyters according to the Rule and Tradition.* Brighton, Mass.: Koinonia, 2012.

Horst, Ulrich. "Christ, *Exemplar Ordinis Fratrum Praedicantium*, according to Saint Thomas Aquinas." In *Christ among the Medieval Dominicans: Representations of Christ in the Texts and Images of the Order of Preachers*, edited by Kent Emery and Joseph P. Wawrykow, 256–70. Notre Dame, Ind.: University of Notre Dame Press, 1998.

Howsare, Rodney A. *Balthasar: A Guide for the Perplexed.* London: T. and T. Clark, 2009.

Hozma, Lu Ann. "The Religious Milieu of the Young Ignatius." In *The Cambridge Companion to the Jesuits*, edited by Thomas Worcester, 13–31. Cambridge: Cambridge University Press, 2008.

Hünermann, Peter, and Bernd Jochen Hilberath, eds. *Herders Theologischer Kommentar zum Zweiten Vatikanischen Konzil.* 5 vols. Freiburg: Herder, 2004–6.

Hunt, Anne. *The Trinity and the Paschal Mystery: A Development in Recent Catholic Theology.* Collegeville, Minn.: Liturgical Press, 1997.

International Commission on English in the Liturgy, ed. *The Rites of the Catholic Church* (*RCC*). Vol. 2. Collegeville, Minn.: Liturgical Press, 1991.

Irwin, Kevin W. "On Monastic Priesthood." *American Benedictine Review* 41 (1990): 225–61.

Jackson, Pamela E. J. "Theology of the Liturgy." In *Vatican II: Renewal within the Tradition*, edited by Matthew L. Lamb and Matthew Levering, 101–28. Oxford: Oxford University Press, 2008.

John Paul II. *Familiaris Consortio* (*FC*). Apostolic Exhortation. November 22, 1981.

———. *Redemptionis Donum* (*RD*). Apostolic Exhortation. March 25, 1984.
———. *Mulieris Dignitatem* (*MD*). Apostolic Letter. August 15, 1988.
———. *Christifideles laici* (*CL*). Apostolic Exhortation. December 30, 1988.
———. *Pastores Dabo Vobis* (*PDV*). Apostolic Exhortation. March 25, 1992.
———. *General Audience*. July 21, 1993.
———. *Vita Consecrata* (*VC*). Apostolic Exhortation. March 25, 1996.
———. *Ut Unum Sint*. Encyclical Letter. May 25, 1995.
———. *Ecclesia de Eucharista*. Encyclical Letter. July 7, 2003.
———. *Pastores Gregis* (*PG*). Apostolic Exhortation. October 16, 2003.

Johnson, Luke T. *The Writings of the New Testament: An Interpretation*. Philadelphia: Fortress, 1986.

Jungmann, Joseph A. *Christian Prayer through the Centuries*. Translated by Joseph Coyne. Mahwah, N.J.: Paulist Press, 2007.

Kardong, Terrence. "Lack of Ministry: A Problem as Old as the Rule of Benedict." *American Benedictine Review* 35 (1984): 97–109.

———. *The Life of St. Benedict by Gregory the Great: Translation and Commentary*. Collegeville, Minn.: Liturgical Press, 2009.

———. *Pillars of Community: Four Rules of Pre-Benedictine Monastic Life*. Collegeville, Minn.: Liturgical Press, 2010.

Karris, Robert J. Introduction to *Works of St. Bonaventure: Disputed Questions on Evangelical Perfection*. Translated by Thomas Reist and Robert J. Karris. St. Bonaventure, N.Y.: Franciscan Institute, 2008.

Kasper, Walter. "A New Dogmatic Outlook on the Priestly Ministry." In *The Identity of the Priest*, 20–33. Concilium 43. New York: Paulist Press, 1969.

———. *The God of Jesus Christ*. Translated by Matthew J. O'Connell. New York: Crossroad, 1984.

Kelly, John. *The Great Mortality: An Intimate History of the Black Death, the Most Devastating Plague of All Time*. New York: Harper, 2005.

Kerr, Fergus. *Twentieth-Century Catholic Theologians: From Neoscholasticism to Nuptial Mysticism*. Malden, Mass.: Blackwell, 2007.

Kilby, Karen. *Balthasar: A (Very) Critical Introduction*. Grand Rapids, Mich.: Eerdmans, 2012.

Knasas, John. "Whither the Neo-Thomist Revival?" *Logos: A Journal of Catholic Thought and Culture* 3, no. 4 (2000): 121–49.

Koerpel, Robert. "The Form and Drama of the Church: Hans Urs von Balthasar on Mary, Peter, and the Eucharist." *Logos: A Journal of Catholic Thought and Culture* 11, no. 1 (2008): 71–96.

Küng, Hans. "The Charismatic Structure of the Church." *Concilium* 4 (1965): 23–33.

Lafont, Ghislain. "The Theology of Priesthood in the Context of Monasticism." Audiocassette. Monastic Institute Tapes: Benedictine Federation of the Americas, n. 8105. Richardton, N.Dak.: Christian Life Center, 1981.

———. "The Eucharist in Monastic Life." *Cistercian Studies* 19 (1984): 296–318.

———. *Imagining the Catholic Church: Structured Communion in the Spirit*. Translated by John J. Burkhard. Collegeville, Minn.: Liturgical Press, 2000.

Landini, Laureito. *The Causes of Clericalization of the Order of Friars Minor: 1209–1260 in the Light of Early Franciscan Sources*. Chicago: privately published, 1968.

Latourelle, René, ed. *Vatican II: Assessment and Perspectives; Twenty-Five Years After (1962–1987)*. Translated by Leslie Wearne. 3 vols. New York: Paulist Press, 1988–89.

Lauter, H. J. "De Ordenpriester." *Ordenkorrespondenz* 13 (1973): 134–38.

Lawrence, C. H. *Medieval Monasticism: Forms of Religious Life in Western Europe in the Middle Ages*. 3rd ed. Harlow, UK: Longman, 2001.

Leahy, Brendan. *The Marian Profile in the Ecclesiology of Hans Urs von Balthasar*. Hyde Park, N.Y.: New City, 2000.

LeClercq, Jean. "Témoinages contemporains sur la théologie du monachisme." *Gregorianum* 48 (1967): 49–76.

———. "Monachisme, sacerdoce et missions au Moyen Age: Travaux et résultats récents." *Studia Monastica* 23 (1981): 307–23.

Lécuyer, Joseph. "L'Episcopato come Sacramento." In *La Chiesa Del Vaticano II: Studi e commenti intorno alla Constituzione dommatica "Lumen Gentium,"* edited by Guilherme Baraúna, 713–32. Florence: Vallecchi Editore, 1965.

———. "Decree on the Ministry and Life of Priests: History of the Decree." In *Commentary on the Documents of the Second Vatican Council*, edited by Herbert Vorgrimler, translated by Hilda Graef, J. O'Hara, and Ronald Walls, 4:183–209. New York: Herder and Herder, 1969.

Legrand, Hervé-Marie. "The Presidency of the Eucharist according to the Ancient Tradition." In *Living Bread, Saving Cup*, edited by R. Kevin Seasoltz, 196–221. Collegeville, Minn.: Liturgical Press, 1987.

Leo XIII. *Au milieu des consolations*. Encyclical Letter. December 23, 1900.

Lescher, Bruce. "Laybrothers: Questions Then, Questions Now." *Cistercian Studies* 23 (1988): 63–85.

Lienhard, Joseph T. "Signs of the Times: Signs, Symbols and Meanings in Religious Life." In *Apostolic Religious Life in America Today: A Response to the Crisis*, edited by Richard Gribble, 91–100. Washington, D.C.: The Catholic University of America Press, 2011.

Little, Lester K. "Saint Louis' Involvement with the Friars." *Church History* 33 (1964): 125–48.

Lochbrunner, Manfred. *Hans Urs von Balthasar und seine Theologen-kollegen*. Würzberg: Echter, 2009.

Lösel, Steffen. "Conciliar, Not Conciliatory: Hans Urs von Balthasar's Ecclesiological Synthesis of Vatican II." *Modern Theology* 24, no. 1 (2008): 23–49.

Löser, Werner. "The Ignatian *Exercises* in the Work of Hans Urs von Balthasar." In *Hans Urs von Balthasar: His Life and Work*, edited by David L. Schindler, 103–20. San Francisco: Ignatius Press, 1991.

Lynch, Joseph H. *The Medieval Church: A Brief History.* London: Longman, 1992.

Mansini, Guy. *Promising and the Good.* Ann Arbor, Mich.: Sapientia, 2005.

———. *The Word Has Dwelt among Us: Explorations in Theology.* Ave Maria, Fla.: Sapientia, 2008.

Marmion, Columba. *Christ the Ideal of the Priest.* Translated by Matthew Dillon. San Francisco: Ignatius Press, 2005.

Matera, Frank J. *New Testament Theology.* Louisville, Ky.: Westminster John Knox, 2007.

McCann, Justin, trans. *The Rule of St. Benedict.* London: Sheed and Ward, 1970.

McCullough, David. *The Path between the Seas: The Creation of the Panama Canal 1870–1914.* New York: Simon and Schuster, 1977.

McDade, John. "John Paul II and His Ecclesiology." In *The Legacy of John Paul II,* edited by Gerald O'Collins and Michael A. Hayes, 51–70. London: Burns and Oates, 2008.

McDermott, Rose M. Part III, "Institutes of Consecrated Life and Societies of Apostolic Life (cc. 573–746)." In *New Commentary on the Code of Canon Law,* edited by John P. Beal, James A. Coriden, and Thomas A. Green, 741–908. New York: Paulist Press, 2000.

———. *The Consecrated Life: Cases, Commentary, Documents, Readings.* Alexandria, Va.: Canon Law Society of America, 2006.

McDonough, Elizabeth. "*De Accommodate Renovatione:* Between the Idea and the Reality; Occasion and Intent and Consequences of Vatican Council II." In *Apostolic Religious Life in America Today: A Response to the Crisis,* edited by Richard Gribble, 67–90. Washington, D.C.: The Catholic University of America Press, 2011.

McGregor, Augustine. "Monastic Life and the Priesthood: A Historical Study." *Hallel* 7 (1979): 101–16.

McKnight, W. Shawn. *Understanding the Diaconate: Historical, Theological, and Sociological Foundations.* Washington, D.C.: The Catholic University of America Press, 2018.

McPartlan, Paul. "The Eucharist as the Basis for Ecclesiology." *Antiphon* 6, no. 2 (2001): 12–19.

———. "Liturgy, Church and Society." *Studia Liturgica* 34 (2004): 147–64.

Mertens, Benedikt. "Franciscans in Parochial Ministry: Past and Present Aspects of a Debated Question." *Antonianum* 75 (2000): 523–54.

Monti, Dominic. "Gospel Preaching and Gospel Life: Similarities and Differences." In *Franciscan Evangelization: Striving to Preach the Gospel,* Washington Theological Union Symposium Papers 2007, edited by Elise Saggau, 9–31. St. Bonaventure, N.Y.: Franciscan Institute, 2008.

———. "'Deservedly Approved by the Roman Church': The Context for Papal Recognition of Francis's *Forma Vitae.*" In *The Rule of the Friars Minor, 1209–2009:*

Historical Perspectives, Lived Realities, edited by Daria Mitchell, 3–31. St. Bonaventure, N.Y.: Franciscan Institute, 2010.

Najim, Michael. "Two Ways in the East: The Marital Status of Clergy." In *Vested in Grace: Priesthood and Marriage in the Christian East*, edited by Joseph J. Allen, 225–64. Brookline, Mass.: Holy Cross, 2001.

Nichols, Aidan. *Holy Order: Apostolic Priesthood from the New Testament to the Second Vatican Council*. Dublin: Veritas, 1990.

———. *The Word Has Been Abroad: A Guide through Balthasar's Aesthetics*. Washington, D.C.: The Catholic University of America Press, 1998.

———. *No Bloodless Myth: A Guide through Balthasar's Dramatics*. Washington, D.C.: The Catholic University of America Press, 2000.

———. *Say It Is Pentecost: A Guide through Balthasar's Logic*. Washington, D.C.: The Catholic University of America Press, 2001.

———. *Divine Fruitfulness: A Guide through Balthasar's Theology beyond the Trilogy*. Washington, D.C.: The Catholic University of America Press, 2007.

Nugent, Robert. *Silence Speaks: Teilhard de Chardin, Yves Congar, John Courtney Murray, and Thomas Merton*. New York: Paulist Press, 2011.

Nussberger, Danielle. "Saint as Theological Wellspring: Hans Urs von Balthasar's Hermeneutic of the Saint in a Christological and Trinitarian Key." PhD diss., University of Notre Dame Press, 2007.

Oakes, Edward T. *Pattern of Redemption: The Theology of Hans Urs von Balthasar*. New York: Continuum, 1994.

Oakes, Edward T., and David Moss. *The Cambridge Companion to Hans Urs von Balthasar*, edited by Edward T. Oakes and David Moss. Cambridge: University Press, 2004.

O'Brien, David J. *Isaac Hecker: An American Catholic*. New York: Paulist Press, 1992.

O'Brien, Mary Judith, and Mary Nika Schaumber. Conclusion to *The Foundations of Religious Life Revisiting the Vision*, by Council of Major Superiors of Religious Women, 177–209. Notre Dame, Ind.: Ave Maria, 2009.

O'Collins, Gerald. *Jesus Our Priest: A Christian Approach to the Priesthood of Christ*. Oxford: Oxford University Press, 2010.

O'Donnell, Gabriel. "The Renewal of Religious Life." In *Called to Holiness and Communion: Vatican II on the Church*, edited by Steven Boguslawski and Robert Fastiggi, 201–14. Scranton, Pa.: University of Scranton, 2009.

O'Hanlon, Gerard. "Von Balthasar on Ecclesial States of Life." *Milltown Studies* 22 (1988): 111–17.

O'Keefe, Mark. *In Persona Christi: Reflections on Priestly Identity and Holiness*. St. Meinrad, Ind.: Abbey Press, 1998.

O'Malley, John W. "The Fourth Vow in Its Ignatian Context: A Historical Study." *Studies in the Spirituality of Jesuits* 15, no. 1 (1983): 1–59.

———. "Priesthood, Ministry, and Religious Life: Some Historical and Historiographical Considerations." *Theological Studies* 49 (1988): 223–57.

———. *The First Jesuits*. Cambridge, Mass.: Harvard University Press, 1993.

———. "One Priesthood: Two Traditions." In *A Concert of Charisms: Ordained Ministry in Religious Life*, edited by Paul K. Hennessy, 9–24. New York: Paulist Press, 1997.

———. *What Happened at Vatican II*. Cambridge, Mass.: Belknap Press, 2008.

Orsy, Ladislas. *Open to the Spirit: Religious Life after Vatican II*. Washington, D.C.: Corpus, 1968.

Osborne, Kenan B. *Priesthood: A History of Ordained Ministry in the Roman Catholic Church*. Eugene, Ore.: Wipf and Stock, 1989.

Papa, Benigno Luigi. "Identità Carismatica Ed Esercizio Pastorale Dei Religiosi Nella Chiesa Paricolare: Questioni Aperte." *Sequela Christi* 2 (2009): 157–71.

Paul VI. "Ai Superiori Maggiori degli Ordini e Congregazione Religiose." In *Insegnamenti di Paolo VI*, 4:574–75. Vatican City: Tipographia Poliglotta Vaticana, 1966.

———. *Evangelica Testificatio*. Apostolic Exhortation. June 29, 1971.

Pecknold, C. C. *Christianity and Politics: A Brief Guide to the History*. Eugene, Ore.: Cascade, 2010.

Philibert, Paul J. "Priesthood within the Context of Religious Life." In *Being a Priest Today*, edited by Donald J. Goergen, 73–96. Collegeville, Minn.: Liturgical Press, 1992.

Philips, Gérard. "Dogmatic Constitution on the Church: The History of the Constitution." In *Commentary on the Documents of the Second Vatican Council*, edited by Herbert Vorgrimler, translated by Lalit Adolphus, Kevin Smyth, and Richard Strachan, 1:105–37. New York: Herder and Herder, 1967.

Pius XI. *Ex officiosis litteris*. November 10, 1933. *Acta Apostolicae Sedis* 26 (1934): 628–33.

———. Handwritten letter to Cardinal Gasparri. January 21, 1927. Quoted in Hans Urs von Balthasar, *The Laity and the Life of the Counsels* (*LLC*). Translated by Brian McNeil, with D. C. Schindler. San Francisco: Ignatius Press, 1993.

Pius XII. *Mystici Corporis Christi*. Encyclical Letter. June 29, 1943.

———. *Mediator Dei*. Encyclical Letter. November 20, 1947.

———. *Provida Mater Ecclesia*. Apostolic Constitution. February 2, 1947.

———. *Primo Feliciter*. Motu Proprio. Mar 7, 1948.

———. *Evangelii Praecones*. Encyclical Letter. June 2, 1951.

———. *Ad Sinarum Gentem*. Encyclical Letter. October 7, 1954.

———. *Address to the Second World Congress for the Lay Apostolate*. October 5, 1957.

Power, David N. "Theologies of Religious Life and Priesthood." In *A Concert of Charisms: Ordained Ministry in Religious Life*, edited by Paul K. Hennessy, 61–103. New York: Paulist Press, 1997.

Power, Dermot. *A Spiritual Theology of the Priesthood: The Mystery of Christ and the Mission of the Priest*. Washington, D.C.: The Catholic University of America Press, 1998.

Pryds, Darleen. "Preaching Women: The Tradition of Mendicant Women." In *Franciscan Evangelization: Striving to Preach the Gospel.* Washington Theological Union Symposium Papers 2007, edited by Elise Saggau, 55–77. St. Bonaventure, N.Y.: Franciscan Institute, 2008.

Przywara, Erich. *Anologia Entis: Metaphysics; Original Structure and Universal Rhythm.* Translated by John R. Betz and David Bentley Hart. Grand Rapids, Mich.: Eerdmans, 2014.

Rahner, Karl. "Notes on the Lay Apostolate." In *Theological Investigations.* Vol. 2, *Man in the Church.* Translated by Karl H. Kruger, 319–52. Baltimore: Helicon, 1963.

———. "The Word and the Eucharist." In *Theological Investigations.* Vol. 4, *More Recent Writings,* translated by Kevin Smyth, 260–81. Baltimore: Helicon, 1966.

———. "Dogmatic Constitution on the Church." Chapter III, "The Hierarchical Structure of the Church with Special Reference to the Episcopate." In *Commentary on the Documents of the Second Vatican Council,* edited by Herbert Vorgrimler, translated by Lalit Adolphus, Kevin Smyth, and Richard Strachan, 1:186–217. New York: Herder and Herder, 1967.

———. "Priest and Poet." In *Theological Investigations.* Vol. 3, *The Theology of the Spiritual Life.* Translated by Karl H. Kruger and Boniface Kruger, 294–317. Baltimore: Helicon, 1967.

———. "The Point of Departure in Theology for Determining the Nature of the Priestly Office." In *Theological Investigations,* vol. 12, *Confrontations* 2, translated by David Bourke, 35–36. New York: Seabury and Crossroad, 1974.

Ratzinger, Joseph. "The Pastoral Implications of Episcopal Collegiality." *Concilium* 1 (1965): 20–33.

———. *The Open Circle: The Meaning of Christian Brotherhood.* New York: Sheed and Ward, 1966.

———. *Theological Highlights of Vatican II.* New York: Paulist Press, 1966.

———. *Church, Ecumenism, and Politics: New Endeavors in Ecclesiology.* Translated by Michael J. Miller. San Francisco: Ignatius Press, 1987.

———. "Biblical Foundations of Priesthood." *Origins* 20 (October 18, 1990): 310–14.

———. *Called to Communion: Understanding the Church Today.* Translated by Adrian Walker. San Francisco: Ignatius Press, 1996.

———. *Pilgrim Fellowship of Faith: The Church as Communion.* Translated by Henry Taylor. San Francisco: Ignatius Press, 2005.

Rees, Daniel. *Consider Your Call: A Theology of Monastic Life Today.* Kalamazoo, Mich.: Cistercian, 1978.

Roberson, Ronald G. "The Profile of Eastern Monasticism Today." *Melita Theologica,* suppl. no. 3 (1994): 91–120.

Roberts, Augustine. *Centered on Christ: A Guide to Monastic Profession.* Kalamazoo, Mich.: Cistercian Press, 2005.

Roberts, Louis. *The Theological Aesthetics of Hans Urs von Balthasar.* Washington, D.C.: The Catholic University of America Press, 1987.

Robinson, Denis. "The Counter-Reformation: Age of Imagination." In *The Tradition of Catholic Prayer,* edited by Christian Raab and Harry Hagan, 89–105. Collegeville, Minn.: Liturgical Press, 2007.

Root, Michael. "Bishops, Ministry and the Unity of the Church in Ecumenical Dialogue: Deadlock, Breakthrough, or Both?" *CTSA Proceedings* 62 (2007): 19–35.

Rosen, Cyprian R. "Fostering the Patrimony of the Order of Friars Minor Capuchin: A Study in the Mutual Responsibility of the Order and the Apostolic See (Canons 576 and 631)." JCD diss., The Catholic University of America, 2009.

Rowland, Tracey. *Benedict XVI: A Guide for the Perplexed.* New York: T. and T. Clark, 2010.

Ruddy, Christopher. *The Local Church: Tillard and the Future of Catholic Ecclesiology.* New York: Crossroad, 2006.

Sacred Congregation for Religious and for Secular Institutes. *Mutuae Relationes* (*MR*). "The Relationship of Bishops/Religious Orders." *Origins* 8, no. 11 (August 31, 1978): 161–76.

Second Vatican Council. Constitution on the Sacred Liturgy *Sacrosanctam Concilium* (*SC*). December 4, 1963.

———. Dogmatic Constitution on the Church *Lumen Gentium* (*LG*). November 21, 1964.

———. Decree Concerning the Pastoral Office of Bishops in the Church *Christus Dominus* (*CD*). October 28, 1965.

———. Decree on the Adaptation and Renewal of Religious Life *Perfectae Caritatis* (*PC*). October 28, 1965.

———. Decree on the Priestly Training *Optatum Totius* (*OT*). October 28, 1965.

———. Decree on the Apostolate of the Laity *Apostolicam Actuositatem* (*AA*). November 18, 1965.

———. Decree on the Church's Missionary Activity *Ad Gentes* (*AG*). December 7, 1965.

———. Decree on the Ministry and Life of Priests *Presbyterorum Ordinis* (*PO*). December 7, 1965.

———. Pastoral Constitution on the Church in the Modern World *Gaudium et Spes* (*GS*). December 7, 1965.

———. *The Basic Sixteen Documents: Vatican Council II: Constitutions, Decrees, Declarations.* Edited by Austin Flannery. Northport, N.Y.: Costello, 1996.

Schillebeeckx, Edward. *Marriage: Human Reality and Saving Mystery.* Translated by N. D. Smith. New York: Sheed and Ward, 1965.

Schindler, David L. *Heart of the World, Center of the Church: "Communio" Ecclesiology, Liberalism, and Liberation.* Grand Rapids, Mich.: Eerdmans, 1996.

———. "Institution and Charism: The Missions of the Son and Spirit in Church and World." *Communio: International Catholic Review* 25 (Summer 1998): 253–73.

Schneider, Francis J. "Obedience to the Bishop by the Diocesan Priest in the 1983 Code of Canon Law." JCD diss., The Catholic University of America, 1990.

Schneiders, Sandra M. *Religious Life in a New Millennium*. Vol. 1, *Finding the Treasure: Locating Catholic Religious Life in a New Ecclesial and Cultural Context*. New York: Paulist Press, 2000.

Schroeder, H. J. *The Canons and Decrees of the Council of Trent*. Charlotte, N.C.: TAN, 1978.

Scola, Angelo. *Balthasar: A Theological Style*. Grand Rapids, Mich.: Eerdmans, 1996.

———. "The Theological Foundation of the Petrine Dimension of the Church: A Working Hypothesis." *Ecclesiology* 4 (2007): 12–37.

Seasoltz, R. Kevin. "Institutes of Consecrated Life and Ordained Ministry." In *A Concert of Charisms: Ordained Ministry in Religious Life*, edited by Paul K. Hennessy, 139–68. New York: Paulist Press, 1997.

Senocak, Neslihan. *The Poor and the Perfect: The Rise of Learning in the Franciscan Order, 1209–1310*. Ithaca, N.Y.: Cornell University Press, 2012.

Servais, Jacques. "The Lay Vocation in the World According to Hans Urs von Balthasar." *Communio: International Catholic Review* 23, no. 4 (Winter 1996): 656–76.

———. "Yves Congar and Hans Urs von Balthasar on the Theological Status of the Laity" ("Congar and Balthasar"). Unpublished manuscript made available to me by the editors of *Communio: International Catholic Review*. The original French essay is "Le statut théologique du laïc en débat: Yves Congar et Hans Urs von Balthasar." In *Chrétiens dans la société actuelle: L'apport de Hans Urs von Balthasar; Actes du colloque du Centenaire de H. U. von Balthasar 17–18 novembre 2005 à Lyon*, edited by Didier Gonneaud et Philippe Charpentier de Beauvillé, 131–58. Magny-les-Hameaux: Socéval Éditions: 2006.

Sheridan, Mark. "The Origins of Monasticism in the Eastern Church," in *RB1980: The Rule of St. Benedict in Latin and English with Notes*, edited by Timothy Fry, 3–41. Collegeville, Minn.: Liturgical Press, 1981.

Skublics, Ernest. "A Contemplative Ministry?" *Worship* 45 (1971): 480–87.

Smith, Susan E. *Women in Mission: From the New Testament to Today*. Maryknoll, N.Y.: Orbis, 2007.

Stickler, Alfons Maria. *The Case for Celibacy: Its Historical Development and Theological Foundations*. Translated by Brian Ferme. San Francisco: Ignatius Press, 1995.

Streider, Leon F. *The Promise of Obedience: A Ritual History*. Collegeville, Minn.: Liturgical Press, 2001.

Sugawara, Yūji. *Religious Poverty: From Vatican Council II to the 1994 Synod of Bishops*. Rome: Editrice Pontifica Università Gregoriana, 1997.

Sullivan, Francis A. *The Church We Believe In: One, Holy, Catholic and Apostolic*. Mahwah, N.J.: Paulist Press, 1998.

Sumption, Jonathan. *The Age of Pilgrimage: The Medieval Journey to God.* Mahwah, N.J.: HiddenSpring, 2003.

Taborda, F. "Il Religioso presbitero: una questione discussa." *Vita Consecrata* 38 (2002): 626–40.

Tanner, Norman P. ed. *Decrees of the Ecumenical Councils.* Vol. 1. Washington, D.C.: Georgetown University Press, 1990.

———. Chapter V, "The Church in the World." In *History of Vatican II*, edited by Guiseppe Alberigo and Joseph Komonchak, 4:270–386. Maryknoll, NY: Orbis, 2004.

Taylor, Charles. *Sources of the Self: The Making of Modern Identity.* Cambridge, Mass.: Harvard University Press, 1989.

Thompson, Augustine. *Francis of Assisi: A New Biography.* Ithaca, N.Y.: Cornell University Press, 2012.

———. *Dominican Brothers: Conversi, Lay, and Cooperator Friars.* Chicago: New Priory Press, 2017.

Thompson, William M. Introduction to *Bérulle and the French School.* Edited by William M. Thompson. Translated by Lowell M. Glendon. New York: Paulist Press, 1989.

Tillard, Jean-Marie R. *The Mystery of Religious Life.* Edited by R. F. Smith. St. Louis, Mo.: Herder, 1967.

———. *Devant Dieu et Pour Le Monde: Le projet de religieux.* Paris: Cerf, 1974.

———. *Church of Churches: The Ecclesiology of Communion.* Collegeville, Minn.: Liturgical Press, 1992.

Tobin, Joseph. "A Great History Still to Be Accomplished?: Prospects for Consecrated Life in the Church-Communio." In *God Has Begun a Great Work in Us: Embodied Love in Consecrated Life and Ecclesial Movements*, edited by Jason King and Susan Schrein, 87–103. Maryknoll, N.Y.: Orbis, 2014.

Torrell, Jean-Pierre. *A Priestly People: Baptismal Priesthood and Priestly Ministry.* Translated by Peter Heinegg. Mahwah, N.J.: Paulist Press, 2013.

Tugwell, Simon, ed. *Early Dominicans: Selected Writings.* Mahwah, N.J.: Paulist, 1982.

United States Conference of Major Superiors of Men. "Formation for Presbyteral Ministry in Institutes of Religious Life: A Statement of the Members of the Conference of Major Superiors of Men." The Conference of Major Superiors of Men, 2011.

Veilleux, Armand, ed. *Pachomian Koinonia.* Vol. 1, *The Life of Saint Pachomius.* Kalamazoo, Mich.: Cistercian, 1980.

Vorgrimler, Herbert, ed. *Commentary on the Documents of Vatican II.* 4 vols. New York: Herder and Herder, 1967–69.

Walsh, Eugene Aloysius. *The Priesthood in the Writings of the French School: Bérulle, De Condren, Olier.* Washington, D.C.: The Catholic University of America Press, 1949.

White, Thomas Joseph. *Wisdom in the Face of Modernity: A Study in Thomistic Natural Theology*. Ave Maria, Fla.: Sapientia, 2009.

Welch, Lawrence, J. "Priestly Identity Reconsidered: A Reply to Susan Wood." *Worship* 70 (July 1996): 307–19.

Wigley, Stephen. *Balthasar's Trilogy: A Reader's Guide*. New York: Continuum, 2010.

Wood, Susan K. "A Theology of Authorization of Lay Ecclesial Ministers." In *In the Name of the Church: Vocation and Authorization of Lay Ecclesial Ministry*, edited by William J. Cahoy, 99–116. Collegeville, Minn.: Liturgical Press, 2012.

Workman, Herbert B. *The Evolution of the Monastic Ideal*. Boston: Beacon, 1962.

Wright, N. T. *Paul: In Fresh Perspective*. Minneapolis: Fortress, 2005.

Wulf, Freidrich. "Dogmatic Constitution on the Church," Chapter V, "The Call of the Whole Church to Holiness." In *Commentary on the Documents of the Second Vatican Council*, edited by Herbert Vorgrimler, translated by Lalit Adolphus, Kevin Smyth, and Richard Strachan, 1:261–72. New York: Herder and Herder, 1967.

———. "Dogmatic Constitution on the Church." Chapter VI, "Religious." In *Commentary on the Documents of the Second Vatican Council*, edited by Herbert Vorgrimler and translated by Lalit Adolphus, Kevin Smyth, and Richard Strachan, 1:273–79. New York: Herder and Herder, 1967.

———. "Decree on the Ministry and Life of Priests: Commentary on the Decree." Chapter II, "Priestly Functions." In *Commentary on the Documents of the Second Vatican Council*, edited by Herbert Vorgrimler, translated by Hilda Graef, J. O'Hara, and Ronald Walls, 4:228–36. New York: Herder and Herder, 1969.

———. "Decree on the Ministry and Life of Priests: Commentary on the Decree." Preface. In *Commentary on the Documents of the Second Vatican Council*, edited by Herbert Vorgrimler, translated by Hilda Graef, J. O'Hara, and Ronald Walls, 4:214–17. New York: Herder and Herder, 1969.

INDEX

Understanding the Religious Priesthood: History, Controversy, Theology was designed in Warnock Pro and Mr Eaves and composed by Kachergis Book Design of Pittsboro, North Carolina. It was printed on 60-pound House Natural Smooth and bound by Sheridan Books of Chelsea, Michigan.